The Crunch of Gravel Under Thrumming Tyres

ON & OFF-ROAD CYCLE TOURING IN THE 1960S

A decade of memories cycle touring from Stoke-on-Trent, staying mainly at youth hostels in the UK, Ireland and in the Pyrenees, Dolomites, and Norway, with adventures at every turn of the pedals.

About the Author

C. A. Green, almost scared of getting on a two-wheeled bike as a youngster, finally became confident when running up and down the village lane on his cousin's little, red bicycle in deepest Lincolnshire. His Uncle Billy's enormous sit-up-and-beg work bike was an adventure but proved hard to ride and even downright dangerous. After leaving school and thoroughly fed up of PT and combative sports on the playing field, he gravitated towards the so-called lightweight 'sports' bike and made many trips from Stoke-on-Trent and into the near countryside. The Potteries in the early 1960s were a hotchpotch of mixed heavy industries; ceramics being the principal manufacturing craft. Although containing a wonderful population of genuine, friendly folk, one was always looking to escape the city environs in search of fresh air. An initial long distance solo tour down to Plymouth, in Devon, staying at youth hostels overnight really lit the fuse for the pastime.

With an interest in photography and scrutinizing maps, he found two hobbies that fully complemented the cycle touring. Continued cycling led to the joining the local YHA, touring wild Wales and, inevitably, meeting a gathering of like-minded cyclists. Finding a note and soggy cigarette in a tin box, high in the Berwyn Mountains, meant an expansion of the club numbers and formation of an organised hostel touring programme in the United Kingdom.

Tours as a group spread to southern Ireland, Ulster and the continent, including the Pyrenees of France and Spain, the Dolomites of northern Italy and the Norwegian fjords. By the end of the 1960s, the cyclists went their separate ways and C. A. Green joined a few friends to continue cycle touring and camping in the Tarn, Lot and Dordogne areas of France, in beautiful Provence and the Cote d' Azur, north Portugal and in Spain's Picos de Europa.

Age and arthritis finally caught up with him, thrusting a spoke in his wheel. He hung up his cycle clips and decided all this history on two wheels – the landscapes, weather, foul and fair, the pleasure and pain and the sheer adventure of it all – should be set down on paper. Of course, with appropriate maps at hand to provide enhanced memories.

The Crunch of Gravel Under Thrumming Tyres

C. A. GREEN

The Crunch of Gravel Under Thrumming Tyres

Olympia Publishers
London

www.olympiapublishers.com
OLYMPIA PAPERBACK EDITION

A CIP catalogue record for this title is
available from the British Library.

ISBN: 978-1-84897-293-3
(Olympia Publishers is part of Ashwell Publishing Ltd).

First Published in 2014

Olympia Publishers
60 Cannon Street
London
EC4N 6NP

Printed in Great Britain

To Garry Hogg (1902 – 1976) for his writing of Explorers Awheel in 1938, a gentle tale of a summer cycle tour in more innocent times and with constant re-reading, pointed me down the traveller's road signposted 'ADVENTURE'.

Acknowledgements

To Zean Fairbanks-Gilbert for her continual, genuine belief, interest and support for the book's production.

To my Stoke cycling friends for all those happy memories gained over many miles.

Preface

This is a book about a group of cyclists and their touring exploits over the decade of the 1960s – a decade of momentous worldwide events. A time of seismic shift from the 1950s, particularly in music, fashion, morals, deference, and behaviour. I was lucky to be interested in cycle touring; lucky to make contact with the local Youth Hostels Association and lucky to meet with a like-minded gathering of cyclists steeped in a keen spirit of adventure. Most unusual in those changing times, especially considering the trends of a society used to post-war deprivation, stilted good manners towards those in authority, the Establishment, holidays at Skegness and the BBC Home Service. One would have expected youth to break free, go jiving to the new, wild music, holiday in Malaga and be constantly obsessed by fashion and appearance. Most did and were.

The decade's main events and my comments are listed at the start of each chapter, merely to provide a backdrop to our travels on the bike – which were far more interesting, in our opinion, than what was happening throughout the world in faraway places. However, it *was* a momentous decade and I feel that it warrants recording.

Our group lived in the city limits of Stoke-on-Trent, so there was, possibly, a good reason to go on spins into the countryside. The popularity and enjoyment of group cycling had reached its peak over the 1920s and 1930s. I think we rediscovered a taste of those times. A collection of jolly souls, laughing, joking and chattering as they whirled down country lanes with the wind in the hair, was the epitome of freedom in those times and again, in our times.

Unlike today, we didn't cycle to keep fit, deliver some important document as a courier, save money or raise money for charity. On the contrary, we enjoyed a pint, a smoke and a laugh. We wanted to see and experience interesting landscapes and constantly seek rough-stuff routes for a challenge of map-reading and trail-blazing. We virtually doubled in membership and friends after finding a note and cigarette left at the summit of a long, lonely mountain crossing. That, I believe, just says it all.

We made good use of the YHA and were, generally, grateful for its being. Not so much for providing inexpensive accommodation, but for running such basic and diverse havens for the casual traveller in, mainly, strategic and attractive places. In fact, both ourselves and many other hostellers were somewhat 'long in the tooth' and could easily afford more salubrious shelter. As time went on, we found the YHA to be modernising, admitting school parties and improving facilities towards 'travel lodge' standards. We actually preferred the old armchair, cup-ringed table top and springy iron bunk beds. Rules, especially in high tourist areas, were becoming suffocating, until, for us, they eventually became intolerable. Nevertheless, we contributed to our local YHA through the production of slide shows and readily attended local hostel working parties and joined the walkers on auto-rambles. Nationally, our group hostel and bed night count over the decade certainly swelled Head Office's coffers.

We were so very lucky indeed to be able to ride through relatively unspoilt areas in the 1960s. Mass tourism hadn't quite kicked off. When it did, most people were venturing to the Costa's of Spain on cheap package holidays, leaving whole swathes of the UK and Southern Ireland countryside relatively untouched. Certainly, areas closer to Stoke-on-Trent, in the Peak District and Cheshire, invited exploration. Shropshire was positively 'wild'! There was a world out there of adventure, forgotten places and quirky characters.

It was all at the end of leafy lanes, indistinct tracks and over windswept hills – unspoilt, seldom visited – for us to go out and find.

Prologue

The torrential rain, streaming off my head, coursed through my hair, flattening it against the forehead and dripped continually into my eyes, making them sting. Eyebrows were rendered useless. Water was creeping under my rain cape collar, too and was inching down, travelling the length of the body, soaking my shirt and shorts until it dripped down into my shoes. We had just descended a long Pyrenean pass, Johnny Bradbury and I and we were mightily relieved to be reaching the flatter roads in the valley. Suddenly, a vague figure appeared out of the mist and, almost casually, sauntered into the middle of the road...

We had been descending from Baños de Panticosa, high in the Pyrenean peaks on an out-and-back two day diversion from Jaca. We had chosen the Pyrenees as, we believed, it was the wilder of the European mountain regions, offering challenge and something different. The mountain chain draped across the land, from Atlantic to Mediterranean, like a continuous curtain of peaks, separating France from Spain. A major characteristic of the Pyrenees wildness was, however, its violent thunderstorms. Hot air masses from the central Spanish plateau intermingled with the cooler Atlantic airstreams to create whirls of rising, spiralling, and invisible columns of air. Our descent from Baños de Panticosa was during one of these cataclysmic storms.

The Spanish Department of Public Works were, high in the mountains, improving the route by first removing any top surfaces of tarmac. Massive plant was reducing the road width by more than half and creating a morass of mud. We had to negotiate floods, landslips, and rock falls caused by the incessant rainfall Baños forming hillside streams as we struggled along a road surface that was rapidly disappearing. With one foot dragging through the runnels of water and mounds of silt to keep balance, it was if the 'road' was moving faster than we were – slipping at right angles, across our path and being swept over the drop into the valley far below. It was becoming frightening. Lower down the pass, where the route cut below and between cliff faces, even large boulders were falling, being toppled into our path, crashing on the road, propelled by the force of the flooding deluge.

But the seemingly endless kilometres of difficult descent finally ended and we rolled onto a flatter, more gentle road that was heaven, surfaced with a layer of solid tarmac, albeit pocked with deep, gravel-filled potholes. Mist clung in a thick mantle to obscure even the roadside trees. Those high mountain peaks whose slopes threatened immediate danger were high above the mist layer, out of sight and almost out of mind. The rain still fell in sheets of stair-rod intensity.

Through glasses that were permanently steaming up, I noticed a vague figure in the mist, wandering into the middle of the road, several metres ahead. At first, I thought that he was a local giving us a welcome to his village. These mountain folk were always friendly – and curious. Suddenly, I recognised the cape and black, shiny headgear. The cap that signified severe authority, the Spanish Civil War of 1936, the opposing anti-Fascist International Brigade and Picasso's *Guernica*. With rain streaming down his stern, olive-complexioned cheeks, coursing down his cape and splattering onto the road, he waved his pistol and ushered us into the stone-arched entrance of the local Guardia Civil headquarters. The lettering, *TODO PARA LA PATRIA,* on a red and yellow-painted patriotic signboard above announced trouble ahead. Oh God, what have we done? What now?

Spain was delivering, living up to its wild reputation – providing something different!

Introduction

Apart from a few days or half-days of cycling around the North Staffordshire lanes on a heavy, sit-up-and-beg, black bicycle, my early cycling adventures were spasmodic. A return journey of thirty miles (forty-eight kilometres).down the A34, to the outskirts of Stafford nearly put me off the idea of cycling forever. Near-death exhaustion caused by hypoglycaemia, almost made me abandon any two-wheeled transport thereafter. My early cycling experiences, therefore, consisted only of the odd, about-town jaunts through the familiar hilly streets of Stoke-on-Trent.

Those city streets in the late 1950s were still bordered by pottery manufacturers (pot-banks), warehouses, coalmine entrances, allied engineering workshops, isolated shops, and the ubiquitous oatcake bakeries. These tiny, end-of-terrace establishments prepared flat, savoury pancakes that no Potteries bacon and egg fried breakfast could be without. Tightly rolled, they effectively mopped up the egg yolk and surrounding moat of the inevitable tinned tomato juice. The chimneys on these bakeries emitted wisps of smoke, just a small contribution to the previous years of heavy polluting smoke from the innumerable grouped bottle kilns. But by this time, the firing of pottery was changing from the pregnant-looking bottle ovens to the relatively clean gas-fired tunnel kilns. The area's coal mines were also closing down; their associated spoil heaps being seeded to form 'forest parks' – open, windy areas where one could exercise (toilet).the dog or fly the kite. The total infrastructure of Stoke-on-Trent, Arnold Bennett's cluster of five towns, was a bewildering mixture of land uses. Pot-banks, coalmines, iron and steel foundries, gas works, light and medium engineering works, marl pits, railways, plate-ways, canal spurs, gantries and even the young River Trent dared to show itself as it fought for open air beyond its confining conduit sections. Apart from the small, relatively modern groups of new developments and a few vast council estates, housing consisted of, mainly, line after line of uniform terraced dwellings, levered in between the industry wherever possible. There were no model villages for the workers, such as at Bourneville or Port Sunlight.

Travelling from north to south, the five towns could be expanded to total ten or eleven. Starting at Goldenhill, wending through Tunstall, Burslem, Middleport, Longport, Hanley, Stoke, Fenton, Longton and Meir, one arrives at Blythe Bridge in the south-east – passing a hotchpotch of townlets with no visible green sward, let alone greenbelt to separate them. Brownfield sites appeared a greyish-black where terraced homes, considered just too decrepit for human habitation, and were swallowed up in the great programme of slum clearance. End-of-terrace properties, serving as the local shops, were temporarily spared, giving their surrounding vacant areas an even more desolate and desperate appearance. However, the general, overall squalor of the city streets concealed a conurbation of craftsmen, artists, designers, innovators and, above all, folk of a genuine, golden friendliness.

Although a hive of industry, the conurbation is only about eight miles from north to south and comparatively narrow – half the distance, in an east to west direction. The borough of Newcastle-under-Lyme borders the city to the west. The surrounding countryside, particularly in the south and west, is pleasant enough and to the north and east, beyond Leek, becomes spectacular, as we reach the Staffordshire Moorlands and southern Peak District. There was plenty of incentive to drag the bike out of the back yard, pump up the tyres, apply a smidgeon of oil and cycle out of those busy city streets, past the ribbon development of the suburbs and reach the 'great outdoors'. The trip to Stafford and back on that heavy, sit-up-and-beg bicycle; that beast with the rubber pedals, rusting rod brakes and obligatory white-painted 9 inches of clanking rear mudguard, made it plainly obvious that I needed a lighter machine. The last few miles returning to Hanley Road, Sneyd Green, were a nightmarish blur of knee-wobbling weakness – a typical attack of the cyclist's 'knock', or drastic fall in blood sugar level with its symptoms of tired, yawning, jelly-like legs and the desire to 'eat a horse between two loaves of bread'. One planned trip out of the Potteries got only as far as the pavement outside a companion's terraced house behind Lichfield Street, Hanley. On a steamy-hot summer afternoon, I had the bike upturned, resting on its wide saddle and handlebars, while I struggled with the punctured inner tube, dipping it progressively into a bowl of water to find the leakage, with the carping, cursing comments of my 'friend' ringing in my ears. "One day soon, mate, we'll start this journey!" Delivered with a broad Potteries' accent and a tinge of sarcasm, this didn't bode well for a pleasant afternoon's ride.

I bought a 'sports' bike from the Hanley branch of Halfords. It had a green 20 inch steel frame, Sturmey-Archer 3-speed gear, chromed wheels and handlebars, white, plastic mudguards and a small, fabric-covered, cardboard saddlebag. After the big black beast, it was, to me, the pinnacle of cycling lightness. Edward Elgar and Thomas Hardy used to gad about the country lanes of Worcestershire and Dorset on their tall, trusty machines but I bet they had to dismount a few times. I can imagine them stopping outside an isolated inn, removing their cycle clips and being served a frothing tankard of ale as they sat on a bench outside, taking the airs and being careful not to spill their drink across their latest created compositions. My Halfords 'flyer' was not left rusting with softening tyres in the garden shed but put to good use as I went on several day tours such as lofty Mow Cop Castle folly, Gawsworth's Tudor Hall and to admire the multiple jetties of timber-framed Little Moreton Hall in Cheshire. A more ambitious journey took me to Lichfield. There, I unpacked the Kodak Box Brownie and took my first photograph – a view of the western façade of the cathedral. My trembling finger hovered over the shutter release, seemingly, for an interminable amount of time before, at last, the composition was correct and the deed was done. A divine power must have seen that the printed image was free from camera shake. Even so, it resembled an early picture taken in Lacock Abbey by the pioneer of photography, Mr William Fox-Talbot.

The rigours of cycling in hot weather were brought home to me on a day's run south-east of Stoke-on-Trent in the general direction of Uttoxeter and Burton-upon-Trent. Clear of the main A50 road down the Trent Valley, I entered a network of narrow lanes through flat and 'ordinary' arable countryside. Around lunchtime, I sat just inside a farmer's field, clear of the growing crop, amongst the wild hedgerow grasses, ate my sandwiches and drained my dust-stained feeding bottle of the last drops of Robinson's Barley Water. The sun blazed down, encouraging the ever-hidden crickets to sound their continual chirruping – a summer sound to almost halt the passage of time and leave it suspended in the heat of midday. Hot airs wafted their mellifluous currents across my flagging, reclining body, threatening sleep but it was time to move on. Wearing khaki shorts, a short-sleeved shirt, no sun cream and no sunglasses, I came home with my thighs and arms taut with sunburn and forehead striped as red and white as the Stoke City Football Club's colours. My day's direction had been east, turning south and finally west; miles and hours of heading directly into the sun and the miles of squinting against its roadside glare had puckered my brow to result in this embarrassing, patterned effect.

Having learned of the existence of the Youth Hostels Association (YHA)., which enabled the 'humble traveller' to seek a night's rest for a mere pittance, providing he or she travels under their own steam, that is, walking or cycling, I sent off for details of membership to Head Office in St Albans. My idea was to cycle all the way to Plymouth where we still had family and friends, not by boring old motor car or train, but to make an intrepid journey – have a *real* adventure. I duly filled-in the necessary application form and enclosed the annual membership fee of 10/- (50p). I received an official membership card, a handbook listing the hostels and their location, a small scale coloured, physical geography map showing general hostel sites, triangles for England & Wales, circles for Scotland, squares for Ireland and two green YHA enamel button badges. The back of the handbook contained the Association Rules, one of the first being that members should travel by foot or bicycle. Cyclists should have no problem with this, but walkers did tend to leave the car at the end of the drive. After signing the membership card and sticking my photograph to the inside, I was holding my 'passport' to a world of two-wheeled adventure. It was summer, 1960. I lived on Hanley Road, Sneyd Green, in a semi-detached house adjoining the area petrol filling station. On its forecourt, I scanned a display stand for the appropriate Esso paper road map of the *Midlands, Wales & the South West...*

The bicycle must have been one of the cleverest contraptions invented by man. After all, it included, probably, the number one invention – the wheel – now that's got to make it a winner. Placing two wheels in line, one behind the other, facilitated balance through steering and various later refinements such as disc brakes, inbuilt suspension, suitable gearing, and the roller chain made it mechanically efficient, while still retaining an overall simplicity. In short, it was easy to maintain, seldom broke down and was ridiculously inexpensive to purchase and use. What other device can you, after a brief repair, ride away after fishing it out from the bottom of the local canal? What other device can you, after riding sixty miles, pack into a bag and take it on the train beside you? Most people would rather ride sixty miles against a rain-lashed gale than catch a train, but that's not the point. What other machine could be ridden into any back street and after setting it on its stand and making a simple connection, could you sharpen an amnesty of kitchen knives for the local housewives?

The very first bicycles, called velocipedes, were made of wood, and were scooted around by the foppish French, no doubt attempting to impress their doe-eyed *Mademoiselles*. Scottish blacksmith, Kirkpatrick Macmillan, devised wood and iron machines. These were improved by Englishman James Starley; making them of metal and having the front driving wheel a ridiculous diameter of about 5 feet (1.5m).and the rear wheel very small. Referred to as a Penny Farthing, their correct name was an Ordinary and the moustachioed rider would come a terrible cropper when he happened to encounter one of the numerous potholes on the dirt roads of that time. This was the era when group cycling became popular and gangs of pill-box capped; liberated, lecherous males would ride to the next village and cat-call every parlour maid who ever dared to venture forth from her mistress's grand house. They sat high enough on their machines to be able to look over most boundary walls. If they could manage a wind-up gramophone whilst terrorising the peaceful countryside, these reprobates could be equated to our modern-day boy racers. The safety bicycle's design was progressed in England where a chap named John Starley, deciding that the two wheels should be the same diameter, 28 inches (700mm)., measured to the outside of the 'new', comfortable, inflatable tyres developed by John Dunlop and sitting within Endrick profiled rims. This became an acceptable design and was named the Rover. The Safety bicycle was considered proper, even for gentile ladies who wore knickerbockers or bloomers, so, creating yet another fashion. A flash of ankle, let alone thigh, was so daring. A wheel measurement of 27 inches (675mm).was eventually considered to be ideal. Tricycles were made for those folk who just couldn't balance to save their lives, or those who were very old and important, like King George V.

Various design changes, some quite recent, have added very little to the bicycle's efficiency. Mr Moulton designed a bike with small wheels and inbuilt suspension. The small wheels gave a jarring ride and therefore, some form of cushioning in the forks was required – both features completely unwanted. The standard diameter wheel, with its tangential spoke arrangement, was a brilliant concept, providing lightness, strength, adjustability, known as 'truing-up' and some suspension qualities – relegating the car wheel, for example, to the realms of the Stone Age. I am constantly irritated by so-called inventors trying to improve the design of both the bicycle and its components. Why cannot they admit that the design has reached its zenith? To try and go beyond spells failure.

In the summer of 1959, I was working for the Scrooge-like architect, Mr Charles Sinclair Green and whenever I ventured into the basement of the building, maybe to tell the housekeeper how many cups of tea to provide, I would catch sight of a colleague 's dark olive-green Viking Mileater. This racing bike had been stripped of any unnecessary accessories such as mudguards, bike stand, tennis racquet clip, and bell and leaned against the cool basement wall, emitting a faint smell of light oil. This sleek thoroughbred had probably been hand-built in the back streets of Wolverhampton by a grease-covered old man – a craftsman – with a pair of brazing goggles pushed on top of his head and a half-smoked cigarette hanging from the corner of the mouth. He probably had a clipped moustache hanging above his upper lip, too. The tyres were minimal in depth and tread; but the centres of those wheels caught my closer attention. The alloy hubs were large-flanged, drilled out for lightness and gave the whole machine an air of racing efficiency, much like the large front brake disks on most modern motorcycles. In the cool, crepuscular gloom of a Victorian basement, this slick, stripped-down machine leaning against the bare wall was built to travel fast and far. My Halford's Sports was similar, but in colour only. Its tubing was painted a middling leaf-green. That was the only similarity to the Viking Mileater.

The summer of 1959 was long and very hot. Heat rose off the city streets in mirage-making waves, bouncing off gas holder and bottle kiln brickwork alike. A pulsating heat that strangled any fresh air was exacerbated by the many emissions of the noxious gases from numerous industrial chimneys. The grass on the two football pitches at the back of the house turned yellow before disappearing into a dusty dirt. That summer ended in late August with a tremendous thunderstorm. The sky turned gradually from a clear afternoon blue, through a threatening bluey-grey, to an apocalyptic, Stygian grey. A sudden fork of blue lightening joined sky with football pitch and a ball of evil yellow, orange and blue fire earthed on the chipped and rusty metal goal posts. Heavy raindrops formed circular dust markings in the arid playing surface before being sucked into the thirsty subsoil. The summer was over. I resolved that next year I would get out more on my two wheels.

I was already mobile on eight wheels, but only in the form of a pair of roller skates. They were a good quality pair with composition rubber wheels, precision ball-race bearings and real leather straps. I would walk from Hanley Road, passing the entrance to Hanley Deep Pit with its ever-winding pit-head gear and clanking, smoky locomotives shunting their lines of coaling trucks. With skates over the shoulder, I tramped towards Hanley town centre. Situated in Town Road, the Ideal roller-skating rink was once a small, flea-pit of a cinema before conversion and now was a flea-pit, fly-blown space with a flat dance floor bounded by a splintered and scuffed wooden perimeter barrier. The dark-grey floor was covered in squashed, discarded chewing gum and ancient, flattened dog turds. Beyond the splintered woodwork barrier was a narrow corridor where non-skating, courting teenagers skulked sullenly, smoking and quaffing bottles of Tizer. Waves of screaming kids rolled in a perpetual rotation of the clear area, learners on the outside scrabbling for the barrier, while the fully proficient lads performed skating tricks, showing-off to their pony-tailed girlfriends. Their juvenile, barely recognised sexual desires were driven to hysteria by the thumping sound of late 1950s pop music, continual and of ear-bleeding intensity. It probably disguised the occasional complaining yelp or slap across the face. *You don't like crazy music/You don't like rockin' bands/You just wanna go to a movie show and sit there holdin' hands/You're so square, Baby, I don't care!* Next summer, 1960, I would suffer the 'Summertime Blues' no longer, but throw my leg over the crossbar of the Halford's Sports and cycle all the way down south to Plymouth.

Chapter One

1960

Cycling to Plymouth and Back – Explorers Awheel – Places of Work – Move to Trentham – My History on Two Wheels – The Go Anywhere Machine – A New Sun Bicycle – Joining Local YHA Early Days Forming the Cycling Section.

Age: 19.
Home: Bank House, Hanley Road, Sneyd Green, Stoke-on-Trent.
(Later: Cherry Tree Close, Trentham, Stoke-on-Trent).
Work: Adams & Green, Architect, Brook Street, Stoke.
Government: Conservative.
Prime Minister: Harold Macmillan.
February: Martin Luther King, the Civil Rights leader arrested.
March: Agadir, in Morocco devastated by earthquake; Britain scraps the Blue Streak missile and Blacks are massacred in Sharpeville, South Africa.
May: American U2 spy plane shot down over USSR. Princess Margaret marries Antony Armstrong-Jones.
August: Olympic Games staged in Rome and East Germany close the West Berlin border. Missiles parade in Red Square, Moscow. J F Kennedy elected US President.
Book: *Lady Chatterley's Lover.*
Films: Hitchcock's *Psycho* and Fellini's *La Dolce Vita.*

Aged 19 and interests restricted to very local subjects; the early days of work; an occasional visit to Stoke City Football Club, the 'Potters', at the Victoria Ground, Boothen; more 'Potters' at the Sun Street speedway and the weekly bout of late-teenage roller-skating, my awareness of world events was severely curtailed. Old 'Edwardian' premier Macmillan visited Africa when many countries were seeking independence from Colonial Rule, preceding a terrible massacre of sixty-seven black locals in Sharpeville, South Africa. The advancement of space exploration held my interest; with Soviets having launched the first satellite, Sputnik I, in 1957 and soon afterwards, launching dogs there on a one-way ticket. America's first attempt to emulate the 'Ruskies' ended in a launch pad explosion and headlines reading 'Phutnik'! The USA's paranoia for anything Red was not helped by the arrest of their spy plane pilot, Gary Powers, in his U2, caught with his high-level camera work. Our government elected to fall out of the arms race by scrapping the Blue Streak Intercontinental Ballistic Missile; countless millions of pounds down the pan, but never mind. (It's trying to take part that counts!). An explosion of global proportions occurred in Agadir, Morocco, with a devastating earthquake. The earth moved, also, for Princess Margaret when she married Antony Armstrong-Jones; Potteries folk collapsed in a bout of sentimental swooning – not! J F Kennedy grasped the poisoned chalice of President of the US when diplomacy with the USSR was growing icy-cold. Somewhere between them hung the Iron Curtain – keeping both exceedingly warm!

*

It was a summertime morning, bright and sunny and I was taking breakfast prior to my grand departure, cycling eventually to Plymouth, but today contemplating the first day's stage to Cleeve Hill on the edge of the Cotswolds. I was sitting at the dining table in the back room at our semidetached house in Sneyd Green, forcing down a second Weetabix despite a queasy stomach due, no doubt, to the thought of the many miles that lay ahead. Sister Sheila and brother-in-law, Fred and my foster parents looked on, probably asking themselves, "I hope you know what you're taking on?!"

For a boy born in 1941, even an age of eighteen years left me still feeling very young, especially when faced with a long-distance cycle ride. Lads grow up faster these days, or that's what we are always led to believe! I was wearing my khaki shorts, silly cloth 'racing' cap of red and grey and my stunning, Hawaiian-style summer shirt with its crazy flecked pattern of black and white darts and swirls printed on shocking scarlet-dyed cotton. I felt its newness and stiffness – a little too conspicuous but at least I would be instantly noticed by passing traffic. I was shod in ordinary leather town shoes over black nylon socks. These were the days before designer labels and stubby, ugly-looking white trainers. Sports footwear at the dawn of the '60s was plimsolls whitened with a weekly application of liquid Blanco. In trepidation, I pushed off and freewheeled down to the foot of Hanley Road Bank before the first turn of the pedals.

Weeks before the day of departure, I had studied my paper Esso maps covering the *Midlands, Wales & the South-West,* marking in the intended route with coloured biro, circling the youth hostel locations and noting the distances in miles between each town to make a daily total. I calculated the total distance from Stoke-on-Trent to Plymouth to be about 240 miles (385k), giving a daily mileage over four days of 60 miles (96k)./day. Starting at 8:00am, I would have eight hours before the hostels officially opened at 4:00pm. I took comfort in the knowledge that I would only have to average a speed of 7 or 8 miles an hour to complete each day's journey. Nevertheless, the map margins were covered in scribbled calculations, trying to convince myself that everything planned was possible. As any weakling should be able to maintain an average cycling speed of, maybe, 10 miles (16k)./hour, I considered the journey to be just easy, or in today's crude parlance, "A piece of p...!" The Esso maps I used lacked any indication of contours, although my generous allowances of time made this fact unimportant. With continual opening and folding, my fragile paper map soon opened up at the seams, became torn and tattered and lines of Sellotape had to be applied. Despite indicating no physical features, the maps contained a wealth of information and an area gazetteer of place names on the reverse.

Clear of the Potteries, I made good time on the road and moving south, passing through Stafford, Wolverhampton, Kidderminster, and Worcester, travelling on the A34, A449, and A38. Of course, this was before the total arterial road system of motorways had been built. There were very few roundabouts (motorists were able to turn right correctly in those days).; the route led through town centres without miles of by-passes, traffic was considerably less, lighter and speed was reasonable. There were very few sections of dual carriageway and the 'B' roads were virtually deserted. Cars with style would pass me, some a little too close but one soon got used to that. Standard Vanguards, Wolseleys, Hillman Huskies, Austin Devon and Somerset saloons, Sunbeam Talbots, Morris Minors and Triumph Mayflowers. Lorries and coaches were of a sensible size, too, the majority being Foden or Bedford. British Road Services held the monopoly for long distant haulage. The uniformed, saluting Automobile Association motorcyclist patrols were starting to disappear and with them, a certain feeling of camaraderie and good manners amongst motorists.

Somewhere south of Worcester but before Tewkesbury, I dived into the network of minor roads with the breeze ruffling my hair and the gravel clattering and skittering under the plastic mudguards. I remember being quite proud of my progress thus far, surprised that the miles had slipped under my wheels so smoothly, with only a slight feeling of fatigue in the legs. Tiredness can creep up insidiously though and I began to have a tendency to stare at the chromed handlebars instead of the road ahead. I was now approaching the Cotswold Edge, climbing to Winchcombe and into more interesting countryside. I was forced to dismount as the road reared up south of the village; my Sturmey-Archer low gear not low enough. I became aware of a hilly landscape and felt a buzz of excitement to be passing through countryside with steeper slopes and longer drops than previously encountered. As the route clung to the edge of Cleeve Common, a wide view opened to the south-west, towards the Severn Valley and the Forest of Dean. Short of Cheltenham and at the highest road point of the Common, I swung into the entrance gates of my very first youth hostel, full of apprehension at what or who I would meet and worried that I wouldn't 'fit in'. After slotting the bike into the cycle shed (there were only two other bikes there)., I found the warden's office and dutifully signed in, handing over my 'passport', my membership card and feeling slightly proud of my signature and the space describing occupation as 'draughtsman'. The warden was perched in his office, a sort of kiosk and I handed my overnight fee through the open, serving hatch window. He was healthily middle-aged and had a demeanour indicating boredom, probably caused by having to tackle the administration instead of strolling the neighbouring hills. Maybe it was his title of 'warden', signifying, to me, the vision of echoing corridors, slamming cell doors and prison bars that caused my unease. The window frame was covered all around with masses of pieces of paper, all stating various rules and regulations of the hostel. Dog-eared bus timetables were attached with lengths of string alongside a list of area maps for sale. The warden took my few pence for the hire of a light, cotton sleeping bag as well as my fee for an evening meal, both previously booked. Overnight stays were about 6/- (30p).and sleeping bag hire was 1/- (5p).–mere coppers compared with today's prices!

As I was having an evening meal in the hostel, there was no need to carry large amounts of food in the saddlebag, albeit snacks purchased at the last-passed or nearest village store. My small, cardboard saddlebag, with its thin fabric covering, barely held the minimum change of clothes, soap and towel and the odd chocolate bar for emergencies. An aluminium feeding bottle was attached to the handlebars, sloping forward like those fitted to the Tour de France racing bikes. The contents, usually containing diluted fruit juice which invariably leaked through the ill-fitting cork stopper, leaving orange streaks of gooey sugar on front forks and bare knees. A yellow, plastic rain cape was strapped to the top of the saddlebag and an all-fitting cycle spanner and puncture repair kit wedged into the incredibly small side pockets, fitted, no doubt, for cosmetic purposes rather than usefulness.

The hostel common room appeared calm; an eclectic mix of furniture, a scattering of shabby armchairs, side tables piled with fusty books, a coloured, wall-mounted area map of the Cotswolds, John Bartholomew's, I think – with the site of Cleeve Hill Youth Hostel obliterated by countless pointed fingers. Casually placed reading material, *The Peoples' Friend, The Countryman, Twenty Sites To Visit In Rural Gloucestershire, Reader's Digest,* were fingered absent-mindedly by a few travelling colleagues. Sun-tanned fellows pointed the chewed end of their pipes at a particular point on their Ordnance Survey Maps, reliving the day's adventures between puffs of Digger Plug. The calming fug of cigarette smoke mixed with the warmth of related touring tales was only interrupted by the clash of cutlery thrown onto the long dining table. A handful of ourselves – hungry, intrepid travellers – sat down at the common room refectory-type table for the evening meal.

In order to help maintain the hostels, members were obliged to undertake hostel 'duties', that is, small tasks taking somewhere in the region of fifteen, twenty minutes– or so; washing-up, window cleaning, grass cutting or the dreaded task – cleaning the self-cooker's kitchen. If members needed an early morning departure, they could do their duty on the preceding night. My first hostel duty at Cleeve Hill was to sweep the floor of the men's dormitory. Dormitories contained two-tier iron bunk beds with thin mattresses and nothing much else. Each berth had a pile of three blankets, all a uniform blue-grey, very much like those used by the Salvation Army and other shelter organisations. A few hostels had three-tier bunks, offering a challenge to the acrobatic abilities of the topmost occupants! The bed frames were a standard design with shallow coil springs. When sleeping in the bottom bunk, one would stare upwards in trepidation at the threatening bulge formed by the sleeper above, listening to the twang of tortured bed springs and the barely-muted sound of snoring. Sound sleep of the innocent traveller in their sea of dreams, be that a sea of calm or calamity. The sight of bare, white, lowering legs and bunion-bulging feet of fellow upper-bunk hostellers was not the greatest herald of a fresh, new day in the countryside. The self-cooker's kitchen was fitted with sheet aluminium work surfaces. Several double Calor gas burners were arranged on top, a harbour for accumulated grease and dust and extremely difficult to keep clean. The burners were connected to several large gas containers by black rubber tubing, often perished, frayed and singed, no doubt suffering from former amateur cooks' culinary disasters. The main self-cooked meals prepared here comprised, in the main, of tinned beans or spaghetti hoops. If a pan fell off the burner grid it would be called "Spaghetti – oops!" Giant brown enamel teapots were on hand to whet the traveller's whistle – teapots probably last seen at evacuation muster-points in World War II. As an enthusiastic cycling group in late years and equipped with large saddlebags, we would always use the facilities of the self-cooker's kitchen. It was cheaper than the hostel meals provided.

The whole institution of the Youth Hostels Association was administered through its National and Regional Councils with representation on a European and worldwide basis. It probably received grant funding from higher organisations who supported health, cultural and educational ideals – in fact, in later years, we were to see hostels used more frequently by school parties on field study trips – too frequently, in my opinion, as traveller's lodgings became school classrooms. I would eventually discover that Stoke-on-Trent was part of the Staffordshire Sub-Region of the Midlands YHA group, had weekly meetings throughout the year at Cartwright House, Broad Street, Hanley, organised activity programmes for walkers and cyclists, and even printed a quarterly news sheet, *The Staffordshire Knot*. Each region would adopt hostels that needed attention by forming working parties, volunteers to stay overnight for free and carry out the more involved tasks such as repainting, drain-clearance or building work. Stoke-on-Trent's adopted hostel was Dimmingsdale, a single-storey cabin-type hostel situated in pine and birch woodland above the Churnet Valley at Oakamoor, beyond Cheadle. A very attractive setting with the turrets and towers of Alton Towers just visible on the opposite side of the valley. An Alton Towers in the peaceful days when the site was noted for its architecture, parkland and gardens, and not the stomach-churning, wallet-emptying playground of eternal noise and queuing that it has become today.

At Cleeve Hill, high on the Cotswold Edge, I finished my 'duty', collected my membership card and hostel packed lunch, opened the door on a brand new day, and went to the bike shed to continue my journey into the south and west. I had bought a black and white postcard of the hostel taken from above, from the slopes of the Cleeve Common Golf Course. It showed a long, narrow, single-storied building with simple pitched roof, abutting an older two-storey structure; probably a former schoolroom or village hall built in the early 1940s style. At the bike shed, I found that the front wheel had a decidedly soft tyre. I glanced around nervously for any assistance, but the only other cyclist that morning made it very clear that he wished to get on his way quickly, not hang around mending punctures, and I was left with a flat tyre and holding a white plastic cycle pump with the thin rubber connector waggling about in almost impotent uselessness. Although I had a puncture repair outfit, I had failed to include any tyre levers. Two at least are needed for the removal of a normal high pressure, wired tyre, and two strong thumbs to put it back on. I dared not to disturb the warden for a loan of two spoons – substitutes essential for levering outer tyre off rim – and just pumped with hopeful enthusiasm, hoping that the wheel would remain rideable for a few miles at least. The tyre stayed reasonably hard for many miles during that second day's ride; in fact I only mended the tube when the journey finished, at Plymouth. It must have been a very slow puncture.

Dealing with the odd puncture was an integral part of cycling. An inconvenience that needed to be attended to for riding on a flat, rear tyre cut the outer cover to shreds and a flat, front tyre made steering almost impossible, if not dangerous. Rustic solutions when caught without a repair kit when miles from anywhere were to pack the inside of the tyre tightly with grass, paper or use a postage stamp to mend the tube. There was always the wit to issue the unfunny comment, "It's only flat at the bottom mate!" The puncture outfit, bought from any High Street cycle shop, was a long, thin tin of delights. Red glue in a small, screw-capped tube, a square of emery cloth, a portion of canvas cover, a collection of red rubber, circular patches in various sizes, and a minute tin of French chalk. One was tempted to take a deep sniff of the glue – it smelled delicious. Mending a puncture properly was a contest between patience and impatience. A competition between brute strength and exquisite dexterity.

Careful positioning and use of the tyre levers was vital to prevent further punctures. Essentially, and often forgotten, the outside, and inside of the outer cover was tested for protruding flints or thorns. The faint hiss from a partly-inflated inner tube was sometimes hard to detect, especially when beside a busy highway or having colleagues shouting and laughing between themselves. After removal, the area around the puncture had to be clean, dry, and slightly roughened to take the smear (not too much) of glue. The backing had to be carefully peeled from the correct repair patch with, invariably, cold fingertips. The patch had to be pressed firmly into position for an adequate length of time and dusted with chalk to prevent the unintended sticking of inner tube to outer cover. Finally, after testing for a successful mend, other leaks and replacing the tyre, the wheel was inserted, and one was on one's way again – whistling with happiness, fingers, face and forehead smeared black with oil.

No, a spare inner tube, carried always, was the best way to deal with roadside punctures. If a rear puncture, one was advised to set the derailleur into top gear before re-inserting the wheel. With the correct technique, (push cover into centre of rim around circumference and watch for the trapping of the inner tube), one could use thumb pressure only to replace the tyre. Later, repair kits contained vulcanised rubber patches with chamfered edges to attain a more successful mend. Yes, mending punctures was a challenge – almost an art – a task to make one's tongue to stick out from the corner of an anxious mouth.

My initial impression of youth hostelling was of a juvenile institution with masses of rules, but run in a fairly friendly manner with the spirit of the intrepid traveller to the forefront. With members' age completely irrelevant, it was a mixture of school, scouts, and an overnight, shelter accommodation for the less well-off.

I pushed off from Cleeve Hill on the descending road to Cheltenham watching the front wheel like a hawk for signs of its softening. A sudden flat front tyre can make steering almost impossible, throwing the rider into a wobble before he's dumped unceremoniously onto the tarmac. My route wended through the Cotswolds by way of Stroud, Nailsworth, arcing into the south-west, through Bath, Radstock, Shepton Mallet, and Glastonbury, before arriving at the youth hostel in the Somerset village of Street. The overall scenery was of undulating, rolling countryside dotted with the honey-coloured stone houses, some rather grand, of this limestone landscape of Old England. Houses of stone-tiled roofs, steep gables, and functional door and window detail; deep mullions and transoms with carved sills, and lintels protected by ornate dripstones. Dry stone walling dividing patchwork fields were similar to boundaries of the White Peak in North Staffordshire. The roads here were lined with dusty, white gravel; the dry, well-drained landscape typically of underlying limestone. One section of road appeared to start to go downhill but I found that I needed to change to a lower gear and press harder on the pedals. I thought I was fighting a headwind but there wasn't even a slight breeze. The road actually climbed slowly, but because of the slope of the adjoining hills, a conflicting perspective caused the optical illusion. A road in Ayrshire, Scotland, the Electric Brae, creates the same illusion, nonplussing motorists who, believing themselves to be descending, think their cars to have drastically lost power. At the time I suspected a soft front tyre to be the reason. Pedalling uphill or down, I was pleasantly surprised how easily the miles were disappearing behind my rear mudguard. Every mile gained was one less to my day's destination at Street, a settlement of Roman origin and now famous for shoe manufacturing, including the sandal. As progress was easy on the flattening roads, I would arrive at the hostel before official opening time of 4.00pm. So as not to be seen waiting on the doorstep, I would tootle around the town or village in question, sit on a convenient wall, maybe light up a Player's Weights cigarette and watch people go by. I was at such an age when I occasionally smoked the odd plain cigarette; had part-inhaled the odd Park Drive or Woodbine in the downstairs toilet at Sneyd Green, and even half-enjoyed the experience. I wasn't, however, sophisticated enough to own a lighter, so the small, angular matchbox had to be teased out of the tight shorts' pocket together with the sweaty handkerchief and odd coins. At a final glance at the wristwatch, opening time had arrived, and I entered the portals and welcoming bosom of my second youth hostel of the journey.

With the whaleback Mendip Hills off to my right, I covered the flat minor roads at speed, passing easily over the King's Sedge Moor with its cross dykes and wild, reed-covered wastes until the Devon moors appeared out of the haze ahead. An important experience of cycling is the fact that one can discern even the slightest change in gradient. With varying pedal pressure required, one 'feels' the countryside passing under the wheels – one is aware of the landscape through the tautness and strain on the calf and thigh muscles. On the more severe climbs, if just a few yards, I would have to rise off the saddle and stand on the pedals. This is known as 'honking', safe enough if toe clips prevent the feet from slipping off the pedals but on the steepest of hills it is probably best to dismount and walk. Beyond Taunton, the roads west began to rear up; Norton Fitzwarren, Milverton, Wiveliscombe, approaching the hill country of Exmoor, and the deer-hunting village of Bampton. I was decidedly early so I had to saunter around the stone-built village, waiting for the hostel to open. A much advertised fact of youth hostelling is the variation in types of buildings available to the weary traveller. The handbook boasted the use of former school buildings, castles, a disused water mill and even a closed railway station – probably a victim of the gradual decline of the branch lines before Doctor Beeching wielded his cost-cutting axe. The majority of disused buildings used for hostel accommodation, especially in rural Wales, was the isolated chapel or village schoolroom – a sign of reduced rural existence – a demographic shift with families moving from the poor farmland to the areas of concentrated, more profitable employment on the coast or in more industrial-based towns.

After signing-in and making-up my bunk bed, I settled into a well used armchair, one of a mixture of begged and borrowed furniture scattered over the uneven boarded upper floor of this barn-like common room. I had proof that I was in the centre for Exmoor deer hunting; there was a dusty, flea-ridden deer's head fixed to the wall. Striking south from Bampton, passing through the wooded Upper Exe Valley, I cleared Tiverton and the quaint thatch and cob village of Bickleigh before reaching Exeter. Here I regained the A38 to Plymouth. Sheila, Fred and I had travelled this road many times in the early 1950s, the last lap of our journey down from Stoke to see Fred's family. Mile after mile in the Austin Seven van, engine ticking smoothly like a well-oiled sewing machine. There were memories of the climb over the Haldon Hills, past the Devon and Exeter Racecourse, followed by an undulating road through South Devon towns, Chudleigh Knighton, Ashburton, Buckfastleigh and Ivybridge. Names evocative of the warm red soil of the southwest. However could there be overcast weather, let alone rain in place names such as these? The A38 now, in the new millennium, is a continuous dual-carriageway, a super fast highway of rushing traffic, a mixture of holidaymakers and goods vehicles, an artery connecting the channel port at Plymouth with the rest of the British motorway network. This frenetic cavalcade of haste is often brought to a grinding halt by the ubiquitous, never-ending road works. The mere sudden, innocent slowing of just one car can lead to a build-up queue of mammoth proportions, leaving the poor motorist with no explanation for the hot miles of crawl when traffic flow resumes a more reasonable speed. In view of the present policy to raise the national motorway speed limit from 70mph to 80mph, would it not mean reaching the back of the traffic queue a little earlier?

In 1960, on the final miles to my destination, the conditions were very much calmer. The A38 actually went through the centre of these towns, passing grocers, garages, confectioners, places to buy a bottle of pop, a wafer ice cream and, if one looked closer, the odd shop, according to *Monty Python's Flying Circus* – The Bicycle Tour (Of North Cornwall), selling bicycle pumps. "I believe one still exists somewhere between Ottery St Mary and Tiverton." Seriously, that manic send-up of a bicycle tour, despite the Pythonesque silliness and diversions, did contain some genuine home truths regarding cycling in those days.

By mid-afternoon, I had reached the estuary of the River Plym and soon was jiggling over the hard granite setts in the back entry of the family terraced house in Lipson. The dazzling white stone walls, the tall washing line posts, wires, and pulleys, and the canopy of a summer azure sky overhead reminded me that I had, at last, finished my journey. I caught the warm whiff of ozone, probably blown on a sea breeze from the Barbican fishing quays a few streets away. I could now relax for two weeks, and get around to mending that front wheel puncture.

My initial inspiration for cycle touring was the book *Explorers Awheel* Written by Garry Hogg, is the story of a cycle tour from near the New Forest to Exmoor and return by a small party of two boys and two girls escorted by their adventure-loving uncle. The children ride tandems and the uncle, a solo machine, covering the southern byways of England, experiencing adventures along the way. It is a warm tale of innocence, of making do, of a hot spell of settled weather, and cooking over an open fire, and sleeping outdoors below the stars, wrapped inside warm sleeping bags. It describes a time, probably in the 1930s, when children had freedom to play in an unthreatening atmosphere, to discover, and appreciate nature, and not to be reliant on electronic games for their entertainment, artificial, toxic foods to eat, or lifestyles promoted by creeping commercialism. It is a mixture of *Swallows and Amazons*, the *Famous Five* with *Biggles Flies Down*.

On the return journey from Plymouth, beyond Exeter, I followed the A3052, connecting the coastal towns of Sidmouth, Seaton, Lyme Regis, until I arrived at the pleasant seaside town of Bridport. The hostel was one of the many cottage-style buildings that bordered the narrow, twisting lanes that laced up the hill away from the harbour. I felt the sun's warmth reflecting off the whitewashed stone walls as I carried the bike down steps and into the adjoining bike/store shed. Next day, another day of dry, sunny weather, I moved north into Somerset and beyond Wells, reached Croscombe at the foot of the long line of the Mendip Hills. This was the country of limestone caverns and wonderful place names: Cheddar, Wookey, Rodney Stoke, Priddy, and Chewton Mendip. Landscape that promised extreme exploration and adventure. Place names, apart from the spectacular gorges and caverns nearby, that brought back memories of all-day mystery tours from Plymouth to Weston-Super-Mare. Why do mystery tours always go to Weston-Super-Mare? I have known coach trips as far away as Manchester, finish in Weston with bewildered passengers staring out to sea, wondering where mud flats end and water begins.

After Bath, my route turned from east to north-east and I regained the Cotswolds through Chippenham, Malmesbury, and Cirencester. Leaving the arrow-straight Roman Road, the Ermin Way, I discovered a network of leafy lanes that wound through the Duntisbournes to arrive at the hostel in Duntisbourne Abbots. Isolated stone cottages crouched behind unkempt hedgerows; woodland copses overhung the almost deserted lanes; it was a rural scene that appeared to have just forsaken the heavy horse and hay-laden wagons; a Cotswold before the cosmetic 'improvements' of the well-off second-homers from down south. On my last day of touring, I made a brief stop in the sleepy village of Bourton-on-the-Water. There were the honey-coloured clusters of roadside shops, there was the Windrush stream bubbling down the centre of the high street and there were the numerous toy-like bridges that playfully spanned this gentle waterway who's depth only climbed up to the top of one's bare, cool ankles – well, in summer anyway. Little hump-backed bridges that resembled those on a seaside crazy golf course, bridges in miniature where toddlers squatted, looking for imagined minnows between the ripples of sunlit surfaces. However, the street was almost devoid of tourists and only a few cars lined the kerbsides. The occasional MG Sports, Wolseley Hornet or Morgan parked behind the tall, narrow, unstable-looking Ford Popular and the large Humber Super Snipe; its owner taking tea or something stronger, behind the mullioned and leaded windows of the adjacent Tudor hotel. The lack of massed tourists was, for me, at that time not noticed, therefore, not appreciated. It was the norm; villages in the Cotswolds, as in numerous other attractive places, received just a few appreciative visitors and had no need to cater for overwhelming tourism. How many times have I needed to resort to long past memories to compare the pleasant qualities of a location with that of today's honeypot mayhem? The difference between 'visiting' and 'touring' in some respects was the difference between chalk and cheese; use of the bicycle was one sure way to remain an undemanding visitor.

I completed the miles back home in a state of dulled fatigue. My plan was to stop the night at Malvern Wells youth hostel but arriving at this grand, converted manor house under the steep slopes of the Malvern ridge, I found it to be fully booked. Full to the gunnels, overflowing with youthful explorers and not one spare bed to be found. I hadn't planned on staying here but thought it a good idea to extend my time aboard the bike and extend the tour. Consequently, I hadn't bothered to make a booking here, so, found my bunk had been claimed by somebody who had, probably, just stepped off public transport. I decided, therefore, as it was still only early afternoon, I could cover the remaining miles home and still have time for supper. The disappointment of being turned away from my chosen hostel would put fire and steel into the pedalling legs. I managed it but only after countless miles of tunnel vision; staring along the road ahead with a fixed, wretched gaze and many stops for chocolate snacks and swigs of orangeade. I freewheeled to a stop outside Bank House in Hanley Road,

Sneyd Green, after over a hundred miles covered and collapsed into the armchair to wait for the encroachment of muscle stiffness and feeling to return to all my hanging appendages!

Overall, I was surprised that the whole journey, there and back, had turned out to be so easy. Cycling those sort of miles made no destination out of bounds. The world, or at least, the British Isles, suddenly were my oyster. My horizons had widened, I could see beyond the end of the lane. My Esso paper road map was splitting down the folds, trailing dried Sellotape with the mileage calculations scribbled in the margins almost obliterated by wear and especially tear. The cycling days had been completely dry with plenty of sunny intervals. I loosened the straps holding the rain cape to the top of the saddlebag and unrolling it, caught a smell of dry plastic emanating from its cracking, custard-yellow folds.

In the summer of 1960, I was working at a private architects in Brook Street, Stoke – the firm, Adams & Green. It was there that I admired the aforementioned Viking Mileater in the basement; the cycle that spurred on my wish to embark on cycle tours and invest in a much lighter machine when I could afford it. In the autumn of 1960, we moved house from Hanley Road, Sneyd Green to another semi-detached house in Ash Green, Trentham. A relatively new estate then, had yet to have its cul-de-sac access road surfaced, but was definitely, for ourselves, a move up the housing and social ladder, albeit a very short step. The estate was opposite the fine park and lake, Trentham Gardens, of Duke of Sutherland renown and had a connecting road, Werburg Drive, to New Inn Lane and Hanford. The new public house on the corner was named The Man in Space, anticipating, no doubt, after America and Russia's recent unmanned probings into sub-orbital space, man would soon follow. No 1, Cherry Tree Close had a single asbestos garage to the side with plenty of room for a red Hillman Husky estate, garden tools and possible space for a favourite bicycle at its far end. Due to lack of funds, that bicycle would have to remain the Halford's Sports for a few more months hence. Mr Charles Sinclair Green, my Dickensian employer, offered an Article of Pupilagewhereupon a contract would be established between us. I couldn't lose my job and any training would be funded but I would only be paid a weekly pittance, although I was allowed to take Christmas Day off! No, it wasn't quite that bad but a post did arise in the city of Stoke-on-Trent Reconstruction Department, advertised in the local daily newspaper, *Evening Sentinel,* for a position of draughtsman. I duly applied for the job and was successful, starting work at offices in Woodhouse Street, Stoke in February, 1961 and seeing an enormous leap in my pay from that offered by the architect, Scrooge. I was working now for the Labour-controlled City Council, preparing maps that outlined areas for slum clearance. Every drawing seemed to be titled, Area Edged Red. I recall on one early winter morning's cycle run to work where, at the end of New Inn Lane, I failed to notice a patch of ice and slammed into the road, taking the fall on elbow and hip. The fall was so sudden, my surprise at being spread horizontal surpassed any feeling of hurt. The instant hurt after a crash is to one's pride; nevertheless, on regaining my composure, I recorded my very own 'Areas Edged Red'!

Falls and scrapes apart, I had always been fascinated with cycling. It was nothing to do with having cheap, convenient travel or a burning desire to get fit. My first substantial Christmas present was a smart scooter with wire-spoked wheels, ball bearings in the hubs and real rubber tyres. I spent hours circling the unfurnished front room in St. James's Road, Cannock; laying down hundreds of concentric tyre burns on the concrete floor, as I circled the room on my journey in the mind.

My horizon outdoors was travelling the tarmac footpath from garden gate to the end of cul-de-sac telephone box and back. A year or so later, I would borrow a tricycle from a neighbour's son (we were too poor for me to have my own).and pedal along the entryway, turning the shiny handlebars, manoeuvring with skill to make tight turns, barely missing to scrape the chrome hubs on fence or house wall. Proficient enough to win the toddler version of 'lorry driver of the year'! I suppose I was in a child's diverse world of pretend. Sitting patiently on the trike at a wayside railway station of the imagination, waiting for my passengers to board and me taking on coal and water, I would eventually start on a journey around the garden. I would stop at the back garden fence station to drop off and take on fresh passengers. In my young mind I was in control, providing a service, following my railway track and getting my travellers safely to their terminus by the front gate. A magic, imagined world far away from reality yet concerning everyday things. A special state of pretend that only a child can enjoy.

Moving to Barkston in Lincolnshire, my cousin, Denhy had a small, red, two-wheeler and we would take turns to cycle down the country lane, avoiding any fresh cow pats and almost reach Elnor's Farm and yet another world of mystery. When it wasn't my turn, I would be patient and relish the thought of the next trip while looking for birds' nests in the boundary hedgerow. My cousin, however, preferred to play cricket and, eventually, I was left with this little bike to come and go as I pleased. With hedges flying past in a blur of cow parsley and berried briars, my horizons were being pushed further and further ahead – if not in linear miles – definitely in expanded flights of fancy. That little, red two-wheeler gave me confidence due to being able to place both feet flat on the road while standing stopped.

An occasional trip to see my Aunt Peggy at Stoke Rochford provided me with the chance to ride a grown-up's bike. Her husband and brother, Will and Billy, working in estate management for the nearby Stoke Rochford Hall. I borrowed Billy's enormous black, sit-up-and-beg bicycle and pedalled down another long lane in the general direction of Skillington. I wasn't tall enough to sit on the saddle so had to ride, standing on the pedals, with the cold metal of the crossbar rubbing between my legs. The distance between the tied cottage and the white-painted section of rear metal mudguard stretched to over a mile before I braked to a halt and, skewing around, returned for tea, cakes and a round of putting golf balls on the extensive lawn. The experience of unlimited freedom was overpowering. Uncle Billy had been worried over the disappearance of his bike; it was his only form of transport and he was surely grateful to see me staggering with it, handlebars at my head level, through the garden gate on my eventual return.

My short time in Plymouth was spent cycling along the impossibly steep side streets off Mutley Plain and around St. Judes, North Road railway station, the fish market at the Barbican and Sutton Harbour. Another borrowed bone shaker of a bicycle and learning to cope with the steep cambers and deep gutters of Plymouth's back roads while train spotting and trawler spotting. A nearby acquaintance, another big-bike owner who possessed a streak of adventure, persuaded me to join him on a relatively distant jaunt along the Kingsbridge Road to Yealmpton. We messed about by a stream below the village. This, I suppose, was a most significant increase in miles cycled. My journeys down in the south west were ceased when my foster parents made an employment-changing move, up north, to Stoke-on-Trent. Besides, a landlord's son's pet rabbit had taken a fancy to the bike's rubber tyres and nibbled them down to the canvas base!

Of course, it wasn't just getting from A to B on the bike but the very experience of moving along the road, moving through the air, as if flying. Something like skiing but not so wet and cold, or being dragged up a mountain by hooking one's backside over a freezing metal bar. Being able, when conditions and slopes dictated, to stop pedalling and freewheel; hear the busy chattering and ticking of the gears, hear and feel the vibration and thrumming of rubber tyres on hard road surfaces. What a marvellous word – 'freewheeling' – moving along with no effort and all for free. When the road reared up ahead, to feel the pressure under the feet and be able to select a more sensible, lower gear ratio. Here, strength, style and stamina came into play. The ultimate experience was climbing high on alpine roads, soaring and swooping like an eagle between snow and sky. I could compare cycle touring to something like cross-country gliding. Although not of a racing disposition, we all experienced a feel-good factor to reach a pass summit first, as it was to cross a town or village boundary sign at the head of a storming phalanx of bounding, leaping, lurching bicycles in a sprint of flashing, shiny chrome and colour.

Another enormous plus for the bicycle, I found, was that it could be taken almost anywhere. Anywhere and everywhere: along main roads, down lanes, some with a strip of grass in the middle, along footpaths, over short grass, through shallow and deeper fords, over tracks, across boardwalks, down cycleways, along beaches (not recommended because of the hard going and intrusive gritty sand)., up mountains and down dales. Even into war! Soldiers on two wheels, acting as messengers, were extremely effective. Being manoeuvrable, silent and needing no fuel, bicycles played their part in many subversive actions.

In Lindsay Anderson's excellent film, *If... A Revelation of Public School Life, Class and Class Perversions and Revolt*, we see the history master riding into school, down the corridor and even into the classroom on his big, black bike, complete with wicker basket! Such is the accessibility of the bike. I remember a character in my village, Bomere Heath, who decided, on a keep-fit drive, deciding to buy a lightweight cycle as his inexpensive form of transport. His friends bet him that he wouldn't keep up this lifestyle but he joined them one evening in the pub's lounge to show off his gleaming machine. He cycled through one door, crossed the room and exited through the door leading to the toilets – not stopping, not putting his foot on the carpet and not missing a pedal stroke! And not even buying a drink. Yes, cyclists can go almost anywhere – rough-stuff cyclists even further. Naturally, boulder-fields and motorways are out of bounds. Who wants to travel a motorway anyway? National Cycling Week!? Overpaid and overweight television presenters pretended to be keen cyclists, wobbling along for a few yards, turning an impossibly low gear as if on a washing machine's fast-spin. With their feet splayed at ten-to-two and on the point of lost balance and displaced style and dignity, the media tended to make fun of cycling. Cycling is, only now, in this new millennium, treated as a serious form of alternative transport. Only now, an organisation such as Sustrans has realised the unique usefulness of the bicycle. In the 1960s, if one preferred a bike to a motor car, they were considered to be on the lowest strata of society – mere lower class or completely loopy, deranged! In London and with the introduction of the congestion charge, many more adventurous folk are defying death to take up the bike, even if it's only to deliver precious packages in the shortest time possible. Bicycle couriers in London's traffic have a special ability alongside their own particular rules of the road. Some of these rules are interpreted in order to preserve life, especially where bendy buses and large lorries turning left are concerned.

Mountain biking looks good fun. Once known as cyclo-cross, this activity offers an exciting, spectator-friendly sport – just about, peering through the trees – but has been grasped by the commercially-driven philistines and portrayed as youth – sideways and airborne, flying down a cliff face with a protective cushioning of fresh-air, against a snowy Himalayan infinity background. Pyjama-clad and covered in sponsorship logos, youth giving cycling sport more zip and pizzazz. Generated, no doubt, from the cult of computer games, these images are both silly and rather dangerous!

After finishing my solo journey to Plymouth and back, I had needed to change my cycle. The Halford's Sports just wasn't lightweight enough, not good enough. I collected a brochure for Sun Cycles and admired the sleek racing models illustrated. Based in the Midlands, Sun Cycles weren't a very small, exclusive cycle manufacturer but produced models above the mass-produced standard. Their factory wasn't a back-street, hand-built frame makers but, nevertheless, produced machines of quality. They had not yet been absorbed into the giant industrial estate concerns, such as Raleigh or Coventry Eagle. It soon became apparent that the more spartan, uncluttered, light and basic the model was, the more it cost. Less meant more! This was, of course, because superior frame tubing and gears were used in the really light, racing models. I poured over the varying specifications until the brochure was dog-eared and covered with oil stains. Wondering how they could show the bikes across the page, having no stands and without them falling over! I admired the sleek frame angles, the low racing handlebars, the large-flange hubs and imagining being able to lift the bike with one finger; I chose to ignore the rake and narrowness of the lightweight saddle! I finally plumped for a mid-range model, something between a racer and a touring machine. The wheelbase governs the responsiveness of a cycle frame – short wheelbase for racing, longer wheelbase for a more comfortable, touring position, where speed and response are not important. I settled for a middle-of-the-range, off the peg model with a 21 inch frame, 6-speed gear block and a Campagnolo gear mechanism. Campagnolo was the quality gear that was made using superb materials, phosphor-bronze bushes and was used by all racing cyclists. What is more, they were made in Italy and that couldn't be bad! This gear didn't have a vast range for the use of ultra-low gears, but looked good and was advertised in the weekly magazine I read at that time – *Cycling*. The gear enabling a really low bottom gear – a cog as large as a saucer that let you climb 'up a wall', was the Cyclo-Benelux with wide-spaced jockey wheels to take up chain slackness – yet another piece of useless information! The frame was of a ruby/purple colour and I hand-painted the name *'Maud'* on each side of the crossbar, very amateurishly, in white, freehand lettering. The handlebars were of light alloy and wound with white plastic tape for grip. Despite the taping, my hands would be covered with black alloy stains after a few miles of riding. The brake hoods and levers were covered with soft rubber sheaths and altogether, I was very pleased with my purchase.

I used the Sun Tourer, *Maud,* for some longer exploratory runs in that summer of 1960. We had joined the Ellis family on a week's holiday in a chalet behind Prestatyn, North Wales. Instead of travelling by car, I opted to cycle there by way of Llangollen, climb the Horseshoe Pass, and reach the coast via Ruthin and St. Asaph. I camped alongside the basic wooden chalet in the small paddock for a few nights. I remember the terrible smell of the septic tank. It kept me awake for hours as I tossed and turned in the cold darkness!

On a day's solo ride into Shropshire, I reached Church Stretton and struggled a few hundred yards up the severely steep Burway road, leading to the top of the elevated Long Mynd. Sheet ice covering the road surface, followed by deep snowdrifts, making an impenetrable white wall. Faced with a return journey of some distance, I took a quick photograph of wintry heights and turned the bike around to cycle home in fading daylight. Nevertheless, my distances were increasing, I was gaining fitness and all I needed now was companions, like-minded explorers.

My account of cycling around and away from the idyllic environs of the Potteries had already been mentioned. With improved equipment, acquiring a skill of mechanical maintenance and a meeting with like-minded enthusiasts, my horizons had widened to virtual infinity. The desire to explore the unknown, whether it be to the end of the lane or to the summit of a long mountain pass, were the things to do. The bicycle was the best thing to do them on. Onto this pastime could be hung another interest, in my case, photography. The two interests could augment each other, feed off each other and provide a basketful of memories. Companionship, comradeship and camaraderie derived from a cycling weekend or, better still, a longer tour, was and is immense. Being a lone wolf cyclist is fine enough; time to set one's own pace and choose one's preferred routes and destinations is good, but do it all within a group of like-minded enthusiasts is far, far better. I was fortunate in Stoke to find my cycling friends through the auspices of the Youth Hostels Association. To use the YHA as an organisation for the provision of accommodation, observe the many rules and regulations, provided they were based on common sense, but not to consider the institution as an exclusive religion. We were within the spirit of it all by travelling under our own steam and not cheating by use of a motor car and besides, we were notching up bed nights and swelling the YHA's coffers in no small way. We even went on working parties to Stoke's adopted hostel, Dimmingsdale. But being of an age when visits to the public house, the occasional smoke and staying out a little longer were part of the enjoyment of it all, by the end of the decade we were older, not necessarily wiser, but felt it was time to move on. There were no more mugs of cocoa and flicking through the pages of *Reader's Digest* while drowning in the scruffy, hugging arms of a collapsingly-old armchair. Our trusty cycles, instead of being neatly stowed in the hostel bike shed, were, invariably, leaning against the wall of the local tavern. With being wage-earners, spending money became available. Most young men would ditch the bike and save for a small motorcycle at that time, the ultimate goal being a cheap, second-hand car. We could afford to become motorised. Pushing boundaries, acquiring wheels, buying tents and camping stoves and freeing ourselves of the constricting rules of youth hostelling. But we still loaded the bikes on to or into our conveyances and continued to enjoy cycling.

Chapter Two

1961

A Tour Through Mid Wales – Some Fellow YHA Cyclists – Christmas at Edale – A Brewery Visit – The Dreaded Cyclists' Knock – Misty Mishaps – The Boggy Wastes of Whixall-Photography the Old Way.

Age: 20.

Home: Cherry Tree Close, Trentham, Stoke-on-Trent.

Work: SOT Reconstruction Dept., Woodhouse Street, Stoke.

Government: Conservative.

Prime Minister: Harold Macmillan.

January: J. F. Kennedy becomes President of America.

April: Yuri Gagarin of USSR is first man in space.

April: America in Bay of Pigs invasion incident with Cuba.

May: Kennnedy pledges America will reach moon and return safely by end of decade. British spy George Blake sentenced.

June: Ballet dancer, Nureyev, defects to the West.

August: Britain unsuccessfully applies for membership of the European Economic Community. East Germany builds the Berlin Wall – 'defending the East Germans from Western decadence'.

Musical: *Oliver.*

Novel: *Catch-22.*

Film: *West Side Story.*

Cosmonaut Yuri Gagarin, the very first man in space, posed for photographs on an access staging of the Vostock 1 rocket. His service greatcoat and enormous, round hat gave him an air of patriotic amateurishness, especially when compared to the clean, high-tech overalls and space helmets of the American astronauts. John Glenn replied with a sub-orbital hop! Nureyev leaps to the West – I don't blame him – Russian women street cleaners sigh whilst leaning on their brooms. Britain just couldn't get into the European club. Geoff Cartlidge, discussing the Common Market, said, "All these Frogs can produce is wine and cheese – what's the use of that?!" He wasn't too impressed with General de Gaulle either! The USA made another pig's ear with their overkill in the Cuban, Bay of Pigs incident. The most significant event this year was the rapid building of the Berlin Wall. The East German Guards relinquished their union tea-breaks to throw up this barrier in double-quick time and form a ghetto with the Communists, protected from the over-indulgences of the West. As Brezhnev displayed his missiles in Red Square, Ban the Bomb marchers formed serried ranks; marching on London and shaking their cardboard placards, but still getting their message over.

*

As my journey down to Plymouth the year before had proved reasonably easy, I studied the YHA map of Britain and decided that a week's tour of mid-Wales and towards Pembrokeshire was quite possible. On a late summer's afternoon in 1961, I departed Cherry Tree Close and took the road to the A53, to the road junction known as Trentham Lane Ends, a convenient meeting place for countless future Friday night departures to use the hostel at Shrewsbury. The distance to be covered was about 34 miles (55k).through Baldwin's Gate, Loggerheads, Market Drayton, Tern Hill, Hodnet and Shawbury. The road was pleasant enough, passing through rolling countryside, the only serious climb being long, rather than steep, from the foot of the wooded Maer Hills to the summit at Loggerheads. I found the Shrewsbury hostel, Woodlands, at the top of Abbey Foregate, a grand former family residence opposite the high Greek Doric column of Lord Hill. The approach to Abbey Foregate was through the streets of Ditherington and Castlefields, crossing the River Severn over the Castle Walk footbridge and winding through the suburbs of Cherry Orchard and Monkmoor. Cyclists are always on the lookout for a short-cut and part of this route led down Queen Street, Castlefields. Twenty-three years and many thousands of cycling miles later, I bought a marvellous Victorian terraced house in this very street! I would be living day-to-day in this

Shrewsbury suburb that I had flashed through on many shortcuts to, first, the Bricklayers' Arms and then the youth hostel. I remember the warden as being taciturn but able to play the squeeze box very well. I gathered later that he was a member of the local folk club.

The overall route of my second YHA tour was from Shrewsbury to Clun, Glascwm, Pentre Cwrt, Poppit Sands, Borth and Corris, to meet a few of my recently found and barely known Potteries cycling friends at Bala. Ignoring the direct route south to Clun, I ventured west, over the Welsh border, on back lanes through Westbury, Chirbury and Montgomery, to reach Abermule. The 'B' road from here reared upwards on its way to Kerry and the countryside opened out to high level moor and grassland with isolated spruce forestry; countryside where the tough Kerry sheep roamed, before being driven eastward down the long valley to the market centre at Craven Arms. The lane descended from the Wales/Shropshire border at Anchor, wriggled through Newcastle-on-Clun, to arrive at Clun itself, the sleepy, one-time fortified small town made famous by A. E. Housman's *A Shropshire Lad*. A medieval stone bridge crosses the stream here, the lowest point of the valley that is surrounded by rounded, separated hills, many clothed with dark-green woodland. The castle holds a prominent position close to the centre, its brooding, ruined battlements on a steep-sided motte enjoying uninterrupted views up and down the valley to west and east – an almost fairytale image of ivy-covered domination. A guardian of the serfs, who lived below its walls, from hoards of marauding Celts of the west. Passing the high walls of the former alms houses and Trinity Hospital, I cycled up to Clun youth hostel, a disused corn mill on the edge of town once served by a now dried-up lagoon feeding off the River Clun. The warden could be contacted at his home in nearby Ford Street. The hostel building was basic in the extreme with thick outer walls, concrete floor and stout, ground-floor, wooden support columns. None of the milling machinery remained. A small mens' first-floor dormitory had a small window at floor level and held just a few wooden bunks. The whole building creaked after its long-past busy working life.

The main road from Clun to Knighton begins ascending opposite the squat tower of the Norman church of St George and climbs steadily into high rolling country with expansive views of bordering hills. The Marches landscape here offers glimpses to the west of unknown hills disappearing into a hazy backdrop of mid-Wales; a child's patterned quilt of greens, yellows and browns, strafed by handsome cumulus clouds on a blue ground. I saw ahead the road dipping into a fold in the hills as if 'collecting' the hamlet of New Invention, with its scattering of small cottages and disused chapel. Beyond, the road swept up again like a giant big dipper – the length and severity of the climb immediately felt in pulling thigh muscles. The final descent to Knighton is bordered by dark spruce woodland on the western hill slope with the letters 'ER' cleverly delineated by the careful planting of yellow-green larch. No doubt a recognition of the country's new queen crowned in 1953. Knighton, straddling the English/Welsh border, is the main town and midway point on the Long Distance Footpath of Offa's Dyke, now having well-signed routes to north and south and a Heritage Visitor Centre, but in 1961, virtually unknown and certainly not promoted to any great extent. We had yet to enter the age of touring, unlike today, when, no matter what the destination, we visited, just as long as a brown sign told you to go there! From Knighton, my route took me through Old Radnor, with the bare, grassy swell of Radnor Forest off my right shoulder, Gladestry and into a network of narrow lanes that climbed into Welsh hills towards Glascwm and another overnight hostel stay. The rich farmland of Herefordshire fell below and behind as I climbed into bare hills, walking on the final steep yards and gained a high level valley with a minute settlement of stone cottages and the roadside hostel. Glascwm youth hostel was one of many disused schoolhouses to be found in unpopulated central Wales. Close by the roadside, the place was sited within its small playground, accessed by a few well-worn rugged steps with a view opposite of grassy mountainsides crossed by many sheep tracks. One could almost sense the scrape of hobnail boots on old asphalt playground, or the scrape of chalk on writing slates. One could almost hear the swish of the girl's skipping rope and the rounds of children's rhyming songs rising, ghostlike, from behind the chants of times-tables learnt by rote.

The warden arrived to sign visitors in. She was old and Welsh but didn't wear the red cape, frilled white blouse or black, pointed witch's hat that's seen in many a gift shop. She didn't arrive on a besom broomstick but had tootled up the cwm from Hundred House on a black bicycle, assisted with a fitted rear wheel Cyclemaster engine. She described Hundred House as if it was the centre of the universe. She didn't play the harp either! Or at least, she didn't carry one up the mountain with her. Now that I'd crossed the border into wild Wales, I began to find the cycling a very lonely pastime indeed. I began to feel like an alien in a foreign land. The main A486 road travels through real bandit country. Builth Wells, north of the Mynydd Eppynt, Llanwrtyd Wells, Llandovery, Llanwrda, before I took a minor route deep into the hills via Llansawel, to cross the bleak Mynydd Pencarreg towards Lampeter. My head was swimming with all those double 'lls' and double 'dds', or was it the steepness of the gradients on this wild and open moorland? The wind bent the clumps of cotton grass and sheep sheltered behind any scant vegetation at the sides of the road, while a chill, misty rain made my glasses steam up. The cloud base lowered in a heavy, scudding greyness. As the rain increased, I had to squint through the steamy lenses and curtain of water dropping from my eyebrows. I noticed a hamlet ahead, so, with water swishing forward off my front tyre, I slewed to a belated standstill outside a village shop. Stopping is always a problem in heavy rain – brake blocks struggling to take hold on wet, shiny rims, only shuddering to a stop when surfaces become dry. The shop was on the edge of the village, lonely, isolated, like the infamous Local Shop in the TV comedy, *The League of Gentlemen:* but this was bleak Rhydcymerau, not evil Royston Vasey. I pressed down the latch and pushed the door open. The doorbell gave an out-of-tune clunk and the door screeched as if a piece of gravel had caught underneath, warning the three shoppers inside to switch, in an instant, from speaking English to a very throaty Welsh. The three women dressed in heavy gabardine raincoats gathered in a close huddle; grey hair bound tightly under headscarves and stout shopping baskets and purses gripped in vice-like fingers. With an appropriate costume change, they could easily have played the opening scene to Shakespeare's *Macbeth!* "When shall we three meet again – in thunder, lightening, or in rain?" Today, it was, thankfully, just persistent rain. I stood with water dripping onto the quarry tiles, wet and pink crinkled knees showing from beneath a shiny, yellow cycling cape and felt intimidated in the extreme. I was afraid – very afraid! Some semblance to a language assured my ears as I heard the occasional recognisable words emerge. Brand names such as Persil, Oxo, Vim and Marmite spilled from the guttural sentences of deep Welsh as the ladies made their desired daily purchases. When my turn arrived, I handed over my 6d (2.5p).and received my Milky Bar from the bespectacled, aged crone behind the counter. I rushed out of this very local shop and set my front wheel in the direction of the Afon Teifi and Newcastle Emlyn.

After a few miles short, I arrived at Pentre Cwrt youth hostel, met fellow travellers and some being English! It was like being rescued from a desert island! Downstream from Pentre Cwrt, I had a rest and admired the coracle paddlers under the old bridge at Cenarth. The day was overcast, the river sullen and the old gents in their round, canvas-covered boats sculling here and there for the benefit of the odd, passing tourist – the scene demanded, nay, cried out for photography using sepia printing paper. My camera at that time was an early folding Kodak 35mm and an opening lens panel with aperture, focus, speed controls and shutter release connected to the camera body with neat concertina bellows. It was an antiquated, miniature work of art. I often wished that I'd kept it, if only for its tactile qualities. Moving westward, I followed the Afon Teifi to the sea; through Cardigan's streets to reach the estuary at St Dogmaels. The hostel clung to the grassy headland above Poppit Sands together with a few other isolated cottages. The name, Poppit Sands, evokes the thought of wreckers and smugglers, swinging their lanterns, luring the unwary ship on to the rocks and rolling those barrels of rum up the beach. Sitting in the common room, sipping my cocoa and listening to the wash of the waves and squeal of the gulls conjured up the vision of swarthy fellows doing dark deeds. The illusion of wreckers was brought into the 21st century with the grounding of a container ship, *Napoli,* in 2007 off Branscombe Beach, Devon, when container goods, including BMW motorbikes and thousands of Pampas baby nappies, were claimed by 'beach cred' locals. One can't help having a certain admiration for such opportunists. The claiming of jetsam was quickly declared illegal, local legislation was rapidly rewritten and the area of beach was soon surrounded by police and customs officials clad in suitably officious, high visibility garb. It is surprising how fast officialdom can work when needs must!

From Poppit Sands, I cycled north following the coast via Aberaeron and Aberystwyth; all main 'A' roads before a turn on to a lane beyond Aberystwyth, which took me back towards the seaside and the long, sandy beaches at Borth. [Early notes typewritten years ago on yellowing, foxed paper indicated a route from Poppit Sands to Nant y Dernol, north of Rhayader. This I mentioned in my *Memoirs*, describing part of the route on that 1961 mid-Wales tour. As those notes were made years after the event, I have to admit that my memory fails me and I must accept that the more likely route was up the coast to Borth. Cyclists don't like going back over the same roads on a tour, therefore a day cycling from Poppit to Nant y Dernol! sounds highly unlikely]. Vague, barely fleeting memories tenuously lodged at the back of my memory help me to recall a fellow hosteller at Borth who, on seeing the sea and flat hinterland thereabouts, raved repeatedly, endlessly, about the cliff scenery at Marloes and extolling the beauty of the Pembrokeshire coast in general.

Next day, I continued north to Aberdovey, reaching the Dovey Estuary and the rainy Machynlleth streets. Welsh architecture shows its solid, dreary best on rain-sodden days. Building stone of mid-grey with purple-grey roof slates, streaming wetness, isn't the best image to set the heart soaring but, at least, it was typical Welsh vernacular. After crossing the Afon Dyfi, I headed north on a slowly climbing main road signposted Dolgellau. The more I climbed, the more the heavens opened up, turning quickly from an incessant heavy drizzle to a spirit-numbing downpour. The road wound into a steep-sided valley with flanks clothed in dense conifer woodland. Wraiths of mist hung wandering and dancing between the branches above and strearnlets of water coursed down the roadside gutters, forming waves before disappearing into kerbside drains. My cycling cape, hanging from around my neck and hooked over the two brake levers, rapidly bulged with water and sagged heavily above the crossbar. Each pedal stroke saw my knees bang into the underside of the bulge, causing the water to slop from side to side in a sad tidal wave. The weighty, watery ullage and monotonous drag of the climb caused me to imagine goldfish swimming around merrily in this mobile aquarium. I could hear, hundreds of feet above and out of sight, the muffled roar of numerous mountain streams, well above the mist, giving this wet afternoon's ride a feeling of deepest gloom. But all good things must eventually come to an end and I rolled to a decidedly damp, splashing stop outside Corris youth hostel. With sloshing steps and water dripping onto smooth, cold linoleum, I headed for the drying room and arranged my socks on the boiler rail, leaving them to, hopefully, dry without burning. Other hostellers' apparel hung sullenly from every available space, waving wafts of hot, moist and fuggy fumes around in the dim atmosphere. Seeking clear, cool, fresh air, 1 went outside to seek life-giving oxygen. The surrounding hillsides were covered in scattered boulders, with the occasional spoil heaps of past slate mining activity. The areas of bracken, moss-covered stone and conifer plantations had an overall softening effect on the general past industrial scenery as did, of course, the blanketing, rounding-off effect of low-lying, rain-penetrated mist. Corris was yet another disused village school. How those rag-arsed, booted kids sitting in their damp, chafmg clothes would fidget uncomfortably as they urged the two hands of the large wall clock to creep around to 4:00pm and the leaving bell.

The rain clouds had blown away by the next morning as I climbed into the valley beyond Tal-yLlyn, over the Cross Foxes Pass, passing a bulky shoulder of Cader Idris before swooping down through woodland, around the many bends, passing abandoned gold mines and into the cluster of stone and slate at Dolgellau. The A494 took a direct route to the north-east for some 18 miles (29k).to finally skirt the elongated Llyn Tegid and arrive at the inland sailing centre of Bala. The hostel at Plas Rhiwaedog was hidden in the network of narrow lanes that finally leads over the Hirnant Pass, to Lake Vyrnwy – an adventurous route, we would cycle over on many a hostelling weekend in the near future. Bala hostel was a grand stone building, accessed by way of an arch let into the defensive outer wall. The site had definitely been fortified sometime in its past history; a history, maybe, involving roving brigands doing darkest deeds. The warden seemed friendly enough though! It was whilst in the hostel that I met with several cyclists from Stoke-on-Trent, cyclists who would become close friends and fellow explorers. With a few minutes of eavesdropping and some brief, passing conversation, I realised that these riders had ideals and interests very similar to my own.

My final day touring was to join the A5 Holyhead Road, east towards Llangollen, following the River Dee. Part of the route followed the narrow lanes from Carrog on the north bank of the Dee; an undulating, lonely road winding alongside forestry and dipping to river level at times. This alternative route to Llangollen provided a view of the brooding Berwyn, a distant view of the hills to the south of the Vale of Llangollen and avoided the summer traffic congestion on the A5 main road. Beyond the Chain Bridge, the route leads into the town by the recently opened and extended Llangollen to Corwen steam railway. I pedalled through Erbistock and Overton before crossing the north Shropshire flatland plain and through Whitchurch to Newcastle-under-Lyme, Stoke-on-Trent and home. Rolling to a halt outside the house in Cherry Tree Close meant that I had closed the circle, finished my solo tour, and enjoyed new scenes and scenarios, despite the full week being a bit on the lonely side.

As late summer progressed, I learned that Stoke had its local YHA group, so, I went along to a few of the meetings in Cartwright House, Hanley. It was through these that I met with the Hazeldine brothers, Roy and Eric. They were living in Boughey Road, Stoke at the time; the street we first moved into, lodging with Edith and Les Ellis, when first moving north from Plymouth. Roy was the elder brother. He had lost most of his hair, wore round, owl-like spectacles, tended to be a little shy, but had a cheerful smile, enjoyed a joke and with his experience of cycling, was the natural organiser to form the Cycling Section of our local YHA group. Initially, we were known as the Stoke-on-Trent Youth Hostels Cycling Club (SOTYHCC).Social programme apart, up until then the group had only a Walking Section. Eric Hazeldine was a real outdoor enthusiast – on two feet as well as two wheels. Sturdy and stocky in stature, Eric could easily have been mistaken for racing driver, Stirling Moss; the

Stirling Moss wearing goggles, face tanned by the slipstream and climbing out of his Jaguar E-type at Le Mans.

Geoff Cartlidge, wiry of frame with freckles and a shock of ginger hair, was about the same age as myself, if not a year or so younger. Over the next few years, we would share the experiences of many cycling tours. Geoff had a bone-dry sense of humour, very much akin to my own and like his father, was a great supporter of Harold Wilson and the Labour Party. His father worked for the Gas Board and Geoff was destined to follow in his father's footsteps. Maybe because of his freckles, Geoff was uneasy wearing shorts, so, at first, wore tight blue jeans on every cycling trip. Joan Hall was a solid, robust lass who could turn the pedals with powerful thighs. Joan was rather worldly and would often make fun of Geoff with a motherly concern. She christened him Banjo – only because, in her eyes, he always 'strung along'. Marian Vyse was of slighter build than Joan, wore incredibly tight denim shorts, and wore horn-rimmed spectacles. At a quick glance, she could have been mistaken for a young Mary Whitehouse, that self-appointed guardian of TV viewers' morals. She also resembled Dame Edna Everage with those glasses, but with a less *risque* and moderated sense of humour. Marian would turn a vivid pink in thighs and cheeks as cold winds buffeted our early in the year cycling days. Miss Vyse also had an alarming swerve when avoiding any road debris or pothole; the following rider left to take the consequences. Her boyfriend, Bill Walshaw, strong, tall and taciturn, was her constant companion.

Derek Latham was tall, well-built and sported a Royal Air Force moustache. Derek was one hundred per cent Air Force – the embodiment of one of The Few! He was a few years older than myself and probably had experience of National Service. He would often be seen grooming each spiky side of this facial hair addition with a nicotine-stained forefinger. He would tweak his handlebar moustache after each sip of beer or to remove the crumbs after a shortcake biscuit. He held himself with such an air of self-importance that, to everyone else, seemed altogether quite comical. Indeed, we would often describe him as Himself or Squadron Leader! His cycle, a Hill Special, was large-framed, ruby red, with fine white box lining and chromed forks front and rear. Derek would smoke a cigarette down to the quick, extracting the last smoky whiff until the stub burned his fingers. Nevertheless, he was a great darts player and an even greater cyclist. Derek had introduced a near neighbour to cycling, Dave Hope, who lived a few doors away at Hanchurch crossroads. Dave, a bricklayer by trade, was of mixed race with a glowing nut-brown complexion, barrel-chest and, like Derek, enjoyed a drink, a smoke and a joke on every available occasion. His occupation must have given him great strength, stamina and the broadest of minds! Apart from his silver Mercian lightweight cycle, Dave was the proud owner of a Manx Norton. He also enjoyed a game of darts.

Ken Hall, another keen cyclist, was an even keener walker. Ken, apart from loving the savagery of the Scottish Highlands, was essentially a Pennines walker. As gritty as the millstone grit of the northeast Pennines, Ken was solid, stocky and would be seen dressed in corduroy shorts and thick, baggy woollen sweater for most of the year. Ken would not be seen on lower, softer mountains. He had a love of 'good old' mild beer and classical music and finally persuaded Geoff Cartlidge and me to attend a concert at the Victoria Hall, Hanley. It was the *Pastoral Symphony* by Beethoven. Bill Barnish was another cyclist who joined the section in the earliest days. Bill, quite shy, lapped up the sometimes dubious banter and near-the-knuckle jokes with a guffaw while retaining a front of complete innocence. He always wore his embarrassment with flushed cheeks of pink. His cycling wear consisted of a green outdoor jacket and a black beret – almost a sort of Frank Spencer character of *Some Mothers Do 'Ave 'Em* fame. Brian Whalley, short, sharp-featured, fair-haired with an Errol Flynn moustache and accident prone, would always be acting the clown. His bush hat reminded one of billabongs and kangaroos. He always wore an oversized blue sweater of such a length that, dragging down to his knees, it appeared he had no shorts on, naked below the waist. Brian, with twitching moustache, had more than a roving eye for the girls.

Uncle Joe Ball, a nickname stemming not from Joseph Stalin, but Uncle Joe's Mint Balls, was a real old timer who must have been everywhere and seen everything in his cycling days. He would always enjoy short runs, attending reunion dinners and New Year parties and even turned up for a future Tramps' cycle ride, (to Rudyard Lake). He was very well-respected, as was Fred Maitland, a stalwart of the local cyclists. Laurie Landon had done some cycling, too and in the 1960s was Secretary of the Staffordshire YHA. He appeared to be rather posh and resembling *Billy Bunter of Greyfriars School;* bumbling, chubby, bespectacled and red-faced, he was, nevertheless, a keen YHA servant. Maurice Such, who courted Joan Hall for a time, split his interests between cycling, walking and wooing.

In 1961, this handful of characters formed loosely into the Cycling Section; everyone interested in cycle touring, planned to embark on the more conservative distances and routes at first, but formed a nucleus for potentially exploring more ambitious routes as experience was gained. Because there was a connection with walking through the local YHA Section's programme, short sections of 'rough-stuff' – cycling along hill tracks and off-tarmac – were considered. Planned routes on tracks linking existing lanes were forming furtively in the minds of the more adventurous. We were a crowd of chattering bikers, laughing and joking as if on a one-off, jolly day's picnic outing rather than a communal group of Lowry's factory workers streaming out of the factory gates when the day's shift was over. We were a tight group of outdoor enthusiasts who were using youth hostels to open up tracts of countryside away from the usual tourist spots. Groups of happy cyclists spinning down country roads; headscarves flapping, flat caps being waved, was an image that had appeared on the covers of early road maps of the 1930s and closely reflected our approach to leisure cycling. Documentary images with a jolly soundtrack backing, although appearing naïve and far too innocent, were styles of touring that we wished to loosely recreate. In view of the events, styles and morals of the emerging decade, this seemingly innocent pastime could be considered a two-wheeled anachronism.

I joined Derek Latham, Dave Hope and Ken Hall for a few days over the Christmas period, staying at Edale youth hostel in the Peak District. The hostel was situated at the very end of the Vale of Edale, north of the Hope Valley, the Peak Cavern and Castleton. I cycled into the Peak District via Leek and over the bleak moors to Buxton in dull, rainy weather. As I was leaving the tight streets of Buxton, pedalling uphill and passing a line of parked cars, I was momentarily blinded by rainwater dripping from my hair to the eyes and collided with a protruding rear bumper. It was only a glancing blow and after collecting my wits and after some confusion regaining the handlebars; grappling for them under the wet cape, I continued to steer towards Chapel-en-le-Frith. It was only when descending through Barber Booth on the hilly lane into Edale that I noticed a build-up of rubber dust clinging to the top of the front forks. It was caused by the brake blocks rubbing on the rubber walls of the tyre instead of the rim. They had become misaligned because, with my altercation with the parked car in Buxton, the forks had been forced backwards. They were only slightly bent, needing only a slight readjustment of the brake shoes. It does, however, indicate the forward rolling force generated in the cycle when the front wheel is stopped suddenly. I arrived at Edale with no further disasters and joined Derek, Dave and Ken for a few days of merrymaking.

Huddled under Mam Tor, known as the Shivering Mountain due to its liability to landslip, the hostel was at the start of the long distance footpath, the Pennine Way, that wound up the very backbone of England. Looming to the north-west of Edale is the foreboding Kinderscout. This elevated area of black, boggy land was the venue for a mass trespass in 1932 when the working class hoi-polloi from the cotton towns revolted against rich landowners and spoiled their precious grouse shooting. We walked over and through this demanding terrain; climbing in and out of deep troughs of slimy peat, until, under compass guidance, arrived at the spectacular cliffs bordering the waterfall, the Kinder Downfall. This was definitely 'Ken Hall country'!

Very much closer to the hostel was the Nag's Head public house. That Christmas would be remembered for the sweet, cloying taste of Tennent's Gold Label and the hours of euphoria that it caused. I was then still a young man without any experience of alcoholic beverages, least of all ultra-strong barley wines. Luckily, I managed to retain my constitution and never disgraced myself – just! There were nights, however, when I fought to control the ever-spinning dormitory's walls and ceiling. In fact, on the protocol of drinking, my experience of entering a pub and ordering a drink was pretty much non-existent. I remember waiting at the bar on one occasion and shyly ordering a pint of *beer* – not a pint of bitter, mild, stout or lager. Generally, us younger members would squat at tables outside, in the beer gardens and not in that evil saloon bar, behind the etched glass, hiding a room full of boisterous singing, swearing and projectile expectorant into the communal spittoon!

We met and got talking to a member of the YHA who was working for Bent's Brewery at Stone, south of Stoke. John Shackerley was the brewery's senior (and only).chemist. John was thin, rangy and wore bottle-bottomed spectacles – just what a chemist fresh out of university should look like. He was responsible for testing the various mixings, mashes, warts and all of the various brews. He invited us all to have a tour of the brewery with his expert guidance. Maybe we were acquiring a reputation for enjoying a drink or two? Derek Latham, Dave Hope, Ralph Salt and Eric Hazeldine, I remember, were the first to put their names down. John's laboratory was a mere cupboard space with a bench covered in dusty beakers, test tubes, thermometers, hydrometers and a cobwebbed microscope. We were all treated to a comprehensive tour of the establishment; mashing room, fermentation hall, bottling plant, with Derek posing for photographs under a dripping beer barrel; eyes closed, mouth open and soaked moustache lathered with the froth of Bent's Best Bitter. I recall the fermentation vats most vividly. Head held over the deep foaming surface of the brew in yeasty agitation, the 'barm'; nostrils assailed with the malted richness of it all, before the complete choking sensation of having nil oxygen whatsoever to breathe made a sudden, involuntary, upward jerk of the head absolutely necessary. Geoff Cartlidge and I cycled back home after the privileged tour while Derek, Dave, Ralph and Eric carried on drinking and finally spent the night in comatose, sleeping peacefully in a corner of the brewery, dead to the world on layers of molasses sacks. The next morning, the foursome cycled on autopilot into the Peak District and arrived at Leam Hall, near Matlock, there, no doubt, to re-enter the land of the living!

Having embarked in the late 1950s on a run to Stafford, astride a sit-up-and-beg beast of a black bicycle and on the return, being stricken with the hammer-blow of the knock, it is timely to describe the symptoms of this debilitating condition. Peculiar, it seems, to cyclists – touring or racing – the knock, bonk, snakebite, or more specifically, hypoglycaemia, is a sudden, massive drop in blood-sugar levels. The French have a word for it – *la fringale*. The initial indications are, when happily cycling along, to be faintly aware of an emptiness deep in the pit of the stomach and a propensity to belch. Another symptom is to want to yawn. Not once, but time and time again with gaping mouth, open to jaw-disjointing wideness. A yawn that indicates a desire to sleep for a hundred years. Very soon, one would feel a desperate need to eat something; anything that could dispel the cavernous void deep below in the stomach; even a desire to chew and swallow one's own tongue in order to supply that aching, vacant space. Your first reaction is thinking that the feeling is a passing glitch and can be put down to indigestion; can be ridden off and forgotten. However, the feeling spreads into the gut, just like having drunk a potion of acid and noting its burning effect coursing through the vast tubular system of the upper and lower intestine. When the feeling reaches the low-slung appendages of the groin, you really must stop.

Very soon, the shakes begin. One's legs lose almost all power; starting at the groin and spreading downwards through thighs and knees, both legs become trembling, flapping pillars of weakness. You are forced to stop, struggle to maintain a footing, while preventing the bike from toppling and pulling you prone at the roadside verge. Try to understand what on earth is happening to you. The legs wobble like jelly and the arms, in sympathy, begin to shake while hands clutch handlebars, reaching for stability. Blood-sugar levels have sunk so low that by now, they are seeping out of the shoes and staining the road. Your whole frame has lost its energy-giving glucose and you have become as weak and useless as a discarded puppet. You're as weak as wastewater. You are close to having the bike tip and crashing on top of your pile of puzzling, uncooperative limbs. You shake with the chill of icy limbs, fingertips blanched to a bloodless white and at the same time, feel as hot as hell, beads of sweat rolling like bullets from the brow, down the neck and soaking the collar and back of the shirt. Why couldn't you have stayed at home, lie back on the sofa and be fed, one by delicious one of plumptious, glucose-laden grapes? Orbs of the vine, peeled by handmaidens!

But a cure is there in the saddlebag. That is, if you have bothered to pack for just an emergency. It comes in a well-known package of deep-brown wrapper, garishly labelled. A chocolatey-covered, caramel-stuffed, toffeely-caressed bar of ribbed confection. A Mars bar. The treat that helps you work, rest and, in this instance, play. That squashed, lint-covered sweetie that has melted and solidified tens of times before you find it in the nethermost regions of the saddlebag – half-caressing and stuck to a dirty, odd sock. Eat this or similar and soon you'll be fit as a flea, strong as Charles Atlas, a veritable Reg Harris and be ready to take up the cudgels to battle those homeward hills of mountainous miles. On second thoughts, an isotonic drink is probably better! To have style and be really sophisticated, a post-knock rest and meal at a Cyclists' Touring Club café would be the very best cure, as long as it included a sweet of apple pie with lashings of sugar and evaporated milk. An invigorating meal, best served if possible, by a comely, smiling, serving wench! The knock will soon be forgotten; a thing of the past; a mere inconvenience, an interruption in the journey – until the next time it strikes!

I have already described the heavy rain encountered in Wales, cycling north from Dolgellau to Corris, on my solo tour of the principality. Weather in all its differing guises would present itself on many occasions along the many thousands of miles of cycling I did in the years to come. On the bike, one is open to all that the weather can throw at a plucky fellow with no protection other than a thin cape or other, so called, weatherproof wear. Most protective gear usually does only half the job. Torrential rain, when the water stings the eyes, to suffocating heat when the sun's ultra-violet stings unprotected winter-white limbs, is all part of the cycling adventure. Discomfort, as with the resistance of pedalling uphill or the wind chill of a fast descent, the vagaries of the climate leaves one feeling to have really passed through the landscape as against just viewing it from the warmth and comfort of an all-enclosing tin vehicle. The car is far too insulating!

Rain and sun, heat and cold, snow and ice; all are met whilst on the saddle and are usually overcome with strength of character and set of jaw. One weather phenomenon that is difficult to deal with, however, is wind. Wind, that is, that blows from an opposing quarter and not wind that blows from behind!! The other is thick mist.

The group, about ten in number, were cycling towards the Potteries after a weekend in north Wales, probably having stayed at Cynwyd. A mile or so east of Whitchurch on the main road that passes the Ancient Britain pub, the weather on this late autumn afternoon was thick with mist. Oncoming darkness exacerbated the difficulty of reduced visibility. Seasonal vapours were rising from the shallow valleys, rendering trees and hedgerows into undefined, ghostly shapes. At the junction short of Burleydam, where one road forks left for Nantwich, we lost sight of the roadside verge altogether and found ourselves in a featureless desert of plain asphalt. Instantly disorientated while riding two abreast, the inside riders decided to swing right while the outside line decided to keep left. The resultant coming-together of some ten cyclists, despite travelling slower than normal, was utter chaos; human indecision personified. We all ended up coming off and running into the intervening hedgerow straight ahead; a tangle of bodies, bikes and pieces of undergrowth. Darkness and thick mist dampened sights and sounds of consternation and we were very soon treating the whole episode as a joke. Luckily, no serious injuries were sustained and after sorting ourselves out, we continued merrily on our way – of course, with no noticeable reduction in speed or formation!

*

One place never to tour when mist cloaks the land was Whixall Moss. We entered this completely flat landscape before taking tea at the CTC café in Quina Brook. The area straddled the border between what is now Clwyd and north Shropshire. A dismantled railway marked the actual boundary and a section of the Shropshire Union Canal (Llangollen Branch).cut across the flatness. Quaint timber lift-bridges, white-painted and counter-balanced, gave a feeling of being in the Dutch Polders. Other canal crossings were marked by steep, hump-backed bridges. The whole area was worked by peat diggers who cut their slit trenches and extracted turf as a fuel for domestic fireplaces. Much like the turf cutters of Ireland. The sphagnum mosses and general peat bog conditions provided a habitat for interesting wildlife. Subsequent mechanical extraction on an industrial scale in order to supply the gardening craze has meant that certain areas have had to be protected through the establishment of Sites of Special Scientific Interest. Yet another example of greed and the need for making vast profits.

We would spin through the lonely lanes of Whixall Moss and invariably become hopelessly lost. All signposts seemed to have been removed, as if the locals had imagined themselves to be still under the threat of a WWII German invasion! We re-arrived at a remembered point several times before, somehow, managing to be spat out of this barren heath and on towards Whitchurch. After several unsuccessful attempts to find a route, we would even begin to have a sense of uneasiness just short of panic – well-disguised by a passing joke. In dull weather with loss of a sun, it was even more difficult to find our direction; the terrain appearing a flat, featureless waste as far as one could see. The scouting ability to use the sun and a wristwatch as a compass was completely negated in times of dull weather. A view from the hump of a canal bridge might offer a vague glimpse of distant hills, but it was very much a hit and miss operation. We would pass the occasional isolated house; detached, bare and anonymous, where a furtive fellow would watch our progress. He would probably have a stack of peat in the back garden – fuel to heat his home lying stark and exposed on this blasted heath. I would not be at all surprised if there were bog burials in these marshy wastes. Early man, trussed and twisted, having undergone some pagan ceremony of martyred sacrifice, skin shrunken to a parchment and sightless eye orbits having stared at a land of aeons past. A land that had not changed too much over the intervening ages. Peat has a preserving quality – it should be bottled! Burials have been discovered further north, in Cheshire and Whixall Moss was that sort of place. Eventually, with no little difficulty, we extricated ourselves from the area and were able to resume our route east and homeward.

The perfect complementing hobby to cycling is, I believe, photography. The camera is relatively light in weight, can be packed easily and the bike can reach locations other forms of transport cannot. I have mentioned my early efforts in taking snaps of the west door of Lichfield Cathedral. My Kodak Box Brownie was but a little more advanced from the camera obscura but for all its awkwardness, used Vest Pocket roll panchromatic film, thereby producing a good-sized negative. The single, fixed-focus lens and crude iris diaphragm control, comprising a thin metal slide with holes of differing diameter, turned out surprisingly sharp photographs. A camera to take images; provide fond memories of Aunt Maud and Uncle George on the beach at Blackpool. I had more artistic work in mind. Taking hours to photograph a stream and vegetation in the Staffordshire Peak District was more to do with being able to see through the viewfinder than waiting for the best lighting! An extra pair of hands would have been useful, too, as I struggled to shield the viewing glass from overhead light, hold the camera steady and press down the basic shutter. The breathless anticipation of waiting for the chemist's processing was just one extra big thrill. Snapshots with an inordinately wide border of white were eagerly perused and most of them discarded!

But the taking of photographs was only half the story, a quarter of the enjoyment. Next door in Cherry Tree Close lived May and Norman Bennett. Norman was the photographer for the Potteries Motor Traction Company (PMT)., taking photos for insurance claim purposes. He processed his work at home and was good enough to show me how the printing process was carried out. Photography was moving from 120-and VP-sized roll film to the new 35mm format. I sent off for a new camera. I duly equipped myself with a Gnome 35mm enlarger, masking frame, set of dishes, print paddles and I believe I made an orange safelight, just buying the glass screen. This light source, fitted with low-wattage bulb and holder, had no effect on the sensitive bromide paper and cast sufficient light for most tasks. I also bought a daylight developing tank for the processing of the initial negatives. The loading of the spiral had to be done in total darkness, resulting in many minutes of groping with the whippy film and feeding it into the take-up grooves. Sweat would pour from the troubled brow if this operation became awkward. A whole film could so easily become fogged with leaking daylight and rendered a deep-black disaster! Safely loaded, the tank could be taken into normal lighting and chemicals introduced for set times and temperatures, depending on the film speed.

For picture printing, having blacked-out the bathroom, I mixed the fine grain developer, stop bath solution and hypo-fixer in correct strengths before tweaking the enlarger controls to produce my first image. The picture arose from the developer like a vague, orange-cast apparition. The densest parts appeared first, followed in seconds by the remaining tones and finishing with the subtlest of detail in the highlights. This was the creative branch of photography and a moment to be proud of. An instance in time had been grabbed, frozen and recorded for posterity and in normal conditions, would give enjoyment as each image presented itself from the black pages of the family album. It is said that a good photograph is worth a thousand words! Until the advent of digital cameras and computing, the camera could not tell a lie.

The ability to print one's own photographs opened up a new world of techniques. Tilting the masking frame to alter perspective, diffusing the image, adding filters and many more tricks would add interest. Even reticulation; an instance of having too great a temperature difference in developing solutions, albeit a mistake, would provide a different, mosaic-like finish. A technique of solarisation produced a curious, mercurial, silhouetted appearance. The choice of printing papers was almost bewildering. White fine lustre, satin, sepia-toned, matt or glossy, single or double weight were just a few different sorts of paper finishes. I learned all these techniques; an ability that would be advantageous in future work. The hobby was fast becoming a craft.

However, my choice of 35mm camera was a disaster! I saw the advertisement on a cheaply-printed, single sheet flyer. It described an advanced model with all the latest features – all-metal body, f-stops, rangefinder, four shutter speeds, and it was called a Halina! In small, nay, microscopic print on the bottom of the box was printed, "Made in Taiwan." This and its ridiculous low price should have given me due warning. In this case, the term, 'you only get what you pay for' was the truest of statements. The film wind-back button, a small, knurled knob, proved difficult to operate. It became stiff and eventually inoperable. The effort to rewind the film's thirty-six exposure length back into the cassette was so great; I had to use a pair of pliers to effect the slightest of turns; the reclaiming of just an inch of celluloid! I have since learned that Sir Alan Sugar's first camera was a Halina when he progressed his own early photographic adventure. I'm sure he had a better model.

My next camera, as mentioned, was a little gem. It was a 35mm, German Kodak model with fold-out bellows and the fullest range of apertures and speeds. Although it looked as if it had come from a museum, it was amazingly crafted, lightweight, with controls perfectly arranged. A more tactile piece of equipment would be hard to find. I bought a range of filters for the lens; green, yellow and orange, additions to immediately improve the black and white images. The green filter lightened the grass foreground and the yellow darkened blue sky, thereby delineating the glorious cumulo-nimbus cloud formations. The use of the mid-orange filter gave an enormously dramatic blackness to the clear sky areas, thereby presenting any middle or foreground detail in stupendous richness, particularly in low-angled evening lighting. The days of bland, blank, white skies were a thing of the past!

I did take colour slides (Agfa and Perutz).and prints at this time but the very fact of being able to print my own tilted me in the direction of monochrome photography. Besides, the colour images just didn't appear as sharp as the black and white. But it wasn't just that. The warm tones of a black and white photograph captured in a landscape, both the warmth of a timeless summer day or the bleak coldness of a snow and icy winter scene – the media was perfect for illustrating both scenarios. Summer images exuded insect-buzzing grassland, rich hayricks and dusty dirt lanes. Winter images the opposite – cold, sharp icicles, crisp, windblown snowdrifts and lumps of snow on every gatepost and telegraph wire.

A third camera was also of German manufacture. When the little folding job finally expired (or did I give it away?)., I obtained a Kodak Retinette. The viewfinder was bright, the lever wind, film transport, f-stops, shutter speed and focussing rings were silky smooth; all together, an extremely good camera. It came in a smart brown leather case. Again, I fitted the lens with suitable push-on filters. By now, Japan was entering the camera market, so, Geoff and I equipped ourselves with the Yashica

35mm. The lens was of multiple elements and could be opened to a wide aperture. Although not a single lens reflex, this model was considerably heavier than past models so, before long, I returned to the faithful Retinette – a model that my brother Ken would nickname 'The f11 '! It lasted me until the end of the 1960s. A disastrous change of camera was made to mark the new decade and also to record our 1970 minibus tour to Marrakech, Morocco. I purchased a stout East German Praktica 35mm. It was built like a tank, heavy as lead and decided to malfunction on my first trip to the Dark Continent. The focal plane shutter failed to operate and I was left with over a hundred slides that showed mainly blackness and only an eighth of the total picture area visible! Luckily, John Bradbury supplied me with those unforgettable, replacement shots. I dumped the Praktica and reverted to the West German Retinette.

Inevitably, digital photography will supersede the old processes and will prove to be much, much better and certainly, much easier. It will satisfy the gadget-loving geek and provide instant results. The photograph will, after all, be able to lie. However, I will miss the fiddling adjustments to the camera when difficult lighting conditions are encountered. Miss the mental calculations of focusing and depth of field. Miss the darkroom, its low-level orange gloom and peering into dishes to see the photographs gradually appear. Miss the smell of the developer and hypo-chemicals and the drying, straightening and mounting of the finished article. Miss the mystery of it all!

Chapter Three

1962

Early Hostelling – Cynwyd and the Berwyns – The Wayfarers Track – Message From the Salts – Down the Towy Valley – A West Country Holiday – The Demon Drink – First Holiday in Ireland – Serious Darts – Wild Times of Youth – Winter Days Draw On

Age: 21.

Home: Cherry Tree Close, Trentham, Stoke-on-Trent.

Work: Stoke-on-Trent Reconstruction Dept., Woodhouse Street/Kingsway, Stoke.

Government: Conservative.

Prime Minister: Harold Macmillan.

February: Gary Power, U2 spy plane pilot, exchanged for Soviet prisoner, Colonel John Glenn, first American in space.

March: United Kingdom still unsuccessful at joining European institutions.

April: Prince Charles enters Gordonstoun's tough school in Scotland.

May: Adolf Eichmann hanged in Israel. Coventry Cathedral consecrated. August: Attempted assassination of General De Gaulle, film star Marilyn Monroe dies, demonstrations at the Berlin Wall.

September: Soviet Union ships missiles to Cuba.

October: The Cuban Missile Crisis as Kennedy faces Khrushchev.

November: Cold War becomes red hot.

Film: *Lawrence of Arabia, Lolita.*

Novel: *One Day in the Life of Ivan Denisovitch.*

Theatre: *Who's Afraid of Virginia Woolf?*

The Duke of Edinburgh sends Prince Charles to back-of-beyond Gordonstoun School in Scotland where a harsh regime of cold showers and naked, early morning swimming in icy lochs was not to the young Prince's taste. But to the shock-horror of the country, his taste for cherry brandy was! I didn't blame him; anything to warm him up! General de Gaulle continued to give Britain a resounding "NON" over entry into the Common Market. Somebody tried to shoot him! Could the hitman have worn a flat cap, plus-fours, tartan stockings and a heavy, bristling moustache? The really serious events arose later in the year when Russia decided to ship their missiles into Cuba, well within striking distance of American cities. Kennedy caught them at it through aerial surveillance and faced-up to the bull-necked Khrushchev to clear out or else! A very brave thing to do as Khrushchev had a nasty habit of banging the table with his shoe. Besides, he hadn't washed his dirty socks! Things finally calmed down but, for a time, global annihilation was on the cards. We could have had our hats knocked off – and no Blue Streak deterrent!

*

With a well-established and growing group of fellow cyclists, I began the New Year, 1962, with the traditional cycle run to Rudyard Lake for the usual New Year's Party. We would join the Walking Section for a meal and jolly party games with a chance to socialise with the YHA's other half. Distances at this time of the year needed to be kept relatively short with road conditions and daylight being an important factor. An early ride to Cannock Chase, to Wandon youth hostel, saw us all together, savouring the warmth and bonhomie of a nearby pub, the Miners' Arms. The hostel was a single-storey building, much like Dimmingsdale, set in a clearing and surrounded by forestry spruce. The pub was just down the road and probably got its name from the small-scale coal mining activity once present in this otherwise attractive upland spread of countryside. We gathered in the small lounge, our group of a dozen or so taking up the whole room. Led by Bill Housley, we started singing a few well-known, mainly repetitive songs while a steady drizzle outside, beyond the chintzy curtains, patted against the dark window panes. The nightly 10:00pm hostel closing time was always a bone of contention for us cyclists as we would rush back with minutes to spare before front doors were bolted and barred. The warm atmosphere of the local inn with a pint of ale on the table and surrounded by a convivial company was much preferred to lying in a cold dormitory bunk bed, looking at that threatening male sleeper's bulge a few inches above the face. We didn't consider ourselves children and unlike the motoring hosteller who left his car down the road, we had earned a pint or two after a day's hot and hard cycling. But YHA rules are rules, so, we generally had to toe the line, although frequent and nervous clock-watching became a fine art. It was a different kettle of fish if the warden was also a cyclist. I have recently learnt that a hostel in the Peak District, Hartington Hall, has its own licensed bar in one corner of the common room. In early 1962 and as part of the draughtsman's course I was attending at the time, I chose to do a part survey of Hartington Hall with a colleague, Brian Sweatmore. The warden was grouchy and followed us round the property as we dragged the measuring tape over deeply-architraved doorways and rich, oak panelling.

Most of the winter season, Saturday nights were spent in visiting the close hostels – those that needed only a few hours in the saddle but saw us, at least, out of the dismal, dank streets of Stoke-on-Trent. Hostels such as Rudyard Lake, Ilam Hall, Oakenclough, Windgather, Hartington Hall and Shining Cliff. Nevertheless, we still explored some adventurous rough-stuff routes and short-cuts such as Lathkill Dale, Monsal Dale, Dovedale and the Manifold Valley. Tracks in the dry valleys of the White Peak involved a good deal of lifting the cycles over and through mud and standing water. Rivers had a habit of appearing mysteriously, even in the dry Peak. Hostels further away but still in the Peak District could be reached, such as Buxton, Leam Hall, Ravenstor, Bretton, Elton and Edale, although it must be admitted that the existence of a convenient drinking house nearby would inevitably steer our choice of hostel. If we felt particularly helpful and club spirited, we could always volunteer to join a working party for some job at nearby Dimmingsdale. The overnight accommodation there was free and the closing time was our own. Many a night would see us stagger and struggle up the steep hillside, walking through the bracken and birch woodland, taking the direct route back to the hostel after a raucous night in the Lord Nelson far below in Oakamoor village. Next morning and through bleary eyes, we would admire the end wall of the common room. A local YHA member of some considerable artistic ability had painted an extensive mural – a wide scene of the Snowdon Horseshoe, the grand spread of mountains as viewed from Capel Curig. Snowdon, Crib Goch and Y Lliwedd gave us inspiration for future activities.

As the days lengthened and spring approached, we set our wheels to the west and into Wales. Alternative destinations and different areas could be accessed, such as youth hostels at Copt Oak in Leicestershire, Chaddesley Corbett in Worcestershire, Delamere Forest in Cheshire and Lichfield in Staffordshire. However, our eyes turned, invariably, to the more spectacular hills of north Wales. Various hostels became reachable, such as Maeshafn, near Mold in Clwyd, Llangollen and beyond, and Cynwyd, a few miles from Corwen on the 'B' road to Bala. Maeshafn had three-tier bunk beds and was useful, being close to the Clwydian Hills and the moors north of Llangollen. Another Miners' Arms nearby provided an evening's entertainment and sustenance – suitable sustenance to climb into those high, topmost bunks! Midnight toilet breaks could prove to be adventurous, if not downright dangerous! Cynwyd was our favourite. The disused mill building at the back of the tight, close-knit community was run by Mr and Mrs Roberts. Mr Roberts, of short stature, balding and slightly hunched, looked like a very rural but strictly labouring-class version of Neil Kinnock, the Welsh Windbag. His wife was homely and would sometimes provide us gratis with a homemade pudding. The couple liked cyclists and weren't too particular what time we returned from the pub! The village had a railway halt and two public houses facing each other on each side of the main street. The Prince of Wales stood defiantly opposite the Blue Lion. Named the *Blue* Lion, no doubt, to distance itself from the perceived, very English name, Red Lion. The hostel was spartan, with pieces of mill equipment remaining. The ground floor was stone-paved and a steep wooden staircase led to a dark dormitory above; a dormitory crowded with bunks where the top bunk occupant's nose seemed to almost scrape the ceiling. I will always remember the first-floor support pillar and cross shaft, with a pulley wheel painted a bright red. It threatened the top bunk, heavy sleeper and early riser with a bump to the head as he awakened from a night of dreams. Downstairs someone had painted a mural on the sky-blue wall in the common/dining room, depicting an Edwardian cyclist on a Penny Farthing, clothed in a tight-fitting, striped bathing suit and Deerstalker hat, and sporting a flowing handlebar moustache. The earnest, straining rider reminded us of a considerably thinner Derek Latham.

Every time we visited Cynwyd, we met the same three, elderly Liverpudlian cyclists. Was it their second home or was it their Merseyside Scouse nouse, realising that hostel fees and evening meals worked out cheaper there as a weekend out than staying at home? They were long in the tooth, worldly-wise and spoke in a gruff, barely understood Liverpool accent. Anyway, they were an admirable example of cycling friendship and camaraderie. I could never have imagined them to have visited any other hostel in the country other than Cynwyd.

Cynwyd village crouches under the northern edge of the Berwyn Mountains, the high land which spreads from west of Llangollen and towards Bala and from Corwen, south to the valleys of Ceiriog and Tanat, to drop into north-west Shropshire. It is a vast, high level land mass that includes rounded slopes of heather and cut with deep, narrow valleys on its south-eastern side. Principal heights include Cadair Berwyn at 2,714 feet (827m)., Cadair Bronwen, Moel Sych and Moel Fferna, with the attractive Lake Vyrnwy (Liverpool's water supply).and the spectacularly high waterfall of Pistyll Rhaeadr (spouting waterfall)., near Llanrhaeadr. The region is crossed by the lonely road, the Milltir Cerrig, from Llangynog to Bala and the very steep Bwlch y Groes road from Dinas Mawddwy to Bala. These places would figure strongly on our programme in those early days of adventure. The rough-stuff routes were gleaned from a booklet titled, *The Berwyn Log*; a small, old-fashioned publication purchased from the hostel at Cynwyd. Within its blue cover, illustrated by a windswept moorland scene, minute print in ancient lettering and the odd grainy photograph described various crossings of the Berwyn heights. With foxing spots to the dog-eared pages and rusted staples, this gem of a book was one of our sources of inspiration! It described, in Edwardian detail, the various mountain crossings to a standard adopted by that lover of the Lake District, Arthur Wainwright. The high level views were missing from the book but would have appeared as blurred, open wastelands and, therefore, unfriendly. One had to be in the midst of that wild vastness to fully appreciate the area – not gleaned while at home looking at grey photographs.

The main ridge, if one can call the lofty, rounded slopes a ridge, is crossed at right angles by a series of long, high tracks – lonely, wind-swept routes once used by drovers and now grouse shooters. From Cynwyd, we passed through narrow lanes, along forestry tracks, until we broke into open country on the mountain pass named the Nant Rhyd Wilym. This pass is known to rough-stuff enthusiasts as the Wayfarer's Track, named after the founder of the Roughstuff Fellowship, Walter M Robinson. Articles signed in his pen-name, 'Wayfarer' and brilliant pen-and-ink drawings by artist, Patterson, featured frequently in the touring section's column inches of *Cycling* magazine.

We walked and pushed the cycles up the long, steady incline on a rutted track to arrive at the summit, marked by a nick in the skyline and a low, rocky outcrop. Below the Wayfarer Memorial and wedged into a nook of the rock was a shallow, square, metal box; its lid held on by a large stone. With the wind moaning through the bracken, rippling the tufted heather and grey clouds scudding across the noble heights, we lifted the box lid to find a few oddments inside. At the bottom lay a squashed and bent Woodbine cigarette, a single match and a note, "With compliments from the Salt Brothers, Stoke-on-Trent," or words to that effect! I recall myself and Geoff Cartlidge sharing the cigarette, although the tobacco was stale and the match was damp and wouldn't strike, but waste not, want not! Eric Hazeldine, Joan Hall and the rest of the group joked at our desperate addiction to nicotine! The existence of this solitary note was our introduction to yet another bunch of great cycling enthusiasts. We continued down the track, splashing through a boggy section; passed the isolated wood and corrugated iron shooting cabin, before the route widened into a green lane and we eventually reached drier, narrow, surfaced lanes, freewheeling towards Llanarmon Dyffryn Ceiriog. We promised to make contact with our smoking benefactors, thereby enlarging the Cycling Section by a few more members and an additional wealth of character.

The Salts, Ralph and Clive, lived on the edge of the extensive Bentilee Estate at Bucknall, below Limekiln Bank and Hanley. Ralph was tall, yet well-built, with aquiline features and had great desire to be a pathfinder, especially on rough-stuff routes through the hills. I remember him to be the proud owner of an enormous sweater that was worn everywhere. We called it his horse blanket! Ralph's heroes were Tom Simpson and Fausto Coppi; both dominating the cycle racing scene in their respective countries around that time. Ralph worked as an auditor's clerk and was brilliant at playing darts and, obviously, calculating his impressive scores on the board. Clive, Ralph's brother, was smaller in statue, wiry, but equally enthusiastic about cycling. He was well-read, the more thoughtful of the pair and loved music. In fact, Clive could tickle the ivories, especially ragtime, without being able to read a quaver of music notation. He was also the proud owner of a Claud Butler – while Claud Butler was still a distinguished frame builder, frames were noted for their intricately-cut joining lugs. They had a cycling friend, Paul Leese, who was swarthy with pointed features. Paul was short, powerful and rode like a demon over the steepest of hills. He could easily be described as being 'built like a Gypsy's dog' – all ribs and d..k! Not the gentlest of expressions but so damn accurate! Paul's competitive nature would make him 'half-wheel' his adjacent cyclist when paired-up and at the front. Half-wheeling is the habit of always being half a wheel in front, whatever the speed. Consequently, this undeclared competition sees the average speed ever-increasing until the rest of the group are left behind. Probably useful in club cycling when training for a forthcoming time trial, but not in leisurely touring where one takes snaps and admires the wild flowers! John Humphreys and Cliff Yates were also friendly with the Salt brothers; all together, making a happy, fun-loving bunch. I suppose we were still just big kids!

The map of central Wales shows a high, mountainous region with few main roads, towns and villages, its centre divided by the young

Afon Towy. The river rises south of a bleak collection of lakes, named the Teifi Pools, west of the Claerwen Reservoir, itself part of the Elan Valley Lakes system. A few miles south-east of the site of Strata Florida, the stream begins its long route, flowing due south for many miles. A track follows its course for some miles, running parallel with, crossing and re-crossing the stream many times in a series of fords. Many miles south, the track leads into a network of narrow lanes, before one joins the main road at Llandovery. Truly a rough-stuff route offering a challenge and many miles of wild adventure! Typically, Eric Hazeldine had proposed this Towy Valley journey, probably after reading some pioneering cyclist's account in the touring section of *Cycling*. Adventurous routes were often learned by casual conversation or a chance published article.

We had a healthy number of members present as we cycled to Shrewsbury on the Thursday evening's run. This was an Easter holiday, promising a few extra days available to make an extended weekend. The route to our first hostel at Ystumtuen was straightforward; pounding westwards through Welshpool, Newtown, Llanidloes and Llangurig, before the steady climb over the Plynlimon mountains and descending on the sweeping, open road to Pont Erwyd. The turn-off lane to Ystumtuen is close to the George Borrow Hotel, named after the traveller and author of the book, *Wild Wales*. In those past times, Wales, and this region in particular, really was wild! The hostel, quintessentially, yet another disused village schoolhouse, just about accommodated our numbers. We were welcomed by the warden's attractive daughter; just the ticket after a good few miles of sitting in the saddle, pedalling along a main road. The area surrounding the hostel was, however, somewhat bleak; open, switch-back lanes, thin soil with ill-looking grasses and scattered with numerous boulders. I believe this area had seen a barely thriving silver mining industry in years gone by. The warden's daughter was a flash of cheerful beauty in the otherwise bleak surroundings. We pressed cups of tea on her, just to keep her talking, but finally, she had to return to her rude hovel and mother's side!

Next morning dawned grey with a persistent drizzle falling from a leaden sky. The main road crosses the River Rheidol where its course squeezes through a narrow and precipitous defile. Here is the spectacular Mynach Falls and a series of three bridges built atop each other, said to shelter the very devil himself! The dull roar, as powerful water bounces off the hard rocks and soaks the clinging mosses and ferns, easily promotes the vision of sheltering, bad-tempered trolls. As the site is so vertiginous, a viewpoint is almost impossible to gain, making photography out of the question. Our road climbs, falls and bends, winding through spruce forestry on a scenic route to Pontrhydygroes and Ysbytty [Yspytty] Ystwyth. The latter hamlet means hospital or hospice by the [river] Ysywyth, I believe. A fine drizzle fell between the pine branches, causing streams of rainwater to trickle down the roadside gutters and sometimes to flow right across the road's surface. A beautiful tang of pine emitted from the many piles of forest log piles; tweaking the nasal passages; another collection of GPO telegraph poles! Ysbytty Ystwyth. A name thought so strange that we had to take a photograph, with most of the group wearing their rain capes, holding their bikes and trying to wrap their tongues around the name on the village sign. The Welsh seem to be able to spell a word without using any vowels! That is, until they spell out a Christian name, where, for example, just about every vowel is used and one encounters a'Ieuan'. It never rains but it pours!

We pressed on through the tiny hamlet of Ffair Rhos and turned on to a rough track just beyond Pontrhydfendigaid, climbing to the ruins of the priory at Strata Florida. Over the climb and spread out before us was the vast, soaking bog forming the catchment area of the Afon Towy. The watershed, the windswept saucer of spongy morass, was cut by numerous channels, slowly winding, joining and collecting to gradually form a defined watercourse. We hopped between clumps of cotton grass, balanced on innumerable tussocks trying to find dry ground; lifting and lugging the bikes alongside with saddlebags swinging and constantly grazing the backs of the legs, with the steel, rat-trap pedals. As we moved south, the barely defined track improved but crossed and recrossed the river many times. In no time at all, the depth of the water and its flow increased until it was swirling by at knee level. We removed our cycling shoes for the first few crossings but as the track had gathered pools also, we abandoned this idea and accepted that soaking leather shoes and socks were inevitable. Besides, to cross barefoot could have caused us to slip on smooth stones underwater, thereby preceding a total, ice-cold ducking. However, we had to keep the cycles lifted above the water level as wheeling them through the fords would see the hubs become quickly washed clear of any lubrication whatsoever. The hubs were packed with light grease when assembled, but we would always check that the bearing cups were packed with enough grease when maintenance time came round. The recent sport of mountain biking has created the phrase, 'a repacking ride', describing a downhill run so severe that the cycle hubs have to be disassembled and repacked with grease after every descent.

The rainy weather ceased finally as we moved downstream on a now, well-defined dirt track; the valley bordered by gloomy hills at an average height of 1,600 feet (490m).; brooding, rounded hills topped with heavy, grey cloud cover. There was a short section of tarmac where the narrow road from Tregaron to Abergwesyn crossed this wilderness; a route of severely steep inclines, as the riders in the Tour of Britain once found out, much to their disbelief, consternation and lack of a low gear.

Known as the Devil's Staircase, the lonely, exposed section, many miles from civilization, was always lined with masochistic spectators; a surprisingly large following who had motored from faraway places to witness continental cyclists suffering on good, honest and outrageously steep Welsh slopes.

The route continued south through lonely, afforested countryside until the tiny hamlet of Rhandirmwyn and a surfaced road at last. The immediate, steep-sided main valley and spurs have since been flooded north of here to form Llyn Brianne, yet another artificial lake to slake our thirsts. It has taken many years (a century at least) for the landscape around Lake Vyrnwy to mellow down and lose its man-made, clean-lined appearance. We finally met civilization again at Llandovery and soon arrived at the small hostel of Llanddeusant to dry shoes, wash bog-stained socks, and reflect on a day of challenge. Our chosen route through the very centre of the Cambrian Mountains; following down their spine, the Afon Towi, was a milestone for our rough-stuff programme, albeit, pursued in dull, inclement weather (a bright, sunny day would have appeared incongruous) although some might view it as a forbidding form of self-inflicted water torture.

*

With the coming of warmer days, in the middle of May, I joined Derek Latham and Dave Hope, the pair from Hanchurch crossroads, on a week's tour of glorious Devon. We decided to cycle all the way down by way of the Cotswolds. I had my almost new Sun touring machine, *Maud*, while Derek used his Blackpool-built Hill Special and Dave, his Derby-built Mercian. Although there was a vast difference in frame quality, there was no snobbery in cycling, just as long as you had two wheels, a range of gears, and, most importantly, a liking for the open road with all its attendant adventures. From an almost expected start at Shrewsbury; which gave us a convenient and reachable Friday night hostel, and moved us a few miles further south; we cycled down to Ashton Keynes, a small hostel in the tiny Cotswold hamlet close to the Duntisbournes – the Duntisbourne Abbots of my earlier, solo return from Plymouth in 1960. Our plan for the week was to tour north Somerset, and Devon using youth hostels at Bampton, Gidleigh, and Instow in Devon, Holford, and Cheddar in Somerset, Cleeve Hill back in the Cotswolds, and home by way of Shropshire and its border town of Ludlow.

An enduring memory of the week was our coffee breaks at elevenses, usually a swift pint at a wayside tavern. After covering twenty or so miles (32k), leaning the bikes by a convenient wall, spreading the map across the picnic table, and holding it down with a full pint of ale at each corner, was a satisfying experience. The first few bitter-flavoured swallows, accompanied with a draw on a cigarette after our early efforts, in my opinion, makes anyone condemning drinking, and smoking an utter toady. Again, our middle-of-the-day lunch breaks were an added pleasure. Taken alfresco, sitting on a grassy bank at the side of a quiet lane, assembling the Primus stove, boiling a kettleful of water, and mashing a brew of tea to wash down the sandwiches, was a cyclist's accepted ritual. We shared the tea brewing duties, as we did the carrying of the equipment. One would carry the small, demountable Primus, usually just fitting into a saddlebag side-pocket, one would carry the kettle of water, and one would have an aluminium feeding bottle filled with paraffin and a small tin of methylated spirit to start the stove's combustion. Cold, windy weather made stove-lighting a tricky operation. After vigorous pumping, with the curl of burning meths dying in its ring underneath, and a cloud of white, swirling vapour above, a sudden combustion would set fire to the surrounding grass, hedgerow, and thirsty operative's eyebrows. Our lunch stops were under Devon's midday sun; in silence broken only by the chirruping of crickets; in dusty back lanes, where the occasional dust cloud was raised by a solitary passing motorist or having to avoid the gravel spat out from under the local midwife's soft bicycle tyres. Idyllic days of rural beauty and peacefulness indeed.

From Bampton bordering the stag-hunting country of Exmoor, we moved south, through quaint cob and thatch villages, to the eastern extremities of Dartmoor. Gidleigh, near the busy little market town of Chagford provided another night's accommodation. After a hastily prepared dinner from the self-cooker's kitchen, we grabbed the bikes from the cycle shed and pedalled our winding way through tree-lined, sunken Devon lanes. A bicycle free of its saddlebag after a long day's journey, is a liberated, lightweight, racing machine that is a delight to ride. No hill is too steep, no bend is too tight as your thoroughbred bears you swiftly to your destination. Passing muddy farmyards, we braked to halt at an isolated inn for the evening's liquid refreshment. The lonely hostelry, half-hidden in adjoining trees and bushes, appeared bleak and desolate with grey cob walls, lack of windows and fading, black lettering under the eaves, spelling out the name HEAVYTREE ALES. The place lacked colourful signage or posted menus, seemingly, wanting to crawl back into the hidden depths of rurality; not seeking any prominence or custom whatsoever. The one, and only room, the bar, had a stone-flagged floor, low, beamed ceiling, had gnarled settles pushed against the walls, with no bar or counter, but a full height, black-painted, wooden glazed screen which provided a poky, separated cubicle. A few local farmers sat on the settles, seemingly melted and welded into their splintered seats. They were deep in discussion but we weren't able to discern any understandable language. The whole place, floor, ceiling, furniture, and locals seemed to be coated in a dark-brown patina of the genuine, earthy charm of times gone by. The landlady emerged, rolling off her stool in her cramped cubicle and informed us that she only had farm-brewed cider for sale. She filled our pint glasses with a clouded, amber liquid from a chipped enamel jug. There appeared to be bits floating around this opaque beverage, sometimes rising to the flat, dead head, devoid of any froth. The cider assaulted our throats with thirst-quenching savagery. It was strong, powerful, and slipped down with consummate ease. We played darts on a worn board, straw filling bursting out from treble twenty like an outlandish growth. We voiced our goodbyes before cycling back to the hostel in a dark blur of rushing hedges, walls and overhanging trees. The cider's overpowering alcoholic strength made us lose all feeling in the legs. Our raucous songs died away to a temperate silence as we knocked on the hostel door, seeking shelter. Sleep came quickly.

Dartmoor wore its welcoming face the next morning. Small, white clouds sailed over the purple heather slopes as we climbed steeply above, and beyond low-lying Moretonhampstead, and followed the main road cutting across the centre of the moor. A gathering of buildings appeared on the horizon, isolated, lonely, appearing almost incongruous in these open square miles of windswept moorland nothingness. A single black saloon was parked outside the Warren House Inn, its owner inside perusing the many grainy photographs hanging on the walls. Photographs of the inn showing it in a rare winter days long ago when snowdrifts piled up against its stout outside walls. The inn lies at about 1,4oo feet (430m) above sea level; not the highest – we could visit that one later on a long weekend in the Pennines, but high and exposed enough to catch the occasional blizzard. At the end of the bar room there was a small turf fire alight in the fireplace, barely glowing inside piles of grey ash, and throwing just a smidgeon of aromatic warmth to anyone close enough to it. The landlady informed us that it had never been allowed to go out for a hundred years. We looked at each other and mouthed a disbelieving, "Yeah, right!"

We crossed Dartmoor, and cycled to the coast at Instow, near Bideford at the mouth of the Taw/Torridge Estuary. From there, we turned back to the east and headed for the uplands of Exmoor. The climb out of Lynmouth via Countisbury Hill was long and steep as it slanted up the cliff with the blue of the sea far below, and off our left shoulders. Direct, and uncompromising, it made us get off the saddles and stand on the pedals to make any headway. With upper bodies arched over the front wheels, tongue almost touching the rubber tyres, we had to strain every muscle and sinew to claw our weaving way upwards. Close to the hill's summit where the road finally flattened out, Derek found that his gears had broken. When he tried to pedal forwards, the gear block spun around freely without engaging any drive. He had to lay the Hill Special on its side, resting on a level area of turf by the roadside, and begin the delicate operation of removing the whole of the gear block. This was the cyclist's equivalent of performing invasive brain surgery.

The procedure starts when the cluster of toothed cogs is removed from the core of the gear by tapping free the circular cover plate. This exposes the front and back rings of small ball bearings set around the centre core – a time for them to drop into the grass and be lost forever. Derek had to spread his rain cape under the rear wheel to catch any errant balls. The inside surface of the gears have a ratchet around the circumference, and a couple of pawl springs force two dogs against the ratchet teeth to create a drive in one direction and a freewheel in the other. This produces the distinctive click-click-click when freewheeling. When the pawl springs break or are jammed with mud, the dogs don't engage properly, resulting in a lack of drive. When new springs are fitted, front and rear ball-races replaced in grease, and the gear blocked refitted, all should function properly. This tricky manoeuvre entails holding the pawl springs in a closed position with a thin strand of encircling cotton to be withdrawn when all is complete. Derek had to swoop back down Countisbury Hill to Lynmouth, find a cycle shop, and purchase the offending springs. He did so but, usually, who can find a pawl spring shop when one needs one? He returned, and with heaving chest, sweat dripping from puckered brow, and a half-smoked cigarette stinging his eyes, he performed the surgery in impeccable style and aplomb. Dave and I sat on the springy turf, smoking, and watching the odd cars struggling up the severe gradient, gears whining, engines and bonnets pulsating with heat, and giving Derek's brow an occasional mop with a dirty handkerchief.

I approached the downhill gradient of Porlock Hill with due care and respect. Even at County Gate, still a good few miles from the dreaded plunge, I was loathe to let my hands stray too far from the brake levers. The hill deserves its reputation, its infamy, as one approaches from the heights of Exmoor and falls to virtual sea level in Porlock village – all in a matter of only a mile or so. The view above the handlebars is of a smooth road ahead lined with the odd, reclining sheep which suddenly disappears from sight with only the distant view of far, blue hills, miles away, across the bay beyond Porlock Weir. You wonder what has happened to the intervening landscape that should have filled the airy gap between road surface and blue sky. In no way could I allow the bike to accelerate and run out of control. The actual descent turned out to be ordinary but hard work. Noting the approaching bends, and various run-off sand traps, the bottom third of the hill was the steepest, when fingers ached due to continuous squeezing of the brake levers. The alloy rims, squeezed tightly between the hard rubber brake blocks, were beginning to get toasty hot. Garry Hogg in his book, *Explorers Awheel,* wrote of the twins, and uncle having to help a floundering motorist, his noisy, frightened family, and their stalled car on the dreaded Porlock Hill.

The remaining days of this tour were through Holford, a small village below the Quantock Hills, on through Glastonbury, with a culture visit to Wells Cathedral, and on to Cheddar at the foot of the Mendips. A pint too many of Somerset scrumpy saw me hugging the toilet pan like a long-lost friend for part of that night before, next morning, a stiff climb through the Cheddar Gorge chased away the accumulated cobwebs. From Bath we re-entered the Cotswolds again, and made a stop at Cleeve Hill youth hostel, high on Cleeve Common above Cheltenham. The run north to Ludlow was uneventful, that is, if any cycle journey is ever uneventful. We arrived there in good time to make an evening's sortie into the historic town. The hostel at Ludford Bridge, is set high above the River Teme with an excellent view of the Lower Broad Street, and the ancient Broadgate. The centre of the town is set atop a hill and the town's cluster of buildings evokes the feeling of a medieval fortress site, hiding behind its encircling walls with the busy, weir-stepped river below. The Norman Castle, and tall tower of St Lawrence's Church break a skyline comprising a jumble of roofs, gables and chimney stacks alongside a Roman, grid-iron street plan. The view of the town impressed me so much, I made it the subject of my first line drawing illustration many years later when working for Shropshire County Council. Of course, I included an old-timer pushing his bike up to the medieval gate, a narrow, arched access in the old town wall. Ludlow has rocketed in popularity, particularly noted for its *haute cuisine,* I hope it doesn't finally get overrun and spoiled. We crossed the narrow, refuge-cut Ludford Bridge and patronized a small beer house at the foot of the hill. Beer houses; merely a room set aside from the family rooms, occupied many a terraced house in Ludlow, Shropshire even as late as the early 1960s. In not too much more than the landlord's front room, and draughty passage, we quaffed a few pints of real ale drawn from the barrel and reflected on a week of brilliant West Country cycle touring.

*

Cycling and drinking have always made good bedfellows. Maybe the two-wheeled traveller feels liberated from the laws on drinking and driving, both legally, and morally. Is it because the 'fragile' cyclist, slightly inebriated, has only himself to blame if injured in an accident? Cycling under the influence of alcohol basically comes down to self-preservation. The fact that the cyclist is open, unprotected, and surrounded by sharp and pointed pieces of metal makes accident avoidance paramount. Is it the desire to cock a snook at overbearing authority, even if only riding off when informed by an officer of the constabulary that, one's back light isn't showing? The clever reply to this is, "No, neither is the front, constable." Cycling is the thirst-inducing occupation in winter, and especially in summer and the welcome of a rest break after hot and hilly miles is hard to resist. Or is it that cycling is enormously pleasurable, like knocking the head against a wall, especially when one stops? Or is it that the cyclist is repeating the age-old practice of frequenting the country alehouse and enjoying a meal just as the original coach traveller would do while the ostler changed the horses? Besides, to keep fit, and save the planet at the same time should always be rewarded by a slight over-indulgence.

A few of us were returning from a volunteer working party at Dimmingsdale youth hostel, and passing through Cellarhead cross roads east of Stoke, we felt that we'd earned a drink in the Bowling Green Inn, a Joules Ales house of some distinction. Les Fenton, a long in the tooth, part-time cyclist, and seasoned drinker, with his mate, coaxed me into the pub to enjoy a pint of what his favourite Joule's Stone Ale bitter. Of course, one pint quickly turned into two, and before long I had consumed far above my alcoholic tolerance. The evening ended at closing time with me having sunk four pints of strong bitter. The lounge bar was warm, snug, and I seemed to impress my hardened drinking partners with my capacity for beer by showing no apparent sign of being drunk. However, when I stepped out into the late evening's fresh, cool air, the effects of the drink invaded my brain, and I only just managing to throw a leg over the crossbar. I freewheeled downhill to Longton, guidance switched to autopilot. I remained upright and balanced through Longton, and headed for Trentham and home. I was just yards away from my estate road when internal guidance deserted me, and I slewed a full ninety degrees to the left, mounted the kerb, crossed the pavement, and embedded myself and bicycle in a garden privet hedge. I had jammed myself, still upright in the manicured topiary, unable to dismount, so sat there, barely suppressing a bout of laughing. The cold air finally persuaded me to extricate myself with machine and I staggered back on to the pavement, leaving a perfect shape of head and shoulders in the neat hedge – as is seen in most comic cartoons. Apart from a few minor scratches, I was uninjured. I quickly skedaddled, or should that be skid-addled lest the property owner caught me rearranging his boundary foliage. I awoke next morning with the drummers from hell beating out a deep, throbbing rhythm, somewhere in the hidden, labyrinthine recesses of my upper brain. Joules Stone Ale had left its skull-aching legacy.

*

I had my 21st birthday party on 26th July. It was a Thursday. It wasn't a boozy do in a local pub; I didn't have to suffer a de-bagging by friends and I already had a door key in the pocket. Sheila and Fred bought me an excellent slide projector. I held a show at Cherry Tree Close for my immediate cycling friends and lashings of good food on the table. It wasn't strictly teetotal and neither were there gallons of lemonade and multi-coloured, quivering jellies. Times were all-together more moderated for me in the early '60s; no wholesale quaffing of pints of lager and being violently ill in shop doorways and unlike my earlier mentioned drunken tussle with a privet hedgerow, I retained appropriate sobriety through the evening. Besides, next day was still a working day; a day of busy draughting in the employ of the Reconstruction Department.

I have often been puzzled by the fact that many cycle tourists are occupied in draughtsmanship – technical or architectural – usually employed in some drawing office or other, bent over drawing boards, busily preparing plans. Is it because of a sedentary occupation leaving plenty of strength and stamina for cycling? Is it a wish to escape the claustrophobic atmosphere of a dusty, Dickensian drawing office for the fresh air and open miles of a verdant countryside? Is it the interest in cartography or because the pastime doesn't necessitate spending oodles of money? In short, many cyclists have had some skill in wielding the mapping pen.

Geoff Cartlidge, he of the red hair, dry humour and socialist ideals, became a great friend and enthusiastic cycling companion. Geoff lived in Wellesley Street, in the Shelton area of the city, the same street, coincidentally, where I was living before moving to Sneyd Green. He, too, lived with his parents and in 1962 was expecting an apprentice's job as, like his father, a gas-fitter in the Gas Board, based in Etruria down the road. Geoff and I decided on a two week tour of Ireland by catching the ferry from Holyhead to Dun Laoghaire and cycling from Dublin in a general south-westerly direction from the Wicklow Mountains to County Kerry. After reading the odd book and magazine article, we thought of Ireland as a somewhat wild country, a country of strong Catholic beliefs, grim institutions and threatening famine; a place of muddy roads and quaint donkey carts; the west coast, a scattered population of rude, thatched hovels and children running about in bare feet. A nation of didicoys; mischievous imps dressed in green and waving crooked sticks! We found that we weren't entirely misinformed. Our expectations would be fully satisfied in this land of myth and magic!

In late August, we caught the evening train from Stoke to Crewe and the night mail boat express through North Wales, to join the Irish ferry at Holyhead. Soon after leaving Crewe and long before we rattled over the Conway and Britannia bridges, the latter crossing the Menai Straits and on to Anglesey, our compartment was empty and we had room to stretch out. Lit only by the weak, yellow lights of the compartment, we nodded off and wondered if the bikes were still safe in the rear guard's van. In 1962, passenger rolling stock was still quite antiquated; net luggage racks and sepia prints on the bulkhead walls. Steam trains were soon to disappear from the network, considered inefficient and too costly to run and maintain. Decimated by Doctor Beeching's keen axe, many branch lines were to be closed a year later, so, old carriages were left to die away as well in the last breaths of rail nostalgia. Modern, open carriages, although clean-lined and up-to-date, exposes us now to the tinny torture of Walkman and mobile phones of the spotty riff-raff.

The sharp, cold sea air blowing over Holyhead's docks jolted us into full wakefulness as we wheeled the bikes into the cavernous car deck and lashed them to bars on the side walls. Grabbing saddlebags, we threaded through the lines of lorries and cars and climbed the companionways to a crowded passenger deck. Even in the early '60s, articulated lorries on cross channel trips were of some considerable size and squeezing past enormous wheels felt overbearingly oppressive. The ship's bar was crowded, exuding a warm atmosphere with the smoke of Irish Sweet Afton cigarettes and the fumes of many pints of Guinness stout and Smithwick's Ales – some still in the glass. A strong Irish brogue arose from a host of wiry characters; a wardrobe of slept-in, grey suits and stained and creased waistcoats. Later into the night, we wandered outside to the taff rail astern and watched the pre-dawn light preceding another sunrise as it picked out a straight wake, swerving gulls and bucking ship's line tachometer.

I'm not too sure when we crossed the invisible time line between today's date in 1962 and the turn of the century. Maybe it was entering Dun Laoghaire harbour; stepping on to Irish soil when we seemed to regress some forty years and into the quaint, but slightly 'used' atmosphere of the twenty-six counties. Passengers streamed from the ferry and immediately swamped onto the already crowded railway station; set at low level in a stone-faced cutting and providing a direct route from the port to Dublin's fine city, *Baile atha Cliath*. The relaxed pace of life we had been led to expect in Ireland was dispelled immediately by the frenetic movement of masses of seagoing travellers, impatient to transfer from ship to shore and meet friends and family in the capital. Our planned destination was in the opposite direction, south and into the foothills of the Wicklow Mountains.

Beyond Bray and Enniskerry, we skirted Powerscourt Gardens, quickly losing any signs of traffic and climbed gradually into the Knockree valley. A collection of buildings close to the top of the valley and tucked under the Wicklow slopes turned out to be a disused film location; a range of buildings having just a front facia and supported at the rear by slender scaffold tubes. A sight to evoke an air of incongruous mystery and falsehoods – a spooky intrusion into this unspoilt landscape. We slept well that night in Knockree youth hostel; in the care of *An Oige*, the Irish equivalent of the YHA, marked with blue triangles instead of green. The climb next morning to Sally Gap brought us on to the Military Road, a narrow, high level route winding and dipping over and through the Wicklows with distant views of windswept moors. Cycling west from Sally Gap, we dropped to the extensive reservoir of Pollaphuca, or Blessington Lakes, and spent a night at Baltiboys youth hostel, a cottage set within the lonely lane network that surrounds this sheet of water; a supply for thirsty Dublin.

The next day we headed back towards the Wicklow Mountains and the Military Road where, it is said, long ago, General Wade moved his armies. The road links several elongated valleys as they carve into the central heights of Mullaghcleevaun and Lugnaquilla, bold, rounded tops at 2,780 feet (847m).and 3,030 feet (924m).respectively – high, but not readily identified. The Glendalough valley is full of history. St Kevin's Bed and the lofty Rattoo Tower, with its high-set entrance doorway, are just two ancient Celtic sites lying in front of the placid lake. Celtic crosses, carved with intricate patterns, crowd together at crazy angles and in unplanned chaos. The lough, this haven of tranquillity, lies deep in the hills and beneath the surrounding cliffs; a finger of water reflecting the larch woods and scree slopes above whose surface is often broken by the lazy mouthed 'O's of rising fish. Insects dance above the deep green water, caught in the shafts of light from an evening's summer sundown. This was a place to stand and stare and reach for the camera.

Aughavannagh hostel, a former barracks, lies at the foot of the Military Road; obviously another site of past conflicts and this evening used by just two other hostellers. We spent a pleasant evening chatting to the girls, adventurous sorts from far away Borehamwood, Hertfordshire. The warden, a bent old lady who emerged from the very depth of the austere building, apart from booking us in, left us to ourselves; relaxing on the scruffy sofa, downing mugs of tea and coaxing the fire into some sort of life. We left our backpacking females next morning and pedalled along the minor roads in a general south-westerly direction, stopping at Foulkstrath Castle near Kilkenny before approaching the Galtee Mountains at Ballydavid Wood. The various villages we passed through had a distinctive plan consisting of a long main street with off-road spaces to each side, where the occasional donkey cart or small tractor had been roughly parked. Invariably, the gutters were littered with the detritus of day-to-day Irish living – piles of donkey or pony droppings, the odd few lumps of dried turf and the cluster of rotting cabbage leaves. The Catholic church had a village centre prominence; its boundary wall lined with numerous big, black bicycles, two or more deep on Sundays! Irish bars, doubling as grocery shops and post offices, lined the town square, ornate, frosted glass doorways and each painted fascia bearing the typical Celtic style of lettering.

West of Cork, the landscape became more spectacular; more hilly after the flat roads in the centre of Ireland, and decidedly with a more temperate climate. After Macroom, we passed through attractively-named places, such as Inchigeelagh and Ballingeary; cut through low, twisting gorges, never too far from the young River Lee and finally reaching the sea on the shores of Bantry Bay. The road to Glengarriff wound around seaweed-choked coves, past rich hedgerows of rose and honeysuckle with scattered pines, with the silver sea in the bay ever-sparkling off our left shoulders in a late afternoon sun. Bantry Bay – the name conjured up images and places on the Spanish Main. Cutlass-wielding, wooden-legged pirates with a patch over the eye and a toothy, evil grin. The area map of Cork and Kerry suggested such illusions, especially with place names reading Roaringwater Bay, Skibbereen, Cape Clear and Mizzen Head. Bantry Bay, seen now in a lowering, afternoon sun, revealed a beaten copper sheen with the hills to each shore fading into an indistinct, warm haze.

From a bed and breakfast stop at Glengarriff, we pedalled up the narrow main road, around multiple bends, slowly climbing past gorse and scrub to cross the summit at the eastern end of the Caha Mountains through a series of short tunnels. Below and ahead, we crossed the end of the Kenmare Estuary by a new concrete bridge before another climb, this time among the Macgillicuddy's Reeks, at Windy Gap. The Reeks contain Ireland's highest mountain, Carrantuohill, at well over 3,400 feet (1,040m).and a famous panorama of mountains, islands and lakes; the Ladies View, looking east to Killarney in the distance, a few miles away and many feet below. Although a fine aspect, the view is towards open countryside; open-ended and, therefore, lacks a distant central focal point. Immediately below the Windy Gap lies an area of special scientific interest, a section of ancient woodland with many differing species in the under storey, protected from any harsh climate by the constraining, steep-sided valley slopes. We descended to Killarney before the next day, passing Kate Kearney's Cottage and through the famous Gap of

Dunloe; rocky, mountain walls towering to each side. The track was rough but not too difficult due to our club's recent rough-stuff history. From Black Valley youth hostel and its immediate mountain setting, we regained the coast road that circles the Kerry Peninsular – The Ring of Kerry – following this adventurous route with its many short climbs and descents, around bends, over a bumpy, wavy surface for most of the time with a surrounding landscape of mountains and coast. Through Parknasilla, Sneem and climbing through a tortuously constricted gap in the mountains, covering half the route before heading inland to Glencar, near Lough Currane, and an opportunity to explore numerous small loughs, many secret and unnamed. We stayed in the area for two days; riding over dirt tracks, resting by lonely stone bridges, smoking the odd Sweet Afton and admiring the long line of central mountains which would become capped with a mantle of dense white mist at the onset of evening. We met the occasional farm labourer or gentleman of the road; everyone would engage us in friendly chat, the Blarney, telling of the area's history, be it ancient or modern; passing the time of day in a land where time is of no importance and having no consequence in the order of things. To meet an Irishman on the road, prepare yourself for a chat lasting, sometimes, hours.

We finally had to depart this idyllic countryside, an explorer's Pandora 's Box, especially for the intrepid cyclist, and head east and north, returning to the Wicklows and Dun Laoghaire. A prevailing, favourable tail wind ushered our bikes along quiet roads out of County Kerry, out of this land of geographic surprises and warm winds, but we would keep the experiences in mind for future tours. Through Glin and Foulkstrath Castle and skirting the Wicklows, we covered the return journey in quick time – too quick a time, in fact, there's a lot to see – before meeting the Irish Sea ferry. Our last views of the Emerald Isles, for now anyway, were the receding harbour walls at Dun Laoghaire and beyond in a hazy distance sky, the long line of rounded, cobalt blue hills of Wicklow. It was the first day of September. The musty, earthy smells and low hanging mists of autumn would see us seek out closer hostels and shorter runs.

We were moving into the social season; shorter days, less daylight hours and the time to draw up to the fire, be it at home or in some public house, close to a Saturday night hostel stay. Darts would become our favourite pastime, supplemented with a pint of Best bitter and a cigarette smouldering on the rim of an ashtray. Summer weekends and holidays had given us plenty of opportunities to throw an 'arrow' or fistful of three. With Derek Latham and Dave Hope, and later Geoff Cartlidge as partners/opponents; with Ralph Salt and brother Clive, and Roy Deakin more than proficient at hand-to-eye coordination, we very soon gelled into a formidable cyclists' darts team. Ralph, apart from being a good darts player, was lightening fast in calculating scores. Scores scored and scores needed. After all, he was working for an auditing company. Roy was a bank teller so he was really fast at the mental mathematics. At the games of 301 and 501, rapid scoring calculations give a team added advantage, kept the team throwers in their rhythm. We played up and down the country in all sorts of conditions, on all manner of dartboards from bulging horsehair to best cork and against all sorts of opposition. Mainly, we would be playing others on their home turf, on their own board and toeing their own line, or oche.

One weekend, enjoying a lunchtime drink to wash down the sandwiches, we were drawn into a series of darts games with the locals. The pub was, I remember, the Horse and Jockey at Stottesdon, in deepest south-east Shropshire, beyond Bridgnorth and approaching the Wyre Forest area. We had probably followed a rough-stuff route over Brown Clee Hill, north-east of Ludlow and the highest point in Shropshire. Where we were heading, I know not – probably homeward on a sunny Sunday. The locals challenged us to a few games, probably thinking that they could beat us easily. Who were these cyclists wearing khaki short shorts, this break-away party from a Baden-Powell scout jamboree, these young whippersnappers on bikes who thought they could play darts? But characters like Derek and Dave possessed that burning desire to win and Ralph, so eager to be at the top of every climb first, certainly wasn't going to lose! Roy screwed up his eyes, twisted the corner of his mouth into a sneer, held a steady arm and maintained concentration as a bank clerk is wont. It goes without saying that we prevailed, even when the winning stakes turned from rounds of drinks to cash on the bar. We eventually bowled away from the Horse and Jockey at closing time while the locals hunched over their pints, left crying into their beer! At least the bar curtains would be drawn and they would be left in peace to enjoy an extended 'locals lock-in'!

On reflection, we all came from Stoke-on-Trent; a place in later years that was to become the capital of darts, producing England players and world champions on an, almost, factory production line! Player's way above our own amateurish abilities in a (then).world of beer, beer guts, and raucous audiences under a cloud of cigarette smoke!

As the year drew to a close, there was only a subtle indication that the winter months would be so severe. Early cold conditions with a November cycle run to Fox Howl, Delamere Forest, spending Sunday morning on the shore of Pickmere Lake, where throwing, running and jumping were more to keep warm than any competitive spirit. Hardy bystanders watched us cavorting on the gravel shore in an event we later named The Pickmere Sports! Later in November, on a Stoke YHA auto-ramble into Snowdonia, our proposed route up to the summit of Snowdon via the Watkin Path had to be cancelled due to a massive overnight snowfall. The coach journey into Wales was a few hours of raucous laughter and youthful horseplay. Firmly ensconced on the back seat, a walker, Dave Trigg, was determined to hang his hat on an attractive, giggling girl's proud chest! What happens to folk when they sit on the back seat of a run-down charabanc? *Didn't we have a lovely time, the day we went to Bangor?* On a toilet break at Bettws-y-Coed, he led us all in a regimented straight line, goose-stepping, saluting and chanting the German war cry, *"Kommen sie mitten zieg!"*Goodness knows what the locals thought! Next morning, we motored over snowy roads into Nant Gwynant, vacated our coach and prepared ourselves for the climb ahead. Even the start of the route was blocked with deep drifts and visibility reduced to yards, not miles. We returned to the hostel at Snowdon Ranger after an ultra low-level wander. It was a long way to travel in that winter but views, when the clouds lifted, were spectacular as ever.

I joined Ralph and Clive Salt, with friends Paul Leese, John Humphries and Cliff Yates, for some very short cycle runs and rambles, usually in the moors above Leek; walking beneath the jagged heights of The Roaches and Ramshaw Rocks. We even sometimes caught a bus to travel above Leek, purely for the experience of walking on deep, frozen snow. The lonely Mermaid Inn appeared even more isolated in those days of wandering around snow-covered moors. I never remembered icy surfaces deterring us from cycling, although distances were severely curtailed, keeping us on cleared, local roads around the city and immediate environs. Social visits to each other's homes kept us all in touch. I remember dropping in on the Salt brothers in Beverley Drive, Bucknall on those short, dark days of winter. Mr Salt, wearing a flat cap, moustache and chain-smoking, would always make us welcome. Their house was council-owned, one of hundreds, cluttered inside and always comfortable. We spent evenings chatting under the yellow glow of a 60 watt light bulb, drinking cider, listening to music and messing about with unplugged electric guitars and getting mildly tipsy to the beat of the Beatles and the Mersey Sound. We would spend evenings talking and looking at maps; planning cycling adventures whilst waiting for better days to come. Ralph was always the pioneering explorer in these days of severe weather, impatient to be out there in the great outdoors.

Recent documentaries of that 1962/63 winter show bleak scenes of snowdrift-blocked lanes, traffic half-buried or struggling for traction on icy estate roads. Scenes of pedestrians slipping and sliding along slushy pavements or negotiating gigantic piles of cleared snow to reach their front doors. The Milk Marketing Board had to appeal to the general public to dig out their empty bottles from snowy, front door mounds. Daylight barely penetrated the winter days with dated Austin vans and Morris Minors polluting an already misty and smoggy atmosphere. Within industrial Stoke-on-Trent, it appeared that we had hardly moved from the Victorian era; lines of bleak terraced houses standing stark and regimental, lining ice-rutted streets of the cold, poor, but ever-cheerful local folk.

It would become a waiting game before the 1962/1963 winter released its grip.

Chapter Four

1963

Winter Cycling – Snow on Thorneliff Hill – Forays into Winter Shropshire – Hot Miles – Pistyll – Rhaeadr Waterfall – Magic of Maps – Rough-stuff Routes – The Cycle Shop – New Bike from Liverpool – Crash – A Lonely Run – Whitsun in the Wye Valley – Another Welsh Holiday – Holiday in Western Ireland – Cycling Versus Walking – Thunderstorm – Les West – Boots 'n Saddles Christmas.

Age: 22.

Home: Cherry Tree Close, Trentham.

Work: Stoke-on-Trent Reconstruction Dept., Kingsway, Stoke.

Government: Conservative.

Prime Minister: Sir Alec Douglas-Home.

Jan: Severe winter; Britain blocked from joining EEC.

Apr: Black Civil Rights campaign begins in USA.

Jun: John Profumo/Christine Keeler scandal.

Jul: Spy Kim Philby exposed.

Aug: Great Train Robbery;"I have a dream" speech by Martin Luther King. Doctor Beeching wields his axe.

Sept: Riots in Birmingham, Alabama.

Nov: President Kennedy assassinated.

Films: *Cleopatra, Tom Jones & Doctor Strangelove.*

What a year. Macmillan, with his 'landed gentry' persona, gave way to an even more privileged country squire in the form of Sir Alec Douglas-Home, a thin, ill-looking premier who reeked of the grouse moor and smoking shotgun barrels. Geoff C. queried if the man was actually alive. Our Minister for War, John Profumo, got caught savouring the naughty delights of London models, Christine Keeler and Mandy Rice-Davies. State security could have been compromised. But these were raunchy days in the early '60s – days of Morris Mini Minors, miniskirts, ladies' long, plastic boots, beehive hairstyles, tight sweaters, E-type Jaguars and Carnaby Street. The Jaguars had been speed-tested on a section of the M1 when it first opened in 1959. A mail train travelling from Glasgow to Euston, carrying nearly 2.6 million in used banknotes, was stopped near Bridego Bridge, Tring, Home Counties. The robbers were finally hounded down by grim detectives in shabby overcoats at remote Leatherslade Farm, Brill due, no doubt, to the purely impossible logistics of hiding such a vast amount of paper money. The Great Train Robbers were secretly admired by the general public and because of this, subsequently sentenced to crushingly-long, thirty-year prison sentences. There were riots in Birmingham, Alabama and other southern states of the USA as blacks suffered the red-necked, gun-crazed attitudes of the evil Ku-Klux-Klan sympathisers – ideal conscripts for Uncle Sam's future war adventures. However, Martin Luther King had his dream. Doctor Beeching, the 'Fat Controller', cut many of the country's railway branch lines, effectively isolating small communities and forcing them to use road transport. For reference, watch the film The Titfield Thunderbolt. Years later, enthusiasts would reclaim many scenic lines, reverting back to the attractions of steam. It was a normal dull, rainy November early evening. I have forgotten were I was when John F. Kennedy was assassinated, although I can safely say where I wasn't. On that grassy knoll. America wept.

*

Cycling on snow-covered roads can be easy or almost impossible. It all depends on having the right sort of snow, a phrase used as an excuse for many of British Rail's winter cancellations. On the roads, if the snow is freshly fallen and free of passing traffic, providing a smooth, ridge-free surface and of modest depth, cycling is relatively straightforward. If, however, the temperature on the surface is below freezing, there is a high likelihood of slipping or skidding. If a snow-covered road is smoothed down with numerous car tyres and becomes frozen, a veritable ice-skating rink is formed and slipping becomes almost inevitable. I remember dismounting from the bike at the foot of a slope in the local housing estate road at Trentham and immediately sliding downhill;

silently and smoothly, standing upright and as certainly as the gliding of a ship's launch. The trickiest cycling on snowy roads is when the surface is lined with frozen ridges; usually after a partial thaw and having seen the passage of much traffic. If one's direction entails crossing a ridge, balance is jeopardised, steering affected and a fall is the usual outcome. Much like having to mount the kerb at a fine angle or getting a front wheel stuck in the tramlines. Black ice is evil and awaits the careless cyclist like a sleeping devil. Dave Hope would like to wear heavy walking boots in snowy conditions, but when he could take to the saddle on clearer sections, he found that he couldn't fit them into his toe clips. A deeper snowfall would see the mudguards choke up with compacted snow trapped between wheel and mudguard, thereby bringing the rider to an enforced halt. Snow building up over the rear gear block would make the chain come off, unable to engage any of the toothed sprockets. Piddling on the chain and sprockets usually solved the problem; body-heated urine having the necessary melting qualities. Bearing in mind these factors, cycling a few miles in snow was fun, if not limited in distance and wrought with hazards.

Of course, riding into a blizzard of wet, cold snow is not pleasant at all. Half-blinded and suffering from possible frostbite, the wise cyclist will soon start looking for alternative forms of transport. There are, however, times in winter when the conditions can be appreciated for what they are; a different, sometimes challenging experience. It's all a matter of having the right sort of snow. I will always remember an evening's ride onto the moors above Leek after climbing slowly from Hartington Hall and Warslow. We were returning from a winter weekend to a relatively close Peak District hostel and the last real climb of the day was towards the Mermaid Inn, an isolated spot overlooking the Roaches. There had been a light fall of snow and in the freezing temperature on these lonely moors and lit only by the fading ruddy light of a sunset, small hillocks of snowdrifts were being formed in the tough tufts of heather. Snowy spindrift was being blown across the road surface, looking like waves of very cold, windblown desert sand. The effect of the swirling, ground-hugging snow transformed the road into perpetual motion, a wide, moving, powdery conveyor. We were silhouetted against a completely clear, cold winter sky; still quite light but revealing the odd, ultra-bright star. With just a smidgeon of imagination and with half-closed eyes, we could very well have been travelling across a Mongolian desert tableland.

The winter of 1962 spread into the early months of 1963 with increased intensity. Again, returning from a weekend in the Peak District, passing the isolated Mermaid Inn and descending the long, precipitous hill to the bottom at Thorncliff, we found that deep snowdrifts had formed on each side of the narrow road. This evening was dark; the road dropped like a brick, its course picked out by the line of white snowdrifts, while ahead and far below, the lights of Leek twinkled in the cold, cutting air. Thorncliff Hill could have been used as a National Hill Climb venue, a sporting branch of cycle competition usually held in the autumn months. The Burway Hill, rising to the Long Mynd in Shropshire, could also have been used because of its length and severity, as was the climb of the Winnat's Pass, near Castleton. The Peak District National Park certainly had more than its fair share of lung-bursting ascents.

We negotiated the hill reasonably easily, but near the bottom, windblown drifts began to block the way. In the gathering twilight, we could see a roadside farm building with a long, graceful snowdrift spreading from its sloping roof at ridge level and totally infilling the sheltered midden yard. Cruel winds from the north-west had transformed the landscape. Close to the foot of the hill at Thorncliff village, we stumbled upon a sports car with its radiator half-buried in a deep, high snowdrift. The driver and his girlfriend were scratching at the mountain of snow, trying to gain just a few extra yards in their journey to the main road and civilization at the Moss Rose PH on the outskirts of Leek. To a man (and two women)., we formed a gang and, part shovelling, part pushing, manoeuvred the car gradually clear of the section of drifting; our intention being to, eventually, see the happy couple well on their way and out of this white hell. Pushing, lifting and steering seemed to last for hours as we finally gained a clear roadway; free of a series of graceful, sculpted ridges and hillocks, now frozen at this late hour to a crispy crunchiness. One of ourselves was even allotted the responsibility of bringing up the bicycles, moving and parking them in turn to be ready when our journey could be resumed. We considered the job a challenge of logistics against the elements as the primary concern, rather than an overwhelming desire to help the couple out of their dilemma. As a fringe benefit for our helpfulness, we hoped that our chivalry went some way to repair some of the animosity that often occurred between cyclists and motorists at that time. We did, however, applaud their sense of adventure for motoring through difficult winter conditions in an open-topped sports car. Being abroad in those severe months appealed to our spirit of adventure; we admired them for challenging the extreme, whatever their transport.

Towards the end of February, Paul Leese and I used Shrewsbury youth hostel as a Friday evening start, allowing us to use Saturday for a snowy journey into south Shropshire at Clun. Although the distance from Shrewsbury to Clun was modest, we needed the extra time in case of difficult road conditions and lack of daylight. Besides, we would be able to possibly tour through some of the narrow lanes that veined this countryside. At about this time, we all had a craze of smoking pipe tobacco. With Paul agreeing, we had a break at Craven Arms; not through a need of a rest, but to search out my small tin of Whisky Flake tobacco, fill the briars and partake in a few minutes of contemplative puffing. We leant the machines alongside a village-centre bus shelter and sat inside, out of the chilly winter wind, going through the rigmarole of charging, tamping, and lighting our favourite smoking pieces. It seemed to be so very damn sophisticated. We all wore black gabardine cycling jackets and dark red tartan, cheese-cutter, flat caps in this early decade of cycling; the smoking equipment packed away in one of the deep jacket side pockets. We both felt very posh and studious as we puffed away, warming the fingers on the pipe's curving bowls. It was all so civilized until, on tipping my head back when laughing at a Paul Leese wisecrack, I received an accidental mouthful of neat tobacco goo; that delightful mixture of green nicotine tar and spittle that always collects in the pipe stem of the pretend smoker.

The main road to Clun strikes due west from Craven Arms by way of Aston-on-Clun. Having time to spare and being of sterner stuff, we ventured to the very south of the county, deciding to make for the hamlet of Stowe and pass over the hills to arrive in Chapel Lawn, situated in an isolated valley to the north. From the slight cover of thin snow on the main roads, posing no problems of progress, we climbed on a narrow, exposed lane and promptly met with deep snow drifts in a land of silent, hilly whiteness. Even the few, scraggy sheep were silent in the blanketing snow; standing transfixed, unmoving, just exhaling clouds of steamy breath. The damping effect of deep snow on voices and sounds rendered the surroundings even more isolated. The field boundaries, mainly post and wire, were hung with fingers of freezing ice; icicles blown into a horizontal arrangement indicating the direction of past weeks of cold winter winds. We retreated from this hostile world blocked by snowdrifts and a feeling of exposed isolation, deciding on backtracking to join the main road to New Invention and our shelter at Clun youth hostel. The hostel is spartan even in high summer; on a February night in the middle of a severe winter, the place held the coldness and dampness of death. Even so, after a day of battling snowdrifts in back-of-beyond south Shropshire whilst trying to stay warm and sheltering in sad bus shelters, we knocked out our last pipes of Whisky Flake, climbed to the dormitory and buried ourselves under piles of mouldy blankets. A deep, dreamless sleep came easily. Hostelling in deepest winter was rough and full of discomforts but had its bonuses, too, in spectacular scenery and lanes to ourselves.

As cyclists can move quickly from the broiling heat of a long, slow ascent to a fast and furious, freezing cold descent, so my memories of these times moved from ice-cold winter to the hot, idyllic, timeless days of summer. The Berwyn Mountains, separating north-west Shropshire from the hills and vales of Clwyd in deepest north Wales, were to become familiar ground for the cycling/hostelling tourists of Stoke-on-Trent. The region is crossed by three intensely interesting road passes. The very steep Bwlch y Groes, situated in the extreme south-west of the area, climbs airily from lowly Dinas Mawddwy with an ever-deepening cwm yawning below the cyclist's right shoulder. It bisects at the summit with a narrow spur lane dropping to Lake Vynwy and finally leads to the south-west end of Bala Lake. This pass caused mutterings of disbelief to Tour of Britain riders on the race's one and only crossing. Not only did racers from all the European countries have to dismount and run with their machines; they suffered the chagrin of having to walk, fighting for breath, up the final, destroying yards of the summit gradient.

The Hirnant Pass emerges from a network of narrow, woody, stone-walled lanes near Bala town and bursts out into an open, U-shaped valley, before clinging and climbing the smooth valley flanks before the summit. The openness and exposure of the immediate surroundings leaves one in awe of the terrific glacial pressures and scourings that must have occurred in some past ice age to form such a landscape. Immediately over the summit, the narrowness of the winding descent is cloaked in dense pine forestry. The Hirnant Pass was, possibly, our favourite climb – a climb that fed our imagination of Tour de France mountain stages. We would instantly become a Fausto Coppi, Charly Gaul or Federico Bahamontes; pedalling smoothly upwards whilst clad in the distinctive polka-dot, king of the mountains, racing jersey. Incidentally, Bahamontes, or *bajas montes,* has the meaning low mountains in Castilian Spanish. How's that for a contradiction of the Eagle of Toledo's climbing achievements?

The third challenging pass that bisected the Berwyn for us intrepid cyclists was the Milltir Cerrig climb from Llangynog to Bala. The climb starts immediately on leaving the main street of Llangynog and rises steadily, passing craggy roadside rocks, to emerge on to the elevated moorland slopes of the Berwyn massif. On a blisteringly-hot day at Whitsun, with the past mineral workings and spoil debris on the adjoining steep slopes wavering in the midday heat, we plodded upwards at a moderate touring pace. As we gained height, the road surface became black, shiny and definitely sticky. The tyres began to make a swishing, sucking sound as if we were on a very wet road. Waves of tar-laden air assaulted the nostrils, rising upwards from the rapidly melting asphalt and as sheer heat bounced off the roadside rocks and dead insects impinged on our sweating brows, we were slowly sucked to a crawl, slowed by the build-up of tar. As we progressed, a healthy layer of loose gravel attached itself, finally jamming between tyres and mudguards. We struggled to the open summit at a walking pace with no time to enjoy the view below and at our backs, of the ever-deepening valley. A waterfall at the head of the vale had been reduced to a summertime trickle. The open, undulating road ahead was lost in a mirage haze of hot gravel, disappearing into the yonder bluey-grey toasted air. An isolated sleeping sheep and the distant flash of a solitary car windscreen was the only sign of life on these sun-dried heights. After descending from several elevated miles, we paused under the cooling shade of the trees to clear the solidified gravel/tar coating from under the mudguards with a deftly wielded screwdriver. We could, at last, continue our travels with our wheels turning freely, but our shorts pulling and chafing at reddening, sunburned thighs.

Several long valleys cut into the south-eastern slopes of the Berwyns. The one that held our fascination in those early days was the deep valley that probes into the mountains, some 5 miles (8k).from Llanrhaeadr-ym-Mochnant to the Pistyll Rhaeadr waterfall. As one travels further into the cwm, the hillside rims become higher, steeper and the bottom slopes are littered with massive boulders, no doubt eroded by past weather extremes, prised from the heights above. Most of the valley floor boulders are of modest size, but one in particular is as big as a house and is used by would-be rock climbers for some low-level practise. The culminating wonder, we found, was at the very end of the valley where cliff-top pines encroach and enclose the precipitous Pistyll Rhaeadr (spouting waterfall)., said to be one of the Seven Wonders of Wales. With a name like that, it just had to be a wonder and a spectacle.

Rainfall collected on the swampy ground below Cader Berwyn eventually forms into a brisk stream and flows out of the mountains and down the valley. At Pistyll Rhaeadr, the water leaps over a high, rocky shelf; a geological step formed by hard and softer strata eroding unequally, and plunges some 210 feet (65m).in an almost uninterrupted drop. Remember those secondary school geography lessons where one had to draw the stages of a river's life – cross sections from 'V' to 'U' shapes? The transition from one to the other here is sudden and dramatic. Two-thirds down the awful abyss, the water thunders into a natural, moss-covered rocky bowl; a furious cauldron of foaming hydro power and wreathing mists, before finding an outlet and falling the remaining feet to the riverbed in a bouncing, lively cascade.

We scrambled to the top of the falls; stepping and reaching over slimy, mossy boulders and loose, bracken-covered earth banks; hoisting ourselves upwards by levering on most of the tree trunks, until we gained the top and very lip of the drop. Standing, teetering on the flat, rocky brink, the fall of water was below and out of sight, gouts of flung spray apart, hidden to the timorous bystander. As one looked into open-air and down the valley, one's knees grew weak and strangely feeble; one's imagination invented a malignant force, a devilish power only too keen to give a hearty shove and send you spinning into space, ending in a hard, soaking and shocking demise. Standing at the top of the waterfall, you were constantly glancing behind, monitoring any possible clumsy tourist whose accidental stumble could nudge you into oblivion. It's a place from which you were constantly considering a cautious retreat. It was a spot on which one shouldn't linger. Sadly, visitors have died hereabouts. How could we have ever climbed behind that thundering waterfall?

The photograph was in black and white with a thin white border, probably taken by a Box Brownie and printed from a vest pocket-sized negative film. It was slightly out of focus, scratched and ragged at the corners. It showed a group of us; Ralph and Clive Salt, John Humphries and, probably, Paul Leese, perched on a narrow, moss-covered shelf, standing at the very back of the waterfall. Severely back-lit with the sun bleaching-out their shirts, sleeves rolled casually to the elbow, they were captured nonchalantly grinning at my camera with a silvery curtain of water in rushing freefall, almost touching their noses. Thundering water and a yawning abyss in front, damp, moss-swathed vertical rock at their backs, the assembled adventurers appeared completely unaware of the danger, congregated in a laughing huddle on that precarious perch. Any comments or jokes would have been drowned out by the continuous noise of plunging water. But these were the times to pursue risky exploits – long before our, now, safety-conscious awareness and a society of nannyish mollycoddling.

To view the falls in their entirety and in full-spate after, say, a week of heavy rain, one wonders how the hell we ever managed to reach such an exclusively dangerous spot halfway down the drop. It appeared well-nigh inaccessible. That photograph has long since gone missing; crumpled, torn, shredded, burnt or probably buried, lost under tons of landfill. The snapshot and those times have gone forever; happily, the memory is still vivid.

In 1963 we were constantly seeking out rough-stuff routes of ever-increasing degrees of difficulty. Our main map usage was the excellent John Bartholomew 1/2 inch to 1 mile Series of England, Wales and Scotland. These colour-layered maps proved ideal for cyclists as they reduced the need to carry a vast collection of more detailed OS maps on a long, cross-country journey. East to west, the map covered about 80 miles (130k).and north to south, about 40 miles (65k).; all, of course, as the crow flies. Besides, by using a range of colour layering from low, valley, deep green, to moor and mountain, dark brown, they gave an easy indication of height climbed or descended. All narrow lanes, even those with a swathe of grass down the centre, were marked in yellow, together with principal tracks, marked by single, dashed lines. However, when we considered a rough-stuff route, particularly in hilly country, we would use the more detailed Ordnance Survey, 1 inch to 1 mile, (1/63360). Series with full contour marking and minor stream courses indicated. The up-to-date metric equivalents are at a scale of 1/50,000th, but in my opinion, although easier to read, somehow lack the style and Edwardian character of the older maps. An early OS map marked 'GR' and with a price of 3/- (15p)., with its seraphed lettering, hachures, subtle colour layering and ornate notations seemed to evoke fonder memories of a historical landscape of long ago. A work of art in itself. The cold, clinical metric version just doesn't have that same quality; Dunkery Beacon, at 519 metres above sea level, high on Exmoor just doesn't sound right. An Imperial height of 1,702 feet seems far more impressive. Despite schools encouraging the metric system, I still believe many older folk are happier with the old Imperial style and system.

Slavishly following the Afon Towy track in Mid Wales and crossing over the Berwyns, by way of the aforementioned Wayfarers Pass, were two serious introductions to rough-stuff cycling. Memories of the wet wilderness of wild Wales and the Nant Rhyd Wilym, with its summit memorial and flat, tin box for donations, will linger in the memory. Other routes over these breezy, rounded heights were by way of Moel Fferna, dropping to the Swch-Cae-Rhiw stream and an extended summer's afternoon bathing almost naked in one of the several, deep, cool pools. Needless to say, we had no female members present – just plenty of male members. John Hall and Brian Whalley needed no encouragement for this skinny-dipping, an act they would later repeat in the busy boating waters of the River Teme, below Ludlow Castle. The Bwlch y Ffeni, crossing from the Hirnant Valley to a lane short of Llangynog, gave views of distant, low, forested mountain slopes below a fine blue sky. This area was definitely planted with Forestry Commission commercialism in mind.

Beyond Shrewsbury and based on the Mid Wales youth hostels of Corris, Kings, Dolgellau and Plas Rhiwaedog, Bala, we used a longer Easter weekend for the long rough-stuff route crossing the shoulder of Cader Idris from the lanes above Tal-y-Llyn. The day was overcast and rainy as we negotiated the faint track around the headwaters of the Afon Dysynni, near the Castell y Bere, and climbed slowly upwards through saturated, boggy ground with only an isolated shepherd's stone shelter for company. An odd barbed-wire fence drooping between leaning, mould-covered posts trailed soaked tufts of snagged sheep wool and droplets of rainwater. Diversions to avoid sloshing through cotton grass and bog were many and time consuming. However, the gloom lifted with the clearing weather and as we crested the long ridge at a height of some 2,000 feet (607m)., the whole length of the Mawddach Estuary came into view. From the Barmouth railway bridge at the mouth of the estuary, to the toll bridge at Penmaenpool, the inlet was spread out before and beneath us, as if we were looking at a map of the area. Warm, late afternoon sun filled the valley, making the sea to the west, off Barmouth's waterfront, glisten with silvery light. Swirling sandbanks, easily identified from this height, indicated an estuary full of hidden tidal currents. A ferry boat had capsized years before, close to the spot where the toll bridge is now sited, drowning many souls and proving the dangers of fast, fluctuating estuary waters. The view to the north revealed a distant Rhinogs and beyond them, just a faint suggestion of high peaks, probably Snowdonia. Cader Idris, the Chair of King Idris, lay along the ridge to our right; 2,926 feet (892m).of rock and scree buttress, looming over the streets of Dolgellau. Our descent, although steep and mainly grassy, was made without mishap, dropping to the high level lane before the short ride to the youth hostel at Kings, Dolgellau.

Sometime in April, my Sun Cycles machine, Maud, with its large-flange hubs and reddish-purple painted tubing, was looking very tired. Through moving in cycling circles, I was learning of newer, lighter components and hearing the names of distinguished cycle frame makers. Scouring the pages of *Cycling,* I soon became knowledgeable on the pros and cons of different touring equipment. I learnt to choose helpful gear ratios and gear-arm ranges; the benefits of rustless, stainless steel spokes; the best saddles for touring or whether to use alloy mudguards. Could they prove to be noisy – rattle when loose? Brookes leather saddles, of highest quality, actually improved with wear. The suppleness of backside flesh was, over many miles, transferred to the saddle's accommodating chrome leather, turning it into a brown, veined and cracked 'perch' that became a faithful friend. Some biologists maintain that bodily atoms are eventually absorbed by the saddle, the bike becoming part-human and bionic, assimilating characteristics of its rider. Some other biologists would consider me crazy. You mould yourself into the saddle – not the reverse and it's definitely not like sitting in an armchair.

Acquaint myself of differing handlebar profiles; straight or Maes bends, the toughest saddlebags and their capacities. All these facts and figures could be taken on board just by waiting at the counter in a 'gen' cycling shop and eavesdropping on other racers or tourists. Swinnerton's cycle shop, considering the status of the family in cycle racing, was remarkably small. After all, Les West and Brian Rourke, both members of Tunstall Wheelers CC, shopped there. A converted terraced house in Victoria Road, Fenton, going through the shop doorway and up to the counter was like entering into a magical fairy grotto. The window was packed with cycling components – jewels of high engineering to put an avaricious gleam in the eyes of all cycle enthusiasts. Purchasing anything from a derailleur gear to a puncture outfit was a delight. In the gloom, shining frames were arraigned in a glittering line, just begging to be ridden – fast. Lightweight alloy wheels displayed their strong but fragile-looking spokes in a spider's web tracery of thin wires. Wheels that relegated the car wheel to the Stone Age of Fred Flintstone. High above, dark tyres in clumps hung like thunder from the rafters, rounded and rolled and displaying their delicate treads, designed to reduce road drag to the barest minimum. The whiff of rubber was overpowering. High pressure touring tyres and racing tubulars of gossamer lightness were there for the tourer or racer alike. What miles would they cover, what speeds would they reach? However, it was the overall smell of the shop that played on the nostrils and invited everyone to ride away on a journey of exploration. The aromas of leather, rubber, grease and oil tweaked the nose with the gathered smells of cycling newness. The oil-stained, splintered floorboards, gnarled by years of cleated cycling shoes, had many an oily, errant ball bearing collected in the dusty floorboard gaps. What level of excitement was enjoyed by the boy or girl wheeling their new, shiny steeds into the street, an early birthday or Christmas present, away from this den of promised joys to come? What future tours were formulating in excited heads?

Accessories apart, the main part of the touring machine was the basic frame. The name Harry Quinn caught my eye and from thereon, he was the craftsman to make my bicycle. On a pro forma returnable sheet, I had to specify the frame's size and angles at seat tube and head tube, brazed-on extras, such as pump pegs, cable stops and carrier bosses. The type of jointing lugs, plus indicate a full colour scheme. In fact, one had to know a considerable amount about cycle design before a correct specification could be submitted. I returned the form and was presently summoned to Walton Road, Liverpool, in order to take delivery of my pride and joy, my hand-built, lightweight frame.

An early April breeze was whipping off the Mersey as I made my way from Lime Street Station and strolled by the giant pier head buildings to the edge of the city centre and into the long Walton Road. Harry Quinn Cycles was just a small retail shop, like Roy Swinnerton's, where the shop assistant handed over my precious merchandise. He was clad in dirty, oil-smeared, brown overalls and coughed a Liverpool accent, as rough as emery cloth, which escaped from pursed lips that struggled to hold a half-smoked fag. I thought at the time that my gleaming cycle frame deserved more than an uninterested grunt as he handed it over to me with no ceremony whatsoever. Such engineering perfection as this fully deserved a ceremonial fanfare. With the frame tucked under my arm, tubing fully wrapped in protective paper coils, I made my way back to Lime Street and trained back to Stoke. I had bought, separately, all the components: wheels, handlebars, and seat and handlebar pillars, in lightweight alloy, with the chain wheels, cranks, and pedals in steel (heavier but more elegant). Brakes, brake hoods, saddle, rear carrier, mudguards, cable covers and all the little nuts and bolts and other bits and bobs, were stored in cardboard boxes at the back of the garage at Cherry Tree Close. I couldn't wait to assemble all these wonderful, clean and shiny things into one perfect beast of a touring cycle.

The frame, 21 inches (525mm)., measured from top of seat tube to centre of bottom bracket, was made of duralumin; well-known as Reynold' s 531 double-butted tubing, where the tubes are thicker in section at the ends than in the middle for strength and joined with Nervex intricately-cut lugs. This 531 tubing was developed for aircraft construction before the war, when lightness and strength were needed. The ends of the front and rear forks were chromed and the rest of the frame finished in a metallic bronze lustre enamel paint. The seat and head tubes were painted in contrasting panels of ruby-red and the distinctive Harry Quinn crest applied. All joints between tubes and lugs were picked out with white, fine lining. When the bike was finished, it looked almost too smart to ever take out on the road. At work, I must have mentioned my self-built bicycle many times to my work colleagues, showing immense, barely containable pride. Alan Walker, bald, red-faced and jocular, lay down his pen and laughing heartily, suggested that it could even be considered the Aston Martin of bicycles. The quality and reputation of a Rolls Royce but with the dashing speed of an Aston. The 'Rolls Royce of Bicycles', although luxurious and the pinnacle of perfection, would seem slow and lumbering when describing my Harry Quinn. It needed a racing cyclist on board, not a tourist.

I hadn't ridden the new Harry Quinn cycle for many weeks before I managed to come off it. The day was sunny and warm as we climbed up the bendy road that snakes south from Newtown, lying in the Severn Valley, to the summit of the climb on the road to Llandrindod Wells. A few miles short of Llanbister, a lane diverges to the right, leading to the Bwlch-y-Sarnau, St. Harmon, and Rhayader, in the Upper Wye Valley. Travelling quickly around a tight bend on the road section over the summit, I hit a ridge of gravel on the apex and found myself flying through the air with bicycle bouncing across the road behind. Cars had rounded this bend beforehand, causing a pile of gravel to drift and accumulate at the outer rim. As in most accidents, it happened in a flash, completely unexpectedly and with no forewarning. One could, perhaps, consider pride before a fall to be the only true indication of an oncoming accident. With my pride severely dented, I found myself skidding across the rough, freshly-gravelled road surface. My right arm took the brunt of the impact with the skin of the forearm being rolled back like the lid of an opened can of sardines. Despite the scarlet rawness of exposed fleshy layers and blood starting to drip, my first thought was for the condition of the bike. "Oh dear, have I scratched the bronze paintwork on my beautiful new bike?" "Have I shredded the neat handlebar tape?" My second emotion was feeling a complete idiot. Geoff Cartlidge ahead, stopped, turned and found me picking up the bike and examining it for damage. No scratches could be seen, just a severely ripped and dusty side-pocket on the long-suffering saddlebag. The enamel mug hanging from the side-pocket strap took yet another range of chips and dents. I sighed with relief before having to try and replace the flap of flesh and wrap a not-too-clean handkerchief around the spongy wound. The remaining journey to Devil's Bridge; over the Bwlch-y-Sarnau, through Rhayader, by the head of the Elan Valley lakes and Cwmystwyth, I suffered a sprained right hand and a sore arm, discomfort exacerbated by the burning sun of a hot afternoon. Blood poisoning threatened. At Ystumtuen youth hostel, I had time to clean the wound and apply my panacea of all ills, SavIon antiseptic cream, before rebinding the hurt. Treatment for my wounds that day finished with a pint or two in the

Geoge Borrow Inn nearby. My arm took several weeks to finally heal, but we were oh so indestructible in those days.

Crashing from a bicycle was an occupational hazard in those days of tight riding in close formation, leaving only inches between front and rear wheels. It is incredibly hard to lose one's balance while cycling, even when at a speed barely faster than walking pace. The technique of balancing by steering in the direction a bike appears to be falling is, once learned, an automatic reaction. The very rotation of the wheels acts like a couple of gyroscopes. Gyroscopic action is a powerful force that is used to keep passenger ships from rolling excessively and space rockets to maintain attitude and direction. A cycle wheel can be spun and balanced easily on the fingertip. Any attempt to tip the wheel sideways, out of the plane of rotation, needs considerable force indeed and only results in a tendency for it to wobble and yaw erratically. The problem arises when a rider touches the rear wheel of a rider in front; a quite common accident when cycling in a close bunch and at considerable speed. An elongated whining sound as rubber rubs on rubber heralds a disaster soon to occur. Balance, normally automatic, becomes impossible and the dreaded scuffing sound of clashing tyres heralds the instant loss of stability and the brief flight onto a hard road, or into thorny hedgerow. The mysteries of the gyroscope have been messed with and the result is a wheel having the sexy curves of a mathematical parabola; an elegant figure of eight and, in short, an impossibly useless, buckled wheel. Wheels, even alloy, have incredible strength. Conversely, when buckled, are almost impossible to straighten to perfection. Many hours with a spoke key are the least that is needed before the wheel can again spin and clear the fork blades.

The most dangerous cause of a crash is the front wheel becoming jammed, either by the front brake assembly becoming loose or a section of flipped-up road rubbish fouling the spokes. Forward motion is stopped instantly and the rider probably ejected over the handlebars. The forces are so great that frame tubes can buckle under the weight of the rider and the pressure of the bike wanting to continue forward. Distortion can occur at the junction of headset and forks, top and down tubes. Greater distortion can happen to the rider, sitting on the tarmac, licking his wounds, whilst fearing the approach of following traffic. We experienced several bad crashes within the group but despite the prevalence of nasty, sharp bits on the bikes (pedals, chain wheels, handlebar ends, and gear levers)., we never had any really serious injuries. Apart from the touching of wheels, the other causes were failing to round bends or accidentally pulling the feet out of toe clips when sprinting hard for that town sign. Falls on gravel, cobbles or ice should have been predicted but the utter suddenness of the event left one more confused than seriously hurt. That instance between coming off the bike and hitting something solid was a strange experience. It was a near-death feeling, a tiny portion of sheer peacefulness, a dream-like state and a miniscule time-lapse of believing one was flying like a bird. Time stands still while the nightmarish scene of whirling sky and road flash across the uncomprehending mind. The brain cannot cope with the rush of information. Ultimately, it is pride that takes a fall, being brought back to earth so suddenly. Hurt to the appendages is more common than head injuries. One always flings the arms out, a natural reaction, in the hopeless desire for damage limitation. Damage to hips, shoulders, elbows, wrists and hands are more common, fortunately, than to the head. Consequently, gravel-rash is common.

The worst accident I ever witnessed resulted from the touching of wheels. In the mid 1970s, on the Pembrokeshire coast road, a new member happened to clip a fellow cyclist's rear wheel and in the effort to regain balance, over-steered and swerved to the other side of the road. Narrowly missing oncoming traffic, he rode up the kerb and was thrown onto the castellated top of a hard, stone boundary wall. The other side of this cliff top walling was fresh air and a hundred feet vertical drop to the waters of Fishguard's old harbour. We delivered the poor fellow to the town's cottage hospital. Several hours afterwards, he emerged, totally wrapped in bandages, virtually enclosed in windings of embalming cloth. To add a comical slant on the otherwise serious episode, he wore a pair of designer sunshades over the wrappings – appearing like a cycling Invisible Man. Both racing and touring cyclists usually display a phlegmatic, fatalistic approach to coming off; a sort of occupational hazard that, someday, is bound to happen.

I'm sure the wearing of cycling helmets will eventually become enforceable by law, followed by other pieces of life-preserving kit. Westminster big-wigs will show effusive concern for our welfare, forcing us to wear those terribly-coloured, strange constructions on our unprotected heads. Their very appearance is comical; like a bunch of bananas or the tentacles of an alien invader. Even the back of the helmet is upturned to resemble a duck's arse. I find it so difficult to accept a helmeted cyclist's appearance to be none other than a figure of fun. Unable to take them seriously. Early, understated racing helmets of leather strips were far more sensible

It's all in the grand Orwellian scheme of things – control! Governments will eventually legislate to make the wearing of body armour and helmets mandatory, ordering us to use dangerous, poorly-designed cycleways, thereby keeping us all completely isolated from traffic, safe from injury, able to work and continue to pay their withering taxes. And yet, cycle proficiency courses will be phased out – lack of money.

Two diary dates at the end of March, the 22nd and 23rd indicated the hostels of Shrewsbury and Ystumtuen (Devil's Bridge). It wasn't a programme weekend; I was just making this long run into central Wales to catch sight of the warden's attractive daughter. Long miles on a gradually rising road to the west of Newtown with a fellow cycling hosteller and all for a fleeting few minutes of stunted conversation with this delightful creature. My male companion found the miles wearing and on the long climb from Llangurig, over the desolate Plynlimmon Mountains, he would dismount, lie on the road and lift his legs straight and high into the air, presumably to disperse the blood supply. My blood supply was overactive in the daughter's lovely presence but, sadly, time didn't stand still and too soon, the moment had gone. My assignation and desirous stirrings remained secret. On the Sunday, as I pedalled the long miles away from Ystumtuen, my vision of Lorna Doone faded below the horizon of the gradually receding hills – disappearing from inside the misty vales of my memory. On the sunny Sunday, a diversion from the lonely Cwmystwyth stream, following a faint track over the grassy hills to the main valley short of Llangurig, offered some compensation. From a grassy indent in the hills I turned east, desperately trying to savour what amounted to only a faint memory.

Whitsun and May Day weekends usually provided hot, sunny weather, with the prospect of long days of cycling. In order to lose the crowds of a typical Bank Holiday, we would often scour the detailed maps for a morning or afternoon, following some vague route that conveniently joined surfaced roads at each end. Whitsun 1963 was no exception as we moved from Shrewsbury to St. Briavels Castle, perched on the steep, wooded sides of the Wye Valley. Next morning, some of the lads had to cut the extensive lawn, some weed the many flower beds. We would often wonder why the cyclists were always given physically hard and time-consuming hostel duties while the hitchhikers were let off with relatively light duties – sorting out the cutlery drawer or re-filling the pepper pots. Maybe the hikers had a bus to catch.

When we had put away the lawnmower, shears and dibble, we finally got away and viewed the river from Symonds Yat Rock; deeply-cut, bounded by dense woods and winding, silently from this height, through a verdant countryside on the borders of England and Wales. Although on the border, place-names, such as Cinderford, Coleford, St. Briavels, and Tintern Parva, with Tintern Abbey itself and hamlets of Michaelchurch Escley and Bredwardine, all evoke a feeling of being solely in England. The Forest of Dean, Wye Valley and the Golden Valley areas form a region geographically on the extreme boundary of England, situated in Herefordshire and butting up to the elongated ridges of the Black Mountains. One has to travel some miles to the west of the valley of the River Wye before we meet the double 'lls'. We, as far away cycle tourists from industrial North Staffordshire, have always considered this region to be somewhat a mystery as it is not on a popular tourist route – may it long stay that way.

From Staunton on Wye's grand country house hostel, we moved north, through New Radnor and joined an indistinct, grassy track that climbed to the heights of Radnor Forest. Just off the main road and following a farmer's dirt track, we noticed a pile of bleached sheep bones including a toothy, grinning skull. Dave Hope, Dave Booth, Paul Leese and Geoff

Cartlidge threw off their shirts and dressed up as natives, using the poor sheep's calcified detritus as props. The skull was attached to a stick and some tribal dancing took place. Dave Hope won this fancy dress parade with little opposition. With his nut-brown skin tones, barrel chest, ample stomach, a colourful, patterned, carefully draped towel and a white bone held under his nose, there was no competition. Now, at noon, the day was really getting hot.

Radnor Forest was now cleared of any trees, leaving us with an open, silky-smooth grass track that climbed and fell as we crossed the beginnings of several west-facing hollows. Aeons of intensive sheep grazing had provided us with an easy to follow, high level track with constant views to the west of the central Welsh hills; vague in the glimmer of a sunny afternoon and making the wearing of sunglasses essential. We completed the Radnor Forest rough-stuff; losing height to regain the main roads of Radnorshire, Montgomeryshire and Shropshire and a very long run home via Shrewsbury, to Stoke-on-Trent. Counties of Wales in the 1960s still retained the older 'shire 'endings. Gwynedd now replaces Caernarvonshire, Clwyd replaces Denbighshire, Gwent was Monmouthshire – Carmarthenshire, Cardiganshire, Brecknockshire, Merionethshire – oh dear, where have they all gone? Poor old Radnorshire is now known as part of Powys. Is this a ploy to separate Wales from England – avoid the Anglo-Saxon Shire and to make Wales appear something special, more Celtic sounding? Or is it a stage in the process of political devolution?

One quaint (or tiresome).fact regarding county boundaries was prevalent in 1960s Wales – some county authorities closed their public houses on a Sunday. Strict Welsh Methodism would not tolerate the imbibing of Bacchanalian fluids on a Sunday. The thirsty, informed locals would always know of a private gentleman's club to frequent on the Sabbath. Consequently, we all had an advanced ability to map read in those restrictive days of Welsh temperance. We would embark on many a mad dash for the border line if a drink was at stake. An awful lot of the local motorists, we noticed, would also have the same idea.

*

In August, after several long weekends enjoying the midsummer, Brian Whalley and I decided to spend a week touring into Mid Wales and Pembroke. Using a club Bank Holiday weekend from Shrewsbury to Capel y Ffin and Glascwm as a springboard, we were well set to push to the south-west in the rest of the week. Capel y Ffin hostel lay in a fold of the Black Mountains, over the border from Herefordshire and not too far from Llanthony Priory. The region has a scattering of small farmsteads and red-brick chapels; places of worship, mostly deserted with iron railings intertwined with invasive ivy – a rather sad reminder of this intensely insular collection of close communities. These elongated, isolated valleys and hills cumulate in a steep, spectacular edge on their northern extremity as they sweep down to the young River Wye. This concave curve of hillside, formed by Hay Bluff at 2,218 feet (676m).can be seen clearly from the Cotswold Edge to the east. Close scrutiny of our John Bartholomew map revealed the triangulation point on Lord Hereford's Knob at 2,264 feet (690m). Ann Hassall and Joan Hall, the group's two stalwart lady cyclists, laughingly drew our attention to the unfortunately (or fortunately).titled prominence. We insisted that its real title was The Twmpa, but they weren't having any of that! Just the usual schoolboy and schoolgirl humour that we should have left far behind in the youth hostel yard.

After a day of pleasant pottering and wandering the streets of Hay-on-Wye, we climbed into the neighbouring hills and to the former school of Glascwm youth hostel. It was just after opening time (hostel, not pub).and while we were milling around in the 'playground', removing saddlebags and making adjustments to our faithful machines, we heard the cutting, strident whine of a small motorcycle engine. The warden, a very elderly lady, leaned her big, black bicycle against the playground wall and shepherded us all into the common room to sign in and pay our dues. The distant, wavering sound of her engine reverberating off bare hillsides turned out to be a Cyclemaster motor set into the spokes of the rear wheel. Mick Bennett, ever ready to utter the humorous, irreverent comment, described her as a 'toothless crone, a fearsome hag'. This little, innocent, wizened old lady who had pushed past him in the members' kitchen. When she proudly announced that she'd come up from Hundred House on her motorbike, Dave Hope suggested that she could be the boastful 'fast' woman who owned a racing MV Augusta. Dave, working as a bricklayer amongst a gang of brassy labourers, was always ready and able to shoot from the hip with a witty, appropriate repost and scathing, jocular observation.

My holiday companion, Brian Whalley, was a year or two younger than me. His devil-may-care, fun-loving character was reflected by his dress. Whenever cycling, he could be guaranteed to be seen wearing a long, blue sweater that draped down to his knees. With a pair of short, khaki shorts underneath, it appeared that he wasn't wearing anything about his loins at all. He wore an Australian bush hat, set on his wiry, fair hair at a rakish angle. Although of limited stature, he sported a stiff, trimmed moustache over the top lip, giving him a swashbuckling, dashing-blade appearance. A sort of stunted, fair-haired Errol Flynn. He certainly had a roving eye for the girls or, for that matter, anything else with two legs, long hair and a skirt. Brian also had a remarkable ability to crash. Even braking to a standstill, he would forget to loosen his toe straps and, consequently, was forced to flop over into the road, on to his shoulder, feet still firmly bound to the pedals.

From Glascwm, we cycled along narrow lanes at the base of the Carmarthen Vans, eventually climbing up the A470 main road to the summit of the Brecon Beacons National Park at Storey Arms. The ranch-style youth hostel was set just off the road, sheltered by a square stand of pines with the broad, bare, sweeping mountains forming a backdrop of cloud-shadowed slopes. From this breezy, sheep-strewn watershed, the main road started to descend, dropping to the South Wales valleys at Merthyr Tydfil. As we didn't want to tour the heavy mining industries to the south, we retraced our steps and passed through Carmarthen and the Mynydd Preseli, to arrive in Fishguard and a few miles beyond the beautifully situated cliff-top hostel of Pwll Deri. Close to Strumble Head lighthouse and on a length of Heritage coastline, Pwll Deri hostel, a simple stone cottage accommodation, almost teetered over the spectacular vertical cliffs by the Pembroke Coastal Footpath. We lingered on the cliff edge as a setting sun tinged the rocky walls below with a subtle pink colourwash. The crash of waves and the shriek of sea birds accompanied the raw natural beauty of the scene. The small beach, a hundred feet below, nestling between two jagged promontories, collected a line of creamy foam and a parallel arc of marine detritus, pushed up the pebbles by a lively high tide. The cast of delicate pink on the rock turned through a deep red, to purple, before fading into a dull grey, as the sun finally set and evening shadows lengthened. After a few colour photographs and the last draw on a cigarette in a twilight gloaming and with a soft slap of a tide now on the ebb, we retreated to the warmth of the hostel common room.

For the rest of the week, we cycled north up the coastal road to above Aberystwyth, stopping at Ystumtuen and Dinas Mawddwy. From Tal-y-bont, a village north of Aberystwyth, we took a narrow, unsurfaced track that climbed towards Plynlimon Fawr, that undefined highland region; source of the Rivers Severn and Wye. At Nant-y-moch, now flooded to form a reservoir, we turned south and wound downhill, still on gravel-strewn rough tracks, until we met relative humanity again at the bridge in Ponterwyd, below the George Borrow Hotel, close to Ystumtuen youth hostel. This day, the warden's daughter wasn't there, just the warden herself – which, for us, was sad and rather a disappointment.

Brian also joined us for a fortnight's holiday in the second half of that August. After Geoff Cartlidge's and my holiday the previous year in the far south-west of Ireland, four of us, regular YHA cyclists who turned out on most weekends, decided to tour the far west of Ireland; the ragged peninsular of Counties Galway, Mayo, Connemara and Donegal. That wild area of Old Connaught resembling a holed, torn and tattered flag fluttering out into the waters of the North Atlantic. So, with Geoff and Brian, we were joined by Peter Boardman and the four of us caught the train from Stoke to Holyhead to catch the Irish ferry. Pete Boardman was an altogether quieter character than Brian; more circumspect, thoughtful, but a keen cycle tourist all the same. He had a completely different sense of humour than the rest of us but obviously enjoyed our company. Pete, when cycling along in the middle of the group already travelling at a sprightly pace, would click his brake levers as if impatient and shout a word of desperate, hysterical panic whenever a motorist came up to the back of the group, honking to pass. However, he was a good sort and we all got on well together.

From Dun Laoghaire, we cycled through Ballsbridge and were very soon in busy O'Connell Street, Dublin. After peering into the River Liffey, here, a turgid, thick pea soup of a waterway that undercuts a series of elegant, stone bridges, we made our way to Amiens Street railway station. The cycle registration completed and cycles loaded, we settled into deep, upholstered bench seats for a long journey over the central bog plains of Ireland. Our compartment was dated, almost antiquated, but comfortable as we rolled through Athlone and Athenry, to Galway. Long before Athlone, our heads were nodding to the rhythm of the train; after a night's ferry crossing with no sleep, we were soon lulled by the lurching, swaying coach into fitful dozing.

On arriving in Galway, that city of high culture and religious study, we were soon wheeling further west on a lonely main road that skirted Galway Bay, bound for the hamlet of Lettermullen. The brisk, ozone-laden wind blowing off the Atlantic coast drove away any remaining cobwebs of traveller's sleep. The sun was lowering to a sunset as the road crossed a series of linked islands, the causeways surrounded by acres of brown, shiny, bladder-wrack seaweed. It was so thick that it covered and subdued the lazy rise and fall of the Atlantic tide, its long, belt-like strands and bulbous pods giving off a distinct aroma of iodine. After, seemingly, hundreds of tiny islets, we arrived at the small hostel run by *An Oige,* the Irish YHA, marked with a rusting blue metal triangular sign on a rough wooden post. The setting sun doused itself, fizzing into the sea horizon and as our first day in dear old Ireland ended, I recalled a line from a past, well-known song that I'd heard as a child; a song sang on a coach trip to Colwyn Bay, North Wales – *If you ever go across the sea to Ireland... ...and watch the sun go down on Galway Bay.* Galway Bay and the mighty Atlantic were out there somewhere, glinting beyond the banks of brown seaweed; barely discernable from the archipelago of small islands grouped around the larger Gorumna Island.

Our route from Lettermullen led us north, before branching further to the west to follow the wild coastline of Bertraghboy and Ballyconneely Bays; a winding, open road, often narrow and bending, faithfully following the much indented coast and comprising a series of sweeping coral sand beaches.

This was a magic shore in a magic, almost romantic piece of Joyce's Country. The isolated, arcing beaches, extremities protected by lines of low, rocky headlands, brought to one's imagination the novels, *Robinson Crusoe and Treasure Island;* clean, dazzling white beaches backed by boisterous, deep blue and aquamarine seas – and all with not another soul, my friends apart, in sight. Not only was the coast a feast for the eyes, but the views inland were also grand and mysterious. The grouped, conical mountains, forming the Twelve Bens of Connemara, lay to the north-east; several of their very tops blanketed by layered Irish mist. Several small loughs shone silvery, scattered over the green and yellow patchwork of boggy landscape. This region, in particular, evoked the very character of rural Ireland; the occasional uneven track winding down to a humble stone cottage; thatched roof tied down with large pebbles on rope lashings; donkey carts left isolated on the road and piles of drying turf stored for winter fuel. In fact, we found many cottages still had dirt floors and some even had chickens penned in a wire enclosure, formed by the table legs. A hole in the tabletop would solve the problem of feeding the fowl with breadcrumbs. Cottage interiors were, generally, dark and mysterious with an ever-pervading, not unpleasant smell of turf fires and paraffin for the lamps.

We cycled in sunny, breezy weather, passing the promontory of Slyne Head and curve of Mannin Bay before entering the lively main street of Clifden. The town is the region's focal point (only focal point).and the dealings and transactions within the market and numerous street bars must have been prodigious; everyone washed down with a thick pint of Guinness stout or a shot of Paddy whisky. We soon found that the bars in Ireland served various functions. A drinking section; where the barman carefully poured out draught Guinness by the use of a wooden paddle to whip off the froth, would be backed, from floor to ceiling, by a fully-stocked grocery store. Anything from a baby's rattle to a tin of anti-potato blight powder could be purchased by the basket-wielding housewife. The other end of the bar would be used as a post office and a convenient spot to place a bet on the horses. An antique bacon slicer would be accommodated in a dusty corner while the gathered customers, whispering behind the hand in secretive collusion, would learn where they could get a tasting of poteen while enjoying the pull on a Sweet Afton cigarette.

Our day ended at the lonely inlet of Killary Harbour with the northern shore backed by the peak of Mweelrea, 2,687 feet (819m).above a very nearby sea level. The hostel was a low, single storey, basic building squatting directly on the quayside. The harbour comprised an ancient stone jetty with a few rusting bollards; lush weeds sprouting from between every crack and cranny. A tangle of knotted fishing nets covered the paving with bleached, seaweed-covered ropes trailing, arcing down into the still water. The wrecked remains of a fishing drifter lay alongside; decking planks twisted and warped like the bones of a dead whale. A rusted, almost disintegrating steel hawser lay on the holed deck, useless and almost reverting to red powder. Killary Harbour may have been a haven for German U-boats in the early days of World War II, sheltering in a neutral country's natural submarine pens, miles from anywhere, while they recharged their batteries before the wolf-pack encounters with Atlantic convoys. Or so the rumours went.

We spent a day walking on Mweelrea, approaching from the inland, eastern side. Due to a lack of any recognisable tracks, our walk was arduous, having to stride over thick, bushy heathers and sloshing through saturated ground in the hillside bowl below the pointed summit. On top, however, we had a magnificent view of sea loughs, islands and individual mountain slopes, all spread out below and stretching away from us in a bewildering melange of sea, sky and tessellated countryside. It was hard to distinguish between mountain lake and open sea. A few miles off the main coastline; if, in this confused geography, there could be a 'main, shoreline, lay the mysterious Aran Islands. Like the Arans, Inishark, Inishbofin and Inishturk lay close. Broad-chested, swarthy sons of the Irish soil fished these tempestuous waters from long, canvas-covered and tarred boats, reliving the customs of thousands of years. When the day's work was over, they carried their upturned craft ashore looking like long, leggy, black beetles.

Leaving Killary Harbour, we pedalled on yet more quiet roads, skirting Croagh Patrick, Saint Patrick's Holy mountain, where he climbed to the summit and threw all the snakes out of Ireland. The countless religious disciples over the years had cut out a well-worn track; wide, eroded and seen from miles away as it mounted the bare, convex mountain shoulder, like a livid, devotional scar. We passed Clew Bay and its profusion of miniscule islets; innumerable stepping stones appearing on the map like a pebble-covered patio. Apart from the detailed, highly ornate Irish Ordnance Survey maps at a scale of 1 inch and $^1/_2$ inch to 1 mile, we mainly used the John Bartholomew, 'A quarter-inch Series, colour-layered and showing an intricate web of minor roads. In any case, Irish miles are a different length to those in England. I don't know which are longer but, like the *laissez-faire* attitude of Ireland, it didn't seem to be of importance.

Moving through Westport, Newport and Mallaranny, Currane, our next hostel, was sited on the sea inlet between the Corraun Peninsula and the large island of Achill. We could cycle into Achill Sound itself for provisions. We shared cooking duties, preparing very basic meals in very basic pots and pans. Most evenings were spent in the local bars nearby. Even the smallest community had its bar, either a tiny grocer's shop, hotel annex, or even a local's converted living room. Fellow hostellers were usually German, Dutch or American. They mainly stayed in the hostel and drank coffee. There was a marked absence of English travellers, especially here in the woolly west. We couldn't leave this area before exploring Achill and its far western promontory that juts out into the Atlantic Ocean. We passed through the tiny hamlets of Doolagh and Keel, both having glorious sandy beaches, before a rough track climbed over to the proud headland at Achill Head. Slievemore Mountain at 2,200 feet (671m).is the highest point on the peninsula. Closer, sweeping almost vertically into a lively ocean, are the great sea cliffs of Croaghaun.

A long-distance cycling gap existed between Currane and our next hostel at Carrick in County Donegal; therefore, we made a bed and breakfast stop in Sligo. North of that lively town, off to our right, rose the peak of Benbulben, a whale-shaped, bulbous and elongated mountain at an elevation of 1,722 feet (525m)., appearing distinctive and overpowering due to its close proximity to the flatter coastal hinterland. Heading further north through Bundoran, Donegal town and Killybegs, we reached Carrick youth hostel, purely to give us a chance to see the Cliffs of Bunglass and Slieve League mountain from near Muckross Head. Geoff and I part rode, part pushed the bikes up a very rough, winding track to the exposed headland where a magnificent view opened out across the bay. Slieve League, very much a towering 1,971 feet (601m).above a seething sea, from a cloud-capped summit, swept in a series of near-vertical scree slopes, down almost 2,000 feet to the ocean. Even more spectacular, from a saddle on the ridge, the Cliffs of Bunglass dropped absolutely vertically for a full 1,000 feet (305m)., a curtain of grey and yellow tortured rock exposing the geological movements over aeons of time. Ironically, at the foot of this massive cliff, a low tide uncovered a glorious crescent of golden sand – small, exclusively private and utterly inaccessible. Maybe an adventurous boatman could make a landing here but the conditions would have to be totally benign. Until then, only a passing seabird could ever alight under this dreadful abyss. Yards off the beach stood the stacks of the Devil's Table and Chair, appearing miniature from our vantage point but, no doubt, standing high when viewed from sea level. The two of us smoked a few cigarettes, gazing onto the stupendous view; sheer rock with gulls of every description circulating in a shrieking carousel around a cauldron of raw nature. The scene deserved a good two hours of contemplation while enjoying our lunchtime sandwiches.

From dramatic Carrick, we pushed inland, eastwards into the Poisoned Glen on a narrow lane that soon deteriorated into a stony dirt track. Ahead of us rose the conical mountain of Errigal, streaked white and grey, consisting of quartz rock and shale screes, having a somewhat industrial, spoil heap appearance. To the south, standing isolated before the backdrop of ragged, cloud-covered hills of the Blue Stack Mountains, stood the first turf-burning power station in Ireland.

On our last day in Donegal, and in Ireland, we started out from Poisoned Glen youth hostel; bumping along a rough track, climbing out of the Glen and cycling east to the border with Northern Ireland. We passed through the border at Strabane in heavy rain with our tyres swishing on a flooded surface. Very wet weather in Ireland is never terrible but referred to as 'soft'. Even a torrential cloudburst is considered 'soft'. Two members of the Irish *Garda* slouched against their border hut struggling to light a cigarette, crouched under its inadequate cover. Dressed in their heavy, black rain capes they paid little attention to four intrepid bikers, let alone stopping us for any searching or interrogation. Several yards up the road, a cluster of the Ulster B-Specials, wearing their heavy, black rain capes and large, round caps, sheltered, smoked, and shouldered rifles whilst paying us even less attention than their Republican neighbours. In these early 1960s, cross-border tensions had yet to erupt into sectarian violence. The modern Troubles hadn't started – they would soon, but not yet. Cross-border smuggling of weapons only existed in the pages of Spike Milligan's hilarious book *Puckoon*. Essential reading for anyone considering a tour of Ireland.

From the railway station at Strabane we caught the most antiquated train I have ever seen. We chugged along at a steady 15 mph behind a coughing diesel locomotive, feeling hot in the shabby compartment, crowded with all the other rain-soaked passengers. The dirty windows; streaked with raindrops, soon steamed up, and hiding a soaking landscape that passed outside with lingering slothfulness. Up in the curved, cobwebbed, and cracked ceiling, the lamps shone a diseased yellow; their plastic globes sloshing inside with rainwater from a leaky, clerestory carriage roof. We inched into Portadown and changed to the Dublin Express, and a faster, drier run to *Baile atha Cliath*. The excellent holiday came to an end with a ferry crossing from Dun Laoghaire to Holyhead, and another train returning to Stoke.

Although the Stoke YHA had separate walking, and cycling sections, some members would mix or alternate between the two pastimes. Laurie Landon, Dave Joynson, Bill Housley, Joe Ball and Sam Hackney would sometimes join the cyclists on their short runs, usually held in the easier social season. Likewise, usually committed cyclists would venture an occasional auto-ramble; using a coach to reach an otherwise unreachable walking area. Brian Whalley, my cycling companion on the holiday to Wales, even led a programmed walk. It wasn't just a question of either cycling or walking but the opportunity to be amongst spectacular scenery, and be able to ascend interesting mountains. As cyclists, we went on several auto-rambles: Moel Siabod, the Carnedds, and the Snowdon Horseshoe from north Wales hostels: Bowfell, and the Langdale Pikes from Elterwater hostel in the Lake District, and even gentler strolls such as around London and along a section of the Chiltern Hills ridge. At Ravenstor in the Peak District and Fox Howl hostel in Delamere Forest we had combined weekends. Several of us cyclists went for a drink at the nearest pub, a few miles down the road from the Fox Howl YH., and I remember Linda, tall, lithe, and looking too pretty to be a rambler, let alone a cyclist, sitting on my saddlebag carrier, balancing, and holding on for dear life as we rushed back before hostel closing time. But it was hardly a Butch Cassidy/Sundance Kid bicycling moment. Our real preference for cycling was aptly summed-up by bricklayer Dave Hope. "With cycling, the scenery changes quicker". Of course, ergonomically speaking, walkers have to strain to go downhill as well as up – cyclists can just freewheel.

On the Thursday evening meets at Cartwright House, the girls made contributions to the slide shows and lectures. Geoff and I indulged in mock enthusiasm at the prospect of a lecture on 'Wild Flowers in the English Countryside' given by Jean Ralphs and Jean Rowley. We turned up and were captivated – really impressed. We owned-up to the fact that we found the subject fascinating over a couple of pints of bitter in the Unicorn inn, yards away in Piccadilly, Hanley. On one auspicious occasion we were treated to a lecture of climbing in the Himalayas by none other than the well-known mountaineer Chris Bonington. Afterwards, we packed into a small back room of the homely pub with its scuffed bench seats, overflowing ashtrays, and yellowed walls, to have a chat with the great man himself over a strong pint of Bass. I sat barely three seats away from this great character, wild beard and gappy, crooked front teeth, as he reeled-off the names of famous Himalayan giants; Everest, Annapurna, Dhaulagiri, within, seemingly, a casual, dismissive conversation. Behold, I have name-dropped and am proud of it!

The year so far had been full of touring weekends and holidays, not to mention Bank Holidays. In early October, we had Ewden youth hostel on the programme, an area beyond Buxton and close to Sheffield that was relatively unknown to our group at that time. We had toured in the Hope Valley, Edale and Castleton regions, but knew little of the high moors that lay to the north. The run to Buxton was over familiar ground. To Leek, the climb of Cat Tor Hill alongside the Ramshaw rocks, and Roaches, over the moors of Axe Edge, and down to the elegant spa town of Buxton. Dave Joynson led our small group comprising Ralph Salt, Roy Deakin, Eric Hazeldine and myself. We had a nominated leader for every weekend; someone who would choose a route whenever a choice presented itself, but apart from trailblazing, and checking on any newcomer, and their cycle's condition, he/she hadn't to show any special leadership traits or duties. We were all enthusiasts, always looking for adventurous tracks and the routes tended to dictate themselves. It was just that a stated 'leader' looked good in the *Staffordshire Knot,* the YHA's local programme.

North of Buxton, the road continued to Sparrowpit before we dropped like a stone down the Winnat's Pass. The deeply-cut dry, limestone valley was typical of this area of the Peak District. In a landscape where surface streams have cut down over the millennia, forming a subterranean world of cave systems, the above-ground surroundings appear incredibly arid. Beyond Castleton we cycled to Bamford, and into millstone grit country. The elongated cliff edges ran in serrated lines across the heights, springing out of the moorland heather, and furze. Stanage Edge on the border between Derbyshire and South Yorkshire was certainly impressive. The brown, rounded, grippy rocks, formed into vertically stacks, were a favourite of rock climbers. Baslow, and Frogatt Edges, nearby, were similar geologically. The rough surfaces offered perfect cohesion for the climber, used to minimum hand, and footholds, to advance, relying on friction with his/her rubbery slippers and hand-jamming techniques. Today, on a fine afternoon, the brown, outcropped stretches of rock, in our imaginations, a miniature wall of a possible Grand Canyon, warmed even more as the sun beamed downed and the air became still and thunderous.

By the time we'd reached the Ladybower Reservoirs, sweat had gathered on the brow in the sultry, heavy conditions. All nature seemed to be taking a slumbering siesta in this unusual heat of an early autumn. Even the occasional bird cry went missing, leaving high moorland country to its lofty, silent brooding. The Ladybower lakes were used by RAF pilots when training for the bouncing bomb raids on the Ruhr Dams of industrial northern Germany. Water capacities, the dams' end towers, and approaches being eerily similar – but, of course, no ack-ack batteries. Or, maybe, just the odd, irate farmer or gamekeeper and their trusty shotguns. Home-based providers of food who worried for their chickens' egg-laying abilities.

As the day became hotter, we felt as if we were toiling through an atmosphere of invisible treacle. After an undulating series of moorland roads, we reached the basic hostel in Ewden village, a temporary settlement specifically built to house the thousands of dam builders that have become permanent. By the time we had eaten, rolls of distant thunder were bouncing off the enfolding hills – a growling, threatening presence that was approaching with disturbing regularity. God was moving His, and His neighbours' furniture, and it was heavy stuff. I remember Ewden youth hostel to be a temporary structure; a mixture of wood, asbestos, and corrugated iron. When the storm arrived directly overhead, a flash of light, and instantaneous thunderclap seemed to shake the whole structure. So violent, it seemed to be lifting the entire building off its foundations. We had been counting the seconds between lightning and thunder, calculating, in schoolboy fashion, the distance and direction of the storm. Light and sound came together in a crescendo of dramatic Biblical proportions. With the surrounding air crackling with chaotic ions and our hair fizzing with static electricity, we received the loudest bang that I've ever heard. A metallic crash of an explosion that had us ducking our heads and setting the ears ringing. Raindrops falling, at first, singularly like balls of lead shot, soon increased into stair rods of intensity; curtains of water streaming down the windows and thrumming on the hostel roof. The continuous roar made hosteller's conversation inaudible and irrelevant. Next morning dawned bright, clear and clean as we cycled back through the hills, now beginning to tinge with the russets of a closing year.

During the first half of the decade, a local hero emerged in the cycle racing world. Partnered by Brian Rourke, Les West was having considerable success in both track and road racing. They both rode in the yellow and green colours of Tunstall Wheelers, the strongest racing club in the Potteries. The news of their successes filtered down, eventually to even us plodding tourists. We often went to the cycle track at Trent Vale and watched sprints, madisons and devil-take-the-hindmost events where Rourkey won nearly every time. The evenings of frenetic laps on the steeply-banked oval reminded me of a childhood visit to Hednesford to watch the master, Reg Harris. He really did win everything! After the last race, usually a 'devil', we would sprint away from the track at breakneck speed; barely noticing traffic lights and leaving motorists well astern of our spinning rear wheels. We were fired-up by the evening's competition and sought to emulate our track racing speedsters. Invariably, we would finish at a local pub, the Rose and Crown or The Bridge in Etruria, to chat over the evening's racing or plan a future weekend.

Rourke and West moved to the more affluent, sponsored racing team of Holdsworth Cycles and resplendent in their orange and blue team colours, gained national recognition. Les West progressed to important road racing events, culminating in several successful rides in the Tour of Britain. We watched him in local circuit events where he wiped the floor with the rest of the field. One race in particular, a multi-lap circuit based on Leek, Tittesworth and the lanes under the Roaches, including the testing Gun Hill, saw him decimate the opposition purely on his strength at hill climbing.

It was time for choosing and forming our national teams for the forthcoming Olympics in Tokyo. Potters to a man, cyclists or not, thought that Les West was sure to be picked to represent GB in the road race. He was the right age, was on the way up in form, a good all-rounder and had a perfect physique for strong sprinting and particularly dominating climbing. I'm not sure if it was the governing body for road racing or the GB Olympic Selection Committee themselves who stopped him being included but, nevertheless, the question of his selection had been kicked around so much that it was eventually 'lost in the long grass'. Whoever was responsible for his exclusion, a chance to seize greatness, was unclear but a promising career had been wasted.

For the Christmas holiday, 1963, I teamed up with Geoff, Ralph Salt and his brother Clive, spending from Christmas Eve to 28th December on a cycling and walking tour of the high peaks of Snowdonia. Staying at Chester, Idwal Cottage in the Nant Ffrancon, Llanberis, Bryn Gwynant and Cynwyd youth hostels, we programmed in the Stoke YHA newsletter, the *Staffordshire Knot,* a "Boots 'n' Saddles Christmas." Nothing to do with the Wild West and a marathon session of line dancing but touring by bicycle into the mountains, equipped with heavier protective clothing and hanging walking boots from each side of the saddlebag.

The peaks were resplendent with an icing sugar coating of powdered snow. On Christmas Day, from Chester, we managed to reach Idwal Cottage, situated at the very top of the Nant Ffrancon Pass. The roads were relatively clear of snow and the temperature remained low with clear blue skies. The hostels opened over the holiday but were somewhat lacking in festive decoration and spirit; the Methodism of the northern Welsh not allowing a totally going overboard with yuletide cheer. This cottage of Idwal is one of a group of buildings dedicated to mountain pursuits, sited just off the A5 main road and beside the cascade that tumbles out of Llyn Ogwen. Reflected in the lake's still, peaty water, the peak of Pen-yr Oleu-Wen plummets in a series of terraced rocks and loose screes. This shattered peak is a sentinel to the lofty, rounded Carnedds Group, Dafydd and Llewelyn, to the north. Our attention was drawn to the immediate south and the peaks of Tryfan, Y Garn and the Glyders. We scrambled up to the jagged summit of Tryfan, but due to increased snow cover on the ledges, refrained from jumping from Adam to Eve; the two gigantic blocks of rock that crown the summit crest. This thoroughly dangerous act is a local custom for visiting climbers – a sort of rites of passage initiation for the challengers of vertigo. We suspected a polished layer of ice; a glazed coating offering nil grip between rock and boot lying on the top surfaces so, with caution in mind, made a careful, callow retreat. The descent of Tryfan had to be made with great care; ever mindful of slippery surfaces, while one eye admired the backdrop of splendid winter mountains.

Next morning, we scrambled up a narrow gully that formed a buttress for the aptly named Bristly Ridge, a typically severe arete. Our destination was the top of the Glyders, a shattered, rocky twin height with a neighbouring cantilever of rock named the Castle of the Winds. As we climbed upwards, a mist fell on to and around the ridge's towers, giving a more threatening aspect to the whole scenario. Every foot climbed saw the gradient increase until it was well-nigh vertical; a frozen, snow-packed gully with dark, encroaching side walls, all exposed rock covered with a shiny layer of hard ice. Solid, slippery verglas did nothing to encourage confidence. Each hand and foothold was sloping downwards and packed tightly with long-standing, frozen snow. As our progress slowed to a desperate crawl, we could hear mysterious voices high above, cloaked and muted in a cloying white fog – obviously fellow walkers who had gained the ridge on a more sensible route. They were probably fully equipped with ice axes, crampons and ropes and despite their ghostly disagreements, probably knew what they were doing. We finally seized-up with indecision on whether to advance or retreat; apart from an encroaching dose of the shakes due to our exposed position, we realised that we were heading for disaster. It is amazing how a short climb can, on glancing down between the feet, suddenly turn to a death-defying abyss whenever any substantial height is gained. At one dodgy point in our adventure, I remember clinging in an ungainly fashion to Geoff s hanging boot whilst scrambling to find a decent foothold. Gradually, we inched back down the gully and returned to the relative safety of a flatter terrain. Sitting on the stone wall by the main road, we eased off our snow-encrusted walking boots and with a relieving gladness of the heart, threw our legs over the crossbars and relished in a smooth road descent, out of the Nant Ffrancon, to Capel Curig. The view of the Snowdon Horseshoe cluster of peaks with a foreground of hillsides and lakes is an enduring scene. The tops covered in a mantle of snow, just like the painted mural on the common room wall at Dimmingsdale YH. The whisky distillers, Glenmorangie, used this scene in one of their advertisements, inferring that their product was made from pure Scottish water from the Highlands illustrated. I wrote to them pointing out the use of a Snowdonian landscape in their advert and "claimed my prize of a free bottle of single malt." As expected, they never replied to my letter. Such is the power of the computer-generated image and extent of corporate greed.

Before taking the Beddgelert road and reaching Bryn Gwynant, we paid a visit to the famous Pen-y-Gwryd Hotel, a roadside inn made famous by being the watering hole for many Himalayan climbers. They used the distinctly Edwardian ambience to warm and recover, after days of winter training on the Snowdon heights nearby. Indeed, Crib Goch's icy buttress rose out of the snowy foreground, high on the slopes above Pen-y-Pass on the Llanberis Pass, its frozen crest a daunting challenge to all-comers. The climber's signatures, still legible after many years, were scribbled on the patina-brown ceiling of the bar, protected now by sheets of glass. The warming drinks and bonhomie of Christmas, together with the marks of past pioneers, gave us enthusiasm to explore even further. Gentlemen of learning, born explorers, would have relaxed in the saloon bar's easy chairs, smoking their briars, quaffing their tankards of ale and reading of challenging routes in faraway Tibet. I gather the successful Everest expedition party of 1953 trained on Snowdon's heights, staying in comfortable surroundings at the Pen-y-Gwryd Hotel. We hoped some of this place's history and spirit would rub off on us mere mortals. Years later, in our motoring days, we would enjoy memorable evenings here with folk singing in full flow.

We moved away from Snowdonia and made a stop at Cynwyd hostel to complete the holiday. Here, we found a far more welcoming hostel atmosphere and vowed to make it our destination for the next Christmas break. It would turn out to be a classic Christmas experience.

Cleeve Hill Youth Hostel, Cotswolds, (YHA Postcard)
My very first hostel at Cleeve Common, on run to Plymouth.

The dark, satanic Mills of the Potteries, circa 1920s
Not quite so bleak in the 1960s, but still grim.

Author on an early run into North Wales on the Sun Cycles bike
Maud.
Khaki shorts, sandals and silly cotton hat.

Working Party at Dimmingsdale YH, Oakamoor, Staffs.
(L to R) Brian Whalley, Ralph Salt, Bob Proctor & Derek Latham

Drumming-up in Devon Lanes
Derek Latham, overseeing and Dave Hope on the Primus stove.

Strolling through Bickleigh on Devon holiday.
Dave Hope in smart cycling gear, CAG in make-do jacket.

The Member's Kitchen,
Gidleigh YH
A recipie for food poisoning!
(left)

The Old Mill, Clun, south
Shropshire.
Outside toilet to the left.
(below)

Burway Hill, Cardingmill Valley & Long Mynd,
Shropshire.
A long, winter day's run from Stokoe-on-Trent

Ralph Salt near Longsdon, Leek, Staffs.
Safe cycling depended on the right sort of snow.

Winter walking near the Ramshaw Rocks, The Roaches, above Leek
There was always rambling when the snow was too deep to cycle.

Grappling with Welsh place names, Towy Valley weekend
(L to R) Bill Barnish, Brian Whalley, Derek Latham, Eric Hazeldine, Geoff Cartlidge & Dave Hope

Deep in the Upper Towy Valley, Mid Wales
*With Phil Robinson on left. Much lifting and carryiong pver
the freezing stream,.*

Christmas spirit with cider – we even wore ties.
*(L to R) CAG, Paul Leese, Ralph Salt, John Humphries,
Clive Salt & Cliff Yates.*

The Common Room at Bridges YH, Shropshire,
(Background, L to R,) Kenny Birks, Clive & Ralph Salt

The Common Room at Ystumtuen (Devil's Bridge)
YH.
*(Back, L to R) Clive Lewis, Phil Hughes, Eric Hazeldine,
Brian Whalley, Kenny Birks * Derek Latham.
(Front, L to R) Geoff Cartlidge, Dave Joynson, Bill Barnish,
unknown, Warden's Daughter*

The Cyclists' Annual Dinner, Consall, Churnet Valley, Staffs.
Laurie Landon & Fred Maitland (YHA stalwarts) to extreme left, Joe Ball (another Stoke cycling hero) on extreme right.

Geoff Cartldige receives Bednight Award from Secretary Roy Hazeldine.
Cyclists' Annual Dinner at the Black Lion PH, Cornwall

Wheathill YH, deep in Shropshire's warm, rustic lanes.
CAG checks his wallet. Joan Hall sixth from the left.

The Old café stop (on right, opposite cyclist) in Frankwell, Shrewsbury. (Shropshire Newspapers, Telford)
A welcome milk bar before demolition & new traffic island formed.

Chapter Five

1964

London & The Chilterns – Palm Beach Purgatory – That Badge – Cojones Calientes Del Perro – Bomber Warren – Holiday in Devon and Cornwall – Potteries Humour – With Whalley in Wales Again – Wild Wilderhope – YHA'sChanging Image – Cycle Accessories – "A Cyclist's Year" – Christmas at Cynwyd

Age: 23
Home: Cherry Tree Close, Trentham.
Work: SOT Reconstruction Dept., Kingsway, Stoke.
Government: Labour.
Prime Minister: Harold Wilson (Oct).
Apr: Train Robbers get severe sentences of 30 years each.
Jun: Nelson Mandela imprisoned on Robben Island, off Cape Town.
Aug: Beatles emerge, causing teenage hysteria.
Sept: Southern Rhodesian leader, Ian Smith, visits Britain.
Oct: Khrushchev ousted as President of USSR by Kosygin and Brezhnev.
Film: *A Hard Day's Night.*

The whole year seemed to have been dominated by the four mop-headed musicians from the Cavern Club in Liverpool. Titles such as She Loves You, I Want to hold Your Hand, From Me To You and many more contributed to the Merseybeat Sound with various other groups. Geoff was a real Beatles fanatic and his enjoyment increased further, in October, when pipe-smoking Harold Wilson was voted into a Labour government with a stinging majority of four seats. Girls had attacks of the vapours when the 'Fab Four' hit the stage and screen scene. Earlier in the year, the train robbers got sent down to what was considered a life sentence and later, few noticed when Nelson Mandela was caged for an indeterminate stretch. Thirty-five years later, everyone had to discard their "Free Mandela" T-

shirts when he was freed to become the leader of the African National Congress. Ian Smith of Southern Rhodesia met Sir Alec Douglas-Home and in his sickly Afrikaans dialect, tried to convince him (ADH).that UDI was a good proposition. Later, Wilson wasn't impressed. Bully boy,Khrushchev, gave way to two Russian bears as they glowered over the Kremlin walls at all those missiles parading through Red Square, Moscow. But it was the Beatles who dominated the year (they even made a film)., although, personally, I thought them sugary and preferred the rawness of the Rolling Stones and The Animals, especially their track, House Of The Rising Sun, led by Eric Burdon.

*

Early in the year at the end of January, the Cycling Section joined with the walkers for an auto-ramble to London, staying at Earl's Court youth hostel. The cyclists dressed up for an evening's sightseeing in the West End. We walked the pavements on a drizzly night; through Greek Street, Soho and admired the bright lights of commercialism in Piccadilly Circus. Myself, Ralph, Clive, Geoff with Dave Joynson and Phil Hughes, dressed in almost smart overcoats and rakish trilby hats, looked like a bunch of reprobate gangsters surveying the city life and if truth were known, appearing rather overcome with this 'den of iniquity'. Looking as incongruous as a hearse at a wedding in this traffic-ridden metropolis, miles away from any hills. Next morning, alongside the Walking Section, we spent a misty morning strolling on the Chiltern Hills; gazing over well-manicured Bedfordshire countryside towards Whipsnade Zoo and every bloke trying to chat-up that delightful, tall and lithe rambler named Linda. We tramped through dead, damp leafs, woundthrough avenues of smooth, grey-barked beeches, all the fellows manoeuvring to be alongside lovely Linda with her pink anorak with the wispy, white, fur-lined collar and hood.

Roy Hazeldine, our secretary, introduced a young lady to the group and thought that she could manage to cycle all the way to Dinas Mawddwy from a Saturday start from Shrewsbury. Riding a very heavy Palm Beach bicycle, painted pink with a flowery decoration, having a wide plastic saddle and a tennis racket clip; she completed the Friday evening run to Shrewsbury quite well, all things considered. Saturday, however, turned out dull with a spitting rain mixed in with a boisterous wind. Although Dinas Mawddwy is only about fifty miles (eighty kilometres).via Welshpool, from Shrewsbury, we had to struggle all day against a headwind of epic strength. Roaring towards us from the west, the wind was increasing, unrelenting, forcing everyone to pedal all out, even when running downhill and in a low gear. Through miserable, spitting rain and a sky full of rolling, slate-grey, cumulo-nimbus clouds, the gale-force wind tore at our muscles, straining every sinew. There is nothing worse in cycle touring than struggling against that hard, unseen force. Nothing matches the gut-wrenching pain of crawling ahead; every mile heroically gained, where even hedgerows and slight changes in direction offer scant protection. Our young lass struggled all day, shielded behind the group and when a gap opened up, I had to gradually 'draw' her back, returning ourselves to the back of the leading cyclists and some precious protection. As we arrived at Dinas Mawddwy, someone stacked her trusty steed in the bike shed and barely conscious, she dragged herself to the girl's dormitory to sleep. We walked down the road and frequented the village pub, relishing the thought of tomorrow's helpful tailwind.

Next morning, we persuaded her to eat a hearty breakfast before the return run to Stoke. We enjoyed the strong tailwind; thrumming along at a lively pace – our killer wind hadn't deserted us. However, our brave young lass found it hard to keep up as the front pair was really scorching along. I couldn't blame them as they'd spent the whole of the previous day fighting that ghastly headwind. Again, I had to act as a sort of chaperone, or escort, as we spun along the return miles; devouring the miles, thankfully in relative ease; pushed forward by that unseen powerful force of nature at our backs. Many times I had to drop back to give some sort of shielding – Sir Gallant Green on his bronze charger. I, for one,couldn't leave her to face empty roads alone. Thereby lay despair. The brave girl managed to reach Shrewsbury where a phone call brought her father out west in the car to give her a lift home – cycle stowed unceremoniously in the boot. The Palm Beach bicycle was really designed for the teenage girl who used it for a trip to the tennis courts, pony club or short journey to the local shops. For that, it was perfect. It was even fitted with a plastic carrier attached to the handlebars. It certainly wasn't designed for a long cycle run into Wales, riding against a near gale-force wind for hour upon hour.

On the 1st May, our local YHA Group Secretary, Tony Garibaldi, was retiring and held a grand social and leaving party at the Borough Arms, Newcastle-under-Lyme. Tickets cost 5/- (25p).and a buffet was held from 8:30pm till 10:00pm. I and a good few other cyclists had to scratch around for some clothes approaching a reasonable fit and befitting such an auspicious occasion. A few weeks before, I, with the agreement of all the other cyclists, had designed, ordered and received a batch of felt Group badges. A bicycle wheel in red thread, with a black, foaming beer glass in its centre, was shown on a blue, triangular background and bore the initials, SOTYHCC. The Stoke YHA Group committee looked down on the sew-on badge as being offensive, considering that such a thing would suggest the YHA members to be out-and-out boozers. Regarding the cyclists, I suppose that opinion wasn't too far from the truth. Those committee members who relished power, however little, voted to have the badge banned. We argued that because the initials didn't show 'YHA', missing out the initial 'A' for 'Association', the badge couldn't be linked directly to the YHA. A rather dubious loophole giving us an excuse to just let the matter die a natural death. Almost unconsciously, we had out-bluffed the committee but, at least, the affair had given them somethingexciting to consider. Something to enliven the monthly cash account discussion and 'any other business'. We sewed the offending article to the breast pocket of our black, gabardine cycling jackets or the leg of the shorts and wore it with pride. It wasn't a case of thumbing our noses at the local YHA Group committee, but just a matter of forgetting that any objection existed.

By the middle of May and in the middle of a heatwave, we used the Whitsun holiday for a foray into the delights of the Cotswolds. We used Lichfield, Broom Hall and Rushall youth hostels for a sun-soaked tour into Worcestershire and Herefordshire. Cycling south from Lichfield and somewhere on the southern outskirts of Sutton Coldfield, still in a predominantly urban area, Tony Ross failed to allow enough room between himself and a parked lorry and his saddlebag caught on the tailgate corner. The impact set Tony into a speed wobble and he came down heavily, causing the front forks and top tube behind the headset to buckle downwards, due, no doubt, to the incredible forces created by such an accident. Along with the frame damage, his front wheel formed an artistic figure-of-eight, a perfect double parabola in diagrammatic form, an academic delight for any tutor of advanced mathematics, but meaning that Tony couldn't continue on this hot, long weekend. He was unhurt, save his pride, but this was the very first outing on his brand new, hand-built bike and I knew how he felt about it.

Tony Ross, introduced to the group by the Salts, was a keen cyclist and always quick to see the funny side of any situation. He came from Italian stock, was of a cheery nature and proved indispensable in 1967 when we toured the Dolomites and finished in Venice. He had dark, tousled hair, a slightly swarthy complexion but tended to be a bit of a 'crasher' – he who often loses control of the bike and visited the tarmac with force. Tony phoned his dad, identified the location and sat on the kerb, waiting for pater to pick him and the bicycle up in the family car.

After sweltering miles over melting road surfaces, we reached the edge of the Cotswolds at Chipping Camden and paused for a break under the honey-coloured stone arches of the medieval market place. Chipping, or *cheeping,*is an early word for market, derived from the Saxon, *cheap.* We licked ice creams in the cool shadows inside this ancient building, sitting on chunky, stone-mounting blocks and people-watched the tourists sauntering along the incredibly long, narrow main street. Under a hot, glaring midday sun, I have often been surprised at how cool, almost cold, the deep shadows were. Outside, under an arc of blue sky, we could almost smell the strong sunlight in the heat of the day. We relished the shade under the curving medieval arches, resting, swigging water and licking ice creams before starting on the hot afternoon miles to Broom Hall youth hostel. In one Cotswold village, our passing excited a local dog who raced along the other side of a dense hedgerow, barking and growling as much as his breathing and lolling tongue would allow. Eventually, the hedge ended and I became aware of a slavering hound bounding off a high stone wall and flying in my direction. Whilst still in mid-air, the acrobatic beast had jumped right through my cycle frame's triangle, without touching anything, and landed on the road beyond. With his paws scrabbling for purchase, the would-be savager of cyclists failed to change his direction quickly enough and we had all streamed into the distance and safety before he could rejoin the chase. Most cyclists have suffered the close attention of chasing dogs and their snapping at the pedalling heels; jumping and lunging at a rapidly revolving ankle; before the accelerating rider is forced to lash out haphazardly and with mounting viciousness. The desperate lashing of a bicycle pump or the scything kick of a dog-hating, fleeing cyclist would, if making contact, surely sever the head of or maim a human being. Dogs, especially the little, yappy types, are definitely not the cyclists' best friend. Balance and direction are severely compromised by a chasing dog – especially for a cyclist who isn't too enamoured by Crufts and the Kennel Club. Besides, who enjoys scraping a dollop of cloying dog faeces from the heel of the Hush Puppies?

On the Sunday morning we left Broom Hall, the warden returned our membership cards and wished us a safe journey. He added a comment about the current hot weather. "It's hot enough to melt yer bollocks off!" A fair comment but one that left us somewhat flabbergasted. We had hardly expected a guardian for the welfare of young children, school parties and older, gentler anorak people to issue such a raw, piercing statement and on a quiet Sunday morning, I ask you? We moved west and into deepest Herefordshire, crossing the Malverns and on to the rural lushness of the Marches beyond Ledbury, to reach Rushall; every mile under the arch of a deep blue sky.

I have forgotten exactly when Chris Warren appeared on the scene. Maybe it was the aforementioned Cotswolds tour when I first noticed his rolling style of cycling, indicating a shortness in the legs. Chris lived in Dresden; not Germany, but a district of Longton in the south-east of the city. Geoff nicknamed him 'The All Round Cyclist'; a short, squat, rotund, giggling character who had a definite leaning to food and fancied himself to eventually carve out a career as a chef (excuse the pun). We also called him 'Bomber' due to a bumbling, bouncy character that could be described as a compressed version of *Billy*

Bunter of Greyfriars School. Chris developed a liking for my sister, Sheila's, coffee cake, correctly considering it to be the pinnacle of baked confectionery. He rode his lightweight bike, a red Mercian, with a rolling style, pivoted somewhere at the hips and considering his shape and weight, had masses of stamina. He lived in a terraced house with his mother in Dresden and obviously enjoyed our diverse sense of humour. Despite being accident prone in a non-dangerous way, he seemed unable to do anything but laugh. Jokes flew about at frequent intervals within the group and his chubby, red face would often be thrown back in some hearty guffaw.

I was pedalling smoothly along Abbey Foregate, Shrewsbury, towards the hostel, Woodlands, opposite the Lord Hill Doric column when a distant shout reached my ears. It seemed to be coming from high above and when I glanced skyward, noticed the very small head and shoulders of Brian Whalley leaning precariously over the railings and waving his bush hat from high above. Above him towered the weathered statue of Lord Hill, a famous general in the Waterloo Campaign, high on his topmost plinth, one hand hovering over a long sword forming a supercilious expression on his face of stone. These were the days when visitors could borrow the monument's door key from the local caretaker and climb the stairs to the highest Greek Doric column in the country. Long before our super safety-conscious overlords considered this unwise. On this summer evening, Geoff Cartlidge, Bill Barnish, Chris Warren, myself and a newcomer, Clive Lewis, were just completing the run from Stoke to Shrewsbury at a sprightly pace and separated, as usual, on the last mile dash to the hostel. Brian had ridden to Shrewsbury in the afternoon at a more leisurely pace. We booked in, made up our bunks and hurried down the road to our favourite pub, the Bricklayer's Arms, where, on every Friday night run, we'd savour a couple of pints of bitter and a cigarette, seated in the covered porch side-entrance and looked forward to two or more weeks of cycle touring. What adventures lay ahead – what experiences lay along those pedalled miles?

It was holiday time again and tomorrow we would cycle to Shrewsbury's magnificently Gothic railway station and catch a direct express service to Plymouth, in deepest Devon. From the 6th to the 20th June, we had fourteen, hopefully, glorious days touring from Devon and into Cornwall exploring countless coves and cliffs along a most rugged northern and southern coastline, before returning to Plymouth by way of Dartmoor.

Bill Barnish had introduced Clive Lewis to our group. Clive was a pleasant youth who seemed to enjoy the company. Sadly, he was partly deaf and dumb; he was unable to express his deepest thoughts and, therefore, remained a mystery to us. However, he obviously enjoyed himself and would gainour attention with an alarming yelp. Sometimes, Clive would laugh at a joke before the punch line, thereby adding even more humour to the situation. Bill, to his credit, made sure Clive was alright as he alone could understand his charge's differing moods.

Somewhere between the hostel and the station, we bought a seven pint party can of beer. I believe it was Ansell's Best Bitter; it weighed a ton and resembled a green-painted depth charge. We carted it onto the train and long before Ludlow, an attached opening tool had been produced and we proceeded to take in refreshments. After the first pint, the brew went flatter than a pancake and we were glad when we'd finished it. The can had to be finished in one session as there was no seal.

On this journey, we enjoyed the luxury of seats for everyone in an otherwise vacant compartment. Several train journeys with the cycles were made where we elected to stay in the guard's van, sitting on the packing cases with the bikes lashed to the van sides. We felt that we could keep an eye on them, ensuring that they wouldn't be off-loaded at some obscure destination. It was our way of staying together and sharing the odd joke or story. Due to the Great Train Robbery the year before, the railway officials would look down on such practice and we had to walk the train and try to find a vacant compartment space, long after every seat had been claimed. Having to oversee the loading of the cycles first usually prevented us from rushing to find sufficient empty adjoining seats or vacant compartments.

Our tour would start from Plymouth and immediately cross the River Tamar on the clanking Torpoint chain ferry, to land in Cornwall. From the Plymouth hostel, situated in the granite surroundings of Devonport, we toured through inland Lostwithiel, to the coast at Fowey; where we had to load the bikes into a small rowing boat and be sculled over the water before visiting all the other little coastal villages, using the intricate network of narrow lanes. Porthpean, Mevagissey, Gorran Haven and Dodman Point, to the hostel at Boswinger.Portloe, Porthscatho and into the almost tropical region of St.Just in Roseland. Fishing villages of character wearing a relaxed, timeless atmosphere; a little more developed than when I first saw them when living in Plymouth in the mid-1950s, but still pleasantly devoid of overwhelming, massed tourism. In the warm, luxuriant lanes, with occasional palms and salt-tolerant plants, we passed many a country gateway of rounded pillars surmounted by iron crosses; a local custom, particularly around Veryan, presumably to keep the devil away from land and properties.

At St. Mawes, we lifted the bikes onto a small ferry and crossed the busy harbour to land at Falmouth. The hostel was in a very small part of Pendennis Castle, an immensely strategic position overlooking the Carrick Roads. Henry VIII established this fortress to guard his properties along the Channel approaches. The entrance to the hostel accommodation was just a small, insignificant postern door, almost lost within the main castle's outer wall proportions. Crossing the Helford River on a small rowing boat ferry gave us views of placid river backwaters overhung with dense, rich foliage. We moved onto the Lizard Peninsular, crossing the flat, scrubby heathland of Goonhilly Downs, with its towering radio telescope, before dropping to the coast at Cadgwith. A line of old salts sat on a bench along the boathouse wall, packing their gnarled pipes with gnarled fingers whilst gazing out to sea. Their fishing smacks, all clinker-built and leaning, had been drawn high up the pebble beach, indicating that the day's fishing had finished hours ago and this was the time for mending the nets and gossiping. We entered the inn at the back of the beach and savoured a fisherman's lunch, washed down with a couple of pints of bitter; laying out the map and deciding where we could spend a bed and breakfast night.

Suddenly, a whisper and a following hush circled the bar; the very air turned from ambient chatter into an electrified, crackling atmosphere; a pulse of expectation looped between the locals; a handful of Hooray Henrys staggered through the door, surrounding a woolly-hatted Rodney Bewes. He gestured towards the barman and a dozen ardent admirers received the drink of their choice. Rodney, playing Bob, opposite the more talented James Bolam, playing Terry, in the new comedyTV series, *The Likely Lads,*had entered the building. Himself and his hangers-on turned the lunchtime quiet into an instant, chattering carnival of 'oops' and 'what-ohs' with their gin-and-its. We had probably witnessed one of the first examples of loaded financiers infesting an area, buying up the few cottages for exorbitant, over-inflated prices. Well-healed city types buying their second or third homes; weekend parasites denying true locals, indigenous families, access to any properties by pricing them completely out of the housing market. Sometimes, I even have a secret admiration for the Welsh Nationalists who invited house-speculating invaders to "come home to a real fire."

We stayed in a bed and breakfast at Mullion Cove, close to the spectacularly jagged cliffs and harbour entrance; stout seawalls where, even on a relatively calm afternoon, the westerly wind forced tongues of seawater to lick over corroded railings. Like Porthcurno, further along the coast, Mullion, or Poldhu nearby, formed the landfall for Trans-Atlantic Communications – Poldhu being the receiving station for radio transmissions from America, pioneered by the radio and telegraphy wizard, Marconi. The station was located here because of the site facing the vast, unhindered expanse of the ocean to the west. We enjoyed improved comfort at our guesthouse and, without the closing time curfew of 10:00pm, cycled back to the pub in Cadgwith for a night of drinking. Rodney Bewes wasn't there but his fame had preceded him and the bar was literally packed to the rafters with sycophantic, expectant admirers. Packed like sardines, those standing at the back who wished to reach the bar or go to the loos would be manoeuvred, supine over the crowd's heads; blokes and girls alike, passed hand-to-hand with, no doubt, many a lingering digit. It certainly proved to be a most jolly evening.

Culture continued as Geoff and I attended the Minack Theatre, a few miles from our next hostel at Land's End; taking our grassy seats in the cliff-top amphitheatre to watch *The Italian Straw Hat*. The stage, was a semi-circle, with performers entering and leaving through rocky gaps formed in the precipitous cliff walls, here used as convenient theatrical wings. Stage background comprised curves of carved balustrades and pillars with a natural distant backdrop of the ocean horizon and the sound effects of crashing waves below and the wailing cries of circling seabirds. However, we couldn't understand the play and with the approach of late evening, dampness was rising from the grass. At the conclusion of events, cold and damp had cramped our Thespian cheeks, so, we made a prompt and shivering departure. The cove of Porthcurno lies nearby; a sandy beach contained between two rocky headlands; the one to the east, Treen Cliff, having a giant, rocking boulder at its end, the Logan Rock. An enormous lump of stone, as big as a house, geologically, an 'erratic' that can be disturbed by the pressure of one finger. "Yeah, right!" I fear, one day there will be an almighty splash and the world's sea level will rise 12 inches (300mm). Porthcurno was the land terminal for the Atlantic underwater cable. A modest shed on the cliff marks where the cable landed – a simple garden shed marking the historic link between Britain and the mighty New World.

We found Land's End fairly quiet. A timber-clad building selling souvenirs and a convenient signpost indicating the distance from there to one's home town; Stoke-on-Trent would now be shown as 325 miles (520k)., but that's when using motorways. The approach to the cliffs at the very foot of England, an open road rising steadily, engendered a feeling of dramatic expectation. The gaunt, granite red cliffs provided that drama and beyond, over a decidedly boisterous sea, lay the cluster of rocks surrounding the Longships lighthouse. With the vast, open ocean spreading away to the west, the horizon showed the part-imagined, slightest of curves, giving the location a suitably daunting scale and setting.

*

Our tour turned from Land's End, heading along the coastal road to St. Ives and to Phillack youth hostel. Today, we had a dense sea mist as the road wound by banks of tough, windblown heather, through St. Just and Zennor, to St. Ives. The disused cliff-top tin mine buildings and chimney at St. Just, half-seen in swirling mists, gave a feeling of sad redundancy.

The dripping atmosphere hid away the inland landscape on this very end of the Cornish peninsula; obscuring ancient village sites, like Chysauster and Carn Euny, giving an air of mystery to the half-hidden, leaning cromlechs and dolmens; early man's prehistoric temples and building constructions. I will always remember having to draw dolmens in history classes at Hanley High School, not seven years before. Having an inbuilt skill for drawing, I found the illustration of rough piles of enormous, leaning rocks as elementary. I even added the growth of lichens in the hollows and surrounding wild grasses around the bases, to give the drawings reality and scale. In today's schooling, that would have earned me an A-Level, at least.

We found St. Ives busy. The blue sky had returned with the midday sun reflecting off wet harbour sand and forming pearl drops of light on seaweed-covered boat lines. The light was brittle and bright; clean and clear; I could fully understand the place being a Mecca for artists. Boat building and bollards, lobster pots and fishing nets, textured light and shadow, all combining to serve up a picture of chocolate-box, marine intensity, almost to a salty fault. Even the fishing detritus; cod's heads and crab claws, demanded a lightning, 6B pencil sketch. Big Mac cardboard meals and Coke cups had yet to spoil the perfection of it all. There is now even a Tate Gallery on the waterfront.

From Phillack, we moved the short distance inland to Truro; to a hostel within sight of the high white walls, buttresses and spires of the Cathedral, before progressing up the north Cornish coast, staying at Treyarnon, Tintagel and Boscastle. These Atlantic-facing shores show a remarkable difference to the south coast. Instead of deep rias flowing into long, green valleys and slack water harbours full of swaying leisure craft, the northern coast has higher, jagged headlands alternating with long, sandy strands strafed by high, demanding and serious surf. However, we saw very few surfing dudes on our travels; no beach cafes selling a forest of surf boards; no lime-green or orange VW Camper vans covered with psychedelic designs and no twang of Australian accents, each sentence ending with a questioning up-talk intonation. Here, in summer 1964, the whole of Cornwall was still more or less free of fit, fair-haired sex machines clad in black, figure-hugging rubber. Tall,

Antipodean Adonises sprinting for the waves and kicking sand into deckchair-slung, ice cream-licking, docile peoples' faces. The weather changed dramatically, too. From a damp, misty and clinging, still atmosphere of a south coast, one could travel a relatively short distance to the north coast, where the mist had cleared to reveal a clear and breezy blue sky – the improvement heralded by the comment, "Good, the sun's coming out and there's enough blue to make a sailor's suit."

We all had to descend the cliff path at Bedruthan Steps and see, at close quarters, the giant sea stacks, now, at low tide, appearing like lumbering mammoths roaming over the dazzling white sand of an untouched, prehistoric shore. In a sea cave on Porthtowan Beach, Clive Lewis decided to emit one of his shrieking whoops and scared us all senseless; the sudden sound reverberating off wet, rocky cavern walls, echoing between a salty shingle floor and dark, vaulted roof. Chris Warren threw back his head and exploded with his usual hearty guffaw. The youth hostel in Boscastle stood by the side of the long harbour, or rather, the sunken, walled stream that leads to it. In August 2004, the whole of this harbour was threatened after a torrential thunderstorm inland turned the stream into a thundering mass of debris-laden water. Even cars and vans were washed down to the sea and out into the bay. The hostel and neighbouring buildings survived, but a long repair programme was needed. The local pub, The Cobweb, set further back in the village, fortunately escaped the inundation. It became the headquarters for the many flood-relief appeals that followed the disaster. On our tour in 1964, the old inn still had its clusters of long cobwebs in the bar. They had been allowed to grow so long, they were nearly touching our heads. Some twenty years after, on another visit, we noticed the cobwebs cut back and suitably sprayed to comply with the various public health acts that were beginning to stifle any such individual character.

Between Tintagel and Boscastle lies the spectacular beach at Bossiney Haven. We discovered this jewel of an inlet at the end of some narrow lanes. Vertical cliffs bordered and towered above this deep cut in the coastline, with a shallow sea washing over smooth sands. This was the stuff of pirates and smugglers; a lonely, secret spot mainly shaded by the overpowering cliffs. A waterfall sprayed down from out of the overhanging vegetation, a sparkling curtain under a bright, backlit sun. The stream gathered and cut a channel in the sand, eventually flowing into the incoming tide. This was a mysterious place for children to play out their lively imaginations. A theatre for their dreams. We enjoyed this magical place, too. There were no other visitors to spoil the illusion of wilderness. We claimed Bossiney Haven for ourselves.

From Boscastle, we pedalled inland, through Launceston and Tavistock, crossing into Devon before climbing up into the high, wide spaces of Dartmoor. A mile or so out of Princetown, I delved into the bottom of the saddlebag and pulled out a much-used Ordnance Survey 1 inch scale map of south Dartmoor. It was a linen-backed edition with some detail obliterated and some areas between contour heights crayoned-in to illustrate land relief. It showed a faint footpath heading across the moors, virtually due east, from Princetown to Hexworthy, near Huccaby Bridge and Dartmeet. The route showed settlements, cairns, bridges and stone circles; ancient villages shown on the map in an antique lettering style; a landscape dotted with historic sites, all conflicting with the clustered contour lines. Our appetite for exploring rough-stuff routes would, here, be fully whetted. The narrow, unsurfaced lane climbed to a small farmstead before giving way to an indistinct path that climbed over the open moorland of Royal Tor. In bright, sunny weather, we part walked, part rode through bracken and heather, disturbing the odd, startled grouse while above, skylarks hovered in a blue ceiling of song. Moving parallel with the West Dart River, flowing in the valley bottom off our left shoulders; from here, its rushing flow seen but not heard, we maintained direction, steering a few points south of due east. High above our chattering voices, the occasional bird of prey, hawk or buzzard, circled in wide sweeps in the column of a heated thermal. We had the entire landscape and skyscape to ourselves, along with the undisturbed wildlife.

The path switchbacked across the side valley, crossing the River Swincombe, breasting the opposite slope before sauntering into Hexworthy with its scattering of stone cottages. We dropped down the narrowest of lanes, bordered by high hedgerows, until we met civilisation again in the form of tourists at Huccaby Bridge and

Dartmeet. Actually, the few folk enjoying the boulder-filled river setting were still more visitors than tourists. There were no cafés or car parking, reserved areas or by-law and safety notices. Thankfully, even these sites retained an air of being completely unspoilt. The modern metric equivalent OS map shows simplified notation with our rough-stuff route indicated as a European Long Distance Footpath; marked with a large, red diamond notation, our carefully selected way glares from the sheet, advertising a must-use facility. Silence author, you are becoming selfishly and snobbishly selective.

We fully explored Dartmoor using Bellever hostel near Postbridge, with its famous clapper bridge, Gidleigh YH near Chagford on the edge of the moor and Dunsford, further north and close to the River Teign, beyond Moretonhampstead. Having visited Gidleigh on the earlier tour of the south-west with Derek Latham and Dave Hope, I was keen to lead the others to the forgotten inn that served just powerful, farmyard cider. After a self-cooked meal, hurriedly thrown together from the chaos of the self-cookers' kitchen, we grabbed the bikes and flitted down lanes shaded by high, hollow way banks, hedgerows and over-arching trees, to find the inn marked HEAVYTREE ALES. Slinging the bikes against an ivy-clad wall, we soon had shuffled into the small taproom, ordered rough cider all round and claimed seats on the gnarled, knotted settles. The floor still had its bare, uneven flagstones, the black, wooden, full-height screen still served as the bar, the patina of age and old tobacco smoke still stained the low, beamed ceiling and, seemingly, ageless, ancient menfolk sat on the settle, their lined and furrowed faces matching the knotty, grained woodwork on which they sat. In fact, the old inn hadn't changed at all, appearing even to have regressed further into the world of a refuge for the poor yeoman farmer. Grasping their battered tankards of cider, the locals gave us a salutation of growled "ooohs" and "aaarghs", with a barely understood comment on, I think, the weather. It wasn't just the pub that remained unchanged but the locals, too. A line of old codgers who seemed to be welded to the settles. We drank our pints of scrumpy; served by a toothless crone, wielding a chipped enamel jug and before getting totally blathered, adjusted the horsehair dartboard and started our games of darts. As the golden liquid took effect, our expertise on the board, instead of suffering, improved until we had reached a point when the bull's-eye became unmissable. We would have to 'bull up' to see who started each game of 301, but with every throw, our arrows kept on landing exactly on target. The display of throwing climaxed when one dart landed in the tail of the first, both in the bull. The locals looked on with the occasional grunt of appreciation – we just turned and gave them a grin, and a shrug of the shoulders.

As most of the weekends spent hostelling involved the invariable visit to a public house, if not at lunchtime, definitely in the evenings (we weren't the sort to fraternise in the common room, chatting and reading the *Peoples' Friend).*,we quickly learned, and played very well, the noble game of darts. 301 was the preferred game, played in pairs or singles. Geoff was the best player on this holiday; Ralph Salt, Derek Latham, Dave Hope and Roy Deakin being the best players generally, with both Ralph, working as an auditor and Roy, as a bank counter assistant, being the wizards at fast scoring. We would often surprise experienced darts players with our accumulated skill and win cash or pints into the bargain. The evening closed with our ride back to the hostel; a dashing flight down dark lanes at breakneck speed. Brian Whalley collided with an oncoming car somewhere along the route but anaesthetised with drink, only noticed a badly gashed knee when his sock became wet with blood. He bound the wound with his handkerchief and carried on with no long-term distress. We were tough untouchable and invincible in those days. Sometimes, if we cycled fast enough, we were even invisible. From Dunsford, we had a relatively short cycle run to Exeter before catching a train back to Shrewsbury and the end of two excellent weeks in Devon and Cornwall.

*

Chris Warren continued to rock and roll; rock on the bike from the hips and roll with laughter whenever anyone cracked a joke and although tubby and squat, always seemed to have stamina. On a weekend from

Lichfield to Stratford-upon-Avon in July, he was the first to jump into a rowing boat and scull beneath the shadow of the Shakespeare Memorial Theatre. We teased him about his trouble with getting fitted for cycling plus-fours. He had sent off his order to the specialist tailor for cyclists, Ossie Dover, but the stylish master of the rag trade had got Chris's 'body length rise' incorrect, probably unable to comprehend his unusual, specified measurements.

The Stoke cyclists' humour, as a group, could be as dry as the desert and sometimes very cruel. We arranged meeting places for each weekend and midweek runs; Badderley Green for the Peak District, Trentham Gardens and later Trentham Lane Ends for runs south and west and Newcastle Baths for runs into Cheshire. At the latter, gathered by the large roundabout in Newcastle's town centre, we watched a mod scooter rider negotiate the junction. With duck-green parka and fur-lined hood, the cavalier of trendy fashion; windscreen festooned with a hundred mirrors and bulb hooters, harassed by passing traffic, dropped his machinery and skidded across the road on his posterior. With a shower of broken glass and sparks shooting from the handlebar ends, the horrible scraping sound of metal was instantly followed by a wit in our group shouting, "You should have looked in yer mirror, mate!" While having lunch on a summer day at the head of Tal-y-Llyn, below the CrossFoxes Pass in Mid-Wales, we were spied-on by a local sex deviant. We sat under the trees, eating our sandwiches, drinking our squash and enjoying a cigarette before the afternoon cycling continued, innocence personified, when we saw a man, half-hidden behind the trees, pleasuring himself with gusto. Dave Hope commented, whispering behind his hand, "So, that's what the locals do on a Sunday." I thought that quite succinct, especially from a bloke who owned and rode a race-prepared Manx Norton.

Brian and myself spent another week in wild Wales, appreciating the small, spartan and very basic hostels of the region. We joined the group on the summer Bank Holiday long weekend at the start of August, cycling from Chester to Lledr Valley, and further into Snowdonia at Capel Curig. We had time on our hands at Capel so decided on an evening tramp to the summit of Moel Siabod. The climb was, from that side, on gradual, easy paths, being long rather than severe. Hence we could wear light cycling shoes; more like slippers than shoes and there was no need for stout walking boots. On return to the hostel, with one eye on our wristwatches and aware of the strict closing time in force, we made haste on a more direct route towards the valley lakes. Before reaching them, we had to pass through the thick Forestry Commission plantation; a dense, sward of dark pine trees that lay between open mountainside and the Capel Curig lakes. There is nothing so dense, dark and dead as the understory of an intensive spruce woodland. We slipped and slithered on dry, brown pine needles, between close-planted trees of tall, telegraph pole proportions, in a floundering bunch of nearly-lost souls. As we struggled to maintain direction, with no visibility or point of reference, constantly aware of the passage of time and failing daylight, all that we could hear was the unbridled chortling and laughter of a thoroughly confused, yet ever-amused, Chris Warren.

Next morning, the main group would return to the Potteries, but not before Ann Hassall found that her gears had wandered into her wheel, jammed solid in a Chinese puzzle of folded chain and it was left to Dave Hope to get his hands oily – again. Dave was the chief mechanic of us cyclists. He dreaded the pleading voice of a cyclist having mechanical troubles but, I think, secretly relished the task of overcoming a problem of wheels jamming, chains parting or mudguards rubbing.

Brian and I headed south to explore the wilder regions of central Wales. We stopped for overnights at Corris, Ystumtuen, Blaencaron and Nant y Dernol, former schools situated in lonely countryside managed by ancient, twisted old ladies, and you can't get wilder than that. At Corris, we were loitering in the back garden, me having a last fag, with Brian calling to the girls at their dormitory window trying to strike up a conversation, when the warden caught us defying the closing time curfew and gave us a stern lecture. We stood shoulder-to-shoulder in the common room where the crusty warden, looking over her glasses, asked us what we were doing, telling us it was long past our bedtimes. Under the wagging finger of the stern governess, never had we felt more like naughty boys and never had a disused schoolroom so quickly and accurately reverted to its former use.

To pass through a sleepy Welsh village, with its streets of low, gathered cottages, stone-built schoolhouse and austere, dominating chapel, made one conscious of what would have been the strict, religious regime of a society not too many years before. With rain falling from a leaden sky, the overriding atmosphere of these insular settlements would be created by the presence of slate. Slate roofs, slate fences and slate walls, particularly in North Wales, gave a place the depressing greyness of tight, narrow-minded inhabitants. Or so it seemed to us. Shiny, wet slated roofs combined with a Sunday closing of public houses, gave a feeling of a lowered, even cowered soul.

The rich sound of a male voice choir, beautiful as it was, couldn't raise the spirit as one sheltered from the incessant rain as it flowed over mounds of slate and down gutters of despondency. The tune of *Cwm Rhondda* (Guide me 0 Thy Great Redeemer).arose from over the mounds of grey. The words were ripe for a different, childish rendering, words remarkably suited to the official line. *"Bread from Evans's, cheese from Jones's, Beer from the Collier's Arms/Beeeer from the Colliers Arms."* Anyone passing through Blaenau Ffestiniog on a wet Sunday will get my drift. The piles of slate bordering and almost overflowing the roadside walls threaten to bury and suffocate the sensitive visitor. The matt, blue-greyness of it all, like a hungry monster, devouring all spirit. Or maybe I was there on a very wet and windy day with too many miles left to cycle.

From Blaencaron hostel, a lonely, disused school hidden in the lanes near Tregaron, with the small, rooftop bell tower the only indication of its former use, we crossed wild countryside on tracks to the east. High in the hills, we found the cluster of small lakes marked as the Teifi Pools and fell gradually to a remote Claerwen Dam, the western outlier to the system of reservoirs in the Elan Valley. The Claerwen Reservoir was the last to be flooded, while further towards Rhayader, the Craig Goch, Pen y Garreg, Garreg ddu and Caban Coch Reservoirs and surrounds had had time to partially naturalise. It was only at the lower, original lake that the unsightly buildings, pylons and overhead wires of a hydro-electric plant became intrusive. After several rough-stuff routes already followed, we now felt completely at ease in such regions of bare, treeless mountains where the cotton grass bent to moaning winds and unnamed streams chattered to unhearing ears. Nant y Dernol youth hostel lay at the end of a lonely lane, cutting into the hills north of the upper River Wye and the pony-trekking centre of Rhayader. Scattered sheep farms apart, we were completely remote from civilisation and that included the lack of a public house. Even the warden lived miles away and made very rare visits to replenish the Calor Gas or deliver more logs. Brian and I made a mental note to bring along a few bottled beers on future visits. I remember enjoying a quiet evening at Nant y Dernol with Dave Hope and Kenny Birks, ruminating on distant, worldly problems, while stirring the log fire into life and savouring bottled Guinness out of enamel mugs. Brian and I finished our week's tour with a stop at Newtown, a town through which we would, time and again, speed through on our tours to and from central Wales.

Kenny Birks, probably the youngest member to join us, was a fit, keen cyclist who had a complete disregard for the distances and arduousness of our runs. I think either Ralph or Clive had introduced him to the group. Or I could be wrong. Kenny was the sort of person who just turned-up. With a cheeky, flushed face and tousled hair, he was always quick with the wit and let nothing faze him. His youthful looks and rascally grin belied the wealth of an experienced, street-cred nature. He seemed to be a person who could talk himself in and out of any tricky situation; if he had already finished school, it would be by only a year or two at the most. Kenny – he could never be called a 'Ken' or 'Kenneth' – was a regular attendee on numerous cycling jaunts, adding spice to the weekends. Arriving at hostels without a booking seemed to present little problem for him.

Shropshire was a much-visited county in these early years of 1964. With hostels at Shrewsbury, Ludlow, Bridges, Clun, Wheathill and Wilderhope, the Welsh Marches were a treasure of interesting places to explore, pubs to frequent and rough-stuff routes to pioneer. Here was a concentrated mass of history, geography, geology, architecture, folklore and legend that, surely, was hard to surpass countrywide. Everything was so genuine, unspoilt, convenient, reachable, easy-going and damn interesting. The Peak District also had its cluster of youth hostels, but the region being the first National Park, they had more visitors and consequently, more rules and regulations.

The manor of Wilderhope, a grand Tudor residence set on the dip slope of Wenlock Edg,e was one of our favourite hostels. The immediate countryside is spectacular; many separated hills in view to the north-west, while below one's feet, a view from the limestone edge of coloured patchwork rurality. Built in tbe second half of the 16thcentury, the old manor is a classic 'E'-plan building with a fronting stone-paved terrace and magnificent Tudor, diagonally-linked, ornate chimneys. The grand bay windows have diamond-patterned leaded lights with the whole front showing a typically balanced elevation. The rear, in contrast, facing the plain hillside slope with no view, shows a high, gaunt, almost fortified wall with just a few small window openings. There was no doubt from which direction potential threat and bad weather came from. Set in deep countryside, the place is hidden from the road and faces a lonely tract of dipping fields and clumps of mature trees. The main entrance is a massive, studded oak door that requires all one's strength to make it swing back on its ancient, iron hinges. A small staircase leads to the warden's private rooms, while the common room is a grand, stone-flagged hall with a massive stone fireplace surmounted by wall brackets, no doubt, to hold early hunting weapons. The high and remote ceiling is decorated centrally with a basic plaster Smallman family crest. A spiral staircase with large, wooden treads winds off the grand hall, leading to the boys' and girls' dormitories. The self-cooker's kitchen is an evil room in the far wing that only the extremely brave would utilise. Being owned by the National Trust, and leased to the YHA, in the hours when the hostel was closed to hostellers, (between 10:00am and 4:00pm), it had limited opening to members of the public. I believe this arrangement exists today. What has changed is that the hostel is now open to school parties, supposedly to study the area's geology; a policy decision I disagree with as it limits the beds available for casual travellers, be they walkers or cyclists. Some beds should have been set aside for the singleton but I doubt if this rule was seriously adhered to.

We found many hostels were beginning to accept large school parties, particularly in the more touristy areas. With selfish motives admitted, we believed that the introduction of such large parties would destroy the quiet atmosphere and camaraderie of individual travellers. The noisy, boisterous behaviour of toddlers, running under one's feet and playing havoc with hostel facilities, would lead to the necessity for yet more petty house rules. Besides, how could weary cyclists like ourselves be able to get our beauty sleep? How would the little, scholarly darlings cope with our clouds of tobacco smoke and beery-breathed fumes? Would not the dangers of a self-cooker's kitchen mean scolding and burning to the little ones? Besides, today's youngsters are hooked up to their mobile phones, iPads and iPods, seemingly unable to exist without the technology of the silicon chip; causing a further alienating of young-stupid from old-sensible. What right-minded person in search of shared experiences in friendly conversation could bear an evening of stupid, disembodied, one-way banter that these devices create? Youth hostels weren't supposed to be nurseries with noisy crèches; they were doss-houses for the travelling gentlemen of the road. Seriously, I have recently seen advertisements for the YHA in various magazines; luxury private rooms with bed and breakfast for just £42 per night in the high season. Single, double, family rooms, some with en-suite, for heaven's sake. Cordonbleu prepared meals provided, or salad bar and brunch. Common room furniture seems to have become designer smart and co-ordinated. Licensed common rooms not bad but better to keep the local pub in business – it probably has more history. Local hostelries are closing at an alarming rate. Whatever happened to the draughty dormitory with the gaunt iron bunks and twangy spring bed-frames? What's wrong with beans on toast and tea from a giant, shared, brown enamel teapot? Self-cooking has become self-catering. Folk liked sprawling on old, beat-up sofas; balancing an ashtray on the bulbous, horsehair-stuffed arm; perching on rickety chairs, peering at the map on a chipped, cup-ringed table. I'm not suggesting that we all should regress to medieval times, squalid conditions and a danger of food poisoning, but I feel a certain 'spirit' has left the YHA in the pursuit of attracting a more demanding clientele – whether they seek posh surroundings or not. The YHA was basically for the mainly solo or small group of like-minded travellers of limited means, turning up on spec' and only expecting the very minimum of facilities. A roof, a bite to eat and a bed for the night, providing a stopping-off place for the intrepid traveller who refused to, or couldn't, spend a fortune. Although the costs have increased, they are far from exorbitant; today's youth can easily cope with the prices. It is the insipient sanitising of the hostels that has probably killed the whole spirit of the thing. It is the creeping increase in rules and regulations that has given the organisation a clinical feel. Why try to compete with hotel accommodation and possibly fall between two (common room).stools? Let's hope some of the original spirit remains, probably found in the simpler hostels. Personally, in many cases, I think the YHA has lost the plot.

The rules and conditions at Wilderhope Manor, in 1964, were far from the above, far from stifling, far from luxurious. We walked down the Edge and spent a lively evening in the Longville Arms at Longville in the Dale. At closing time, we trekked up the hillside on a direct line, through a young forestry plantation, before staggering into the Manor past a heavy, grating front door. The warden, far from complaining of our tardy return, invited us up into his private room to help him drink his latest brew of homemade beer. He was probably an acting warden, a student doing voluntary work out of term time. I suppose any sort of company was welcomed in his long evenings, shut inside that old manor house with its creaks and groans, sudden bumps and sad sighs in the darkness. I remember awakening in the middle of the night at Wilderhope. It may have been an unusual sound; a cooling-down movement of some ancient ceiling beam; an unsecured floorboard, or a creak of a bedspring signalling the irritable sleep of a fellow hosteller, tossed on the stormy seas of his agitated dreams. I rose from under the gritty blanket, let my feet plant on the cold, splintered floorboards and crept over to the deeply-mullioned window. The diamond window panes dripped with a film of sad condensation, gathering on the thick strip leading, while outside, an ill-looking, pale-yellow full moon, rose in a sickly arc from above a layer of dense, white, layered mist. I'm sure I saw a party of horsemen riding across the vale, parting the swirling vapours, in hot pursuit of a hysterically-squealing hog. Wilderhope Manor was that sort of place – an unspoilt hostel with spooky, serious atmosphere.

Wheathill was yet another very basic Shropshire village and hostel, set above Corve Dale in the high Clee Hills. Situated a few miles from the future Acton Scott Working Farm Museum, the building was built of rugged stone and had a frugal but comfortable common room, above which lay a bare, floor-boarded dormitory. This had probably been a granary barn before being converted into its present use. The whole building breathed hay and horse manure. The door between boys' and girls' dormitories was a shaky, planked barrier, nailed tight shut with added cross-planking, but with a very large keyhole. Many an eye, wan and watery, was pressed close to that hole. Whoops and cheers filtered through the knotty pine until general lights-out, when the hot, heady pollen of summer hay fields wafted through the open window and lulled everybody into deep, satisfying sleep. You should have heard the language filtering through that barrier to sexual desires; all coming from the girls' side, I might add.

In October, we went to Clun youth hostel, already mentioned, a hostel that was even more basic than Wheathill. As it was October and I had purchased a front wheel Dynohub, I used my black Viking cycle to test its efficiency in the drawing-in evenings at that time. Although the hub was heavy, it powered a rather streamlined headlamp and adequate rear red light. On the miles to Clun, via Shrewsbury, Church Stretton and Craven Arms, I kept stopping to test the apparatus and couldn't wait for the onset of darkness. In the chilly air of autumn, I would stop in lay-bys, lift the front wheel and spin it to see the light beam shine bright and true, making microscopic adjustments to see that the headlamp lit the road at the correct spot ahead. My cycling was brightly lit for the remaining late evening miles to Clun, but the weight and added friction made the going oh so laborious and tiring.

The preferred front lighting was a neat headlamp made from thin metal, with simple screw-down or lever top switch and holding a twin-cell battery carried on the front right-hand fork of the bike. It was reasonably light, dependable, simple to reach and use, and lit the way ahead for at least 5 yards. Cycle front lights were only meant to warn oncoming traffic. The lamp was almost perfect and being so, just had to be altered and redesigned by governing legislation. In days of yore, cyclists used carbide lamps where drips of water onto charcoal produced an exceedingly bright burning gas. Probably the very best form of cycle lighting ever. The Ministry of Cycle Lighting, in their unbounded wisdom, changed the design to plastic. Heavy, cumbersome and unreliable were just three of the many defects. The rear lights were even more ugly and heavy. Consequently, the tin headlamps became unavailable. The only disadvantage of the front forks lamp bracket was that this area received maximum vibration and many a night's ride would see the front lamp shaken loose, skittering and bouncing down the road, emitting a final, dying flash before spewing top, battery and casing into the obscuring curtains of darkness. A folding and wedging of cardboard inserted in the bracket slot solved this problem. Invariably, a leather toe strap was used to secure the lamp, wrapped around casing and bracket to keep it from shaking off on bumpy roads.

Another accessory I fitted at about the same time was a speedometer. A toothed ring screwed to the front wheel spokes drove a worm-geared flexible cable that connected to a handlebar clock. With an odometer included, it was a chunky piece of nonsense that kept me occupied on the boring miles of a cycle run; that is, if any stage of a bicycle journey could be considered boring. The small Cyclo milometer driven by a spoke striker turning a small star wheel was the usual distant recorder, simple and efficient as long as the rider could tolerate a constant tick-tick-tick. Somehow, that ticking was strangely comforting. Yes, we had out-grown the habit of wedging a piece of cardboard in the forks to produce a motorbike sound effect. Many days would pass us by before miniature, battery-powered milometers, with microscopic, mini chip electronics, would come into the cycle shops. They would become an actual cycle accessory improvement.

The old cycle bell, at first a bulky dome of rotating gears, pinions and hair springs, weighed far too much in our opinion. We fitted the minimal Spring-Ding, a small, alloy bell with a simple sprung striker arm that proved to be basic, light and perfectly dependable. However, it was, to the casual, jay-walking pedestrian sauntering in our road, completely silent and useless. Better still was a bulb horn that hung from the saddlebag side-pocket. It was loud and its raucous, pap-papping, yelping tones would give adequate warning and reply to the impatient, beeping motorist.

With larger and heavier saddlebags, we had to fit lightweight pannier carriers or uplift frames clipped into the saddle strap eyes. Apart from facilitating the fitting of panniers, the carriers, made from thin metal rods, prevented the saddlebag from pressing on the rear mudguard. We usually managed with saddlebags only – panniers tending to be an excuse for carrying more kit. The overriding requisite was to carry as little as possible, keep weight to a minimum. Pounds multiplied by miles was the important factor, but at least we carried the load on wheels. Wearing a heavy rucksack while cycling was not to be recommended.

*

By October, we were approaching the social season. After our holiday in Devon and Cornwall, Geoff and I produced a slide show of the holiday to the members at Cartwright House. It was titled, *Cornish Coast and Dartmoor*. As we were none too keen on public speaking, we recorded a taped account, complete with sound effects of heavy seas and the cry of seagulls, and set it to a good collection of slides. Gaps in the dialogue were filled with appropriate snippets of music, mainly sea shanties for harbour scenes and light classical for dramatic coastal situations. Using my Grundig TK/20 reel-to-reel tape recorder to good effect, the show was applauded with genuine enthusiasm. The sound effect LPs of seagulls proved a real winner. At that time, sound effect discs were available from BBC Sound Recordings. We resisted the temptation to acquire further effects, like wild beasts, apocalyptic explosions, steam railway sounds or haunted houses. The show was used as a testing ground for a follow-up slide show of much grander proportions.

In December, all of the cyclists contributed a selection of slides from our many weekends and holidays to produce *A Cyclist's Year*. Produced again on tape, it was billed – *"Don't miss this one-the biggest laugh of the year."* All sorts of slides were included; even the scene of nude bathing at

Swch Cae Rhiw cascades on the Berwyns, the commentary inviting Laurie Landon's wife, Dorothy, to come up to the screen for a closer look. The dialogue also contained the piece by Ralph when he read out the line, "Here we see the peak of [Mynydd Mawr] at *approximately* two thousand, three hundred and forty-seven feet." Again, the show was appreciated, the audience realising that this sort of presentation was a welcome lift from the, sometimes, expected drone of a boring speaker. A week or so later, we took the show to the Stone Wheelers club night in Stone, where it was a welcomed escape from the general racing club conversation of gear ratios, split-times attained and race conditions. I later received a thankyou letter from their secretary, enclosing a postal order for £1 as a donation towards expenses. We moved in big money circles in those days.

At the local YHA's Annual General Meeting, where officers were elected to the various committees, Roy Hazeldine continued to represent the cyclists. The Cycling Section's interest was in the presentation of the Bednight Award; the most number of overnight hostel attendances in the programme's year, from October 1963 to October 1964, well won by Geoff Cartlidge and presented on stage by secretary, Roy. I was determined to win this award the following year.

Fred, at this time, was running his business of typewriter supplies and other office equipment from a small shop in Liverpool Road, Stoke. For deliveries, he bought a Bedford van and I painted Ellis Typewriter Services on both sides in white lettering against a mid-blue background, enhancing the seraphed capitals with black edging. He kindly allowed me to use it to transport a dozen or so members on a Christmas holiday; four days from Christmas Eve, to Cynwyd youth hostel between Corwen and Bala. I hadn't learned to drive myself, yet, so, Dave Hope, Derek Hambleton and Phil Hughes drove us on wintry roads to one of our favourite hostels, the disused mill at the foot of the Berwyn Mountains. I had sent off the block booking and the returned receipt card from Merseyside Youth Hostels Ltd accepted the reservation of forty-six male bednights over the four days, showing that the total cost was £6-12s-0d (£6.60p).

Other members from our Stoke group made their own way there and we all met in the back room of the Blue Lion. The small room with simple bench seating remained our mustering point for the four evenings of enthusiastic folk singing and general jocular banter. Dave Joynson, our teacher/walker/cyclist, had brought along his guitar and was joined by Roy Deakin, playing mandolin and a tricycle-riding chance acquaintanceand Andrew Ovenall from Darwen, in Lancashire, playing an efficient banjo. Roy Deakin, dependable Trustee Savings Bank clerk and ace darts thrower, celebrated his birthday on Christmas Day and the wardens kindly made us all a grand tea and Roy a fine cake. He followed Roy Orbison and with his dark hair and heavy sunshades, resembled the great entertainer himself, albeit it as a rather stunted version. Our mandolin player had the peculiar habit of smelling all his food before eating, even in posh restaurants. Roy was a careful, wary character, an ideal attribute, I should think, for someone working in a bank. Sadly, on the Christmas at Cynwyd the following year, we heard from the warden that Andrew Ovenall had been knocked from his tricycle by a car and killed instantly. It had happened at night when, I suppose, the extra width of a trike could have been confusing. Roy Deakin, co-incidentally, was to purchase a tricycle himself some years later.

With singing so many folk ballads, we would soon write out notebooks full of lyrics and although suffering the stresses and strains of pub singing, quickly became our 'Bibles'; the first items to pack on every weekend and the item that could easily be left on the seat when we had tramped our weary way homeward. The favourite drink of all concerned was Black Velvet (Guinness and champagne, but the bubbly being substituted by cider). After the evenings descended into late-night raucousness, we ceased the pints and switched to shorts; due to the continuous queue at the bar for our vodka and limes, a queue all line-astern and always on the move, we gave the drinks a nickname – Russian Convoys – each tipple celebrated by the salutation, "*Nostrovia!*"Well, that's what it sounded like. The correct Russian salutation was, probably, "*Na vashe zdorovie!*"At that time of night, at that level of wassailing, most conversation sounded Russian anyway. Ralph and/or Clive wore a distinctive porkpie, Trilby hat. On several occasions, it was handed around to the assembled company and worn at a jaunty angle. It also saw the reappearance of a few Black Velvets, giving the felt interior a baptism of second-hand alcohol. In the small hours, we crawled into our bunks, pulled up the heavy blankets and drifted into a dreamless sleep of anaesthetising beer fumes.

The following mornings were clear, bright and invigorating. We walked over the snow-covered slopes of the Berwyns, breathing in air of cutting sharpness and exhaling steamy clouds that hung in the stillness of a freezing afternoon. Sheep stood motionless on the lower slopes, appearing to be frozen solid to the snowy hillsides. The views towards Bala, glimpsed over the dark-green density of snow-dusted pine forestry, showed lowland clumps of trees being rapidly swathed in creeping, clinging mist. The higher tops of the mountains, looking towards Cader Berwyn, were bathed in a flushing of pink light while overhead arched a clear sky approaching a hue of acid blue-green. The pale, full moon, clawing itself over the snow-covered, heathery horizon, added a feeling of open isolation. We stamped our booted feet, removed our mittens and blew on hands before wiping our nipped, runny noses. The fresh, cold air of afternoon, walking through a winter landscape resembling Bruegel's *Hunters in the Snow,* gave us an appetite that made modest beans on toast seem like a meal fit for a king. A brew all round followed, poured from a giant, brown enamel teapot – pure nectar!

After the evening meal, we ambled down the lane and straight into the pub. Another pub lay across the lane, directly opposite the Blue Lion. This was the Prince of Wales; appearing somewhat posher, but we never went in. As 'foreigners' and totally taking over the back room in the Blue Lion, we kept our seats as locals before rising in chorus as the drinks kicked in. *The Wild Rover* became our opening song, then *Whisky in the Jar,* followed by various boisterous sea shanties. It was about now when I started to write down the lyrics to several folk songs; mostly Irish, songs by Ewan MacColl, followed by the American folk of Woody Guthrie, Bob Dylan, Pete Seeger, Joni Mitchell and Joan Baez. Our music was, thankfully, becoming more sophisticated, more grown-up.

A day spent motoring into Snowdonia had to be curtailed due to worsening weather. By the time we'd reached Pen-y-Pass on the summit of the Llanberis Pass, wet, large-flaked snow fell out of an overcast sky, reducing visibility to just a handful of yards. Crib Goch hung above us, hidden for now by a low blanket of snow-filled cloud. Our intended ascent of Snowdon was considered to have been foolhardy and potentially dangerous, so, kicking the snow off our boots, we piled back into the cramped van and made a judicious retreat. A call for petrol on the high, exposed moors between Betws-y-Coed and Cerrigydrudion saw a visiting car skid on slushy snow and slam into the filling station petrol pump. We knew it was time to return to Cynwyd and get warm and dry in the Blue Lion's lounge. Public houses take on a more welcoming appearance and attitude to locals and visitors at Christmastime. The austerity of saloon bar and smoke room are decorated sparingly. Large plates of sandwiches circle the room to keep the punters impressed. After a cold, invigorating stroll in the crisp snow, the visitor enjoys a warmer, inclusive ambiance. There is room at the inn and wanderers are always welcomed into the bosom of the spirited atmosphere – even in Wales.

Chapter Six

1965

Age: 24.

Home: Cherry Tree Close, Trentham, Stoke.

Moved to Shrewsbury Road, Bomere Heath, Shrewsbury, Shropshire. (October).

Work: Reconstruction Dept., Kingsway, Stoke.

September: moved to Shropshire County Council, The Square, Shrewsbury, Shropshire.

Government: Labour.

Prime Minister: Harold Wilson.

Jan: Winston Churchill dies.

Feb: United States bomb North Vietnam. Black Muslim Malcolm X shot dead. Mar: First Soviet space walk.

Aug: Civil Rights riots spread across America.

Oct: Anti-Vietnam War demonstrations. Search of Saddleworth Moors for Myra Hindley/Ian Brady's victims, Wilson talks with Ian Smith. MBEs for the Beatles.

Nov: Death penalty abolished, Rhodesia declares UDI, Cassius Clay/Muhammad Ali defeats Floyd Patterson.

Films: *The Spy Who Came In From The Cold, Dr Zhivago, The Sound of Music.*

Winston Churchill, our British Bulldog, dies; serving soldier in World War I and commanding hero of World War II, this inspirational leader was thrown out of office in the election of 1946, the victim, probably, of a changing class society, failing expectations and the lingering privations at the end of wartime hostilities. Replaced by a Labour Government, then Tory, the politics have changed and changed again with a long run of Conservatism. Now we are back with a pipe-smoking, Gannex overcoat-wearing Labour man whose chuckling, chortling, northern voice seems to have the beating of a landed gentry, in carping parliamentary debate. America, in their typical paranoia of Communism, enters North Vietnam, replacing the French, and begins a war of fire and defoliation in a fight against the running sore of the Vietcong. Ever keen on banner titles, they call the war Rolling Thunder. It will last a long time! [Since, they have invaded Iraq, under the titles, Desert Storm and Shock and Awe. As I write in 2007, their president, George W Bush, could be described as Strutting Stupidity. The Soviets continue to dominate in space travel technology with the first extra vehicular activity – or 'space walk' to the unscientific – by Alexei Leonov. The Vietnam War demonstrations increased in intensity, both in the United States and Britain. We had grainy television images of the sombre search for children possibly buried on Saddleworth Moors, High Peak. The clusters of caped policemen and lines of Black Marias, drawn up along lonely moorland roads, gave an impression to the lover of countryside of sad, hopeless incongruity. Myra Hindley and Ian Brady had tortured and murdered several children in a Manchester suburb. Capital punishment was abolished later. Harold Wilson gave MBEs to the Beatles four, much to the consternation of the gentry swathed in their privilege, grand estate and high office. Our ears were assaulted by the boastful ravings of a coloured American upstart, Cassius Clay, as he whipped peek-a-boo Floyd Patterson to claim the world heavyweight boxing prize. Few people remembered that the Louisville Lip, later naming himself Muhammad Ali, had, beforehand, won a gold medal in the 1960 Rome Olympic Games.

*

Ralph Salt and Roy Deakin gave another taped slide show to Cartwright House; an account of their 1964 adventures in Scotland, on the *Road to the Isles.* Our very first weekend of the year was a tramps' cycle run to

Rudyard Lake youth hostel. Led by a decidedly scruffy Phil Hughes, a good turnout of fifteen 'gentlemen of the road' gathered on the garage forecourt at the bottom of Limekiln Bank, Bucknall. An *Evening Sentinel* photographer was on hand to record the scene. Joe Ball wore a top hat with the top hinged like a lid and smoked a clay pipe, the very image of a quintessentially down-at-heel bum! Paul Leese and Clive Salt smeared their faces with burnt cork; looking more like Middle Eastern terrorists than tramps. Ralph Salt and Pete Boardman sported trilby hats in advanced stages of disintegration and Cliff Yates, a flat, 'ecky-thump' flat cap, looking like he had just finished a hard shift at t'mill. In quite deep snow, thankfully turning to slush on the road to Leek, we whirled along with the flapping of old macs' and wind whistling through our holey trousers. In the Leek branch of Woolworths, Phil Hughes stalked the wooden aisles asking girly, blushing counter assistants if he could purchase a bar of soap! Dutifully, from behind the trays of dolly mixtures and love hearts, they extended a shaking digit and with fluttering eyelashes, pointed towards the pharmacy section.

The Cyclists Dinner had, since January 1964, been held at the Black Lion pub set deep in the Churnet Valley, at Consall Forge. Mr Thomas Plant, the landlord, welcomed us *en masse* for an increase in custom in January, in an otherwise slack time for visitors. The inn faced a scattered group of cottages beyond the Cauldon Canal and disused railway, no doubt from where he drew his wintertime drinking locals. Mrs Plant provided us with a grand lunch, served upstairs at a long table; basically meat and two veg and a sweet of tinned fruit and thick yellow custard. Each cyclist had a pint glass of bitter beer at his and her elbow, but the meal took on a special character, merely because it was close to Christmas; it was our very own Dinner and we had to run the gauntlet of a certain landowner, Mr William Podmore, to even get there! The easier approach to the place was down his private drive; we crept, quiet as mice, down the dirt track with a strictly enforced silence, not daring to breathe, exhaling only when we'd passed the hillside property of Consall Old Hall and clear of any confrontation. I believe he allowed the valley dwellers to access their cottages, but any other visitors were unwelcome. This did not stop him opening his 'no through road' to visitors some years later when he would charge them for visiting his hidden Consall Hall Landscape Gardens.

After aperitifs of pints of ale in the bar, at a signal from Mrs Plant, we would shuffle upstairs and feed ourselves between bench and table to wait in bated expectation for the forthcoming meal. Roy Hazeldine, as secretary, took the head of the table, with his brother, Eric, getting involved in a good-natured scuffle for a seat at the other end. Despite the mass catering, the meals were always piping hot and tasty. So hot, in fact, that Derek Latham once burned the roof of his mouth on a scalding Brussels sprout! Elbow to elbow, thigh to thigh, we fed off plain plates on a vast paper tablecloth, conversation flowing with the drinks, interspersed with the scrape of cutlery on pottery. Outside, through bare, plain sash windows, the daylight faded in the short, cold, winter afternoon. Presently, we all went down to the lounge and carried on drinking; singing away the afternoon until opening time again. It was closing time, but we were considered residents! With afternoon fading into evening and drinks taking their effect, our folk singing degraded into bawdiness, culminating in utter lewdness. A popular song was *The Wild West Show* where each verse being a monologue, was enthusiastically orated by each member in turn. *Ladies and Gentlemen, here we have the oomigooli bird/ The oomi-gooli bird has a two foot neck, but legs only two inches long/And when it lands on a hot, tin, corrugated roof it shouts/Oooh, me goolies!* The chorus was cheerfully bellowed, *We're off to see the Wild West Show/The elephant and the kangeroo-oo-oo/Never mind the weather, as long as we're together/We're off to see the Wild West Show.* Another popular song sung with beer-lubricated larynges and suitable lascivious zeal, was titled, *Oh, Sir Jasper.* The first line of the verse, *Oh, Sir Jasper, do not touch me* [sung three times], was followed by a last line, *As she laybetweenthe lily-white sheets with nothing on at all.* With each verse, the last word of the line, *Oh, Sir Jasper, do not touch me* was subtracted in sequence, progressing through, *Oh, Sir Jasper, do not touch,* to the very last verse merely comprising the word *Oh!* Due to fervent, beer-fed enthusiasm, the last word would end with a drawn-out, climactic *O00000000gh!* With the song's chords reaching their dying conclusion, we returned to the beer and fags. What children we were in those heady days! Typical male hedonism and machismo. But they were just funny songs. *Oh, Sir Jasper* conjured up a vision of a caped, hunch-backed pervert sporting a twitching moustache straight from the Vaudeville stage. Regarding his terrified mistress or quaking French maid, I couldn't possibly comment! It just shows how one's behaviour could degenerate after drinking one too many.

While Dave Joynson played his guitar with a Dylan-style harmonica halter strapped to his chest, Clive Salt kept us all in perfect time with his tambourine accompaniment. Brother Ralph was the chief vocalist, while Roy Deakin added quality and style to the proceedings with a tight, lively mandolin. Songs from English, Scottish and Irish folk history reverberated around the lounge while songbooks were in danger from beer spillage and overflowing ashtrays. Songs of civil wars, songs of the seven seas, protest songs of these Ban the Bomb times. Every Irish rebel song was sung with an enthusiasm where we imagined ourselves behind the Thompson gun. *Young Roddy McCorley* was delivered while we imagined The Troubles and the Black and Tans. Every sea shanty was belted out as if we were hauling on the mainsail sheets. *Shoal of Herring* relived the cold tang of the sea and the bulging, dripping nets. Deep Southern American protest ballads rang out in titles such as *Pick a Bale of Cotton, All My Trials* and the mercenary soldier's song, *With God on Our Side.* Even the southern US States protest song *Corn Bread Peas & Black Molasses,* although relatively unknown, gained popularity with our crowd.

It was while watching Dave strum to our songs that I had the idea of making my own guitar. I had become quite handy at elementary woodwork; notwithstanding my school workshop efforts and proceeded to gather the materials; plywood and softwood for the fingerboard and fret wire, bought from a music shop, together with tuning machine heads. To space the frets correctly, I took a tracing off Dave's guitar and armed with crosscut and tenon saws, chisel and clamps, I steam-bent the sides and fixed everything together with strong glue. The finished product couldn't be described as beautiful, but, apart from the fingerboard warping into a banana-shape, was playable and capable of providing reasonable chords. Dave was aghast at my efforts and heaped on bountiful praise, although his laughing probably hid a genuine incredulity. Most important of all, it gave me the concentrated enthusiasm to learn to play chords, accompany the singing and I duly purchased a proper instrument a year or so afterwards.

A couple of the cyclists, Roy Deakin and Ralph Salt, bought handmade tricycles from Jack Taylor Cycles, built somewhere in Yorkshire – Leeds, I think – and finished to a fine standard. Fondly nicknamed 'barrows', the three-wheeled trikes were even raced, but mainly against the clock. A road race involving a mass pile-up would be too awful to contemplate – a chaotic tangling of metal that could easily end in multiple dismembering, if not beheading. On a late March weekend, we went to Chaddesley Corbett, an interesting, large village in Worcestershire full of quaint, timber-framed buildings. We all had to try out Roy's trike (Ralph's being far too large; his seat pillar extending a good ten inches out of the frame)., and trundle up and down the High Street. My efforts proved pathetic as I was unable to steer out of the nearside gutter; forever being pulled by the camber and stalling by the kerbside, the front and nearside wheels jammed and were immovable. Dave Hope spun up and down the street wearing black shorts, white socks and a confident, supercilious grin. I had ridden a kiddie's tricycle many years before at home, tootling around the lawn and along the garden path, fully in the childlike land of pretend, but this awkward adult brute proved impossible to control!

At Easter any year, a toss of the coin to experience good weather, we decided on cycling on the Isle of Man. The island, being about 30 miles (48k).long and 12 miles (20k).wide, was considered an ideal place to tour on the bikes over an extended weekend. The choice of this Irish Sea island proved popular, with a party of at least a dozen cyclists stopping at Chester youth hostel on the Thursday night before Good Friday and covering the shorter distance to Birkenhead with relative ease. We chose the island on three occasions, in 1965, 1967 and 1968 respectively; having an unconscious fascination with the governing independence of the place, its rich folklore and historical associations with Norse explorers and raiders. I, personally, knew of Ellan Vannin by not just the Manx cat, the administration of the birch to miscreants, but my brother Ken's interest in the June Tourist Trophy motorcycle races. I knew of toast-rack trams, Ramsey hairpin, Snaefell mountain and Creg-ny-Baa corner by reading articles in the magazine, *Motorcycling*. With Ken following the races so enthusiastically, I knew of Bray Hill, Ginger Hall, Ballaugh Bridge and Kirk Michael, but the rest of the island remained a mystery, especially to the south. Those were the days of Bob McIntyre, Geoff Duke, Mike Hailwood, Phil Read and later, John Surtees and the Italian Agostini on fabulous machines like the MV Augusta and Gilera. The days of scratchy celluloid showing the racing ukulele player, George Formby, followed by Manx Nortons were beginning to disappear.

The ferry across the Mersey saw a bright, brisk and bracing morning with the river shining silver upstream towards industrial Ellesmere Port; the sun reflecting off the freshly painted boat's railings and the occasional dip of a seagull's wing as it slid alongside, above the brown, tidal waters. The massive Liver, Cunard and Port of Liverpool Authority Buildings, concentrating the importance of the shipping port and trading of merchants and men; stood tall and domineering above the horizontal warehouses, wharfs and piers of the marine terminus. We walked the bicycles down ramps and stepped onto the wooden jetty before boarding the Isle of Man Steam Packet Company's vessel. Liverpool's buildings, derricks and chimneys receded astern as we were soon out of the widening estuary and sailing into the wide expanses of the Irish Sea; bows pointing resolutely towards 'The Island' and Douglas. Just as we would stay in the guard's van on train journeys, we congregated on the poop deck of the ferry, at the stern railings. The Isle of Man was, obviously, a popular venue for the group, as a photograph shows no less than sixteen of our party clustered together and wrapped up in hats, scarves and long trousers to withstand the rawness of the open sea breezes in mid-channel.

From Douglas, our route north followed the Manx Electric Railway through Laxey, the narrow gauge rails, ornate support poles and overhead wires crossing and re-crossing the roadway, until we reached the hostel on Ramsey's seafront. The building was one of a terrace of typical seaside properties four storeys high and a basement for the bicycles. Our initial experiences of the Isle of Man, particularly the architecture, were of a place barely emerging from the grand days of Victorian seaside society.

It wasn't long before we had left the main coastal road and turned into Sulby Glen, passing the reservoir for the gradual climb to The Bungalow, under the misty top of Snaefell, 2,064 feet (620m)., and serviced by a mountain railway from Laxey. The Isle of Man is so compact that even the run south to Port Erin, including a stop at Peel, is an easy afternoon's ride. Peel Castle and harbour is the fortified site for past Viking landings; the town organising an annual orgy of torch-lit, horned-helmet parades, the burning of long boats and the quaffing of gallons of ale. There may have been pillaging, raping and ravishing, but behaviour such as that probably went on behind closed doors! Just like another usual Saturday night in any English town really! The amalgamation of horned helmets, waterfalls of beer, studded ornaments, tattered clothing and lashed-up Manx motorcycles probably explains the cartoon character,*Ogri,*that lovable, rough 'greaser' and his comic strip adventures in motorcycle magazines.

The extreme south end of the island is dominated by South Barrule and beyond Castletown, the cliff scenery becomes more spectacular, with the rocky island of the Calf of Man forming a bold punctuation mark. We found the landscape and architecture of this area similar to Cornwall, with its dry stone walling, heather-covered slopes and longhouses reminiscent of, say, Bodmin Moor. There was also a scattering of cottage curio shops claiming associations with witchcraft and the occult, pentangles and John Barleycorn; again, similar to Cornish folklore. The third and last hostel visited was at Laxey. The Laxey Wheel at the back of the small town towers precariously from its wooden scaffold and stone tower within the slopes of the glen; an overshot waterwheel with a diameter so large that it beggars belief! A contrivance that more resembles a Ferris wheel. It would have been great to see it turn under the force of water, but I suppose, considering Health and Safety regulations, even in 1965 this was out of the question that day. Or maybe it wasn't even meant to turn, being merely a spectacular replacement for a former, smaller millwheel? I gathered later that it is set to work on a few days throughout the year for demonstration purposes. Using the hostels of Ramsey, Port Erin and Laxey, our tour was complete and we boarded the ferry at Douglas Harbour and bade a fond farewell to the independent land of the three legs.

*

Ralph had mentioned the Roman Steps on several occasions previously. He really was the driving force behind our rough-stuff explorations; probably spending hours crouched over a detailed map, looking for the slightest trace of a dashed line, preferably miles from anywhere and leading through wild countryside. He, Dave Hope, Geoff Cartlidge, Pete Boardman, Tony Ross and I cycled out to Harlech by way of a usual Friday night's stop at Shrewsbury. Our aim was to climb the Roman Steps, an ancient miner's track through the Rhinog Mountains.

The approach road near Llanbedr is narrow, twisting and constantly undulating; passing small farmyards and barns, hillocks and ponds, in a crazy route into the hills. At times, the route seemed to double back on itself in an effort to dive between old, stone farm buildings en route. At one point we were confronted by a loose bullock. The steps start in the Rhinog Mountains, close to the shore of Llyn Cwm Bychan and ascend by a series of flat stones resembling a very rough staircase bordered by scrubby heather, to a gap in the skyline. The visitors to the Llyn are soon left behind as the uncertain route starts its climb. The area was probably mined for ironstone by the Romans, with this link forming a sort of Welsh *via ferrata.* We struggled upwards, constantly lifting the bikes over high steps; banging and cutting the backs of the legs on the vicious, steel, rat-trap pedals, an excruciating pain to the fleshy calves made worse by, invariably, the smearing of oil from an errant, unshipped cycle chain. With a loaded saddlebag pulling the rear of the bike down, we would have to wrestle with a front wheel bucking madly into the air. As we gained height, the adjoining mountainsides encroached; an incredibly shattered landscape of loose boulders, mostly hidden by thick clumps of bracken. Larger platforms of rock, smooth-surfaced but for wandering cracks, lying alongside the steps at canted angles, were begging to be scaled if we were just walking; carrying rucksacks and not wheeling bicycles. We often enjoyed the sport of 'bouldering', i.e. scrambling over large rock boulders with little risk of personal injury, therefore, these ramped, mountain erratics offered an attractive diversion. Back home, in the confines of a temporary darkroom, I could process my own black-and-white photographs. Any easy walking over a rocky, almost horizontal slope could be turned into the scaling of a death-defying overhang by the right-angled twist of the masking frame!

At the summit of the stone staircase, we regrouped and took a break to rest the arms, rub sore legs and admire the view east towards Trawsfynydd and the moors above Ffestiniog. No doubt a slug of water from the feeding bottle and draw on a cigarette would be enough to celebrate our conquering of yet another classic rough-stuff route; studiously discovered by Ralph's enthusiastic map scrutiny. The pass opened out on to a boulder and heather-strewn stepped mountainside and it wasn't long before we had lost height and navigated a course between young forestry, finally reaching rides between more mature pines and the main road from Dolgellau to Ffestiniog. The difficulty of negotiating Forestry Commission plantations of young trees is coping with the numerous drainage ditches; not too deep, but banked with loose earth; ever ready to cause stumbling. Eventually, forest tracks can be found in the more mature sections of the plantation and their wide, stony routes ridden with ease. Owning vast areas of land, the Commission have cloaked millions of acres with their woody cash crop. Only recently have they incorporated slow-growing, wildlife-friendly broadleaf species at their coop edges. Their primary aim then was to produce fast-growing, marketable timber and hang the consequences! The ground under Norway spruce is virtually dead and no benefit to wildlife whatsoever. Perhaps the Kielder Forest is the worst example – and they even construct visitor centres to acknowledge their landscaping achievements – a feeling of guilt perhaps?

We turned east and climbed the moors on our way to Bala. The day had been bright with occasional sunny intervals but now, by late afternoon, the sky had cleared completely to leave an arc of blue to the horizon. We looked over our shoulders towards the mountains just left and the Rhinogs ridge, comprising three shapely peaks in line, were visible as blue, inverted anvil-shaped monoliths against the bright, hazy, western sky. Shadows were cast in front as we spun along the open miles to Bala, swooping over the exposed roads between the Arenigs and Llyn Celyn, towards our last hostel of the weekend; those receding blue hills behind us so well remembered.

The very next weekend was a route so completely different. Lichfield on Friday evening and the long haul to Houghton Mill in Cambridgeshire, taking most of Saturday. Located beyond Huntingdon, the hostel was a typical clapboard-clad water mill so often seen in the lowlands of Cambridgeshire and Suffolk, sitting astride the river with a granary lift set at second floor level. The mill and setting was similar to John Constable's paintings, *Flatford Mill* and *The Hay Wain;*the landscape typical of slow-running waterways, sculling waterfowl and riverside osiers.

At Lichfield hostel, we collected the cycles from the bike shed, including the tandem ridden by Ralph Salt and Derek Latham, and checked saddlebags and tyre pressures before our long miles heading south-east across the Midlands. The tandem was acquired from Derek's girlfriend's family and was, therefore, another form of cycling we had to get used to. A youth wearing a duffle jacket; a duffle bag slung over the shoulder; walked up to the shed and manoeuvred his little Honda monkey bike out the door and followed us down the road. We told him of our destination and he said that he'd race us over the distance. Not the true spirit of the YHA, but a challenge nevertheless. The monkey bike led the tandem and the rest of us were drawn along in the slipstream of a fast-moving express. With knees drawn up to the chin and chin pointing resolutely over the handlebars, our friend coaxed his 50cc machine to its optimum speed, looking very much like the gauche, spotty youth who rode a moped in the motorcycling comic strip,*Ogri*. Derek as helmsman at the front and Ralph as engine room stoker behind, pedalling a large gear and tucked into a streamlined position, streaked down the road, inches away from the Honda's rear mudguard. In contrast to the motorcyclist's urgent, upright and begging position, Derek and Ralph resembled hungry greyhounds close on their prey and baying for blood! Or could they be wolfhounds slavering at the mouth? They were two tall, well-built and fit fellows who found no problem in powering the tandem along at a staggering rate, hour after hour.

The rest of us, pedalling in grateful ease, taking advantage of this fast-moving pace, were drawn along in the slipstream eddies created, careful not to touch wheels in front, or saddlebags to the side. Years before, while trying to learn mathematics at Hanley High School, I listened to our form master, Mr Johnson, trying to explain aerodynamics, as he related his tale of a dangerous cycling interlude. In keeping behind a fast moving lorry, he found himself drawn along at a frightening 50 miles per hour (80kph)., sucked along by the slipstream, unable to escape! Being of a gentle but scatterbrained nature, Mr Johnson was respectfully listened to before the whole class muttered, "Yeah, too right", behind the hand.

Mile after mile, we covered the tarmac at a blistering pace. Signposts, road signs, hedgerows and houses flashed by in a bewildering procession. We shifted up through the gears, pedalling with fury and sometimes having to freewheel when pumping legs became a blur. Overtaking cars were finding their manoeuvre taking an agonisingly long time. The Honda's engine screamed at top revolutions and the rider's arse was only inches away from the hot blacktop! I'm sure our average speed exceeded 20mph (32kph)., a pace described as 'evens' in cycling club parlance; probably reaching over and above that speed in short, downhill bursts. When the valiant Honda and rider needed refuelling, we carried on up the road at a greatly reduced speed, waiting until our motor pacer rejoined and battle could be recommenced. The whole of the ride resembled the motor-paced derney race often terminating the professional six-day, indoor track meetings. We swung through the entrance gates at the mill, tyres crunching on the gravel drive and braked to a dusty stop with the monkey bike's engine glowing in iridescent heat. As it cooled in quiet, ticking rest, our brave rider stalked into the hostel, po-shaped crash hat hidden behind his back, well away from the warden's inquisitive gaze.

Not everything was friendly; not everyone 'got on' within our group. Some of us resented the boisterous behaviour of Phil Hughes at certain times; his over-enthusiastic joking and rough-and-tumble horseplay not going down too well with Brian, Geoff, Chris and myself. But this was Phil's whole character – loud and laughable – taking over and dominating the total spirit of any situation. The atmosphere between us degenerated, as often happens within a tightly-knit, mixed group, until, one evening in the Unicorn Inn, Piccadilly, after one of the Cartwright House meetings; I mentioned to Phil that he was getting on peoples' nerves. Standing alongside at the toilet urinal, he accepted my opinions and actually applauded me for being straight with him, being man enough for bringing the problem to his attention; speaking candidly for the others and acting as their collective voice. I was humbled and appreciated his graciousness and had to ask myself, "What on earth is this business all about?" Phil was the life and soul of the party on many weekends and it was, probably, our behaviour that had been unreasonable! Shaking off the drips and adjusting my dress, I rejoined the group, lifted my pint, but said nothing of our cloistered discussion in the toilets.

I recall another disagreement occurring at the Cyclist's Dinner one January. A few of us became alarmed at the sheer number of hours spent drinking through the afternoon after the midday meal and decided to leave the Black Lion, and make our way home while daylight remained. Six of us moderately temperate souls, fuelled with numerous pints of bitter beer, tried to climb the steep staircase of snow-covered steps out of the Churnet Valley and make our way to the nearest road. Unfortunately, we had taken the wrong direction and we couldn't face the struggle through deep snow to reach civilization. In gathering gloom and with the threat of snowfall, we returned to the Black Lion and resumed drinking as if nothing had happened; drowning our dented pride in Mr Plant's excellent Double Diamond. We finally left the inn on the easier route, later and this time, all together. These were the only times I remember being particularly disagreeable. Considering the innumerable occasions for conflict; difficult and arduous routes, sweltering weather, drenching rainstorms, crashes and mechanical failure; I can't remember any other serious arguments. Considering the occasions for disagreement, there were very few times when cross words were exchanged.

I believe it was Ralph who suggested we tour on the Continent in July, 1965. Dave Hope was keen to improve his suntan – even though, being of mixed-race,he was already nut-brown, but wanted to show-off to his brick-laying colleagues. I also think that he wished to name-drop and boast about his Mediterranean tan. Introduce a touch of sophistication by mentioning some South of France place names. Ironically, we would not even reach the Med on our proposed itinerary. We decided to tour a route through the French and Spanish Pyrenees, following the Route de Haute Pyrenees, and climb several of the Tour de France passes. The thought of including Spain added a touch of the unknown, apart from the prospect of ridiculously low prices for food and accommodation. The assembled cyclists, therefore, were Ralph Salt, Dave Hope, Geoff Cartlidge, Roy Deakin, Tony Ross, Pete Boardman, Chris Warren and myself; eight keen and fit pedallers excited in expectation of climbing the famous cols of 'Le Tour'; feeling the gradients that tested the great mountain climbers, Federico Bahamontes, Fausto Coppi, Charly Gaul, Louison Bobet, Englishman, Tom Simpson and, of course, our very own Ralph Salt.

Ralph booked the relevant tickets using a service provided by the Cyclist's Touring Club (CTC).and I purchased the detailed Michelin maps covering a route from Pau in south-west France, into Spain and the minute mountain-ringed country of Andorra, terminating again in France, at Carcassonne. The CTC provided, and still provides many services for the downtrodden cyclist; route details, ticket reservations, insurance, legal representation and arranges graded, local club runs in midweek. Locally, meetings and socials are also arranged and cyclists' cafes listed in a useful handbook; in short, a very worthwhile organisation formed exclusively for the two-wheeler.

Each year, a CTC rally is held on the Knavesmire Racecourse at York. The camping weekend includes various competitions, demonstrations, exhibitions and even parades of Bicycle Belles for the girls and Knobbliest Knees for the boys. There are even prizes for the furthest person to cycle to York. Together with the grandness of York's Roman walls, streets, museums and the Minster – the York Rally is a meeting of enthusiasts, a marvellous event indeed! Our cycling members' interests and allegiances fell, metaphorically speaking, somewhere between the YHA and CTC.

The Michelin maps, distinctive with their yellow covers and using metric scales, were flimsy in comparison with the Ordnance Survey. Unfolded, they stretched out in multiple folds to a great length, their thin paper liable to be caught by the merest zephyr of a breeze. In detail, though, they were more than adequate for our purposes and showed the multiple hairpin bends of the famous cols with all heights in metres and all distances in kilometres. To study the map's key provided a lesson in French, while the constant calculation from kilometres to miles and metres to feet kept Ralph and me sharp in literacy and numeracy! Not that Ralph's skill as an auditor needed any honing. As regards to usefulness and having studied Spanish at school, I suppose I could be considered a language expert, although Roy Deakin was our chief interpreter in French, being a bank clerk and having the right sort of mouthed sneer. Further expertise existed and character traits abounded with Geoff Cartlidge, who provided a sufficient hatred of everything Gallic, thereby keeping us on our guard, delivered with a dry sense of humour; Chris Warren kept us all in stitches of laughter; Pete Boardman followed our every move with dogged trust and Tony Ross, being of Italian descent, contributed with enthusiasm and snippets of useless Latin. Sorry, Tony! (A few years later, our group, re-named as the Wayfarers with its diverse professional experience, could be jokinglyconsidered the perfectly qualified gang to pull off a significant bank raid). [Myself, being a draughtsman, would have been suitably qualified to provide both mapping and forgery, if and when required.]

With travel tickets booked for trains and ferries, our individual responsibility lay in gathering full ten year passports. We received those large, dark-blue ones that breathed British Empire appeared exclusively officious and where the Queen herself asked for the bearer's due assistance and safe passage. Not those miserably small, red, EU ones that we had to accept years later. A small amount of French francs and Spanish pesetas were provided through the good offices of Roy and his employer, the Trustee Savings Bank. In 1965, the rate of exchange for France was Ff16.6 (1,660 old francs).to £1, and for Spain, 160 pesetas to £1. Paying lip service to first aid requirements, I packed two cartons of Beechams Powders; considered the panacea of all ills, be it blocked-up or too loose and a packet of Silvasun sun protection tablets. I wasn't sure how these could give protection from the glaring Spanish ultra-violet rays, but the others informed me that they were the latest thing and obviated the application of oil. Two thin Collins phrasebooks were added to my list of items to take, although, on glancing through the pages, they were more suited to a holiday using hotel accommodation and luxury travel.

Passport, money, tickets were acquired – the essentials not to forget when packing the saddlebag and looking forward to a holiday on the Continent. Seven of us caught the train from Stoke station in early afternoon on Friday 9th July after meeting at the Roebuck Hotel nearby, close to Glebe Street bridge. Arriving at Euston, London at teatime, we cycled across the city via Piccadilly Circus, Trafalgar Square and Westminster to meet Roy Deakin on the Embankment. He had travelled down a day before to meet up with a long lost friend and we joined him later as prearranged. Victoria Station was as chaotic as ever when we located the Goods Registration office and duly booked and labelled eight clean and shiny bicycles. The hurried, frenetic atmosphere of a London rail terminus; scurrying travellers, departing trains, blurred, barely audible public announcements and the hurried checking of baggage, in our case, saddlebags, brought it home to us provincials that this was the main link with the Continent. A few years before, we had revelled in the glory of the Golden Arrow, the Southern Region's Thanet Belle and years before that, trunks and battered valises marked the Dover Boat Train. We identified with what must have been the romance and excitement for the prospect of travel to foreign lands. Victoria Station, despite a more modern setting, still held that excitement. The atmospheric golden age of travel was almost tangible, soaked into the smut-covered station stonework. Our train pulled away from the platform and the busy scurrying of passengers, carrying us through Kent to the Channel ferry at Newhaven.

The CF *Villandray* sailed at midnight and our crossing was spent either at the ship's bar or being astounded by the low prices on display in the duty-free shop. Ralph couldn't believe how cheap were the cartons of two hundred Gauloises Caporal; stubby, plain cigarettes loosely filled with dark tobacco, having a distinct flavour of working-class France; a taste that turned the mouth into a searing furnace and the back of the throat into a sheet of course emery cloth. I enjoyed them in moderation, but, in comparison, they turned an English Player's Number Six into a soothing balm! Ralph unpeeled one of the two packs of two hunded, extracted a decidedly loose blue paper pack of twenty cigarettes and offered them around. We didn't like them at first but I accepted a few so as not to appear churlish. Ralph thought them horrible but persevered as he had another three hundred and ninety-eight to draw on! In the cold, small hours of Saturday morning we docked at Dieppe, disembarked and crossed the few yards to our train at Dieppe Maritime. French railways, the *Societé Nationale de Chemin de Fer Francais,* (SNCF)., have a system of ticket numbering where one can easily find what coach and couchette must be accessed. Coach number and destination are clearly displayed in mid-coachpanels. The low platform and steep steps to enter the *Wagon-Lits,* together with the severe, utilitarian grey-green colour of the rolling stock, gave an instant atmosphere of past, wartime privations, if not thoughts of Fifth Columnist travelling spies!

We settled onto the two green, plastic bench seats as our train jerked twice before starting out on its long journey to Paris. Our initial progress was at a snail's pace as the long train rumbled over quayside dock rails and points and appeared to travel down the middle of harbour-side streets.

Chris Warren, always ready to see the funny side of any situation, laughingly pointed out a typical French gendarme; black cape, pill-box hat, swinging baton hanging from the belt and whistle to the lips; a perfect example from the *Pink Panther* film's depiction of lower-ranked officers, gave a yelpof derisory laughter. He asked why we were moving down the street before collapsing in spasms of mirth when we passed a flashing miniature traffic island! Geoff commented in supercilious tones and with a desert-dry wit, "It *may* take a very long time to reach Paris!" I nearly choked on my precious bottle of orangeade, a drink with the off-putting label, Pshtt! – a title, no doubt, to mimic the sound of the gassy drink being opened. It was all going to be very strange and foreign. The strangeness of being on foreign soil for the first time saw us descend into nervous silliness.

After a snatched period of sleep, interrupted by the occasional clanging bell of a country level crossing, it was daylight and morning as we rolled over the flat plains of northern France. Basic ablutions were attempted in the end-of-coach toilet – a cramped, dirty, bucking hell-hole of a place where one could peer down the lavatory pan to the rushing gravel and sleepers below. It was to be a fitting introduction to French sanitary conditions with city street *pissoirs* and squatting toilets. We lifted the bunk beds, snapping them shut against the compartment walls, collected together our belongings and readied ourselves for the arrival at Paris, St Lazare at 6:30am.

After reclaiming the bicycles, strapping on the saddlebags and exiting the station, we prepared ourselves for the first few yards on French streets. Number one rule was to 'keep right'; keep right at all costs, a rule instantly forgotten as we were swept along the station's concourse in a rushing tide of hooting cars and jay-walking pedestrians. We headed downhill, towards the Seine, along busy, narrow streets of cobblestones, surrounded by a flurry of scratched and dented traffic, while Parisian street facades squeezed in on both sides, decorated at kerb level with a kaleidoscope of cafés, tables, chairs, advertising signs, street signs, notices and kiosks. All this instant, French chaos was just visible in the corner of the eye as our main attention was focused on the back of a bus. It was one of those antiquated buses with an open platform at the rear; overflowing with blokes waving and shouting, calling out names of famous French racing cyclists and pointing in our direction. The sense of sight apart, our noses were assaulted by that typical smell of Gauloise, blocked drains and freshly-baked bread. Other senses were sharpened by the cacophony of sound; revving, honking cars, Gallic expletives and, yes, even accordion music. We felt the juddering roughness of the cobbles, transmitted through the forks, to our handlebar-grasping, sweating hands.

From the claustrophobic clutter of tight streets, we found ourselves spewed out into the open spaces of the Place de La Concorde. The morning was sunny and here, close to the River Seine, a breeze sprang up to cool the fevered brow. But not for long. We were changing stations; crossing the Paris streets to cycle from the Gare St Lazare in the north, to the Gare d'Austerlitz across the river.

Dismounting, (we unwisely considered it safer)., we dashed between five lanes of concentrated traffic, over two busy junctions, to gain a perceived route across the Seine towards the Gare d'Austerlitz. Changing traffic lights provided a few seconds of opportunity to enable us to make a desperate lunge for spaced gaps. Four or five roads intersected here and in a blinkered, almost suicidal dash, aware of snarling radiators and a symphony of irate horns, we somehow avoided the swerving motorcade to gain the sanctuary of refuges, before attaining our final deliverance, the far pavement. We crossed the bridge to reach the south bank while behind, the cavalcade of motorists rushed in a continuous, lemming-like determination to reach their desired places of work. Our next problem was not the traffic, but the language barrier.

Cycling parallel to the Seine, we approached the Gare d'Austerlitz and saw the words *ARRIVEES* above the grand entrance. Our attempts to register the cycles for the train to Pau met with uncomprehending, blank stares from the clerk behind his glass screen. Even Roy found it impossible to make him understand what we required. As time ticked towards the departure of our long distance express, at 8:05am precisely, Ralph became almost manic with frustration, cursing France and everything French. I distinctly heard Geoff mention de Gaulle and something about the war! It was only when the clerk pointed vaguely towards the other side of the platforms that we twigged. We had thought that *ARRIVEES* meant those turning up at the station to catch a train and not crack SNCF expresses reaching Paris from distant, exotic places. Although basic stupidity, we had succumbed to the nervousness of being confronted with a strange language. We dived out of the station and quickly located the entrance marked *DEPARTURES*. Registration was quick and efficient and soon we had found our *Wagon-Lits* and were sinking onto our couchette's benches, melting into piles of relief and wiping away sweat from the puckered and perplexed brows! After the hassle of traffic, station layout and passenger flow, even a proffered Gauloise from Ralph tasted of Heaven! French rail keep to exact time and so we were soon gliding away from Austerlitz, out through the suburbs; the flash of arcing electric reflecting off grim tenement walls, the roar of the powerful locomotive reverberating amongst the lines of not too clean washing. Leaning out of the window, our train seemed to be miles in length; passenger coaches, car carriers, goods wagons and, hopefully, an enclosed van containing our precious bicycles; the whole, snaking length clattering over innumerable points.

It was a very long journey from Paris to Pau, an elegant town almost at the foot of the Pyrenees. Mile after mile, hour after hour, our long train bisected the French countryside; the scenery getting ever hillier and the weather definitely getting hotter. Paris, Orleans, Tours, Poitiers and south to Bordeaux. Thick, midday cumulus clouds slowly shrank to cotton wool-sized puffs of white, numerous at first, but gradually separating and disappearing, in stark contrast to the ever-bluing summer sky; the temperature climbed inexorably within our compartment, creating an atmosphere of tobacco smoke stuffiness. Beyond Bordeaux, we passed through the region of the Landes Forest; the largest forested area in Europe. Dense swathes of close-planted pine trees alongside the railway had their boughs beaten backwards by the air pressure from the racing express – bending to the march of progress. From Dax, we turned in a south-easterly direction and finally, under a completely clear blue, late afternoon sky, slid to a halt beside the low platform at the Gare de Pau. At the front of the train, our locomotive stood quietly ticking; motor idling and turning the surrounding airwaves into a distorted heat mirage.

The heat bouncing off the bright, sun-baked platform was enough to take the breath away. After reclaiming the bikes and still wearing our long trousers, the short ride uphill into the *Centre Ville* brought globs of sweat to gather above the eyebrows. After booking bed and breakfast at a cheaper town hotel, the Hotel de Paris, we had time to find the famous Boulevard and admire the view to the south. We had to surrender our passports at the desk and fill out a travellers' form each for the French *Bureau de Tourisme.*

A complete chain of mountains could be discerned, shimmering out of the late afternoon sunshine ahead; spreading from horizon to horizon, with the upper slopes between vertiginous rock walls glinting with the reflections of un-melted snowfields. The High Pyrenean chain, with peaks spreading over the French border and deep into Spain, appeared as a continuous curtain-walled barrier, shimmering in the haze of a lowering sun. My thoughts turned to the time of the Spanish Civil War, before my time in 1936 and the International Brigade on their smuggled march over these mountains, guided over rock and snow, through high-level rain and blizzards, to fight General Franco and for the causes of anti-Fascist freedom. According to Agatha Christie, in her autobiography, the view of the Pyrenean Chain was positively overrated.

Having minimal French, we copied Roy and purchased bags of peaches for late sustenance; at least we wouldn't starve and would stay regular! The hotel bill came to Ffl0.50 (about 15/9 in old money – '75p in new).

Our route lay due south from Pau, passing up the Valle d'Ossau, through Gan, Rebinacq, Sevignacq, Louvie-Juzon and Bielle, to Laruns. In the village centre we found a grocery and apart from peaches, our vocabulary extended to cheese! Roy flourished his language skills by asking for a *sac de cord,* a string bag in which to carry his shopping. The wizened *Madame* gave him a polythene bag. So much for trying to be clever. Ralph bought tomatoes and what he thought was celery to supplement his intended salad picnic. It turned out to be some form of French asparagus shoots. The group's language abilities were progressing in jumps and staggers and would definitely improve when the ordering of drinks was required!

From Laruns, the road began its climb of the Col de l'Aubisque with the looming limestone peak of the Pic du Midi d'Ossau appearing in breaks of the forestry, at a height of 9,470 feet (2,886m).way ahead and above. Past the small spa town of Les Eaux Bonnes, the pass reared up in a serious manner. I remember looking upwards at one point where, through sweat-stinging eyes, I could perceive a crowd of people at a roadside bar. Their cheerful, faint chattering drifted down a thousand feet to my ears as they looked over the café's terrace railings, no doubt commenting on the plucky distant cyclists, many hairpin bends beneath them. I remember asking myself, "This road surely doesn't go up there, does it?" The pass, the Col de l'Aubisque, was our very first experience of continental mountain roads and with perspiration dripping onto the crossbar, I was quickly persuaded to select a lower gear, start 'twiddling' and avoid any desire to rush headlong towards a distant summit. Eventually, we passed the café at the hamlet of Gourette. A French cyclist stopped me here and tried to ask if I possessed a puncture outfit. Due to sweating waterfalls and feeling dizzy through being out of breath, I couldn't understand him at all, so had to pretend ignorance. It really was the fact that, without warning, I was embarrassed by being confronted by a foreign language. Despite his frantic, imploring signals, cupping my front tyre with one hand, I wasn't able to make sense of it. The brain seems to shut down when confronted by such sudden situations. Besides, the café's wall-mounted thermometer was registering F95 degrees (C38)!

Mile after mile, we slowly gained height; Ralph leading and the rest of us strung out over several kilometre stones. At last, the roadside trees thinned and we rolled out onto grassy alps with the shapely limestone peaks, the Pic de Ger and Penemadaa, both over 8,000 feet (2,468m)., protruding from the grass and scree like teeth at the heart of the range in the south. When one climbs above the tree line, the heart takes a leap when the brain knows that the summit cannot be too far away. Despite a sun-soaked landscape, barely cooled by high level breezes and clear views of the cruel, climbing road stretching ahead, we were relieved to be on the bare mountainside and making good progress. The top of the Aubisque arrived after innumerable low-gear pedal strokes and we passed the summit sign showing an elevation of 5,608 feet (1,709m). Arriving in dribs and drabs; or, should I say, dribbles and drabbles, seeing how much everyone was perspiring, we sat on the grass verge, pleased that our first serious climb had been conquered. Pete Boardman felt weak and sickly, so I immediately knew he lacked salt through sweat loss and with my miniscule knowledge of anything medical, advised him to drink a glass of salted water. Geoff sprinkled salt into his feeding bottle (Geoff always carried a double-ended salt and pepper container for seasoning picnics)., and Pete quaffed the mixture with gusto. After which, he immediately threw up into the roadside grass. However, it cured his nausea and we were ready to continue.

From the Col, we descended briefly to the Col de Soulor before crossing the Corniche, a cliff-hugging, high level road that passed through several cool, dark and wet tunnels. The road surface in these tunnels was pitted from the constantly dripping roof and although relatively short, they included a bend; not the easiest of conditions due to being blinded by plunging into blackness after being in bright sunlight. In fact, the experience was alarming as one struggled to catch a glimpse; a spark of light, indicating the point of the tunnel's exit before crashing into the rocky side walls. To compound the difficulty, several cows grazed outside the tunnel portals! We stopped for the night at the Hotel Edelweiss, low in the Valle des Arrens where bed, breakfast and an evening meal cost Ffl4.0 (£1.1s 0d in old money – 105p in new). Before taking a shower, I peeled off my racing vest of vivid red, white and blue banding, noticing the streaks of salt staining the armpits and back, and propped its stiffness up in the corner of the bedroom!

Next morning, Monday, we cycled through Argeles Gazost, Luz and Gedre, to the Ponte Napoleon in the Gorge de Luz St. Saveur. Deep in the valleys, the temperature and humidity were becoming unbearable and we sought drinks while Geoff had his camera fixed. I remember Ralph dousing himself in bottlefuls of tepid water; his soaked racing jersey providing a cooling effect when the dampness quickly evaporated. He shouted while shaking his streaming hair; shaking like a drying dog while the water splattered and steamed on the melting tarmac! We stayed the night in Gedre, having well-earned beers in the Hotel de la Grotte. The locals wanted to take Chris Warren on a donkey ride and snap his happy, laughing face! He was that sort of guy. On the morrow, we would cut deep into the mountains and visit the Cirque de Gavarnie, a half-circle of vertiginous rock faces; a natural, snow-shelved rampart close to the range's high Spanish border.

After passing the Chaos de Courmely and shopping in Gavarnie village, we took the well-worn track through scattered forest pines to rejoin the young Gav de Pau stream. The water was icy cold, but ideal for soothing hot feet. Many ponies passed by, having been hired back in Gedre and considered the ideal transport for approaching the Cirque. We, however, stuck to the bicycles and found the well-worn dirt tracks easy to ride after a history of past rough-stuff. Even from a distance of two miles, the Cirque de Gavarnie presented a spectacular, almost belittling scene. The enclosing, high amphitheatre of vertical, clean rock, at least five miles in length around the rim, was dissected horizontally by parallel terraces of snow banks. The topmost crests were being teased by small cumulus clouds, making their jagged outline disappear and reappear, giving them an air of mystery. The Breche de Roland; said to stem from a legendary sword cut; offered a summit doorway south and into the Spanish Ordesa National Park. We called at the hotel for drinks before walking over the snow slopes and towards the base of the cliffs. Our objective was to reach the foot of the Grande Cascade, a one thousand foot sheer drop of a waterfall that gave birth to the Gav de Pau. Of course, with that sort of drop, the water had been atomized long before the cliff's foot and we were left with just a fine cloud of soaking mist. The stream re-gathered and disappeared under banks of snow; crevassed and semi-melted to give the immediate area the threat of danger and a reason to be sure-footed. Not the easiest thing to be, considering our slipper-like cycling shoes. Dave Hope's camera wind-on broke, so, from then on I would take his holiday photographs, too. The day had provided scenery of the most spectacular kind and some months later, I would win a local YHA photographic competition using, as a subject, the Cirque; its eternal snows glinting in the midday sunshine, with a foreground of cool, green pine trees and pony-riding visitors. A superb day was rounded off by a stay at a small hotel in Bareges – B&B and evening meal costing Ff15.60 (£1.3s.6d in old money – 117p in new).

Today, Wednesday 14th July, Bastille Day in France, we climbed from Bareges to the summit of the Col du Tourmalet. Behind us towered the Pic d'Ardiden group of sharp peaks, 9,800 feet (2,986m)., splattered with last winter's snows and forming a suitable backdrop for cycling action photographs. The notorious Tourmalet, a lofty 6,960 feet (well over 2,000m)., was finally reached; the pot-holed road snaking its final hairpin bends to a summit defile between stone retaining walls. Walls that held back the shale scree slopes of neighbouring jagged peaks. The Col du Tourmalet had figured in many a past Tour de France race route, its steep, unfriendly gradients reducing hardened cyclists to gasping despair. We took an unsurfaced road from the summit, leading in a direct line to the base of the Pic du Midi de Bigorre. The going was hot and hard along this elevated, narrow and dusty track. Because of its narrowness, the route operated a timed, one-way system for cars and the yellow trackside dust had been swept into banks on the outside of each bend. Ahead, I noticed the route ascending the final mountain slopes in a series of ramps and hairpin turns; leading ever upwards to the towers and turrets of the Midi de Bigorre Observatory. The telescope domes flashed a reflected blazing sun in the clear blue sky. Ralph made the final climb but the rest of us, hot and thirsty, were content to turn back after appreciating the wonderful distant views. Besides, time was passing, we were getting hungry and our elevation had made the air thin. Lack of oxygen apart, Geoff, Dave and I still enjoyed a contemplative cigarette!

Back at the pass, a distinct-looking Frenchman (beret, agricultural-blue trousers and Gauloise clamped in his mouth).clambered out of his Citroen 2CV, unbuttoned his fly and answered the call of nature, relieving himself over the roadside safety barrier. We were shocked to the core but just had to accept the fact that this was France, and Bastille Day at that! As it often tended to do, my trusty Primus stove blazed out of control and had to be extinguished with a mighty kicking away. The trusty kettle-boiling companion was, however, brought back into service with a good greasing around the pump piston! In late afternoon, the clouds were forming a blanket of white in the valley below. Dropping towards Ste. Marie de Campan, we entered the mist and noticed the dramatic fall in temperature. Suddenly, road surfaces became greasy, bends had to be treated with respect, and hands and knees quickly became red and chilled. We were soon running through the tight streets of Ste. Marie, an attractive old town nestling deep in the valley between the Col du Tourmalet and Col d'Aspin, and seeking out a hotel with modest prices. Surprisingly, it was named the Hotel des Pyrenees!

The subsequent climbs of the Cols d'Aspin and Peyresourde would occupy us for the whole of the next day, 36 miles (58k).over two gentler and more verdant passes that gave us more time to gaze over the Pyrenean, mid-range peaks. Today we had climbed 4,890 feet, (1,490m).and descended 5,635 feet (1,717m)., arriving in Bagneres-de-Luchon after a lunchtime stop in Arreau. As it was drizzling at the time, we ate a basic meal whilst keeping dry under a convenient bus shelter roof.

Next day, in high humidity, the short but steep Col de Portillon brought us through dense roadside trees, wreathed in cloying mist, to cross the border and descend into sun and Spain at Bosost. On Spanish soil at last, I was keen to show off my abilities in the language. Show off to Dave Hope, in particular, when I kept asking him if there was anything he needed from the grocery shop in Las Bordas. Having, by then, a decent vocabulary, I was urging him to ask me for even the smallest item! Having attended Hanley High School for Boys and struggled to comprehend the acerbic whisperings of our Spanish master ,'Crowbait', my painfully acquired knowledge could not go to waste! I even tried out my Spanish on two inquisitive policemen who stared at us suspiciously through squinting eyes. *"Hay une sitio de camping cerca de aqui?"* I don't know why I was asking for a camp site – we carried no tents. They were stern Guardia Civil, dressed in smart grey-green uniforms, firearms at the ready and wearing those curious, shiny, jet-black hats that facilitated the slouching against a hacienda wall and able to take a siesta much easier! They answered with a stony, olive-complexioned silence while pointing vaguely up the valley! After the relative sophistication of the French villages, Las Bordas; sounding like the stereotypical, Western 'one-horse' town, was as rustic and run-down as its name suggested. The grocer's shop was a dark, confined cave overflowing with bucolic hardware; rat traps and barbed wire, as well as basic foodstuffs and sweeties, colourful enough to widen the dark eyes and whet the pleading desire of any young and little Spanish lad and lady. We were looking for sliced bread but the shop's closest equivalent was a sort of bread-like sweet cake.

Chris Warren, pointing at the rusticity of it all, particularly the outside electrics; wires joined and suspended in a spider's web of questionable safety, had us in continuous stitches. We paused by the banks of the Rio Garrona, below the Maladetta peaks, to take a lunch break. Chris opened his recently purchased tin of peaches in syrup and spooned the slices enthusiastically into his grinning mouth. Geoff Cartlidge told him a joke and we were treated to Chris, laughing and bent with choking convulsions, eject the offending peach-piece down his nose and back into the tin! In a time-stopping, breath-taking pause, we witness this unlikely anatomical feat in a mixture of concern and hilarity. Chris, with cheeks red and glistening, finally recovered his composure and we were ready to press onwards along the rougher roads of Spain.

It was sunny again when we eventually rolled into Viella, found accommodation at the Fonda Turrull, and used the Banco International de Luchon to convert our unused French francs into spare Spanish pesetas. As it was after nine o-clock before we would dine, Ralph, Dave, Chris and Tony joined me for a café omelette – *una tortilla* – and liking them immensely, I introduced them to the potato and onion edition. *Una tortilla Espanola con cebollas,* with, of course, a few glasses of *cerveza* to wash them down. Our night's stay with evening meal came to 120 pesetas (15/- in old money, 75p in new).

One week into the tour and we had already covered one hundred and seventy-one cycling miles (275k).in the French Pyrenees; not a vast distance, but it did include the climbing of five seriously long and high mountain passes. Today, Saturday, after a break in Salardu, we climbed the unsurfaced pass, the Puerto de La Bonaigua, 6,770 feet (2,063m).at its summit after innumerable hairpin bends. With eagles souring into a clear blue sky and the midday sun bouncing in a hot glare from the roadside rock and dirt, we climbed into the Parque Nationale de Aigues Tortes, enjoying excellent views of the Maladetta Massif with the Pic d'Aneto rising to 11,170 feet (3,404m).in all its snow-covered magnificence. From the pass, we descended towards Esterri d'Aneau and our night's stay in a very basic fonda.

From the grey and cream rock of limestone mountains; sharp and clean in outline, we were dropping into the red-brown sandstone country of more rounded peaks. We gradually descended into the deep canyon geography of the Noguera Parallesa river valley. Regaining a surfaced road, our accommodation at Esterri was as basic and quirky as to provide an essence of rural Spanish living conditions in their extreme. Crossing the bare floorboards of the bedroom, one was pitched forward, then back, as the timeworn building had sagged and settled through many a freezing cold mountain winter and boiling summer heat. Geoff, washing off the dust of the pass, caught an arm-jerking electric shock from his basin of cold water. These were the spartan, genuine conditions I relished when visiting a foreign country. Not for me the clean, antiseptic conformity of the expensive hotel, where one pays the earth and is mollycoddled in a blanket of falsely concerned commercialism. Myself and I believe the rest of the gang, preferred to smell, taste and feel the cultural differences. Regarding basic conditions, our bill for bed and evening meal totalled a staggering 75 pesetas (9/6d in old money, 48p in new).

Next day turned into an epic. From Esterri d'Aneau, we dropped slowly through Llavorsi and shopped in the tiny hamlet of Sort. After a brief rest, we unfolded the smaller-scale Michelin paper map of the area to find our intended route marked as a very fine line snaking between obscure, isolated hamlets, such as Vilamur, Las Lascunes and Rubio; crossing the watershed at a remote spot named the Col del Canto. Spidery roads shown as dashed lines wound across the sheet, barely connecting obscure hamlets, winding around vague areas of forestry, deep in hilly terrain but without contoured notation, hard to interpret. One hamlet, hidden in the fold of the map, was named 'Sex'! In a 'land that time forgot' tract of country, wedged between the Haute Pyrenees and the small Principality of Andorra, we searched for a road of some kind to take us in the general direction of Seo d'Urgell. After climbing on the narrowest of tracks, struggling through wiry scrub, we reached a flatter plateau. Suddenly, and to our surprise, we found a section of new, four-lane carriageway; smooth tarmac and freshly painted lane markings leading from nowhere to nowhere!

Unfortunately, the open highway ended after too few kilometres, blocked by a series of garish wooden barriers. Beyond lay more sandy tracks, slowly climbing through a barren landscape, until we thankfully gained the elevated Col del Canto. It was now late-afternoon and the sky was darkening by the minute. A dense blanket of white cumulus cloud filled the valley below, its angry edges spilling like cold fingers into the steep, forested side slopes. The sky overhead turned a sullen iron-grey; clouds rolling, billowing and pressing down upon our heads, threatening to enclose us completely. A wind whipped dust into life and we felt the first splosh of hail. Struggling with our plastic rain capes, we ducked as hailstones as large as golf balls, some even bigger, thudded into the ground, bounced off our capes and rapidly formed a deep layer of frozen, dirt-streaked mush. Heavy rumbling thunder approached from the Maladetta mountains, echoing off the surrounding heights, followed by forked lightning, dancing over the valley cloud beneath our feet. The surrounding air was streaked with thin lines of static electricity, zinging and fizzing in all and no particular direction at the same time. It was then that I looked down and noticed I was grasping the bare, un-taped part of the handlebars and thought, "This *could be so unwise – so dangerous!*"Quickly grabbing a section of the cape, wrapping it around the bars, I made sure that I was at least partly insulated against the thousands of volts that streaked around and about in this haphazard fireworks display. The hail turned to drenching rain, dripped off the skirt of the cape, turned knees and calves into icy, red raw appendages and flowed unremittingly into soiled socks and shoes. It was time to lose altitude – and fast.

The descent was a never-ending rush through stinging rain and failing light, negotiating bend after bend of loose gravel, struggling to stay upright and in desperate haste to arrive at a reasonably surfaced road. With eyes stinging from the ceaseless rain and water dropping off the overhanging forest branches, we were barely aware of flying past lonely, rude cottages. Hovels of rough stone with small windows showing yellow light from gutting oil lamps; homes for dwellers of the forest, self-sufficient and living miles from any built-up community. Any locals, bending from the torrential rain outside to collect wood for their fires, must have wondered what these crazy cyclists were doing rushing headlong downhill at a frightening speed and in semi-darkness. I was vaguely aware of passing a gathering of poor hovels. In the gloom of the storm, I managed to just to make out a battered sign reading Pallerols. Rainwater, having sluiced through my hair, tasted salty, metallic and second-hand, before dripping off my chin and pooling in the sump of the cape! Storm-water flowed across the track, eroding the surface even more and formed rutted channels to test our balance and bike handling. It was completely dark before we eventually found a surfaced road. The rain fell in stair rods, pooling across the tarmac and with no lights whatsoever, we finally swished into civilisation, finding food and shelters, at Seo d'Urgell. We dumped the bikes outside the Hotel Andria and padded across the restaurant floor with wet socks, leaving footprints across the polished wood. The meal of steak and chips with ice cream to follow was most welcome. Maybe our bedraggled appearance prompted the waiter to splash an extra large moat of whisky around our ice cream dessert servings. A whisky and a cigarette or two afterwards celebrated our epic journey as we relished being warm, dry and out of that dreadfully persistent rain. A bill of 90 pesetas (11/- old money, 55p new).was a pittance to pay after yesterday afternoon's water torture.

Monday morning was wash day. We borrowed the hotel's hose pipe and water supply to hose down the bikes; rid them of any clinging gravel and re-oil all the bearings. After yesterday's chaotic descent down uncharted dirt tracks in torrential rain, it was time to replace washed-out lubrication and make the bikes again, all bright, ship-shape and 'Bristol Fashion'. I often have to smile at cyclists ploughing through floods with water above the wheel hubs, just to make a splasb for the cameras. If their machines are left to rust, a resultant squeaking bearing makes for hard pedalling!

We progressed up the main road to the capital and only town, of Andorra – Andorra-la-Vielle. The tiny principality straddles the

Pyrenean border between France and Spain, and seems to be the area trading post for the purchase of duty-free goods. We found accommodation at Las Escaldes and took a day off for some shopping and eating. A pleasant café, the Café Nikko, offered chicken and chips, while Chris Warren, firmly settling himself on a counter barstool, kept the chefs busy ordering Spanish omelettes with fried onions. Chris was hoping to pursue a career in catering, possibly progressing to be a chef in the Royal Air Force. The supermarkets, stocked to the rafters with cheap wines and spirits, tobacco and cigarettes, caught our attention, making shopping for such low prices almost a guilty occupation. I acquired a bottle of Cointreau orange liqueur and to save carrying the heavy glass bottle, emptied the contents into my feeding bottle. Not the best of moves as a desperate swig of what was thought to be water could result in being suffocated by orange-flavoured alcoholic fumes! The half litre bottle cost just 56 pesetas (7/- old money, 35p new). It was a sin *not* to buy anything! Ralph was able to restock his supply of cigarettes with a brand approaching smokeable. The change in climate, food and water claimed its victims after the first week of the tour; Ralph, Dave and Tony Ross suffering from gyppie tummy, with Geoff feeling off-colour. So far, I had escaped any symptoms of 'Montezuma's Revenge', feeling the assurance of those boxes of Beecham's Powders in the bottom of the saddlebag. The road, totally urban, climbed slowly up through Andorra towards Port d'Envalira. Continuous warehouses full of cheap goods lined the route, while above these towering emporia, the surrounding jagged mountains, sharp and shale-strewn, cut a crisp, blue skyline. Overall, I wasn't too inspired by the scenery. The deep valley was full of motor fumes, made worse by the trapped humid air collected within the close, confining, steep mountain walls. Any side roads led to a narrow, torturous climb to some lonely village, but the very nature of the landscape gave us little enthusiasm for further exploration. I recall using a roadside toilet and noticing how open to the world it was. There was no graffiti though – the days of aerosol-powered, painted pop art on blank walls was not a regular pastime of these mid-1960s!

I changed £2 into pesetas at a bank in town and received 332 for my stirling. My word, we really did shift big money! Leaving the glass and concrete edifices of Andorra-la-Vielle behind, we all followed Ralph up the Port d'Envalira, all of 7,897 feet (2,407m)., admired the view of the Cirque de Font Negre, before dropping down the slopes of the upper Ariege Valley. Ralph was always leader up the high passes. His tall, lean, yet muscled frame could always be seen a few hundred feet above us, cutting an athletic profile, not so very unlike the famous Fausto Coppi. His long legs tapped out a regular cadence, while us mere mortals, at least, had a distant target to look up to – to try and reach. We regrouped and crossed back into France at the Pas de la Cas and spent the night at a hotel in Ax-les-Thermes. This elegant spar town at the foot of the Pyrenees, famous for its healing waters, was bathed in a gentle evening warmth. After a cooling shower in the Hotel de Parc and a leisurely evening meal, it was heaven to sit outside the Café de Casino d'Ax and enjoy a few beers. To quench the thirst, people-watch, swap a few adventure stories and see the evening daylight fade into streetlight glow. At night, the day's sunny, accumulated warmth releases, radiating from streets and houses and gives a feeling of overall wellbeing. This, with a deep draw on a well-earned cigarette and most of the Haute Pyrenees ridden, was to us eight what cycle touring really was all about.

On a damp road and with light mist swirling through the trees, we climbed the short, but steep Col de Chioula. To our left and below, within the tight, ancient streets, people in sickness, on stretchers and in wheelchairs were being trundled through the town streets to take relief in the many thermal baths. We counted our blessings – one by one. Bright sunshine reflected strongly off a lowered cloud base, giving us spectacular cloudscapes through the deep, tree-clothed valleys. We dived into thick mist on the descent; passing Belclair, before this lifted for the remaining miles through Quillan, to Alet-les-Bains. The Hotel La Main d'Argent (Hand of Silver)., was an old building in the town centre's narrow streets. Several recommendations from past CTC members were pinned on the noticeboard. We asked if they served

English food and the waiter proudly announced, "Yes, tonight we 'ave Irish stew!" Irish stew, potatoes and peas, with bed and breakfast, totalled Ffl 8.10 (27/- old money, 135p new).

It was Friday, our last day on the bikes and we only had to pedal nineteen miles (30k).through Limoux to arrive at our railhead in Carcassonne. The Old Cite, with its curtain walls, battlements and candle-snuffer-roofed corner towers, stretched across and enclosed the townscape, magnificent in its overpowering, defensive length and strength. The attacking Moors would find it virtually impregnable. The narrow, cobbled streets within the walls contained a wealth of souvenir shops; but it was oppressively hot and at the end of the two weeks, we were short of spending cash. After finding the Gare Carcasonne and registering the bikes, we spent our remaining francs in the station's café; enjoying a few beers in the lively atmosphere of clinking glasses, clattering cutlery and chattering classes. A French station restaurant, full of drinkers, diners or just folk wanting to sit and talk, has an ambient, plebeian atmosphere where visitors meet before or after long journeys. The clamour of sociability is all around. Far removed from British Rail waiting rooms where customers, struggling with their curling sandwich and polythene cup of ersatz coffee, wait in pained anticipation for their transport through hell. Rid of the francs, we decamped to the station entrance steps and in the soft warmth of a summer's early evening, pumped the Primus stoves into life and brewed many mugs of thirst-quenching tea. English as ever. Our SNCF express departed at 10:55pm precisely and thundered into the night, north to Paris and the Gare d'Austerlitz, arriving at 08:20am on Saturday morning. See also Appendix for holiday details.

This first Continental cycle tour had been a tremendous success. We had seen our first seriously high mountains, scaled our first long, high passes, just about coped with the language and food, and with Ralph's organisation of route and ticket bookings, reached the Pyrenees in the first place. I will remember the enthusiasm for cycling expressed by many of the locals. When climbing through the winding turns near a col's summit, being cheered on by children standing on the seats of their 2CVs and with heads poking through the roll-back canvas roof, wave and chant the names of famous Tour riders. When descending at breakneck speed down a well-known pass, we noticed approaching cars pull to the side of the road or into any passing places in order to give us road space. Where would that happen in Britain? At every overnight hotel stop, our bikes were well cared for; locked away and not tampered with. Their handling by French Rail was accident-free. Overall, travel by SNCF, comfort, speed and timing, was the height of efficiency, relegating anything by BR to the Stone Age.

Memories of France included the aromas of Gauloises and Gitanes, the countrymens' agricultural *bleu;* peaches, fresh, tinned or second-hand and struggling with the tins of cassoulet – pallid butter beans and hairy pork meat chunks in a thin, watery tomato sauce! In Spain, the discovery of omelettes, the potentially dangerous mixture of plumbing and electrics, and cycling under the torrential rain of a Pyrenean thunderstorm, in darkness and on disintegrating gravel tracks.

Back in Stoke-on-Trent and having recently visited some exotic Continental towns, Paris and Pau being two, Geoff and I playfully asked an apparently callow youth, a junior, assistant stationmaster at Cobridge Railway Station, if we could get return tickets to Toulouse. Cobridge Station, part of the long defunct Potteries Railway, saw the passing of short, colliery goods trains and then only once in a blue moon! Not the sort of place to depart from when visiting such exotic destinations! The poor lad, dressed in an ill-fitting, regulation BR uniform, plus greasy waistcoat and dirty boots, informed us that we best ask at Stoke Station. Much humbled, we acknowledged his good advice, considering his reply as being most sensible!

In September, brother-in-law, Fred, obtained a job with Bullock and Bosson office suppliers to manage their shop in Wyle Cop, Shrewsbury. He covered the Shrewsbury end of their business empire and with Sheila, started looking for a house in the area. After looking at a few houses on the edge of Shrewsbury, including the rough Comet Drive, Ditherington, they found a suitable semidetached in Bomere Heath, a satellite village some five miles (8k).to the north. I successfully obtained an office job with Shropshire County Council, a Planning Department draughtsman's post, working in their town centre offices in The Square, adjoining the medieval Market Hall. After a couple of weeks commuting with Fred from Stoke to Shrewsbury, he to set up shop and I to start my new job, the house purchase details were finalised at Cherry Tree Close and we upped roots and headed for Shropshire. The house sales hadn't been completed in time, so, we took temporary accommodation at a bungalow on Redhill Drive, Hook-a-Gate. Although only a few miles from Shrewsbury, the place appeared to be out in the sticks, deep in rural Shropshire, deathly quiet and icy cold in this cooler than usual autumn. Luckily, we only had to stay in this refrigerator for a short while before we moved into Shrewsbury Road, Bomere Heath. Sheila and Fred reached the house, then named *See Devi,*and found a flock of sheep on the front lawn.

Despite the moving house and job change, I found time for a quiet cycling holiday in Cornwall with Dave Hope. It was for a week only; training from Shrewsbury to Plymouth and spending a relaxing break, touring Cornish fishing villages on both coasts and enjoying a late Indian summer. The morning mists cloaked the glass-like calm of the River Tamar as we crossed into Cornwall on the Torpoint Ferry. Condensation gathered on cold metal chains before dropping to pool on an oily deck. Above the mist layer, a clear blue sky heralded a week of gentle warmth in an unusually fine season. The autumnal mists hung over quaint harbours before rising at noon to reveal limpid waters, disturbed only by the mirrored reflections of clinker-built fishing smacks. Folk unloading boxes of fish from deck to quay appeared so very genuinely engaged in work, instead of the normal fiddling-about for the benefit of tourists. Late September into October and the months of mists and mellow fruitfulness, warmed by a welcomed, albeit lower sun, are, I believe, one of the best times to holiday in England. School is back in term, tourists have returned to their grindstones and the landscapes of the coast and countryside have turned from green, through ruddy brown, to gold.

Having learned photographic processing from Norman Bennett in Trentham, he who was chief photographer for the Potteries Motor Traction, I took advantage of the low, mist-diffused lighting to capture the atmospheric conditions surrounding the harbour scenes of Looe, Polperro, Mevagissey, Padstow, Port Isaac and Boscastle. A rusted anchor chain, seaweed-draped quayside rope, the multi-coloured, swirling pattern of engine oil on still water; all were noticed, recorded and subsequently printed out on large, sepia-toned, sheets of white fine lustre. We soon retraced our route back into Devon, through Tavistock, to Plymouth, our train speeding north from autumn and into winter.

From October, 1963, to October, 1964, I had been keeping a record of hostel attendances by our group members. Slavishly listing every hostel on every weekend in the vertical column and every member's name across the top, the large sheet of graph paper faithfully recorded a whole twelve months of YHA Cycling Section activity. The cyclists had a prize for the most bednights. Geoff won the previous year and I was determined to win now. My prize would be presented at the next Cyclist's Dinner at Consall Forge. Geoff achieved thirty-six nights to come second in the table. I thrashed him, gaining thirty-eight nights to come first. He must have been on his deathbed to miss those two nights! At the risk of being called an anorak, I persisted in this accurate exercise and over the years, looking back, it has released a treasure of memories and provided a fascinating source of information. Having said that, I only recorded attendances for this one year. In total, over this period, we recorded three hundred and twenty-one nights staying at thirty-nine separate hostels on club weekends and by twenty-six individuals. An average of over eight persons per hostel bed night certainly swelled the coffers of the YHA! There were, obviously, many more nights recorded when various members were on holiday or on extra weekends not shown on the cycling programme. Details of other years' cycle touring was obtained from the many collected membership card hostel stamps. (See also Appendix for full details).

We rounded-off 1965 with three nights at Dimmingsdale. Having spent an uproarious time at Cynwyd Mill for the previous Christmas, we tried again to book the hostel but found it not to be open over the festive holiday. I don't think it was because of our enthusiastic celebrations of last year. Never mind, the wardens, the Blue Lion and the village girls would still exist without us – just. Dimmingsdale was only about twelve miles (19k).from the centre of Stoke-on-Trent; beyond Cheadle and in attractive surroundings, close to Oakamoor. The pull of wassailing as a group of cyclists with repeated visits to the Lord Nelson was our main consideration, despite, myself apart, the closeness and convenience of home!

*

Chapter Seven

1966

*Shrewsbury – A Welcome Café – Easter on the Lleyn Peninsula – High Cup Nick –
Moonlight over the Mynd – Night Riders of the Berwyns – A Wet Scottish Tour –
Limping Loneliness – Sunny Autumn in the Lake District – Christmas at Cynwyd –
Popular Folk Music.*

Age: 25.

Home: Shrewsbury Road, Bomere Heath, Shropshire.

Work: Shropshire County Council Planning Dept, The Square, Shrewsbury.

Government: Labour.

Prime Minister: Harold Wilson.

Jan: United States accidentally drops bomb off Spanish coast.

Feb: Freddie Laker forms first cut-price airline.

Mar: Labour win landslide vote.

Apr: Hovercraft service starts across Channel.

May: Moors murderers jailed for life.

Jul: US spacecraft lands on moon. Wage freeze. England win Football World Cup.

Aug: Cultural Revolution in China. Francis Chichester embarks on round the globe voyage.

Sept: South Africa's Prime Minister, Verwoerd, assassinated.

Oct: Disaster at Aberfan, schoolchildren buried by coal tip slide.

Nov: Floods in Northern Italy and Florence.

Dec: Rhodesia leaves Commonwealth.

Novel: Truman Capote's *In Cold Blood*.

Film: *The War Game*.

The United States loses one of its nuclear weapons just off the southern Spanish coast. It had dropped from a USAF plane, splashing down barely out of site of the beach. Probably not armed but surrounded by American Marines' paranoia, scared that any Spanish yokel could have been a red Ruskie spy. The threat of nuclear war and its terrifying aftermath was brought home to the general public by the BBC-sponsored film, The War Game. The film's gritty reality, treated in a bleak, documentary-style, proved to be so macabre, offering no hope of survival, that it was banned a showing on television. I saw the film at the cinema, but it would be over twenty years before it was considered suitable viewing in the living room. Harold Wilson receives a strong endorsement in a landslide General Election. As beehive hairstyles rose higher, so did miniskirt hems; so short, in fact, to be called pelmets or deep belts. White, thigh-length plastic boots climbed up the expanses of leg – either a sight to turn the head or turn the stomach, depending on the girl's or boy's figure! This was the time when hippie blokes wore long, multi-patterned kaftans, rimless spectacles and droopy moustaches and slinky, doe-eyed girls gave away flowers to strangers or poked them down the barrels of rifles. "Peace man!" Midsummer was dominated by the World Cup football tournament. World Cup Willie, a lion in football strip and boots, pranced over every mug and teacloth in the land. England won. I believe that they never will again. Too many foreign footballers have been signed in recent years by top league clubs, thereby suffocating homegrown talent. Chairman Mao Zedong announces his Cultural Revolution and immediately sets out to destroy all vestiges of culture in China. His Little Red Book is waved enthusiastically but doesn't come in loose-leaf edition. South Africa's Prime Minister, Dr. Verwoerd, was assassinated. His Nationalist Party advocated apartheid in all its evils. The latter part of the year was affected by the days of rain. Continuous rainfall in the South Wales coalmining valleys, together with an unrecorded stream course, caused a gigantic spoil heap to slide down into the tight streets of Aberfan. Many primary schoolchildren were buried alive as the oozing, black moraine enveloped their school. Persistent torrential rain in the northern Italian mountains caused devastating floods, washing away a cemetery at Cencenighe and culminating in the flooding of the River Arno, in Florence. We would see these effects while cycling in the Dolomites next year.

*

I settled in to working for Shropshire and was pleased to be able to do drawing work that was far above any required job description. Mrs Ann Malam, Area Planning Officer for Shrewsbury and Atcham, had acquired not just a filing clerk, but a draughtsman who was able to illustrate design advice and plan housing estates. On an unusually warm spring weekday, I cycled back to Stoke-on-Trent to give my workmates in the Reconstruction Department a surprise visit. Descending to Whitmore, a passing car clipped my saddlebag and I only just avoided coming off in the kerb. Maybe this was a well-timed omen. Despite being away for only a few months, the atmosphere was awkward beyond the usual pleasantries. The cycling had been hot and humid, and it took ages for my perspiring to subside. This didn't help as I chatted about the work in Shropshire, continually wiping away beads of sweat with a soggy handkerchief. The experience taught me that one is soon forgotten after disappearing from the scene. Like lifting the fingers from a cup of water – the ripples quickly subside, the liquid flattening back to calmness in no time at all. I was relieved to get back on the bike and wend my way home to Shrewsbury and Shropshire.

We found Shrewsbury a world of difference to Stoke-on-Trent. Instead of the urban sprawl of dying industry; a confused mixture of township developments and an area scarred by the extraction of raw materials, we were living on the edge of an historic shire county town. Almost completely surrounded by the River Severn, the hilltop town was packed with architectural gems, ranging from the Norman and Tudor, to Georgian and Victorian periods. It even boasted a castle, an abbey and flax mill/maltings, being iron-framed, the forerunner of the modern skyscraper. All this and set in the varied and attractive setting of the Border Marches. The town was surrounded by a complicated network of country lanes with tempting views of all those 'blue, remembered hills' in every direction. One of the first impressions of the town was seeing and experiencing the effects of the all-encompassing river in flood. The past winter had not been particularly rainy, but, even so, the height and force of the river was startling. To walk over the Welsh Bridge and glance down at the flood water burrowing underneath its arches, surging against the stone abutments and barely able to find a way through, was an almost frightening experience. The swirling torrent, brown with sediment and writhing in angry eddies, seemed to be only inches away from the road level. It conjured up a feeling of being in danger and in a place best avoided. Frankwell people had to step along planked walkways to reach dry streets; Abbey Foregate folk had to use rubber dinghies to reach the dryer parts of town. Flooded basements and lifting drain covers were the norm; problems faced with a dismissive nonchalance. A cheerful Dunkirk Spirit prevailed; quite appropriate with all the water flooding through every low-level street. Even the town's football team, playing in normal conditions, had to employ a boatman to retrieve a heartily struck football from the Severn. With the river in flood, the ground, Gay Meadow, could only host water polo. It was all very exciting; fully reported in the local newspaper, however, one's trip into the town centre had to be carefully thought through. Cycling through deep floodwater was not to be recommended, despite the comic effect. 1966 was becoming the year of persistent, unending rainfall.

Another discovery for me was the importance of Shrewsbury as a busy railway junction. The main railway station, built partly over the river, had a magnificent entrance facade. The Gothic structure with its grand frontage canopy, reflected the status of the former Great Western Railway, with lines approaching from Crewe, Chester, London, Welshpool and Hereford. A disused station by the Abbey had, in its heyday, been a terminus for lesser routes from Stoke-on-Trent, north-west Shropshire and the Welsh border country (The Potts Line). By 1967, railway modernisation had removed most of the steam locomotives nationwide. As I cycled into town and gravitated towards Betton Street, Belle Vue, I was surprised to see lines of rusting locomotives, buffers to buffers, stretching along sidings adjoining the main Welshpool line. There must have been about thirty of them, forgotten by the march of progress, laid to rest in the sidings, providing only a memory of past railway activity by the once busy Back of the Sheds Locomotive Works. I was impressed by these lines of dormant monsters, but also felt a twinge of sadness at their decline into retirement. Rough grasses and tough thistles forced their way up through oily ballast, between rusting rails and rusting wheels; corroded footplate cabs had taken on the grey-green hue of lichen-covered obsolescence, providing a schoolboy's dream playground, but soon to be towed away and broken for scrap metal.

Although living in Bomere Heath, I continued to cycle along the A53 to Stoke whenever we visited the Peak District hostels. On many a weekend, I would cycle the thirty-five miles (55k).through Market Drayton and turn at Trentham Lane Ends, to continue towards Longton and stay at Chris Warren's house in Dresden. On shorter destinations, I could reach the hostel on the same day. Most of the weekends, however, were in Shropshire or Mid and North Wales, where I could tootle down to Shrewsbury and meet the lads in the Bricklayer's Arms on a Friday night, staying there so as to be ready in the morning for an early departure. Shropshire itself provided a wealth of rough-stuff routes and lonely lanes to satisfy the keenest of cycle tourists. Clun, Wilderhope Manor, Bridges, Wheathill and Ludlow were, in those days, relatively undiscovered hostels with public houses near or on route of the basest facilities and rural obscurity. No acres of tarmac parking, no fancy meals, no laws on not smoking, no adhering to strict opening hours; plenty of character, full of history and just the way we liked them.

On late afternoons or early evenings, usually on a Sunday, returning from some location in Wales, we would approach the suburbs of Shrewsbury and arrive at a small café in Chapel Street, Frankwell. Close by the ancient timber-framed inn, the String of Horses, just before a set of traffic lights, we would lean the bikes against a wall and dive into the smallest of milk bars to feed ourselves egg, beans and chips. The street was narrow and the deep shade afforded a cooling place to retreat from the hot afternoon and recharge our batteries. The cool plastic chairs were salve to our saddle-sore posteriors. After a second mug of milky tea, we would return to the bikes, swish through the Tudor streets of Frankwell, cross the Welsh Bridge and set our wheels on the final miles towards Stoke. The String of Horses has long since been moved to Avoncroft Museum of Architecture; providing a magnificent reception building there, together with the original Co-Operative Wholesale Society shop front. At least it hasn't been lost! Chapel Street and the café where we sat at formica tables to the clatter of cutlery and ringing chatter, has long since been flattened; cleared with other Victorian propertie for the formation of a giant traffic island. Despite the loss, we found an even better eatery later; a CTC-recommended café in rural Edgebolton, near Shawbury, seven miles along that A53 road of sunny evening miles to Stoke and home for my friends. For me, a saunter through narrow, leafy lanes, through Astley, Hadnall and back to Bomere Heath.

For the Easter holidays, we cycled to hostels at Llangollen on Thursday night, Harlech on Friday and a bed and breakfast overnight stay at Llithfaen, beyond Criccieth, on the Lleyn Peninsula on Saturday. The last night, Sunday, was at Lledr Valley hostel, a timber-clad building on the edge of forestry within the Snowdonia National Park. Subsequent Stoke YHA auto-rambles used this hostel whenever we walked on Moel Siabod. A notable part of the weekend was to descend a valley near Nevyn, close to The Rivals mountains, Vortigern's Valley, where we discovered a deserted village overlooking the coast, important in its day for being a port for the handling of slate exports. Lines of empty, roofless workers' cottages spread along the slopes, slowly choking with the spread of errant grasses and foliage; a sad and lonely place enlivened only with the moan of onshore winds and the shrill cry of a startled black crow. Gaunt apertures, without windows and doors, gave framed glimpses of utter desolation. Past cottagers' gardens, bounded by upright, slate panels, linked by rusty wire, once alive with vegetables and flowers, lay bare save the thick, rough seas of untidy grass.

The route into the heart of Snowdon led through the Nantlle Valley; squeezing below the bulk of Mynydd Mawr (The Elephant Mountain).on its way to join the Beddgelert-Caernarvon Road at Rhyd Ddu. The peaks close in on either side; scarp faces and screes, with the occasional tree growing out of the narrowest of rocky cracks. The bulky, convex mountain slopes leading up the Snowdon Ranger Path to the very summit of Snowdon form the distant focus of attention, almost mirroring the 19th century artists with their cloud-filled abysses and cows in water. Overbearing canvases in russets, browns and dun oils; illustrating the mountainous scenery as an exaggerated, forbidding, dangerous place, grazed by shaggy, long-horned beasts.

For many a loose hour, we had searched for the really spectacular rough-stuff route. The Towi Valley in Wales, the Lairig Ghru in Scotland and the crossing of High Cup Nick in the Pennines were the most gruelling; they were often referred to in copies of *Cycling*. The magazine in those days was still printed on thin paper and in monochrome – more of a newspaper than a glossy. Moreover, as well as reporting the stage races and most local time-trial results, they devoted more time to printing touring articles and including Patterson's atmospheric sketches instead of today's garish designer advertisements. I, for one, am not too impressed by a mountain biker dressed in multicoloured pyjamas, covered in sponsors' logos, flying over cliff faces against a background of Alpine proportions.

Therefore, by word of mouth or reading about it somewhere, we chose to cross High Cup Nick and continue into the Lake District for the Whitsun holiday. This meant catching a train north to Lancaster and cycling up the valley of the River Lune, to spend a first night in Ingleton youth hostel. I remember meeting on Crewe Station platform where Ralph, in joking mood, asked us if we had received the tickets and knowing full well that he had already purchased them, holding them in safe keeping. There were eight of us, Ralph Salt, Roy Deakin, Pete Boardman, Tony Ross, Kenny Birks, Geoff Cartlidge, a lad named Steve and myself. Steve was a tall, slim, bespectacled youth, quiet and rather studious; introduced by Geoff, I don't think we ever learnt his surname, but he'd been to the Lleyn Peninsula at Easter and enjoyed himself. Some of our group just tagged along; there was no need for everybody to be a leader or a character. That was what made the whole thing tick. From the station in Lancaster, we pressed on towards Ingleton with the three peaks, Ingleborough, Whernside and Pen-y-Ghent merging into the general moorland landscape with the prospect of some grand cycle touring to come.

Riding in pairs, the valley stretching before us, we could see the bold Yorkshire Pennines in the distance. It was a fine summer evening with just an occasional passing car to disturb the peacefulness. As we swished along empty roads, a policeman pulled us over and demanded we ride in single file. "You must be ready for the big build-up". We were the only road-users to be seen. He, like most traffic cops, was overweight, balding and grew a clipped moustache. Why do traffic police all look the same? Wielding his incredible power, he warned us of the expected build-up of Bank Holiday traffic. We heeded his advice until he'd disappeared up the empty road, then resumed our normal riding arrangements. He had the 'blues' and we were still 'twos'. We reached Ingleton in good time, not bothered by massive traffic congestion and spent a pleasant evening in one of the town's hostelries.

Regarding blues and twos, on viewing, sadly, road and other accidents on television, I have noticed the emergency services, police, ambulance and fire brigade, insistent on keeping all their lights flashing continually, no matter the length of the rescue operations. During daylight, this doesn't pose a particular problem. However, at night, this practice, in my opinion, creates a distraction of blinding, strobe lighting, surely making steady vision difficult and more confusing for rescuers immediately involved. I agree with massive, efficient, steady floodlighting giving ample illumination and due warning to others who may be approaching the site, but the continuous, glaring blue lights emitting from police vehicles must be a disadvantage. Certainly not helpful.

I remember the air crash on the motorway embankment near Kegworth, Leicestershire. I counted a queue of at least thirty ambulances, every one with blue lights flashing. Surely, protection to the rear could have been organised needing fewer warning lights. It appeared to me that the police, especially, took great delight in switching on their blue flashing lights – and keeping them on. A sort of morbid fascination with death and destructive chaos."Look at us, people, aren't we heroes?""You can tell by the continuous, blindingly-blue emergency light reflecting off our flashy,high-visibility tabards." There is no doubt that the emergency services are heroes undertaking, sometimes, the most dangerous of duties. It's just that their flashing advertisement of the fact with incessant strobe, night-club lighting is sometimes overdone. Grousing over.

The B6255 climbs through cave country to Chapel-le-Dale with Ingleborough off the right shoulder and Whernside opposite, across the valley. These peaks, together with Pen-y-Ghent, are the venue for the strength-sapping Three Peaks Race, a gritty test of stamina for all keen fell runners. The limestone scenery is shattered and boulder-strewn; grey-white rocks indicating the mysterious world of caves below. High on the open, bleak moor, the Ribblehead Viaduct straddles the boggy watershed, its numerous tall arches appearing incongruous on such a windswept, unpopulated tract of land. It is widely told that a railway gang man working on the line in a gale was blown over its parapet to disappear under an arch and be blown back to his lofty trackside perch by the sheer force of the wind! And that apart, he still held on to his billy can and packed lunch! Our road dropped through Hawes, to Hardraw in beautiful Wensleydale. Behind the inn there, we walked a few yards through the beer garden to explore the lively waterfall and stand behind its cooling spray. The surrounding trees cloak the site in cooling shade, while the falls leap over an undercut shelf of harder rock, providing a curtain of water to refract sunlight and produce an ever-present rainbow.

Soon we were climbing again on the steep but shorter route to the Buttertubs Pass. So called because of the deep grikes; cool, dark shafts between the flat clints, a geological feature peculiar to the limestone pavement landscape of the area. Teetering on the brink of these dark, seemingly bottomless pits, admiring the tough, clinging plant life, we were afraid of tripping, loosing our footing and possibly breaking a leg. With Great Shunner Fell and Lovely Seat (what marvellous names for hills).alongside, we descended through Thwaite and Keld, before the next climb up Stonesdale to the isolated pub at Tan Hill. To the north-east, desolate, nameless moors rolled away into Durham, as far as the eye could see. The Tan Hill, not unlike the Jamaica Inn of Bodmin Moor, Cornwall, save being so much smaller, stands at a lofty 1,732 feet (528m).above sea level. The highest licensed premises in England. Its very isolation engenders a spooky feeling; a veritable Local Shop from the black TV comedy, *League of Gentlemen.* I bet they have some lock-ins there, in summer or, if reachable, in winter! The day included a gated track which led down to Bowes and Barnard Castle in Upper Teesdale. The day's destination was at Middleton-in-Teesdale, where we booked in at a comfortable bed and breakfast in the middle of a busy main street. It had been a hot and hilly day, so, we took advantage of the relaxed closing time at our guesthouse to fully sample the local beers.

After mending a blow-out puncture for young Kenny Birks, we paused at the massif bluff of High Force where tons of water thundered between strata-layered rock buttresses; a powerful, voluminous jet of peaty brown water providing yet another geological example to excite the geography teacher, if not his class. We followed a track to Cauldron Snout, the highest waterfall in England, though more of a stepped cascade over black dolerite than a sheer, vertical drop. Here, three counties met, Yorkshire, Westmoreland, and Durham. After cycling along lonely dirt tracks we eventually climbed onto open moorland, heading due west between Dufton Fell to the north, and high Mickle Fell at 2,592 feet (790m) to the south. Light breezes ruffled the spiky cotton grass on the sun-drenched waste as we struggled, following a stream course, the Maize Beck, thereby avoiding patches of swampy ground. I have since learned that our route forms part of the Pennine Way Long Distance Footpath, but on this warm afternoon, there was very little evidence of a beaten track. Maybe forty years of tramping boots have marked a clearer route. We paused for lunch; sandwiches, and a brew of Primus tea. Boiled in a Dixie pan, the brown, peaty water making the drink appear stewed before any tea bag touched the sugary brew. Tea always tasted better when having the lingering taint of paraffin and sipped between scalded lips from a chipped, enamel mug. We dipped stained socks in the stream, rinsing out clumps of peaty mud before gathering our chattels together and pushing west towards a hazy, shallow 'V' in the distant horizon. It is surprising how many chattels a touring cyclist can unearth from the depths of his or her saddlebag. Rain cape to sit on, food, feeding bottle, Primus stove (dismantled), mug, alloy pan, powdered milk, sugar, salt and pepper container, maps, camera, light meter, lens cloth, handkerchief, insect cream, matches, lighter, cigarettes, lipstick and so on. That's just for one person!

Generally we sought to keep the weight in the saddlebag down as much as possible. On longer weekends, and tours we searched for ways and means to reduce the load. While on tour, we could parcel up dirty clothes and post them home, although we were more likely to throw them away or burn them. Tools could be reduced to a minimum. A thin cone spanner and appropriate Allen keys were essential together with a dumbbell spanner with its multiple sockets. They could be used, rather than packing various-sized spanners. Steel spanners were heavy, and awkward to carry. Two tyre levers and a spare inner tube saved carrying a puncture outfit. I do remember taking a half filled toothpaste tube, and even cutting a few inches off the toothbrush handle to save weight. As previously mentioned, Geoff carried his salt and pepper in a tiny, double-ended plastic container. I would mix the salt and pepper together, and carry a small amount in a 35mm film cassette pot. Empty cassette pots had multiple uses for the cycle tourist. Our metal knife, fork, and spoon companion sets were made of light alloy and could be reduced to just a spoon sharpened on its one side. Of course, many items could be shared among the group particularly when campimg and having to carry Primus stoves, and dixie pans. Most items performed a dual use. Our overriding theory was every extra ounce x the miles ridden meant a mathematical calculation of total miles/pounds expended per journey. Effort that could be reduced or avoided. One Tour de France racing cyclist, Rene Vietto, a good climber, even amputated his big toe to cut down on the load. We thought this far too extreme – like cutting off his nose to spite his face. Quite rightly, the saving of weight was an unspoken obsession.

Shortly, the going became drier, firmer, and we could ride for a few yards at a time over a springy grass as we crossed the watershed. Now full of confidence, we rode heartily over the remaining mile and reached our objective, High Cup Nick itself. Spreading beneath our feet, the west-facing valley, 'U'-shaped in plan and cross-section, was a deep, glaciated basin with a horseshoe-shaped top rim of terraced rock faces, interspread with relatively flat grass slopes. These high valley platforms fully surrounding the abyss beneath, resembled a row of a natural, overhanging circle seats of a grand theatre. Water oozed from the boggy ground beside us, clattered down over rocky slopes to disappear, and reappear hundreds of feet below in the valley bottom. A silvery thin ribbon of light indicated the winding snake of a stream flashing in the late afternoon sunshine. Mountains – detail obscured by the glaring sun – loomed in an interlocking vagueness far ahead. Faintly blue-grey, and indicating the distant Lake District. We could cycle with relative ease along the terraces, humping over sheep-nibbled grass, and along the northern rim of the valley, to finally lose height, arriving in the tiny village of Dufton. High Cup Nick had fallen under our wheels. A long but not too difficult traverse called for a celebratory cup of tea in the local café. Our glorious day of adventure was completed by riding through Penrith, and following Lake Ullswater to its very southern end. The youth hostel of Goldrill House, Patterdale provided a well-earned night's accommodation. Pleasure boats reflecting on the cool, evening water while we reflected on our trek across the lofty moors of the Pennines. Sunburn had tightened the skin on arms and legs as we washed off the smears of chain oil from the calves and alloy stains off the hands – an occupational hazard when coaxing the bikes over difficult, tussocked ground.

On the final day in the area was yet another half day of rough-stuff cycling into Grisedale, and climbing over the pass by Grisedale Tarn, between Helvellyn and Dollywagon Pike. The pass was topped at 1,800 feet (548m) below St. Sunday Crag and the serrated crest of Striding Edge. We were now in the land of the fell walker who, no doubt, looked on us cyclists, struggling with our bucking bikes, as being completely loopy. We gained height on a rocky pathway, constantly snagging the pedals and grazing the sensitive skin on the backs of legs – a most excruciating pain that fades slowly as we curse ourselves for being so clumsy. We hauled the bikes upwards over boulders until we could climb no more. Although steep, the route had not been too long, and we were soon taking a break by cooling the feet in the Tongue Gyll as it pooled and splashed its leaping course down the mountains towards Grasmere.

Back in the place of poets and crowds of Bank Holiday people, we wasted no time in turning the pedals on the busy roads to Ambleside, and Windermere. Time waited for no man, so with one eye on the wristwatch, we were in danger of missing our train. The twenty miles (32km) to Lancaster had to be covered in an hour, therefore we had to cycle at 'evens' pace. The roads were, thankfully, flat and in true, organised team time-trial fashion, we hurried along doing 'bit-and-bit' to swing into the station car park with a handful of minutes to spare. Buying bottles of Corona pop each, we filled a compartment as the train clicked, and clacked south, towards Crewe. Sitting back in the deeply upholstered bench seats, feeling itchy to the backs of the legs in the warm afternoon, we reflected on the weekend's experiences. A dose of sunburn, scratches here and there, and a back pocket stuffed with tattered, sweat-soaked maps. It was a small price to pay for a memorable weekend in some of the most spectacular scenery of Northern

England. The sunburn and scratches would heal, the aches and pains would disappear, the maps would be replaced, but the memories were etched permanently into the rough-stuff cyclists' minds.

Four years later, in summer, 1970, I submitted a piece to the *Cycling* in response to one of their writing competitions, an essay about our crossing of High Cup Nick. To my surprise I won and they printed my work – uncut – unabridged, unexpurgated – unadulterated, and duly sent me a postal order for £12. They even printed three photographs that I'd included to illustrate the piece. There's something spooky about seeing one's work in print; being read (hopefully) by countless cyclists throughout the country, and seeing your name in a larger, bolder type, acknowledged as the author. You see your name printed there, bold and black, but only in the corner of the eye as any longer gaze could be thought of as self-indulgence. Almost embarrassing really.

Come the longest day when the setting sun leaves a lasting gloaming, a cyclist's thoughts turn to, amongst other things, late-night rides. We enjoyed pedalling down country lanes in the late evenings, especially after a hot summer's day. Twilight shadows making the countryside seem uncertain and mysterious; a cooling-down of the earthy fields, and border hedgerows produces a time of peaceful tranquillity. The remaining miles of the day, usually making one's way home after a drink or two in the favourite inn, is a time that the cyclist hopes will never end. A thoughtfully smoked cigarette or pipe of tobacco while the daylight fades, and the midges cease their dancing, is a really nice feeling – a feeling that all officers and gentlemen should relish. A recent TV advertisement (for a cider drink) conveys this atmosphere of summer evening enjoyment. A sporty cyclist rolls up to a wayside tavern, lurches to a halt outside the beer garden entrance to join his friends. A drink is thrust into his hand and he instantly becomes one of the crowd. In just a few fleeting seconds, the enjoyment of (finishing) the ride, and the prospect of a convivial, warm summer evening is perfectly conveyed. It's a social thing. The advertising agency certainly knew their job.

In those early summer days of maximum daylight, we decided to stage an all night ride. We knew that lights would be needed for a few hours of darkness only, if at all. Our first night run was planned for early July, 1964, about two weeks after the longest day. The run from Stoke-on-Trent to

Shrewsbury was the same as the numerous past Friday night starts. This night, however, we could stay in the Bricklayer's Arms, Abbey Foregate until closing time. Pub closing time in 1960s Shropshire weren't strictly observed, even in towns, so it was well past eleven before we took to the A49 main road south. Eric Hazeldine who should have led the run didn't turn up (probably delayed in his local, the Roebuck Hotel, Stoke,) but we all knew the main A49 road south, through Bayston Hill, Dorrington, and Leebotwood.

I was joined by Brian Whalley, teacher Dave Joynson, his close friend Roy Deakin, timorous Bill Barnish, 'Bomber' Chris Warren, and the ever-present Geoff Cartlidge. We turned right at the turning for All Stretton and took the back road that tucks itself under the broad, convex slopes of the Long Mynd. Into Church Stretton's deserted streets we rode, the normally busy streets crowded with both antique shoppers and shoppers of antiques, now utterly deserted, and a pale full moon rising in the south. Despite being totally alone, we whispered directions to turn uphill, and make for the steep Burway road. Why do folk whisper to each other when completely alone, at night or in the very early morning? There's hardly any danger of waking people. Halfway up the long climb, we paused to look down into Cardingmill Valley, now in heavy darkness, and the bordering hills opposite faintly outlined against a clear, dark night. On a summer's day, this tourist trap is swarming with families; parents in deck chairs, and children mucking about in the lively stream. Just as it should be. Stars tended to disappear as a rising moon turned from an ill-yellow to a dazzling silver. The sun had set some hours before with a faint smear of pink light turning to pale-green somewhere below the horizon. Sun usually sets in the west but in these midsummer nights the afterglow could be seen hours later, and in the north, if not the north-east.

Still on the Burway, we stopped in a shallow lay-by and leaned the bikes against the nearside banking. Across the road the land fell away dramatically, sweeping down steeply into the darkness of the valley floor. A level section of turf formed a place for assembling and placing the two Primus stoves. Accumulated miles, fresh air, and a pint or two of ale back in Shrewsbury had given everyone a raging appetite. Out came the dixie pans, bacon and lard. Several rounds of medium sliced bread were produced, squashed, and flappingly plasticised. The priming meths in its cup beneath the Primus burner plate curled a hot, blue flame; wavered in a genie-like mystery before lowering, fading and extinguishing. Vigorous pumping produced a misty vapour before a timely match brought the stove into roaring life. Rasher after rasher of bacon sizzled and sputtered in the hot fat, spitting, and crisping to perfection with a smell that tweaked the nostrils; a heady aroma that drifted through the cool night air, lingering briefly, to make mouths water. We loved the smell of bacon in the morning.

Bacon sandwiches had never tasted better, augmented by the faintest suggestion of paraffin. We followed the bacon with an attempt at fried eggs but these tended to stick like crazy to the thin aluminium pans. In its stark simplicity, this bacon buttie was one of the best meals that I've ever tasted. The aluminium kettle was filled with water carried on the cycles. Drinks of strong, hot tea followed. We scolded our lips on the roughly chipped rims of individual enamel cups. Most of the time, these mugs hung from the saddlebag side straps, occasionally scraping, and bouncing off stone boundary walls, and car wing mirrors. When the stoves had cooled sufficiently, they were packed away, checking first that the brass filler caps had been screwed home tightly. Cigarette-ends winked like glow worms as we sat on the banking, upon our rain capes to keep the bum dry, and watched the dying glow of the past day's sunset. The shapely Stretton Hills across the valley from the Mynd were outlined faintly against a velvet black sky. Ragleth Hill, Caer Caradoc, and the Lawley were the trio of conical heights that lay on a strong geological line, southwest to northeast in a thin finger of hills that pointed to the outlying Wrekin. Their grassy slopes, stepped variations in gradient, were lit by a now brilliant silver moon. In fact, this area of Shropshire was one of the most mixed systems of faults and rock types in the country. The shape of these hills suggested long-past much-eroded, volcanic plugs. Stratum contorted, up-thrusted, and buried over aeons when the earth was young. The area was rich in legend too; the very name Caradoc evoking tales of ancient kings now forgotten in the veiled mists of time.

Coming up to date, we looked down to Church Stretton where a few street lights still glowed orange, and one or two houses still showed yellow windows upstairs. Looking north, up the valley towards Leebotwood, a string of lemon-yellow lights crept silently along, moving towards the town like an illuminated caterpillar. A two-car diesel train glided through Church Stretton station, probably the very first early morning sevice south to Hereford. Still silent, the vision had a surreal quality. It was only when well beyond the town did any sound reach our ears – a faint clattering and roar of bogie wheels on distant steel rails.

We packed the saddlebags and moved further up the Burway, stopping again on a flatter saddle of land, two-thirds up the climb. Here we watched for the coming dawn. An almost indiscernable light underneath the horizon in the eastern sky, beyond Ragleth Hill, indicated the beginning of a new day. The sun had only been under the horizon a few hours, moving its compass position only a few degrees from setting to rising. After another brew-up of tea, we reached the broad back of the Long Mynd and headed for the solitary signpost indicating Boiling Well. By now, the sun had appeared as a lurid-red ball in a clear sky. Far distant views showed wreaths of mist gathered in the valley bottoms. The top of this broad land mass was crossed ny smooth dirt tracks where sheep huddle half-under clumps of bracken and wiry heather. The whole immediate area showed a surprising change in landscape, rising from the deep, luxuriant valleys to this open, harsh moorland was yet another interesting diversity in the Shropshire countryside. The eastern side of the Mynd was cut by steep streambeds, called hollows. Populous Cardingmill Valley apart, other valleys were named Ashes Hollow, Callow Hollow, and Minton Batch – wilder, rougher, adventurous ways that certainly gained our attention. The western side, a long, steeply-swooping edge was the ideal geographical scarp for the establishing of the adjoining Midlands Gliding Club. All summer long gliders whispered overhead, rising effortlessly on a combination of upsweeping airs, and warming crop thermals. We would spend hours on the Long Mynd on summer days, watching the continuous winch launches, and powered aeroplane tows, evoking memories of one of the first books I ever read, *Silent Flight,* a tale of two children learning to fly in gliders. A story of adventure, looking at the chequerboard countryside far below, dodging playful cumulus clouds, and the challenging thrill of the summer thunderstorm. After landing safely, tea on the lawn, of course!

We rested on the turf, warming-up in the morning sun after a short but cold night. Careful to avoid the scatterings of sheep droppings; shiny-black in their tight clusters, we smoked, joked, and tried not to fall asleep. Skylarks climbed and fell on the wing, and maintained a continuous twittering song as we lounged in slothful inaction. The sun was well above the horizon as we dropped to Bridges, and in Ratlinghope (pronounced Ratchup) in the Onny Valley. The slow climb of Cothercote Hill produced distant views of a rock-crested Stiperstones to the west, and Shrewsbury town far away to the northeast. We clattered over the summit cattle grid and started the long, fast descent through Church Pulverbatch, Longden, Annscroft, and Hook-a-Gate, to Shrewsbury – yet another discovered byway free of heavy traffic. Homeward bound on familiar main roads, we had to prop open the eyelids with matchsticks. Riding along in a tight group, line-astern, we found ourselves being hypnotised by the rider-in-front's rear mudguard. Collisions were avoided and after a refreshing sleep back home, the new day's daylight hours seemed unusually long.

Our second night ride was to be over even more spectacular terrain. We rode out through Llangollen and Corwen, to Cynwyd and made a crossing of the Wayfarer's Track over the Berwyns. After success with the *Cycling* article on our crossing of High Cup Nick, Yorkshire, I submitted a written piece to the magazine titled *A Day to Remember*, adopting the club's new name, The North Staffs Wayfarers.

A DAY TO REMEMBER

A day to remember, or, in our case, a night to remember. Meeting point: Newcastle-under-Lyme. Time: Saturday, 7:00pm.Venue: the Wayfarer's Track from Cynwyd, over the Berwyns, from Cynwyd to Llanarmon-Dyffryn-Ceiriog. (Our club: the North Staffs Wayfarers).We had covered this route, as we had most of the high Berwyn rough-stuff passes, many times before and, indeed, we had named our club after its pioneer, Cycling's Wayfarer, but never before at night.

We visualised rain, cloud and strong winds on a truly miserable venture, but it turned out that we were to be pleasantly surprised. The evening miles through Woore and on to Whitchurch were uneventful and at 9:30pm, the club wheeled into Hanmer with its beautiful lake and adjoining church. We had plenty of time here – after all, we had the whole night in front of us – so, we had a few drinks in the local inn. At 10:30pm, or thereabouts, we were ushered to the door and found ourselves on the deserted village street. Hanmer was bathed in a full, but as yet, yellow moonlight. One by one, the cottage windows clicked into darkness and we were left to the eerie silence of the churchyard, the moon casting an ashen light upon the sturdy church tower and forming inky-black shadows among the gravestones. The lake offered a splendid scene – silvery silent.

We were not a splendid sight. We pummelled front and rear lights into working order, slipped and crashed the gears and pulled unsteadily up the hill out of Hanmer away to the west and the Vale of Llangollen. Our pace was sober to Llangollen. We swung over the town's bridge and pulled over the gentle climb on the A5, towards Corwen. The night was keeping very fine so far, with trace mist in the valley hollows. Sleeping Corwen came and went before we branched left, just west of the town, on the minor road towards Bala. We lost our friendly moon beyond the northern slopes of the Berwyns now and halted to insert new front batteries.

Of course, a stop means a rest and a rest, a bite to eat, so, before long, we had the stoves roaring for mugs of tea and rashers of bacon between the good, old, thick-sliced bread. (Usually, when we think we need a rest, someone accidentally drops the map). Well, we were one mile short of Cynwyd – making very good time – so, felt we could afford this half-hour roadside stop. Greasy frying pans were cleaned with gravel and swilled in the cold stream beneath us, battered mugs returned to their car-scraping position in the saddlebag side-pockets and we slipped into the night again.

We eased through Cynwyd's silent lanes, over the bridge near the Old Mill Youth Hostel (an excellent hostel, incidentally, offering a warm welcome to cyclists)., before fading into the series of steep, uphill lanes that lead to the Wayfarer's Track proper. If anyone had seen us at this unearthly hour, they would have thrown the door bolts, slammed the shutters and with upturned eyes, sighed – "Ah, the spirits of the dead are on a pilgrimage to their mountain abode."

We were in good spirits. As we climbed higher on the mountain, we could see the valley stretching away to the west, towards Bala and beyond, the faint outline of the Arenig Mountains. Fingers of mist were forming above the River Dee and starting to roll up the bordering hillsides like an oncoming tide. Somewhere down there were still-warm farmhouses, nodding cattle and a sheepdog growling in fitful sleep. We were warm as well – the slowly climbing track saw to that. We could ride for a couple of miles on a good solid surface but had to be wary of some deep, isolated potholes and channels, shaded as they were by the bordering stone walls. A mile or so from the Wayfarer summit, on open hillside, we could see the high Berwyn slopes. The line of tops were covered with a well defined mist mantle, reflecting the strong light of a cold, isolated moon. Although we were all together on our well-known track, we remained silent. Perhaps we felt we were trespassing on the sleeping mountain and thought it best not to wake her.

We reached the summit at 3:30am, signed the visitor's book and looked south-east, down the Nant Rhyd Wilym. Our track, or to be more precise, the pools of water in our path were lit faintly by a yellow glow, the glow of an approaching dawn in the north-east sky.

The group reached the conveniently placed shooting cabin in the half-hour and once again pumped the stoves into life. (The cabin is situated at OS Grid Reference 105363 on the Bala & Welshpool 1 inch to 1 mile sheet). Early morning eyes peered into the blue flames and jokes and comments died before they were heard. Sandwiches were made up and wrapping paper used as tablecloths. Inevitably, the eats became tainted with a mixture of paraffin, meths and burnt paper.

It was cold now. Too cold to sleep, so, we left the cabin, splashed peat-stained water on our faces and climbed the hill opposite to see the fast-approaching sunrise. A disturbed grouse took to wing in front of us. Yellow and orange light in the east turned the sky at our backs a steel blue. The pale moon was setting. The large, dull-red sun shouldered itself up from the distant horizon layers, somewhere beyond Llangollen and picked out the lower hills of north-west Shropshire. We descended the remaining track with colour returning to the narrowing hill slopes and were soon on tarmac again for the remaining three miles into Llanarmon-Dyffryn-Ceiriog.

The village was still asleep on this fine Sunday morning. Extra night clothing was discarded a little too early as we had ten cool miles of slow downhill through Glyn Ceiriog, to Chirk. The café was just opening there and so, we were able to warm up with a few mugs of tea. The miles through Ellesmere to

Whitchurch and back to the Potteries were long and vague. Heavy eyelids peered at 'too close for comfort' rear mudguards and I still maintain I heard snoring from the back of the group!

We had traversed the Wayfarer's Pass before, both in driving snow and staring sun, but to pass over there in cold moonlight and fiery dawn was a totally fresh experience. The cold, silent aloofness of the broad mountains made us feel very small and insignificant, indeed. Our first night rough-stuff was a success – no mishaps, perfect weather and a wind-assisted return on the following day. We were to look on it as an experiment, for, since then, we have repeated the route in the opposite direction and also covered the Long Mynd in south Shropshire. Several factors should be considered by prospective 'moon-flitters' – a well-known west to east crossing, a fine moonlit night in midsummer, good views to make it worthwhile and a touch of moon madness in the assembled party!

Apart from the ideal conditions stated above, further necessities could be included. A Primus stove, kettle, mug, dixie pans and most importantly, a supply of bacon and sliced bread. I sent in this masterpiece of nocturnal adventure, hoping for it to be published without question, but, sadly, I heard nothing further from Cyclingmagazine.

*

We decided, for our main holiday, to cycle in the Highlands of Scotland. Ralph Salt and brother Clive, Roy Deakin, Pete Boardman and Tony Ross were planning on reaching the very northernmost point of mainland Britain, at Cape Wrath, a bleak outpost marked only by a solitary lighthouse. The cape was one of those destinations so often written about in Cycling and, therefore, catching Ralph's eye as a definite challenge. Geoff Cartlidge, Chris Warren, Brian Whalley and myself would join them for the long train journey north, to Inverness, and the first three hostels at Cannich, Glen Affric and Ratagan. From there, we four would cycle on the Isle of Skye and reach Torridon back on the mainland, before a planned, leisurely return to Inverness.

Unlike our Whitsun tour of the sunny Pennines two weeks before; June was to turn out wet. The long, overnight train to Inverness was uneventful and by Saturday lunchtime we were well on the road down the Great Glen, that massive geological split in the Scottish Highlands. Loch Ness loomed long and gloomy, but with no sighting of 'Nessie'. At Drumnadrochit, we turned away from the loch and found our hostel at Cannich.

The following day was spent on rough tracks, cycling carefully through scattered Scot's pine forestry, on a loggers' dirt road alongside Loch Affric, heading due west into an even more desolate landscape. Even in June, the mountains lying parallel to Glen Affric; numerous, nameless peaks, jagged in outline, had gullies still holding last winter's snows. Eventually, our indistinct track disappeared altogether as we found ourselves on an expanse of soaking wet bog. The only sign of civilisation was a small, corrugated iron building – walls and roof looking like a built pack of cards, sitting in the middle of a squelching morass. This was the hostel of Glen Affric; a mere shelter, miles from anywhere, looked after by a reticent, old fossil who only communicated with the odd grunt. We spent an unfriendly night by the light of a solitary oil lamp, barely warmed by the meanest of turf fires and listened to the sound of the moorland silence, while distant hills glowered in their covering of rain-bearing, stratus-nimbus. It didn't bode well for the holiday.

Early next morning we were given a collective hostel duty by our grousing guardian. He told us to pull a tree out of the bog and saw it into burnable sections. We pulled the slimy, black boughs from the sucking swamp, and with a blunt cross-cut saw, tried to make an impression. A tree buried in such wet ground for the past millennia will not cut too easily, the wood reverting to the consistency of rubber. We tried but finally had to give up the task. With mouthed grumblings of "Bugger you Jock!" we collected our membership cards and headed for the hills. We were heading for a high pass at the side of the peaks, the Five Sisters of Kintail. We struggled over difficult, boggy terrain, slowly gaining height, avoiding lying water and stream courses until there was no more climbing to do. By now, a persistent rain beat down on our heads, and with adjoining mountains cloaked in dense mist, we slithered down wet, steep tracks, crossing slivers of fresh, run-off water, to reach sea level on the Glen Shiel road. A steep but short climb led us over the Mam Ratagan Pass, through dripping larch woodland to the youth hostel at Ratagan. We padded into the common room with shoes squelching, fingers pink and crinkled, and knees, blue and knocking with cold, asking where we could find the drying room. The small room, full to the ceiling with sodden clothing, sweltered with a steamy fug; an un-breathable, vapour-filled atmosphere of walkers' soaking socks and damp, juicy jockey briefs.

We crossed into Skye at Kylerhea. The continual crossing of the little ferry across the narrow inlet, and the busy, quayside fishing community diverted our thoughts from the wet weather as we queued for the next ferry crossing. Our plan was to tour the Isle of Skye, and no incessant downpour would change our plans. By the time we reached Broadford, the rain was easing, and, from the hostel, I took the opportunity to cycle around to Torrin and take an atmospheric photograph of the peak, Blaven, outlined in dark silhouette with shafts of setting sunlight bursting upwards like searchlight beams. Below, at the end of a lonely, unfenced road; telegraph wires and posts giving an atmosphere of remoteness, Loch Torrin shone silver-plated at the base of the mountains. At last, the rain had ceased.

Skye has a variety of rock, colours ranging from the red of Lord Macdonald's Forest and the Red Hills, to the black gabbro of the Cuillins. The latter, the oldest rock in existence, forms a cruel semi-circle of shattered, sharp arêtes and tests the skill and bravery of the most experienced scrambler. Our lonely, winding road, passing-places provided at intervals, passed the Sligachan Inn. We paused to admire its location with the backdrop of the Cuillins beyond. Sgurr nan Gilean (The Paek of the Young Men) pointed and wholly unfriendly, and the isolated peak of Marsco, yet another mountain in this rocky, stream-coursed desolation. Our hostel for the night was at Glen Brittle, a small community at the head of the sea loch of the same name. As we returned to Broadford and the ferry at the Kyle, the torrential rain returned.

There is something sad about getting soaked, and not being able to change into dry, clean clothes for a day or so. To wake in the morning, and pull on damp socks, and slide the feet into wet cycling shoes has an instant downer effect on the spirit, and the holiday. Looking outside another damp morning, the heavy rain gave us little enthusiasm to drag on the capes and cycle towards the ferry at the Kyle of Lochalsh. Apart from collecting a reservoir of water in the hollow formed by the drapes of the cape over the handlebars, they make braking and steering awkward, are hot and clinging to the thighs, and one usually gets the feet wet anyway. When one stops, and slides off the saddle, and stands astride the top tube, that bulge of rainwater cascades down the legs and into the shoes. Wearing jeans is almost as uncomfortable; wet jeans cling to the legs, and after getting soaked, are no protection against the cold. The railhead at the Kyle was a buzz of activity. Torrential rain splattered on the station platform, and we must have been sorely tempted to bundle the bikes on a train and nestle down in a warm and dry railway compartment, to journey south to a place, any place, where it didn't rain.

The Cape Wrath party had left us at the Kyle of Lochalsh. They would be pushing north, and west through the indented geography of sea lochs, fresh water lochs, mountains and glens, known as Assynt, to reach the far northernmost and perhaps, loneliest place in Britain. Struggling to keep dry, we cycled to the YH at Kishorn. These were not days of mammoth distances with the weather so inclement. We felt it a great pity to a race through such a spectacularly scenic landscape with mist covering the peaks and being partly blinded by rain. The keen photographer, with his lens misting up every few minutes, will always curse the weather – although extremes of climates can produce the most stunning images.

Next morning I strained my knee. We were climbing the Beulach na Baa (Pass of the Cattle) from Kishorn's shores to Applecross, when, on nearing its summit, I felt the slightest of twinges in the joint. The pass is spectacular as it climbs in graceful curves and hairpins to the open plateau above. The cliffs facing Loch Kishorn from a grand buttress; an amphitheatre of, now, rain-lashed rock and swirls of mist. The climbing was hard and I found myself choosing a low gear, having to get out of the saddle, and honk around the summit bends. Wet surfaces and gravel made the going difficult. On cycling over the summit, we were exposed to the cold, west winds, and the combination of the wet and cold, descending briskly to Applecross, with the wind ruffling the heather and our hair, did little good for my poor knees. We bought provisions in Applecross before starting on the unsurfaced track that wound all the way round the peninsula to Shieldaig. Our overnight stop would be at Lonbain YH, a basic hostel in a tiny community, several miles out of Applecross, facing the Inner Sound, separating Skye from the mainland. On the remaining miles of rough track, around the headland to Lonbain, I felt the joint begin to stiffen, although turning the pedals, at least, kept it flexing and mobile. We spent a peaceful night at Lonbain YH., savouring the rest and quiet of isolation, reflecting on the tour so far, and trying to dry the clothes. I even tried a few available-light photographs – time exposures of Geoff and Chris under the yellow glow of a gutting oil lamp, camera steadied on a chair back. My ideal subject would be a coquettish Scottish lassie in a daring kilt, handing me a healthy tot of single-malt – preferably Talisker. Dream on! I had to be satisfied with mugs of tea and a shortcake or two. Images such as those were for the well-healed traveller who patronized the hotel – and not an isolated, forgotten youth hostel.

By morning's early light, my right knees had locked into un-bendable stiffness. Chris, Geoff and Brian soon disappeared along the rough track but I found that I couldn't bend my knee sufficiently to turn the pedals. Even half-pedalling with the right foot hanging down and limp proved impossible as the rough, rutted track made any freewheeling or forward progress impossible. With the left foot clamped tightly in the straps, I could lift the pedal to the top, dead centre and make the down stroke, but this one-legged pedalling made proved to be quickly exhausting, particularly on such a difficult surface. Unbalanced pedalling with one leg only was causing pressure and pain to my groin. Dismounting and pushing the bike was my only option. After a mile or so, my strained knee barked pain every time I put weight on it. Progress became painfully slow as I used the bike as a crutch, applying the brakes whenever it threatened to run out of control on downward slopes. The others drew miles ahead, and I was left to the rain, cold, and desolation of that godforsaken route for, seemingly, endless miles with the thick nimbus cloud dumping loads of water down the back of the neck. Despair is an accelerating process. One's morale can be quickly demolished when, for hour after hour, the route leads one along miles of unending desolation. The track wound around the coast; not by the shore, but a mile or so inland; thereby denying me any visual relief. At one point, a pack of snarling dogs crossed the track in front, further adding to my concern. They had probably emerged from a group of hovels away to the west; a lonely, forgotten fishing community. Luckily, the leading hound had a hunk of raw meat in his chops; the other chasing beasts interested in their goal and not me. A plastic bicycle pump would have proved too fragile to beat off those hungry canines. Not a dog lover at the best of times, this incident did nothing to bolster my confidence. Slowly approaching Loch Torridon, where the track turned the corner, and headed east, a herd of deer sauntered between clumps of scrub, glimpsing my way with typical distain, before continuing their grazing. After a night in Lonbain, with its lack of washing facilities, and a day of perspiration, despite the cold, they probably smelled me. My bike pump would definitely prove inadequate if these monarchs of the glen decided to charge. Despair, and now fatigue crept through my limbs as the never-ending track dipped and climbed and wound around the countless bends. The other three had waited for me to catch up but because I was so far behind, they had to keep moving when the chill of a wet and windy Scottish afternoon started to take root. I didn't blame them. Pain from the knee had now fused into a dull ache, but, at least, I could admire the outline of Beinn Alligin, despite a good part of its sloping bulk cloaked in thick mist. I was reduced to a blubbering, cursing wreck when, finally, my track opened on to a tarmac road. Opposite the road sign Shieldaig, there stood Chris, Geoff and Brian, sheltering under a scraggy tree. Rejoining fellow humans made one realise, and be aware of, the past miles of painful loneliness; the limping along with no encouragement in a wild, almost alien landscape. The misery of the circumstances, when alone, and with no listening, sympathetic ear, is bottled inside one's furrowed brow. The bottom jaw is thurst out and the upper lip is stiffened in a particularly English way. Only in company will the tears well-up and sorrow for oneself manifest itself. A passing motorist in a spacious Volvo gave me and the bike a lift into Shieldaig village, and we were soon getting warm in a bed and breakfast cottage. I saw the village doctor; a rotund, bespectacled character reminding me of Doctor Cameron in *Dr Finlay's Casebook*, who promptly admonished me for cycling at my age. Good grief – I was barely 25 years old and cycling was supposed to be healthy! Well, wasn't it? I refrained from blaming his country's abysmal weather for half-crippling me – he was far too grumpy. That evening, I lay in bed, staring at the ceiling. The others were down the pub taking the waters. That was the measure of my swollen knee joint, my pathetic unhappiness, my lowly depth of spirit – missing a last pint in the local hostelry.

It was a great pity to miss admiring the grand mountains around Shieldaig. The slatting rain next morning, forming a mist as it rebounded from the road's surface, precluded the sight of noble Beinn Alligin's slopes sweeping into Loch Torridon, or Liathac, 3,458 feet (1,054m), its summit shrouded in a thick mantle of mist. The camera was firmly stashed at the bottom of the saddlebag. Geoff, Chris and Brian continued on their travels further north. Unable to pedal, I held my bike with one hand and saddlebag with the other and would put it down occasionally to thumb a lift with torrential rain creeping down my collar. Traffic was scant in this lonely part of the Highlands. Soon, a small, open-back lorry emerged from the curtains of rain, and stopped a few yards up the road. I lifted the bike over its side, and climbed into the cramped cab.

Cycling in any form was postponed from Lonbain YH, yesterday morning's limp around the coast, and would remain so for the next two days. Today, I would journey east, through Kinlochewe, Achnasheen and Connon Bridge, to Inverness. My driver was an ancient Scot who remained 'drunk as a laird', and made numerous juddering halts to buy yet another bottle of whisky, barely disguised in brown paper bag wrapping. We careered acrossed the road on many an occasion, while I stamped the floor in alarm, with my good left leg. Regaining control, he would crunch the gears on every incline until I feared the lorry would shake itself apart. Any conversation was relegated to grunts and curses. The long journey; not in distance but time, reminded me of the film, *The Wages of Fear,* where ex-pats drive a cargo of unstable nitro-glycerine over dangerous mountain roads in decrepit lorries. My chauffer was last seen staggering into a town centre off-license. I had finally reached Inverness, and the railhead for further travel.

I found a bed and breakfast at a cheap hotel in Inverness and checked the train times south. I would need to wait until the next day's evening train before I could start the journey home. Fortunately, I met a commercial traveller in the hotel bar, and he offered to drive me around the Cromarty Firth area where he was selling equipment to whisky distillers. I believe he just wanted someone to talk to on his day of driving and pressure selling. There was no signs of sexual intension, or, at least, none that I detected. My train sped south through the night and by next morning I was wheeling the bike out of Shrewsbury station's Gothic entrance. The sky was blue, the day warm, I found that I could pedal, albeit, tentatively with my right leg, without pain, and cycled the four miles home. Bomere Heath felt virtually equatorial after the cold and wet of the Scottish Highlands. I sunbathed in the back garden all afternoon, sipping freshly-made lemon barley water – safe, warm and dry at last. It wasn't all a dream. No visions of awakening and finding myself incarcerated inside some Russian gulag in pouring rain to trouble my brow. *Monty Python's* future cycling comedy sketch, an end to A Bicycle Tour of North Cornwall, was not to come true. I never imagined dry, sunny weather to feel so good.

Returning to weekend cycling, we had sunny visits to Herefordshire, viz. Shrewsbury to Broom, and a long August Bank Holiday tour to Staunton-on-Wye, Crickhowell and Glascwm. A long run to Penmaenmawr on the North Wales coast saw us late back from the pub, and Ralph having an argument with the warden. When asked for his name, Ralph replied, "Jake Hicker!" and brother Clive, always keen to back his brother, added, "Yes, and I'm his brother, Harry!" Harry Hicker, a stupid name plucked out of nowhere that implanted us all into the world of silent screen comedy. Disagreements with hostel wardens were, fortunately, few and far between, and arose mainly by being minutes late, knocking on the front door after the 10:00pm closing time. Other contretemps arose when we walked into hostels without removing our cycling shoes. Made without racing plates fitted and as light and fragile as slippers, we often wondered what all the fuss was about. On the return from Penmaenmawr, following the A5 trunk road, I passed Derek and Dave, who, apparently, were resting in a lay-by and cycled the many miles trying to chase them down, thinking them just in front. Seperations such as this could easily happen without having pre-arranged meeting points.

A fitting compensation for the partly washed-out holiday in Scotland was travelling to the Lakes in the middle of September with Geoff and his friend, Steve in Steve's Reliant three-wheeler. The shuddering, steady drive up the recently constructed M6 motorway was an experience in itself.

The enjoyed unseasonable, pleasant weather, rambling for one week on all the area's high spots; when the bracken was at its most colourful, turning the fells into swathes of russet and the lakes into bottomless mirrors of deepest blue.

Last year, 1965, Cynwyd youth hostel, beyond Corwen, had been closed. This year we made sure to book early. We presented Mr and Mrs Roberts with a framed, black and white photograph of a scene in Grisedale, Lake District; Roy Deakin cycling along the track with Dollywagon Pike in the background. This was taken on the last day of our Whitsun tour of High Cup Nick. The image, although set in walking country, illustrated the intrepid, or crazy, adventures of the off-road cyclist. I was pleased to see my photographic efforts hung on the common room wall. Days were spent rambling on the snow-covered Berwyns while the evenings were spent folk singing in the lounge of the Blue Lion. Our repertoire was diverse in the extreme. From patriotic Irish rebel songs like *Young Roddy McCorley,* to rip-roaring fun songs like *Putting On The Style.* From sea shanties, such as *Drunken Sailor,* to dour Scottish ballads like *McPherson's Rant.*Southern American black protest songs like *All My Trials,* to re-released ballads of low life in New Orleans, *House Of The Rising Sun.* Raw Woody Guthrie classics, such as *Cornbread, Peas and Black Molasses* and *Pick a Bale o' Cotton,* unknown to us at first, soon became established favourites. Bob Dylan's rendering of *Times They Are A-Changin,* through Donovan's *Universal Soldier* and *Colours,*to even the Seekers'*Morningtown Ride* and Peter, Paul and Mary's *My Granndfather's Clock* went down well with the ale. I will always remember the brilliant lyrics of Donovan's *Catch the Wind. In Chilly Hours and Minutes of Uncertainty, I Want To Be/In the Warm Hold of Your Loving Mind* – sheer genius and written by one who took a piggyback on a policeman! Our choice covered ballads of England, Scotland and Ireland; written in our personal songbooks, of subjects almost inexhaustible. Our singing went down well with the locals, especially those of a younger generation. There were many a times when they joined in and the landlords had no complaints either, as their cash machines continued to ring. There was no nonsense of seeking the correct music licence. We were, I suppose, filling in the dead evenings after Christmas when everyone was fed up with turkey, sprouts and pudding, and the mock admiration of useless, unwanted presents. The socialising each night filled that dreary gap between Christmas and the New Year. Kept the party up and running.

Fuelled by the songs and drink, the atmosphere in the lounge would soon create a different scene for the locals. We were always very aware of not singing in a 'hand over the ear', folk song dirge. An air of keep quiet and listen to this very serious music was to be avoided at all costs. I was perched on a high stool by the lounge's serving hatch when three local girls pressed up tight and close. We were playing a particularly upbeat song and when playing any instrument, one is apt to tap the foot to keep in time with the song. My knee was bouncing; moving to the music of time when, pressed by the throng, the lovely lasses clapped and swayed with evident enthusiasm, pushed in even closer. I was becoming overwhelmed by their swinging curls, soft and frothy party dresses and delightful perfume. Verily, my cup did runneth over! The only thing between me and being totally engulfed by these delightful creatures was my boxy guitar and some fancy fretwork.

Our singing was always well received by other pub-goers. Be they climbers, walkers, casual tourists or, on one future occasion, a whole coach party, we could get the room rocking. On one session in the Pen-y-gwryd climbers' room, fellow singers had to access the bar by first climbing through the window, crawl through the garden and enter by the main doorway. Having made the effort via a devious detour, they returned with a tray full of pints for their own consumption only. Years later, one older couple even sent me a letter of thanks for the evening's entertainment. We knew so many sea shanties I eventually got a book printed, a collection of twelve ballads with all the words, annotated with the chords and illustrated the blanks. There was no need for music notation as everyone knew the songs and the band could play by ear. When printed, I sent a copy of our *Songs of the Salt Sea* to the appreciative couple. And so, another memorable year was burned into the memory bank.

Chapter Eight
1967

Walking in the Lake District – Old and New Shirehall – Tour of Dolomites to Venice – Tom Simpson on Mont Ventoux – Music on the Move – A Way Through the Lanes – CTC Café at Edgebolton – The Mainwaring Arms – Other CTC Cafes – Foot and Mouth Disease – Christmas at Home.

Age: 26.
Home: Shrewsbury Road, Bomere Heath, Shrewsbury.
Work: Shropshire County Planning Department, The Square/Abbey Foregate, Shrewsbury.
Government: Labour.
Prime Minister: Harold Wilson.
Jan: Donald Campbell dies when his boat, Bluebird, flips on Coniston Water. American astronauts die in Apollo launch pad fire.
Mar: Tanker Torrey Canyon spills oil off Land's End.
Apr: Foinavon at 100-1 wins Grand National.
May: Boxer, Muhammad Ali, avoids the US Army draft. Sir Francis Chichester circumnavigates globe.
Jun: Six Day War between Israel and Arab States. China explodes H-bomb. Jul: Tom Simpson dies on Mont Ventoux.
Aug: Pirate Radio banned.
Sept: QEII launched.
Oct: Labour MP, Clem Attlee, dies. Che Guevara killed. Foot-and-Mouth infection breaks out.
Nov: De Gaulle vetoes Britain's entry into European Economic Community.
Book: *The Naked Ape.*
Film: *Bonnie & Clyde.*
TV: *The Forsyte Saga.*
Music: *Sergeant Pepper's Lonely Hearts Club Band.*

My recent memory of the Lake District was of calm, water-reflecting, blue, cloudless skies. The footage of Bluebird somersaulting almost 360 degrees on a dull, rainy January morning saw the antithesis of the vision and the demise of a great pioneer. Stupidly, 1 thought that if the boat had completed the full circle, landing back on its sponsons, he just might have survived. With the United States pushing for a moon landing, NASA's space programme got ahead of itself, resulting in the horrendous capsule fire on the launch pad, killing three highly trained astronauts. An oxygen-rich atmosphere and faulty electronics caused the disastrous flash fire. The sudden incineration in a sealed chamber, like three turkeys in a locked oven, didn't bear thinking about. The oil tanker, Torrey Canyon, bound for Milford Haven, struck the Seven Stones Reef off Land's End and spilled some of its load on the Cornish beaches. To reduce oil pollution, the RAF bombed and napalmed the divided wreck, burning off millions of tons, but not avoiding the terrible consequences for wildlife. At least the RAF got some real practise in. The sad sight of oil-covered birds and other sea life, such as crabs, struggling up the beaches in globules of thick, black tar turned the heart to ice.

Soon after the start of the Grand National at Aintree, no-hoper Foinavon was the only horse to make Jump 7, avoiding a massive equestrian jam. Foinavon is also a Scottish peak and I considered, after the wet holiday there last year, placing a bet on the horse's nose. I didn't and it won at odds of 100-1. Brilliant boxer, Ali, refused to join the United States draft. A part of me thinks, "Good for him!" although this single act would not stop America's commercially-prompted adventures in foreign countries – especially in the Middle East and against the Communist threat of North Vietnam. Francis Chichester sailed into Plymouth after a solo rounding of the world on his small yacht, Gypsy Rose – a brilliant achievement considering the then, lack of ultra-sophisticated navigational aids. US-funded Israel attacked Arab's coalition aircraft while they were still on the ground. Black, eye-patched, Moshe Dayan, corsair Defence Minister, viewed it all with his good eye. The British Government banned another set of pirates, the pirate ship, Caroline, which had been broadcasting popular music from off the East Coast. China joined the nuclear club. An ultra-modern cruise liner, Queen Elizabeth II, was launched, providing luxury travel for the Americans. Che Guevara's head adorned millions of t-shirts. The devastating foot and mouth outbreak, starting in an

Oswestry livestock market, lingered over the dank, dark autumn with thousands of cloven-hoofed beasts having to be destroyed by burning and burial. The infection spread over several counties through central England.Our Gallic friend, Charles de Gaulle, looked down his enormous nose yet again as we begged to join the EEC. Never mind, it was the Summer of Love, the Permissive Society had arrived

*

At Easter, 1967, we sailed over to the Isle of Man; our second trip utilising the extra days available at this time of year. The long weekend's turnout was staggering. Friends of friends, Derek's wife, Vilma and her sister, friends briefly met on some past weekend, even ace cycle frame-maker, George Longstaff turned up; all grouped at the taff rail for a crowded group photograph. Two had brought a tandem. From Douglas, the round of hostels followed; Ramsey, Port Erin and Laxey for a popular, well-supported outing. Rod Taylor, a friend we met at Cynwyd, also joined us.

On a long-distance weekend and staying in a hostel in the Conway Valley at Roewen, I managed to break my glasses. After a particularly heavy evening's drinking in the inn nearby, I sat on them while collapsing on a bottom bunk. The long ride next day, returning along the A5 into Shropshire, was a bit of a blur; not from our sheer speed but balancing a broken pair of glasses on the bridge of the nose, while trying to avoid touching the wheel ahead. As ever, sticky tape came to the rescue-tape technology. The problem of wearing glasses whilst cycling is that, in hot weather, they are liable to slip off the nose, lubricated by a film of perspiration and when one enters a warm room after the cold outside, the lenses fog-up, resulting in instant blindness. A cycling crash means that they fly off and are in the greatest danger of being crushed under the wheels of a following rider. However, the visually afflicted tend to cope somehow.

Before our main holiday, we decided on a walking tour of the high Lakeland peaks. Ralph Salt, Tony Ross, Dave Joynson and I spent an excellent week youth hostelling at Kendal, Patterdale, Wastwater, High

Close, Keswick, Buttermere, Black Sail and Grasmere. The train journey north was spent crouching in the guard's van. It was a punishing, adventurous and ambitious itinerary, as were most planned by Ralph; walking over High Street, Helvellyn, Great Gable, Skiddaw, Fleetwith Pike, High Stile, Red Pike and numerous other lesser known heights. Our week of rambling ended on the relatively low Loughrigg Fell above Grasmere. Crowds in the valley below were eagerly devouring Wordsworth's poetry. I caught a horrendous cold at the isolated Black Sail hostel, a former shepherds' hut in the middle of nowhere and didn't recover until we had boarded the train south from Kendal. At the end of this marathon ramble, I felt like a bunged-up mountain goat. Apart from the stunning scenery, my main recollection was of endless hostel rules and the overpowering taste of Kendal Mint Cake. My bulging rucksack seemed to weigh heavier each day and at the end of the week, I wished to be back on the bike.

*

The daily ride to work was no problem; a journey of four miles (6.5k)., passing the parkland of the Berwick Estate, or the undulating back lane route into Shrewsbury. Many a morning I would stop and pick a dead pheasant off the carriageway, a low-flyer from the Berwick Estate's flock. Stuffing it into the saddlebag, I continued the ride with a limp head and neck (the pheasant's) swinging to and fro. My work colleague, Linda Brannan, could hang and cook the game bird and also use its feathers to make stunning feather/flower arrangements – a truly countryside craft. Waste not, want not. The Planning Department offices were situated in The Square, immediately adjoining the ancient Market Hall. This building, plus the surrounding shops, formed the main set for the 1984 film, *A Christmas Carol*. Little alteration had to be made to the scene in order to create that Dickensian feel. The neo-classical County Council building had large offices and deep, tall windows, giving views of the arched undercroft of the Market and the immediate town centre. I stored the bike in a small room at the rear, off High Street and climbed the grand staircase to the department's first floor. A lattice-gated lift was always busy. My drawing office, high-ceilinged and dusty, I shared with eight others. Most of the room was filled with large, splintered plan chests containing drawers overflowing with detailed Ordnance Survey maps. The County was split into six administrative areas and the planning officers all toiled in this one large room. The assistants who progressed planning applications would suffer a complaint called 'record-checkers' knee'. If a map drawer had been left open at groin height and a clerk happened to make contact with its hard edge, his attention having been diverted, this was called 'record checkers' knee' no matter what part of the anatomy was hurt. The complaint brought instant tears to the eyes of victims and tears of laughter from the onlookers.

Clearly, the entire County Council couldn't operate efficiently in such antiquated surroundings; a move to their new offices in Abbey Foregate was required, so, they employed Casserley & Sons to make the mammoth move in one fell swoop. Their entire fleet of vans were employed over one day to make the move. I had noticed the ongoing construction of the new Shirehall across the road when visiting Woodlands, the Shrewsbury youth hostel, on all those Friday night starts. We were treated to a site visit, conducted by the County Architect himself. It was the grandest example of 1960s-style architecture. Mainly square, gaunt and predictable.

On a brisk, spring morning, Her Majesty, the Queen, escorted by the Lord Lieutenant of Shropshire, Algernon Heber-Percy officially opened the Shirehall. The organisation was stupendous. Our offices on the first floor led onto the foyer and entrance approach to the Rotunda; a round, futuristic structure serving as the Council Chamber. A team of cleaners, armed with brushes, dusters and polish, followed the Queen and entourage, repeatedly removing any footprints from the shiny wooden floor. I likened this procedure to a possible re-enactment of a scene probably set in Henry VIII's Court; a show of extreme subservience. Senior officers were posted at the junction of corridor and foyer, trusted local government officers employed as guards, to ensure none of the hoi-polloi trespassed into Her Majesty's presence. Ian Ridgeway on our floor held back the pressing, deeply-sycophantic monarch watchers. We were instructed to tidy our planning office and provide a display of typical work as there was talk of the Queen making a short tour of the building. This show of work took a few days, a diversion for us workers, but she was running behind schedule and never showed up to admire our efforts.

Part of my work involved use of the extensive store of Ordnance Survey maps. The 25 inches to one mile sheets (1:2,500th Series).used for towns showed extreme detail. A delegation of town planners from Sudan – so black they shimmered with a grey sheen, like yeast on a black grape,wondered why we called them Ordnance sheets, wondering if they were used to show the position of weapons used in warfare. We had a hell of a job explaining why they were named so and decided that it was too complicated. After the Battle of Culloden in 1746, the Military, on chasing the scattering remnant army and finding the Highlands of Scotland an uncharted wilderness, undertook to finally survey the region and produce an accurate map. Hence the military involvement, connection and word 'ordnance'.

When the party had departed, we joked between ourselves, trying to explain the impossible meaning of ordnance and trying to imagine what OS maps of the Sudanese Desert would look like. Sheets of utter blankness – devoid of any detail save the regular longitude and latitude grid lines. It was all part of the office humour.

Apart from the climb through Shrewsbury town centre, the run from Bomere Heath to AbbeyForegate was mainly downhill and, consequently, a long drag on the return, if cycling beside a country estate, lined with grand trees, on a road littered with felled pheasant could be considered a drag. The cycling at the start and end of the day was pleasant enough. It was and is surprising just how many days remained rainless, being sunny and dry throughout the year. I could never remember having to wear the cape more than a few times on weekend tours. It was seldom used and remained tightly rolled under its saddlebag straps – yellow, stiff and smelly.

At last, we were with the bikes again and travelling down to London, stage one of our journey to the Dolomites of northern Italy; basically cycling from Bolzano to Venice. The seven of us spent the night at

Holland Park youth hostel in Central London. A hostel of convenience, a transit hotel for use by the numerous foreign tourists who continually take in the capital, move north to Stratford-upon-Avon and finish in Edinburgh. Ralph S, Geoff C, Dave J, Roy D, Chris W, Tony R and myself rushed through the London streets to Victoria, gateway to Dover, English Channel, Ostende and the Continent. On the station platform at Ostende, having transferred from ferry to railway, we had reached the very end of our long train; the last of the many *Wagons-Lits* marked by buffers, rear light and a closed carriage connecting bellows. Hundreds of yards ahead, snorting and throbbing, waited the powerful diesel-electric locomotive, anxious to start on its long journey across France, Germany and Austria of mainland Europe. Beside us stood a platform notice-board indicating the many cities this train would be passing through; grand European capitals, Cologne, Stuttgart, Budapest, Bucharest and Munchen, where we had to change, the train finally terminating in Istanbul, the gateway to Asia. We thrilled at boarding this veritable Orient Express and searched for the correct coach and compartment number. We settled in for a long journey, hoping that the absent bicycles were being transported somewhere in our wake. Munich Station's vaulted roof echoed to throbbing trains at rest and the clatter of cutlery in the platform's outside café. We grabbed a quick coffee while waiting for our connecting train that would carry us through Innsbruck and over the Brenner Pass, to Bolzano. Our waitress was slim, trim and wore rimless glasses, fair hair tied back in a tight bun and a smart black and white uniform. She showed a superb, typically Aryan efficiency. The pulsating throb of long-distance locomotives and the bustle of rushing passengers melded with the Germanic public address system and shrieking whistles to give an atmosphere as seen in all the best Cold War spy films. Outside Munich Central Station, Roy rushed to the train window to photograph a rare, rack and pinion steam locomotive. I didn't know that he was a train spotter. Our train creaked and screeched around tight rail curves as it chugged steadily up to the summit of the Brenner. The wait at the top was time consuming and baffling, as we were shunted into one of the multiple sidings and inspected by groups of uniformed authority, both Italian and Austrian border guards, transport inspectors, immigration and secret police. Their bureaucratic severity and administrative bearing wasn't appreciated by Chris Warren, who tended to laugh at everything, especially officialdom. Uniforms and specifically, enormously wide, peaked army caps brought about a twinkly-eyed grin across his red, chubby cheeks. I hope he never considered going to Russia, North Korea or China.

The descent to Bolzano was an equally contorted railway route that passed several, barely camouflaged pill-boxes and redoubts. Seemingly, there had been a cross-border conflict between Austria and Italy that had lasted for many years; an aftershock of WWII, probably instigated by mountain men as a decoy, to disguise any illegal boundary trading. By late afternoon on a summer's day, we drew into Bolzano and learnt that the bikes would be delivered the next morning. The crossings through several country borders had slowed up the luggage transfers; considering the distance travelled, we thought the railways had done an excellent job. After all, the last time we saw the bikes was in the registration office at Victoria, London.

Dave Joynson, the early bird, went down to the town centre, into the station and found that the bikes had already arrived. With help, he wheeled them back to the guest house, all present and correct. We were soon packed and on the road to the start of the Passo Mendola. The morning mists had burnt off to leave an absolutely clear blue sky. Cliff faces bordering the valley were lit by the morning light; white and pale cream, glowing brightly in elongated lines and following the contours above thick, green forestry. The Mendola Pass was steep and relatively short with multiple hairpin bends, giving an ever-changing aspect on the hot Italian countryside. I noticed the tarmac was beginning to melt under our wheels; black and shiny in the heat of approaching midday. Over the summit, we descended into a wide valley laced with several lakes. Villages of clustered, red pantiled roofs and churches with onion-capped towers squatted between orchards of apples, pears and plums. This land of plenty was alive with the constant sound of chirruping, a sound that spoke of hot sun and a stillness of pleasant, sleepy torpor. Our second climb of this opening day was up to the top of the Passo di Tonale, a longer, steadier and straighter road. A convenient roadside hotel afforded overnight bed, breakfast and evening meal, with, of course, many a cool beer in the bar.

On day two, we descended the Passo di Tonale, reached Ponte di Legno, crossed the long Gavia Pass into the Valle dell'Adda and cycled north to Bormio. The Gavia was mainly un-surfaced, remote and afforded grand views of snow-capped mountains in the Ortler Group, part of the Parco Nazionale dello Stelvio. Although a dirt road, it was well graded and defined, lonely and traffic-free for the most part and presented few difficulties. However, it was time-consuming and we stayed overnight in Bormio so as to be at the foot of the very long climb to the high and famous Stelvio Pass next day.

A sunny, clear morning sky soon filled with billowing cumulo clouds. Perspiration rolled off the brow as I had to stop, towel down and have a rest. Clearly the time to take photographs, after waiting for the hands to stop shaking. As we climbed on a surfaced road that bore the scars of last winter's snows, we managed to climb out of the humidity of the lower valley and still under hot, sparkling sunlight, progress upwards. The group split up on the long ascent; now over rough dirt and diving through numerous avalanche tunnels, before we reached the open, scree-covered slopes of the Passo Stelvio. Slate-grey scree banks stained an otherwise glaringly white, snow-covered landscape with the large Stelvio Refugio, standing defiant on an elevated and isolated, rocky bluff, aloof above its surrounding skirt of frozen snow. The solid, reassuring building resembled a small version of the Overlook Hotel, as featured in Kubrick's horror film, *The Shining*. The most curious building passed was the Piccolo Tibet Refuge, standing isolated but somehow, wholly appropriate.

We sat on a wall and looked into the deep valley below. The Ortles, over 12,800 feet (3,905m).and the Cima Verona, over 11,600 feet (3,544m).dominated the right-hand side of the valley. The grey, bare rock vertical walls led the eye to summit shoulders capped with a cowl of thick snow. The whole towering massif seemed to squat, threatening, like a ponderous beast and always present in the peripheral vision. Our road laced down the opposite mountainside in a bewildering contortion of hairpin bends, ever turning, ever falling, like a long, twisted bootlace.

We dropped with some trepidation around countless bends; a kilometre stone on every other apex, into the green valley below. I made frequent stops to let the wheel rims cool; constant braking of both front and rear wheels to deter the bike from running out of control superheated the alloy rims. The Ortler mountain hovered above, appearing even higher from here, halfway down the pass. The lower giant buttress, a vertiginous wall, fell straight into the verdant grassy slopes above the hamlet of Trafoi. My fingers were cramped with the constant squeezing of the brake levers, bent into stiff claws by the sheer effort of slowing down. It was only after freewheeling past the church at Trafoi; its tall, narrow steeple dominating the valley, that I could relax, sit up and fully enjoy the surroundings. We headed for the main Val Venosta, the River Adige and a direct route back to Bolzano. Short of the main valley, we found a comfortable *gasthaus* in the little village of Prato allo Stelvio, welcomed by a typical Austrian *fraulein* dressed in her Bavarian pinafore dress with tightly wound, flaxen locks. Twelve years later our group travelling by minibus under the name of the North Staffs Wayfarers would join in the celebrations at Prato, the centennial anniversary of the opening of the Stelvio Pass, all of those thousands of feet above.

A 2007 edition of the television programme *Top Gear* saw the blokes in search of The Best Driving Road in the World. Wanting to fully test their powerful, yet ugly sports cars, they were seeking a demanding road with scores of tight bends. On reaching the summit of the Stelvio Pass, and gazing down its multiple hairpin loops, they had found their perfection in challenging roads, and endorsed their choice without need for further discussion. In 1967, sports cars came with wire-spoked wheels, fold-back bonnets, split windscreens and swooping mudguards. They had style, The blokey boys, Clarkson, Hammond and May, driving their low, wedge-shaped, unstylish macho machines were barely born, probably still filling their nappies; certainly weren't old enough to drive, when we plunged down that heart stopping staircase of the Stelvio Pass.

We cycled through Bolzano, staying at a small guest house in a narrow valley below Nova Levante, before climbing a series of passes to reveal ever more spectacular mountains. The small *gasthaus* here was overseen by a jolly, rotund chef who shared jokes with Chris and was determined to show us his prize jukebox. The bulbous, hackneyed machine churned out similarly-aged antiquated Bavarian melodies. An evening of rounded, rumbustious, oompah music assaulted our ears. Steins of German beer; a golden, refreshing drink in arm-straining, heavy, knobbly glasses, quenched thirsts and lubricated the evening's entertainment.

Above Nova Levante, a view framed by pine trees of incredibly jagged crests had me reaching for the camera. The long arête of the Latemar Group stood in silhouette against a morning sun, its walls falling vertically in sheer flutes, straight into a milky-blue lake. After capturing the scene, I found a roadside trader's shelter and bought a very well-carved wooden eagle to take home as a present. Carved from cedar, it was one of the better examples of a typical touring souvenir. But photographs would always be the best. We stayed in Canazei, meeting Clive Salt and friend, Alan Machin, at the local camping site. They had motored through Germany, Switzerland and Austria in Clive's old Vauxhall to meet us in the heart of the Dolomites. On a back road near Canazei, we had a view of the region's highest mountain, the curiosly named Marmolada; covered in a snowfield streaked with dirty screes and unknown crevasses, at a height of nearly 11,000 feet (3,343m). Our next pass, the Passo Pordoi led to the islanded Sella Group of sheer rock faces. At the summit of the Sella Pass, the grouped cluster of mountains rose like a gigantic, square skyscraper. This enormous monolith of dolomitic limestone, several square miles in base area, pushed out of the white moraines like a giant molar. It was difficult to imagine that this elevated rock was once part of the seabed, constituting trillions of carbonated, aquatic crustaceans, highly-compressed crabs, lobsters and seashells. Subsequent calcification, bedding, up-thrusting and glacial erosion had provided us mere mortals with this stupendous landscape. We had to tilt the head backwards to admire the towering heights where streaks of snow clung in vertical gullies and small, misty clouds played between pale, creamy rocks and brilliant blue sky. The scene has often been portrayed in car advertisements; a fittingly spectacular backdrop to a very ordinary vehicle. A millisecond of geography glimpsed within minutes of trumpeted car detail, all set on curiously traffic-free roads.

We circled the Sella mountains, crossing the Gardena Pass and made the hairpin descent, back to Canazei, before pushing east towards Cortina d'Ampezzo over the Falzarego Pass. Giants of the Dolomites, Le Tofane, Tre Cime di Lavaredo and Civetta punched the skyline in this incredibly jagged landscape. A distant view of Monte Civetta hangs in the memory. Our road rounded a hillside bend where an ancient residence clung to the very lip of the gorge. Beyond the framing hillside slopes, the Civetta formed a full-stop to the panorama. It was evening, and the lowering sun's rays were catching the vertical flanks of this attractive, triangular-shaped mountain. It glowed a pale orange and then a dull crimson in the waning light, reflecting a setting sun, and could almost be an illustration from Tolkien's *The Hobbit* or a *Gormenghast* fantasy setting. A flying dragon, swooping over the peaks, would not have been out of place. Cortina, having played host to a winter Olympics, was a busy resort with a wonderful backdrop of snow-covered mountains. However, it was a highly touristy town, like Chamonix in the French Alps, a fact that reflected in the high prices of everything. The detritus of out-of-season ski-lifts, ski-jumps, bobsleigh runs and skating rinks, together with the aimlessly posing of wealthy tourists being fleeced in more ways than one, gave an air of well-heeled artificiality. We stayed on the outskirts, preferring to move south as soon as possible, into more isolated countryside. We did, however, have time to climb the Passo Giau, a short ascent to 7,335 feet (2,236m), south of Cortina. The way then was just a dirt track and we had to dodge docile snakes spread across the track on the lower approaches. The summit pastures were extensive, and the skyline pierced by strangely shaped, distorted peaks, appearing vague and alien-like in the grey, misty distance.

Beyond Pieve di Cadore, on a lonely minor route, we cycled around a bend to find the road ahead completely missing. What had been a road hugging the valley side, following the windings of the river below, was now a deep hole and a mound of loose earth. Looking ahead we noticed deep bites taken out of the road at intervals, making any progress forward impossible. All the trees alongside the opposite river bank had been flattened and lay horizontal, all aligned downstream. The previous year's excessive rainfall had over-filled lakes; the dam bursting under pressure and the resulting wave of flood waters scouring the lower valleys. The village of Cencenighe downstream was unfortunate to have its local graveyard completely washed away; coffins, bodies and gravestones displaced in an extreme example of gruesome natural forces. It was in the same year, 1966, when the river Arno flooded, threatening the timeless treasures of Florence.

We retreated and joined an alternative route, out of the mountains, into flatter countryside, cycling through parched agriculture, towards Venice. A roadside café halt in a hamlet in the Veneto region brought Tony to the fore as he used his Italian, ordering cooling beers all round. The family were pleased to see cyclists from England dropping in on their humble abode. Group photographs were taken in their back garden. Overall, we found the Italian folk very welcoming; their preparation and serving of food, perhaps, being their favourite occupation. Everything was done with a smiling cheerfulness, an artistic flourish. Every word uttered was accompanied by a wild waving of arms. Nothing was understated. One of the most endearing facets of Italian life was of handling their currency. With so many thousand Lire to the pound, their paper money; although showing a staggering amount of lira; a line of noughts stretching across the tatty paper; was, in pounds sterling, really not much at all. When proffering a note to the raven-black-haired supermarket checkout girl, our change often came back in part coin, part couple of sweeties, both delivered with delicate hand and alluring smile.

We cycled along the causeway towards Venice with mounting anticipation. We weren't to be disappointed. After finding a suitably inexpensive hotel, closer to the station than the Grand Canal, we stored the bikes and began our exploration of the city. The attractive descriptions of Venice were well deserved. St Mark's Square, the Basilica and Campanile, the Doge's Palace, the Bridge of Sighs, the Rialto Bridge, and the Grand Canal, all impressed. There were tourists; not too many in 1967, but Venice could more than accommodate these, all dissipated between countless classical sites, waterways and alleyways. The bewildering layout of canals and passageways, connected by short, humpbacked bridges, have all been well portrayed in the film, *Don't Look Now* from a short novel by Daphne du Maurier. The wealth of abandoned churches, relatively unknown and slowly rotting, their artwork gradually disappearing, didn't bear thinking about. From the cool, narrow alleys, scuttling rats underfoot, one suddenly burst into open, square piazzas, lined with lively cafes and having central public drinking fountains. Mangy cats streaked over warm stone paving, chased by equally mangy dogs, as a lively language reverberated off ancient walls and from under every surrounding café parasol. We sampled the famous Italian ice cream,; numerous flavours, arranged on tall counters and took a canal trip on the *vaporetto*, Venice's local waterbus service. Venice was touristy but being a working city with no traffic allowed, and packed with genuine historic architecture, was well qualified to handle the additional influx of travellers. Gondoliers glided through hidden backwaters; that stunted paddling action appearing awkward to the untrained eye. Green water, littered with detritus of a working city, cast shimmering reflections on the stone undersides of ornate bridges. A lingering smell of slime tweaked the nostrils, though not unpleasant, gave a certain added ambience to the whole experience. Venice is slowly sinking. We were pleased to see it in all its splendour as it may eventually be gone – sunk under the rising water of global warming or the weight of increased tourism. After a full day of sightseeing, it was time to leave this city of the winged, golden lion of San Marco, register the cycles, and take the overnight train through the Alps, and back to England. Back to an England of flimsy kaftans, diaphanous dresses with little worn underneath, beads, bangles, ribbons and bows. Blokes with moustaches, playing sitars in some Far Eastern dream. India became very popular with the overland tours being arranged. The Summer of Free Love – we missed some of it back home – we were amongst the architectural treasures of Venice.

It was the thirteenth day of July and the Tour de France was travelling from Marseilles to Carpentras on a sweltering hot day in southern France. Tom Simpson, riding for the British National team, instead of his usual trade team, Peugeot, was chasing the leader, Jiminez, on the cruel climb of Mont Ventoux. When the road left the shade of forestry, it emerged onto the bare, stony slopes of the mountains; glaring bright in the blisteringly hot afternoon. Simpson, always playing the English gentleman with his brolly, bowler hat and cups of tea, had been taking something far more serious than Ty-phoo to get him through these difficult stages of the Tour. Like all the other Continental riders, he was injecting a drug, probably EPO., amphetamines or some other performance-enhancing potion. He had to do it just to keep the playing field level. He was a professional racing cyclist, and he had to earn money.

On our grainy television at home, I watched a news report showing his slow progress in the blinding heat of a Provencale summer afternoon. He had soon slowed to a crawl and was lurching sideways across the white road. With dust sticking to his sweat-soaked arms and legs, head and tongue lolling from side to side, he clawed his way ever upwards in that stark, exposed desert. Eventually, he flopped over, still attached to the toe clips and his mechanic Harry Hall had to lift him upright before pushing him onwards. The image of his further swaying uncontrollably and falling, limp like an exhausted fish, reminded me of brave Jim Peters as he struggled to cross the finish line after a particularly hard, hot marathon. He finally collapsed in a pile of floppy, useless limbs and was dragged to the side of the road. Oxygen was administered but it was too late.

Tom simpson died near the summit of Mont Ventoux – Mountain of the Winds – with a burst heart, due to heat exhaustion, having, through the use of dope and brandy, cut off his body's safety valve. We in Britian at the time didn't quite realise or understand the use of drugs in sport; it was play, lose, and shake hands like gentlemen after every game for us Brits. Lord Baden-Powell, Earl Haig and Jim Peters had been our heroes, as read about in *Boys' Own* Magazines – taking part and losing were accepted priveleges. Use of drugs is prevelant still in the Tour de France, as well as in athletics and many other sporting competitions. I have climbed steep, long hills in very hot conditions. The mind is determined enough to suffer the sweat, blood and tears, and carry on regardless, but only up to the point; finally, the mind will say, *"No, that's enough, this is stupid, I'll stop and have a drink, smoke a cigarette, look at the map or take a photograph, or better still, do all of these things."* Psychology can keep you wanting to climb that hill, physiology, acting as a safety valve, can stop you in you tracks. Unless that bodily function is bypassed using health substitutes – performance-enhancing concoctions.

After a stay at Maeshafn YH in the Clwydian Mountains, one of our younger members was descending at speed through the sweeping bends of the Horseshoe Pass near Llangollen, when he lost control and hit the tarmac. His presence divided into three, rapidly separating units. Him, his bike and portable radio. The radio skidded across the road, spewing pieces of plastic, batteries, and coiled wire. He had been catching up on the pop-pickers' hit parade; one hand holding radio clamped to ear, the other on the handlebars. As he rounded a fast bend near Valle Crucis Abbey, he finally lost control. The radio was still playing a tinny tune and reader, you will never believe what that title was – *Hit the Road Jack* by Ray Charles. It was one of those curiously ironic occasions that seemed to follow cyclists.

As summer rolled into autumn, our weekends used youth hostels closer to home, hostels like Bridges in the Onny Valley, Wilderhope Manor on Wenlock Edge, and the small farmhouse cottage at Wheathill. I had the crazy idea of carrying this recording machine on a weekend to Wilderhope and both playing some music and taping the fruity Shropshire accents. I had recently bought a Philips portable tape recorder and proceeded to transfer favourite tracks into dinky, clear-plastic three inch reels. Although a portable, the tape recorder was quite heavy, taking six U2 batteries, and it would only just fit in the saddlebag. The Philips tape recorder, a light cotton sleeping bag and a few packets of dried soup. I recorded the gnarled tones of Shropshire farmers as we all enjoyed lunchtime drinks at the Plough Inn on Wenlock Edge. "You wipe that bugger off" was played back, barely audible above the general clamour of a Sunday lunchtime drinking crowd. Considering the weight of the recorder – what a stupid item to put in the saddlebag – but we did such silly things then. Thirty years hence, in the new millennium, we have Walkmans, compact discs, I-Pods, I-Pads, and even music on mobile phones. The up-to-date cyclists is, no doubt, fully wired for sound. But therein lies danger. Awareness, attention and particularly the sense of hearing play an important part in cycling safety. Being deafened by the squawking of modern pop music is not good.

With so many weekends based on Shropshire and mid Wales hostels, the return run to Stoke was always marked with a teatime meal at Edgebolton, near Shawsbury on the main A53 road. Preceding this pleasant interlude and cycling through Church Stretton, between the bulk of the Long Mynd and the shapley Stretton Hills of Caer Caradoc and the Lawley, we would scour the local map for a route to by-pass Shrewsbury. Our deviously chosen way would take us through quiet country lanes starting as far away on the A49 trunk road as underneath the Lawley, many miles south of Shrewsbury. The indistinct lane, hedge-lined and extremely narrow, craftily diverged from the main road at the slightest of angles and heads towards Acton Burnell, passing through the hamlet of Frodesley (pronounced Frudgley). The uncanny straightness of the lane indicated a former Roman Road, and passed over a couple of dry stream beds before inching past the small, wayside inn, The Swan. A glance to the rear at this point revealed the attractive hills of the Strettons; cone-shaped and shaded blue in the afternoon light, before we ran into the main street and scattered cottages of Acton Burnell. The Castle at the back of the village is partially ruined but still offers sufficient architecture to be of interest. A distant ruined barn building in the grounds of the Concord College, a private school, was once the site of early parliament sittings. The whole site, adjoining little church, and hilltop forest included, gives an instant atmosphere of appearing straight from the times when kings hunted the woods for wild boar.

The next rural gem on the route revealed a glimpse from the lodge gates of half-timbered Pitchford Hall. The magnificent 'E'-planned Tudor residence, equalling Little Morton Hall in Cheshire for overall splendour, was once partly open to the public; now, sadly, a strictly private property. The past owner was a Lloyd's 'Name' who, after the financial crash, had to recoup some of the losses. Pitch was mined in the Hall's grounds, hence the place name. Leaving Pitchford, we would join the main A458 Shrewsbury – Bridgnorth road and amble into Cross Houses. The junction between lane and main road was marked with a thin copse of trees and a partly-hidden gypsy encampment. In the 1960s, I remember seeing the old horse-drawn wagons and tethered ponies, with clothing spread over the hedges to dry. Shoeless children; girls in garish dresses and boys in long, short trousers minus the arse end, would scutter along, waving their snotty handkerchiefs. Dogs with noses sniffing the dirt, tails waving high, would lope along behind. Such were the sights and sounds of those times.

With the spires of Shrewsbury closer, we cycled to Atcham and paused on the older of the two bridges there; the A5 Watling Street road spanning the River Severn, resisting the temptation to call at the Mytton and Mermaid Inn across the willow-edged water. At our backs spread the shapely hills of central Shropshire; the Strettons, Long

Mynd, Stiperstones and Long Mountain. How could anyone with an ounce of sense and landscape appreciation contemplate the crass erection of gigantic wind turbines across the hills of Shropshire, or the Welsh border to the west? Sheer lunacy! Frequent views of The Wrekin, that geographic sentinel for mid-Shropshire, were to be glimpsed over wild hedgerows as narrow lanes turned, rose and fell on our deviating route. Pedalling along the boundary of Attingham Park, we wound through further lonely lanes to Upton Magna, Roddington, Roden, Poynton, skirting the eastern swell of Haughmond Hill and finally through Great Wytheford, to Shawbury. Just a mile remained along the A53 towards Market Drayton before we were slewing across the road, dismounting and levering open the garage doors of our favourite tea place at Edgebolton. Our route would vary sometimes but only by a mile or so, passing quiet, leafy Condover or Berrington and Upper Cound; unspoilt countryside of the highest quality. One deviating route took us through a deep ford near Cantlop; a steep hill approach from either direction propelling us through the fast-flowing Cound Brook, across the stone streambed and hoping to remain upright, not slipping on hidden, slimy weed. On one occasion we were freewheeling down a narrow lane in a disorderly group, laughing and joking, when a car suddenly appeared from around a tight bend. We had to split into two lines and crash into the bordering hedgerows, left and right, to avoid clashing with the alarmed motorist. Some of the group landed in the bordering drainage ditch before coming to a halt. The by-passing of Shrewsbury was hardly worth the many twists and turns of deepest rurality, certainly not gaining any reduction in distance. Nevertheless, to miss those varied scenes, burned into the memory and always remembered, would have been a lost challenge of mapreading, a discarded opportunity to discover byways a long way off the beaten track. For readers keen on tracing routes, the OS Landranger Series, Sheet Nos. 126 and 167 show this attractive network of traffic-free lanes.

The Cyclists' Touring Club café in Edgebolton was particularly welcoming. An enamel sign set above the garage doors; a bicycle wheel with three wings and the letters CTC set in gold on a black background was a trusted nationwide sign for the casual cyclist. A sign that indicated a wash and brush-up, an inexpensive, wholesome meal and a rest. Chunky, steaming mugs of tea would be provided, a thirst quencher on both hot and cold days. Mrs Haines's café at Edgebolton was no exception. We would lean the bikes line astern against the garage walls, wander down the rear garden path and into a single-storey outhouse to have a quick wash. The dilapidated building was probably once a pigsty but now provided a place to wash off the accumulated road dust and perspiration of hot, afternoon miles. This stone and tile shack contained a shallow ceramic wash basin and a simple cold water tap waggling on the end of an insulated lead pipe, the unlikely plumbing protruding from the sandstone wall. The garden was mainly laid to vegetables with a disintegrating stone and timber greenhouse at the bottom boundary. Broken glass, peeling paintwork and a tangle of spiders' webs indicated it having being there for years. Nevertheless, its insides always seemed to be crammed full with strong, leafy plants and succulent, juicy-red tomatoes. I'm sure a quick peek beyond the rickety door would leave one reeling from the bittersweet, iron-tangy smell of plump, savoury fruit. An aroma that always tweaked my sense of smell, reminding me of cottage gardens, old plant pots and decrepit, wooden wheelbarrows.

Mrs Haines ushered us into the rear lean-to conservatory, seemingly always drying her hands on a well-used floral apron and mentally noted our individual meal requirements. Here, in the cool shade, seated close together and in two lines at the long dining table, we registered the growing effect of the past miles of sunny lanes. A slight soreness could be felt between the rough material of chafing, khaki shorts and sensitive skin. Sunburned knees and thighs started to tighten, rubbing together, while healthy, tanned elbows and arms nudged, some slyly, maybe, conveying secret messages between boy and girl. Outside, the late afternoon sunshine painted a chrome-yellow light onto the lawn and flower garden; lupins, hollyhocks, daisies and marigolds rendering the visits as halcyon days; days of warmth, timelessness and peace.

Mrs Haines arrived with a tray full of steaming pint mugs of tea – nectar for the travel-weary cyclist – and we helped ourselves to milk from a chipped jug, and sugar from an overflowing bowl. I reflect with pleasure at these sensible, no-nonsense table accoutrements and compare them with today's mean and fiddling paper sachets and miserable plastic pots. Plates of beans on toast and eggs, chips and peas soon followed. The younger cyclists emptied their loose change onto the table, having to take care of pocket money and seeing if they were rich enough to afford a dessert of tinned fruit with evaporated milk. The camaraderie of cheerful conversation flowed to and fro across the oilcloth, interrupted only by the bite of a sausage or rudely-sounding squirt of the salad cream bottle. Our gathering together in that shaded garden room resembled a painting by Auguste Renoir. The *Luncheon of the Boating Party,* that wonderful image of a certain bourgeoisie, a socialising crowd seated at a table groaning with delicious food and wine; a scene of jollity and part-alfresco summer warmth. Just substitute posh dresses, string vests and straw boaters for oil-stained shorts, socks and torn Aertex shirts and a comparative picture could possibly emerge. Swap clear red wine and lead crystal glasses for large pottery mugs of tea and glasses of lemon barley water and the reader will imagine a scene of similar conviviality. Although similar in summer geniality, our lot didn't entertain a yappy dog on the tabletop. As plates were cleared and drinks downed, the filling meal engendered a somnolent dullness; conversation would flag, a fly caught in the dusty web of a corner window pane would buzz and shake in impotent frustration, and it would be time to leave before we all fell asleep.

Pedalling the remaining miles back to Stoke, the sun casting long shadows ahead of the front tyre, we passed through Hodnet, Market Drayton (then, in the early 60s without a by-pass).and over the climbs of Loggerheads and forested Maer Hills. Through Baldwin's Gate, the road climbed and descended to a lovely country inn at Whitmore. On the crossroads there, the homely Mainwaring Arms provided a last stopping place before we would disperse to different parts of the city. A parting pint of hop-infused bitter beer was sharp and cool enough to cut the severest of thirsts. On most summer evenings, the weather was sufficiently warm to enable us to sit on the low, sandstone boundary wall; all in a line with legs spread over the pavement, chatting over the adventures of the weekend. The telling of a joke or humorous anecdote was only delayed by a quaff of ale, undisguised burp or draw on a cigarette. Self-deprecating tales of the weekend's experiences led to interjections, comments and funny side-stories, conveying an atmosphere of innocent fun. Sitting on that warm boundary wall, engaged in witty conversation could almost be equated with childish innocence – sitting on the kerb, letting dirt fall through the fingers, telling tales to a young friend.

We drew up our legs to the chin; brown, dusty, knobbly knees, some smeared with chain oil, to allow a middle-aged man to pass along the pavement. He had stopped in the car park across the road and listened to his noisy wife and kids' refreshment demands. On passing, he commented on our hilarity, adding that he'd never seen such a happy group of people. We raised our glasses in a toast, replying, "We're ok, now we're drinking this." He had probably suffered miles of traffic jams, nagging wife and quarrelsome offspring on a typically hectic, crowded and stifling getaway weekend to the coast. We could imagine his envy of our situation and his vague remembrance of past, idyllic days of single-status freedom.

One evening pause at the Mainwaring Arms was certainly well-earned. Geoff s bottom bracket spindle had shattered a few miles north of Shrewsbury and he had to be push/pulled along the remaining miles home. I would expect the bracket cups to break with a jamming of ball bearings, but the spindle is a heavy, thick piece of engineering. Both his pedal cranks became useless and we had to take turns to push and pull him up hills and along the flat for some miles of close-combination riding and astute manoeuvring. Needless to say, he bought the first round of drinks at our favourite, weekend-closing country alehouse, the Mainwaring Arms.

Other CTC cafés evoke similar memories of pleasurable interludes over a busy meal table. A small café in the village square at Loppington, near the Dickin Arms, provides recollections of being served sliced pears in syrup with a surrounding girdle of evaporated milk. I also used to buy cans or tubes of Nestle's Milk; that thick, white taste of heavenly viscosity would cure any vicious attack of the knock. Loppington's other pub was the Blacksmith's Arms, a minute, ramshackle building with a corrugated tin roof. There was no bar, as such, and the drinks were served from an open counter beside the rear doorway. The room was filled with dark, enveloping settles with back rests climbing from quarry-tiled floor to low, beamed ceiling. Wem Ales bitter, clear and bright but not of skull-shattering strength, was poured from an enamel jug. In clement weather, hot and heavy afternoons, we would invariably take our drinks and sit in the wild back garden, attacked by rampant, triffid-like plants or buzzed by curious, winged and stinging insects.

The café at Quina Brook, the small hamlet at the end of a dismantled canal branch and desperately close to Whixall Moss, specialised in lashings of currant cake. Geoff would make yet another dry joke of this, referring to the contents of the cake stand as another serving of 'funeral bread'. Something to do with the black currants resembling dead flies embedded in the yellow slabs of 'cemetery gravestone' bread. The fusty private lounge, deep in heavy furniture and even heavier curtains, gave a distinct feeling of a creeping, body-sagging doom. On the enormous dresser, an array of silver competition cups flashed, threatening to lift the crepuscular darkness and gloom of the place. Cups of every size, bowls with deep, moulded swags, awards and certificates, press clippings and photographs of a statuesque duellist proudly shouldering his trusty firearm. They had been won by a national champion, Mr Brian Bailey, a local deadeye-dick of a rifle shooter who had even been considered an Olympic choice and gold medal certainty. The Moss, that mysterious fen of disappearing signposts and bleak prospects with a very real danger of swallowing the unwary visitor, lay immediately to the north. Our adventures in that flat waste of sphagnum moss, water-filled dykes and lonely timber lift-bridges has been a story already told.

Another gem of a café was situated in the Staffordshire village of Acton Trusssell. Not a name of a hamlet in a local melodrama of inter-family derring-do, but a (then).quiet backwater south of Stafford, close to the Trent & Mersey Canal where now, alas, the M6 Motorway roars with traffic nose-to-tail on careering journeys to nowhere and back. From inside the timber lean-to, the wild cottage garden threatened to encompass everything; tall hollyhocks and towering foxgloves pressed their heady flowers against the glazing. In fine weather, we could sit outside on rustic pine benches and take tea in fragile bone china cups. It was all so very genteel, civilized and English. That was, until a sharp shard of splintered pine bark would pierce the bare, tender flesh at the back of the thigh. We would often make fun of the village's name. Spinning along country lanes in the general direction of Stafford, we would call to each other in the cut-glass voice of Noel Coward;"Where have you ridden from this day, my fine man?"

"Oh, I have just taken my leave of Acton Trussell,that delightful haven three miles and ten minutes since, don't you know?"

With the coming of the cold, misty days of October, a farmer from Nant Mawr, near the Tanat Valley, took his pigs to Oswestry Market. From that popular venue, livestock was transported across several counties, unwittingly spreading the virile foot and mouth disease to masses of cloven-hoofed beasts – mainly sheep, pigs and cattle. The farms surrounding Bomere Heath had to slaughter many of their herds; the constant smell of disinfectant in the nostrils by day and the sickly smell of burning flesh by night. Each farm entrance had a long mat of disinfectant-soaked straw to cover the wheels of all passing vehicles. The leaping flames of burning cattle pyres reflected off the ever-glowering nimbus-stratus cloud bases on those long nights of the pestilence. The sad scene was like a painting of the charnel houses of hell by Hieronymus Bosch. The seemingly everlasting days of cloud and drizzle did not help; some folk believed that the dull climate spread the disease. Or could it have been through the water courses? Others thought that the birds caused the spread as most of Cheshire, Shropshire and Staffordshire fell under the strict control of animal movement. I will always remember the severe red and white-lettered government warning notices tacked to every farmyard gate. The clinical whiff of disinfectant solution on those straw mats, all squashed and thick with mud and cow manure; the guarding of farms by dour, helmeted and caped policemen stamping their feet and clapping their hands to ward off the wet, raw coldness. It all illustrated the misery of that period and I wasn't even remotely connected to farming. The final total slaughter reached the hundreds of thousands as the Ministry of Agriculture pursued its policy of eradication, not vaccination,all to keep the price of beef high. Foot and mouth finally burnt itself out in the following spring as the warmer, sunnier and clearer days brought an end to the disease. We continued to cycle in those grim times, but never ventured onto rough tracks or crossed farmland.

As Sheila, Fred, nephew Andrew and niece Julie were spending Christmas down in Plymouth, a few of the group stayed over at Bomere Heath. Cynwyd wasn't available and at least we could keep the house lived-in over the festive period. We did little cycling, apart from a meal in the expensive Prince Rupert Hotel in Shrewsbury, a run to the Bridgwater Arms, Harmer Hill and the then quaint Red Lion Inn at Myddle. The singing continued at the Bridgewater where we fraternised with the pub's rifle shooting team, our combined choral efforts echoing off the tiling in the mens' toilets. Some wit named us the Urinal Choir. The Red Lion at Myddle was, in 1967, a very, very rural public house. There was just the one narrow bar room fitted with a single bench settle along the back wall. The lounge was just a chintzy living room where one sank into comfortable, deep armchairs while downing the pints of Wem Bitter. Other pubs in the area were equally basic. The Cross Keys at Burlton always appeared closed; the timid landlady having to stand on a box to reach over the high bar. The Railway at Yorton, run by mother and daughter, vibrated whenever a train passed and the mens' toilet was a brick-built thunder box at the end of the (then).garden. The Railway hasn't changed over the years, winning awards for good, real ale.

Geoff and Gloria were courting at this time. They would shortly marry in Stoke-on-Trent and buy a house on Fearn's Avenue, Porthill. I had to buy a suit for the wedding from, I think, the Fifty Shilling Tailors. It was off the peg, ill-fitting, with turn-ups dragging on the ground and a crotch that hung down like a sack of sand. I was never the world's best-dressed gent – not even a reasonably dressed tramp.

No damage resulted from our Yuletide stay at Bomere Heath, save the inflatable Santa being accidentally punctured by an errant cigarette. After all, this was hardly your usual teenagers' party rampage. We enjoyed the Christmas but it wasn't a patch on our usual stays at Cynwyd. We were far too close to home and far too close to local acquaintances. A Christmas holiday such as ours needed a suitable country setting and, more importantly, to be a good distance from Stoke-on-Trent.

*Sadly, George Longstaff died of a heart attack in October, 2003 while riding a tandem trike.

Tramps' Run to Rudyard YH from Limekiln Bank. (Photo: Evening Sentinel, Stoke).
Combined New Year weekend with the Stoke YHA Walking Section

The New Harry Quinn – The Aston Martin of bicycles!
Frame collected lovingly from Walton Road, Liverpool

Crash south of Birmingham.
The incredible forces created to distort frame and front wheel.

Wilderhope Manor, a magnificent Tudor mansion.
(YHA/National Trust Postcard)
Stays here were always memorable albeit very spooky

Celebrating Christmas in the Blue Lion PH, Cynwyd, Corwen.
Black Velvets and Russian Convoys became the favoured drinks.

Folk singing in the back lounge, Blue Lion.
*Top: Roy (Orbison) Deakin on Mandolin, Below: Andrew
Ovenall on banjo.*

Ralph Salt (Mr Intrepid) crossing the Roman Steps (top right)
Rhinog Mountains.
One of the classic rough-stuff routes he pioneered.

Cirque de Gavarnie, Haute Pyrenees, France.
Magnificent scenery on our tour in July 1965

CAG on the climb of the Col du Tourmalet from Luz-St-
Saveur.
*Nearing the summit at 2115m (6,939 ft) on this Tour de France
classic climv.*

Hirnant Pass from Bala to Lake Vyrnwy.
Textbook glaciated valley & prospect of a hard climb ahead.

Peter Boardman at the summit of High Cup Nick,
Dufton Fells, Pennines.
Another rough-stuff route conquered and an article for Cycling magazine.

Below Dollywagon Pike in the Lake District.
Peter Boardman thinks, 'How can I protect my wheel rims?'

Completing the Wayfarer's Pass near Llanarmon Dyffryn
Ceriog, Powys.
(L to R) Geoff Cartlidge, Chris Warren (in distance), Dave Hope.

Rough-stuff desperados high on the quartzite Stiperstones
ridge.
*(L to R) Roy Deakin, Clive Salt, Ralph Salt, Tony Booth, Brian
Whalley, CAG (front) Geoff Cartlidge, Dave Hope & Ken Hall.*

Upper Glen Affric on a rainy & cold Scottish tour.
*(L to R) Geoff Cartldige, Rory Deakin, Clive Salt, Ralph Salt (sitting)
& Tony Ross*

On the Passo di Stelvio, Ortler Group, Dolomites,
Italy.
The multiple hairpin bends descending to Trafoi (lower right)

Upper Lake at Glendalough, Wicklow Mountains, Southern Ireland.
Probably one of my most favourite places.

John Bradbury at the summit of the Cold d'Aubisque at 1709m (5,
607 ft) on our May, 1969, early tour of the Haute Pyrenees.
Looking west towards the Col de Soulor and Arrens.

Early rough-stuff from Hirant to Llangynog.
(Leading, L to R) Tony Ross & Derek Latham

On the Isle of Man ferry at Easter, 1968. A clutch of Stoke cyclists.
(Standing, 4th from L) George Longstaff, cycle frame maker supreme, died in 2003.
Geoff Cartlidge (on George's left) wears the controversial club badge.

Chapter Nine

1968

Touring Norway's Fjords – Sectarian Divide in Ulster – An Alternative Route into Shropshire – Boycle's Country – Over the Hills of Central Shropshire – Bottle & Glass, Picklescott – Public Houses as They Once Were – CAMRA – The Morris Travellers – Becoming a Motorist – Christmas at Cynwyd Again.

Age: 27.

Home: Shrewsbury Road, Bomere Heath, Shropshire.

Work: Shropshire County Council, Abbey Foregate, Shrewsbury.

Government: Labour.

Prime Minister: Harold Wilson.

Jan: In Vietnam, the Viet Cong launch the Tet Offensive.

Mar: First man in space. Yuri Gagarin killed in air crash. Ronan Point London tower flats collapse.

Apr: Martin Luther King assassinated. First decimal coin minted (full issue in Feb, 1971). Enoch Powell warns of mass immigration.

May: Students riot in Sorbonne, Paris.

Jun: Robert Kennedy dies after shooting.

Jul: Dubcek continues progressive policies.

Aug: Soviet tanks enter Prague, Czechoslovakia.

Oct: Olympics open in Mexico City.

Nov: Richard Nixon elected US President. Novelist John Steinbeck dies.

Dec: Apollo 8 first manned orbit of moon.
Film: *Oliver*.
Music: Simon & Garfunkel write *Mrs Robinson*.
Rock musical, *Hair*.

And the Vietnam War drags on and on. Bitter fighting in Saigon and Hue forces the US to use yet more defoliants in a war they can never win. Anti-war protest marches culminate in violence outside the American Embassy in Grosvenor Square, London. Flying police helmets, brandished truncheons and placards become airborne as the upholders of law and order drag duffle-coated beatniks through grass and over hedges – backwards! Soviet cosmonaut, Gagarin dies in a plane crash but America advance in the space race with further development of their Apollo programme. The Saturn V rocket, developed by German technician, Werner von Braun, proves to be brilliantly reliable at lifting even more metallic junk into orbit. Meanwhile, in London, a granny demolishes a corner of her high-rise tower block by merely lighting the gas cooker! Britain's quick, prefabricated building techniques, always ugly, prove to be dangerous as an outer wall collapses like a stack of cards at Ronan Point. Although not a member of the European Community, we take the first steps to decimalise our currency. The 2/- florin will become 10p. Other changes will surely follow as we convert from imperial to metric measurements to align with the rest of Europe. The hoodwinking of the general High Street shopper has begun. Old Mrs Arkwright will have to double check her change. What's more, her voluminous bloomers will be coming from Paris next season. Far more skimpy. An unlikely alliance between students, rubbish collectors and factory workers protesting about poor social conditions sees chaos erupt on the streets of the Sorbonne, Paris. Nightly clashes with riot police causes the flying of cobblestones, spraying of CS gas and force of water cannon. The French riot police are an alarming sight, dressed in helmets, body armour and wielding batons across full-length shields, resembling a Samurai invasion in ancient Japan. Definitely not the French gendarmerie of The Pink Panther films.

More assassinations in America with black Civil Rights leader, Martin Luther King and Robert Kennedy falling to the bullet. Czechoslovakian leader, Alexander Dubcek, is brought to heel as Soviet tanks invade his country. The Communist bully boys cannot tolerate those progressive policies. The National Aeronautics and

Space Administration (NASA).launch the first astronauts to orbit the moon. Apollo 8 sees the mysterious dark side and its surface is not made of green cheese. The view of earthrise on Christmas morning provided a seminal moment – a blue, living planet that could be destroyed so easily. If only the world powers would realise that. The space programme costs billions of dollars, while here on Earth, in Biafra, wide-eyed, despairing children with distended bellies wonder where their next meal will come from. Tony Hancock, self-deprecating, yet aloof comedian, commits suicide in Australia, thereby ending a distinctive style of comedy. Apart from a few exceptions (comedians such as Ken Dodd, Frankie Howerd, Morecambe & Wise, Les Dawson and Tommy Cooper)., many would lack his genius.

*

Our 1968 programme started, as usual, with the Cyclists' Annual Dinner at Consall. The springtime hostel destinations were in the Peak District, Shropshire and Denbighshire. Weekends to explore the rough-stuff tracks in south Shropshire; the Stiperstones, Long Mynd and Caer Caradoc hills, around Llangollen and the border valleys, and Maeshafn further north, where we explored the moors around World's End and the Eglwyseg Crags. We toured the Isle of Man for a third time at Easter, staying again at Ramsey, Port Erin and Laxey YHs. Soon enough, our thoughts turned to the summer holiday and a suitably interesting and different area to tour. After the French and Spanish Pyrenees and the Dolomites, markedly hot places in which to cycle, we decided on Norway. The imaginations of deep fjords and snow-covered mountains offered a suitably diverse scenario of potential interest.

Ralph Salt, Geoff Cartlidge, Pete Boardman, John Bradbury, a relative newcomer named Ken Hodgkinson and I met on Crewe Station for the first leg of the journey; north to Carlisle. Our intention was to cycle across the narrow neck of England, travelling from Carlisle to Newcastle-upon-Tyne and once there, taking a boat across the North Sea to Bergen. This was considered far easier than reaching Newcastle directly by rail, a journey involving many awkward train connections. The train to Carlisle was on time and after what would be our last journey sitting together in the guards' van, we found Carlisle YH and turned in early, contemplating the following day's ride. We had to cover the distance following a parallel line to Hadrian's Wall and be on time to catch the evening ferry. On paper, we had time to spare, but any unforeseen delays could have made us late.

Our day cycling across the narrow neck of England, a landscape of grand, rolling hills in Northumberland, was achieved with relative ease. The bright and breezy conditions with the west wind in our sails and the sun reflecting off hillside streams was an enjoyment in itself. Reaching the halfway point of Haydon Bridge, a quick time check told us that we were on schedule and need not rush over the lunch stop. Although the approach road to Newcastle was much hillier, with long, gradual and exposed drags, we finally plunged into the great city and arrived at Wallsend in good time. We boarded the MV *Leda,* found our cabin berths somewhere in the deep bowels of the vessel and returned to the passenger deck on a fine and clear Tyneside mid-July evening. Once underway, high crane jibs and gantries glided past the ship in an industrial procession of steelwork. Warehouses and coal yards clung to the waterway, connected by filthy basins, dry docks and wharfs. Our tug, painted all red with smutted funnel and throbbing, water-churning power, drew us down an ever-widening estuary to open water and fresher sea breezes. Soon, we had altered course, our bows pointing to the north-east and we sailed into a cool North Sea night.

Next morning, emerging from the warm fug of a claustrophobic cabin, I happened on John Bradbury as he jogged along the deserted deck. The cold breeze blowing off the North Sea pinched the cheeks and whipped away the breath. John, a strong, stocky, confident character, a picture ofglowing health as he pound the decks, was a very keen jazz follower and cyclist. He was a sheet metalworker by trade and often used his skill to make 'foreigners'; accessory items for his bike that, if not works of art, were certainly strongly fabricated. I'm sure John's work would appeal to the East German light industrial standards for solidity and practicality. John also had the reputation for being extremely careful with his money; suffice to say that he plunged short, muscled arms into the very deep pockets of his cycling shorts. Ken Hodgkinson was fair-haired, slight, taciturn and sported a Harris Tweed jacket, cycling shorts apart, making him resemble an Edwardian explorer of the Edward Whymper style. Ken was so quiet and reserved, it was difficult to assess his feelings, but I believe he just liked to go with the (ice).flow.

We approached the Norwegian coast and navigated between numerous islets before tying-up in Stavanger Harbour. While mail, freight and passengers were landed, we paced the quayside to stretch our legs. Within a couple of hours we were on our way again, cruising north through calm waters along the coast, between more islands too numerous to count, until, by late evening, we had docked within Bergen's busy harbour. The maritime haven was a tumult of water-borne traffic of every conceivable kind; a bewildering mixture of inlets, wharfs, dry docks and even the historic settlement of Bryggen. The timber-clad houses, shops and chandleries accessed by cobbled alleyways was a fascinating area asking to be visited, but time was passing and we had to find the Bergen YH before it closed. This involved catching the cliff railway to Floyen after storing the cycles at the railway station overnight. The night view of Bergen from these heights was spectacular in itself. The tracery of street lights led down to the harbour where navigation and ships' lamps winked in wavering reflections of many colours; a gathering of jewelled patterns; clusterings of illuminated activity, echoing the stars above, in a clear, blue-black sky.

We collected the cycles and caught our Bergen to Oslo express train. It was punctual, fast, smart, with comfortable airline-type seats and we were attended to by uniformed young ladies. A landscape of undulating hills and lively streams in spate slid past the train windows. Scattered houses, timber-clad and painted red and green, dotted the lower slopes looking like property pieces on a Monopoly board game. We soon arrived at Voss, a small country station, retrieved the cycles and set out along unsurfaced roads towards Gudvangen. Reaching Stalheim, the road became hillier. Waterfalls laced down hillsides and rushed in boisterous haste under the road in thunderous roar and churning foam. Roads were tarmac-covered inside town and village limits, but on reaching the outskirts, were left as well-graded but unmetalled. This didn't slow us down too much as the surfaces consisted of, generally, smooth dirt. Nevertheless, all nuts had to be well tightened or they would soon shake loose. The small nuts and bolts securing the rear carriers to the rear fork ends were particularly liable to become unscrewed and fall free. It was mid-July, dry and sunny but the conditions weren't sultry as are many days in July in England. Of course, we had moved from 53 degrees of latitude to over 60, making conditions fresher and cooler, more bracing for the enthusiastic cyclist.

We found bed and breakfast accommodation at Gudvangen, a village at the end of an inlet; a narrow arm of water on the south side of the extensive Sognefjord. The accommodation was homely; heavy furniture with a lacy tablecloth and warm, thick curtains. The evening light outside seemed to last forever in these higher latitudes. Our jolly hostess served tea; a table crowded with large slabs of goats cheese, larger wedges of green-veined stilton, bread, pots of jam, sardines and hard-boiled eggs. I remember expecting a hot meal to be served that evening, considering we were in more northerly climes. Our table was groaning under the weight of food, all cold-served and arranged on a 'help yourself; smorgasbord style. This was all substantial, although we reacted with surprise when the breakfast seemed to consist of these very same foods – as if the table hadn't been cleared from the last evening. In fact, all domestic meals in Norway were to be the same – cheese, fish, eggs and jam. We certainly didn't have enough Norwegian money to enable us to be more adventurous in our eating. There was one consolation. The lashings of jam seemed to have a subtle alcoholic effect, making us all chatty and humorous and even making the tongue-twisting language almost understandable. Every day we would have lunch; 'drumming up' mugs of tea using Primus and boiling the water in the dixie pan, eating our bread, butter and hard-boiled eggs. Sitting on grassy, wild flower banks in the sunshine, Geoff and Ralph would, when asking what was for lunch, yelp in surprise and mock delight on being told there were loads of yet more eggs and jam.

From Gudvangen, we caught the local ferry into Sognefjord, the vast sea inlet that reaches inland for well over a hundred miles (160k).between high, steep mountains, their outlines perfectly reflected in deep, calm waters of an intense bottle-green. A landscape photographer's heaven. In mid-fjord, we met with another ferry; another local service where mail and passengers were transferred. When seen in the context of the mountains and fjord, the ferry, after pulling clear and continuing its journey, appeared toy-like in size and importance. A little plastic boat in a deep bathtub. Our bows cut the glassy surface for a few miles more before we were slowing and inching alongside the quay at Kaupanger. We took to the road again and cycled several more miles, until reaching the end of the fjord at Skjolden.

No breakfast of bacon, eggs, beans and sausage, nor croissants and coffee, but cheese, eggs and jam! Today we climbed over the wild upland region; part of the Jotunheimen National Park, descending to Lom. As the route gained height, we passed through Turtagro, with views in the distance of the group of sharp, triangular peaks; severely black crags and white eternal snows surrounding the peak Galdhopiggen, rising to 8,104 feet (2,470m).into a leaden sky. The road, consisting of dirt and heaped gravel, clearly showed signs of the wear and tear of last winter's snow cover. It narrowed drastically and became lined with slushy snow. We passed numerous semi-melted lakes partly covered with jumbled, greeny-blue blocks of ice; a bewildering array of ice, snow, rock and watery pools as far as the eye could see across this bleak prospect. Gradually, we lost height and dropped into a deep valley; a glaciated landscape that became greener by the minute. The road surface improved also, a fact that brought me contentment, as I had started to feel the effects of a gippie tummy; probably the change in diet! Bouncing over potholes perched on a narrow saddle and riding along a rough track is not the best practice with a fragile constitution. We arrived at Lom on the eastern side of the mountain plateau and were surprised to see a drier countryside with grassland being irrigated by powerful water pumps. Obviously the region was situated in a typical rain shadow area; that dry land beyond rain-capturing hills as learnt in any good geography classroom.

We shopped at the Big S supermarket in Lom and were astonished at the high price of basic foodstuffs. John, ever careful with his money, let a few tinned shelf items fall into his red duffel bag; sardines, pilchards and unappetising whale meat chunks disappearing into the gloomy depths of this canvas 1960s carrying accessory. On yet another lonely road beyond Lom, John's seat pillar snapped, no doubt a result of the continual bumps, and he saw his saddle topple to the ground. There would be no cycle shop nearby; no Halfords selling bicycle pumps or seat pillars. No dedicated seat pillar shop as seen in *Monty Python's* bike pump emporium in A Cycling Tour (of North Cornwall). However, we stopped on the edge of a village to find ourselves directly outside a blacksmith's shed. Not only did the smith have a piece of steel of the correct, frame-fitting diameter, he also had a lathe and tools to pare down the rod's top so that the saddle could be reattached. The new seat pillar had been turned and fitted within the half-hour. In John's case, in view of the earlier supermarket dash, the saying: "God helps he who helps himself," although not entirely in the full spirit of the meaning, became very, very true.

The Norwegians, whether hostel wardens or otherwise, were extremely friendly. The children especially insisted on practising their English, which turned out to be quite extensive, although, as usual, gravitating towards football terms. They seemed to know more about English teams than ourselves – not surprising considering our lack of interest in the national sport. Our evenings were spent in the local cafés enjoying a few beers and talking to the local girls. John, his radar and twinkling eye ever directed towards the lasses, asked them what they did for entertainment. They understood and informed us that a discotheque was arranged, but only when the ferry visited. In this countryside dissected with innumerable fjords between high mountains, the local boat service was the main form of travel. Further north, the only form of travel servicing and supplying even more isolated communities. Due to the astronomical prices of drinks, our evening sojourns in local drinking houses were brief and at a minimum; usually with just six English touring cyclists talking amongst themselves amid the plastic seats and Formica-covered tables. The Rose & Crown snug atmosphere of an English pub were nowhere to be seen here. Back at the youth hostel, we had extra rounds of bread and fermented jam with the warden speaking faster Norwegian and, due to the effects of the alcoholic conserve, it becoming almost perfectly understandable.

From Olden YH, we cycled to the north and west, traversing a countryside of part pine forestry and part scrub. The valley opened out to bordering low hills with our road crossing and re-crossing simple planked bridges. Streams dived under these wooden structures with a cold, racing urgency. Occasionally, we passed roadside cabins, some having grassy turf roofs sprouting wild flowers of many species. Isolated timber houses dotted the land; usually close to coops of forestry with all of them having a flagpole nearby, proudly and patriotically flying the Norwegian colours. The weather on the holiday so far had been generally warm and sunny; we had expected days of wind and rain. On the contrary, occasionally a tanker would pass, spraying water to lay the dust. Our shift several degrees to the north had a marked effect on the daylight available. On one midnight visit to a hostel toilet, a shack down the garden, a dim light still glowed on the northern skyline. This gloaming in the small hours of a clear July night was bright enough to enable one to easily read a newspaper. That is, if one could understand Norwegian.

From Hellesylt YH, we were close to the Vatnajokull ice cap, thus warranting a short diversion to the very toe of the glacier. The icefall, glaringly bright in the distance, swept down between neighbouring mountain slopes like a high, frozen staircase of irregular, chaotic ice blocks. The painful whiteness of the glacier, exaggerated by a cloudless blue sky, made us squint and reach for the sunglasses. A lake of milky-blueness formed below the ice cliffs – a meltwater pond of Wedgwood-blue translucence. At intervals, the wall of ice splintered, collapsing outwards, sending car-sized chunks crashing and splashing into the semi-frozen water. The silence of the area was repeatedly shattered by the sound of pistol-shot cracks of splitting and calving ice, echoing as it reverberated between enclosing walls of bare rock. On hearing these explosive shots for the first time, we wheeled around, assuming that someone was shooting at us. The whole experience of being so close to the glacier, that ever-moving geographical feature, impressed on us the sheer creative and destructively powerful force of nature.

Beyond Hellesylt, we climbed into wilder country, into the Jostedalsbreen National Park and as altitude increased, the surroundings became bleaker, more tundra-like, with banks of roadside snow formed in the shadows. In treeless terrain, seemingly just feet below a lowering, rain-bearing cloud base, we reached the summit of the climb. After days of warm, dry weather in Norway, it began to spit with rain and the grey solidity of thick cloud brought a feeling of cold rawness to the senses. We pedalled with caution over the rough road surface, passing between bordering snow banks until a stunning view of Geiranger Fjord opened out ahead and below. The sheer mountain walls plunged from flat, snowy mountain tops suspended under an angry, grey cloud mantle, straight into the deep-set fjord. High falls of water like slivers of silver ribbon laced down the rock faces; silent from this distance, but adding to the drama of it all. The whole scene resembled a mountainous plateau savagely cleaved by a giant's axe. Far below our feet, the fjord's cold green water cut through the narrowness of the scar, finding its contorted route somehow to the open sea. A glaciation of the most extreme proportions. We descended to Geiranger on a looping road; hands and knees freezing in the overcast, late afternoon. It became so cold; I slipped a pair of socks over my hands, making any further braking difficult. In fact, it was nearly dark when we finally reached the town and sought accommodation. All the guesthouses were full to overflowing. We were resigning ourselves to sleeping in some wayside bus shelter when, fortuitously, we met with a group of young people, a friendly crowd of Christians attending an organised Fellowship Convention. The reason for the lack of accommodation was just this religious gathering. The boys allowed us to kip down for the night in their hostel's loft space. Amongst the jumble of sleeping bags, boots, climbing ropes, and bibles, we hit the hay, reflecting on a long, arduous, and later freezing ride through the mountains.

We followed the shores of Geiranger Fjord, heading for the coast via Stranda and Skodje in the Romsdal hills, to arrive at Alesund. The smell of the pine woods gave way to that of ozone as we neared the jetty. A short ferry journey took us back into Bergen where an overnight stay at Montana YH gave us a full day to savour the port's distinctive character. Our last day in Norway; a brilliant sunny one; gave us ample time to tour the quayside market, admire the harbourside tall ships, and take a short trip across the water to take a look at the old port of Bryggen. The day off the bikes gave plenty of opportunities for creative photography. The hustle and buswtle of this frenetic, Nordic port (if anything so laid-back as Norway could be described as frenetic) showed in the resulting slides. As we took lunch, sitting at tables in front of the quayside café, we chatted with youngsters; all clad in rubber gumboots, corduroy jeans and Fair Isle sweaters. We remarked on their friendly nature, and desire to speak English. The adults had shown a phlegmatic friendliness; a guarded openness that probably mirrored our own nature. We caught the MV *Leda* on the evening tide, navigated the busy harbour waters, and coastal islands before heading back to Newcastle in the gathering gloom of a late July night. The evening meal was laid out on a typical smorgasbord table of groning magnitude – but still fish, cheese,eggs and jam. Being good, upright English gentlemen, we held back before serving ourselves. We were nearly trampled to death in the resultant crush.

*

Ralph and I managed to squeeze in another week's holiday before the year was out. He was keen on visiting the historic sites of Northern Ireland, spending a few days in the Province, before cycling south and into the Wicklow Mountains, south of Dublin. Having visited Ireland on two occasions previously – Cork and Kerry with Geoff Cartlidge, and Connemara, Achill and Donegal with him, Brian Whalley and Pete Boardman – in 1962 and 1963, my knowledge of Ulster was scant. Other than a few miles cycled over the border from Donegal, before catching a train to Dublin, we had barely heard of Mourne Mountains, and the Antrim coast.

The evening train arrived at Lancaster, and with the aroma of fish, chips and vinegar tweaking the nostrils; the appetising fumes spilling out from town centre cafés, we rode the short distance in darkness to Heysham Docks. The overnight crossing to Belfast was cold, with a choppy sea slapping the ship's sides; rolling waves arriving with regularity from out of the dark to make the voyage uncomfortably rough. The convivial warmth of the bar, with the harsh rattle of Ulster Irish voices booming in cheerful banter, slowly but surely drew to a silence. Voices well lubricated by glasses of Guiness, ceased, as the ship's motion began to make stomachs heave. I stayed on deck, trying to avoid the warm, sickly blasts of air issuing from saloon bars and toilets. The sights, sounds, and smells of a rough sea crossing are epitomised by the swinging, and banging of a vacant toilet door, the slippery deck, and the fretful crying of a babe in arms. I stayed on deck, stomach churning, freezing cold, and gripping the ship's rail with white knuckles.

A cold, early morning light saw us approaching the Belfast waterfront; the lone seagull, flying in station for the past hour finally wheeling away as we glided between forests of gantries, and closed on the berth. Boggle-eyed through lack of sleep, we attached the saddlebags, and wheeled our way up the wet ramp and out into the streets of Belfast. Seemingly, after only yards cycling through a drab dockland streetscape, we were brought to a halt by a mass crowd.

I had never before witnessed the enthusiasm for and seriousness of sectarian marching bands. The marching to fife and drum which, towards the end of the decade, was becoming a more common event, had seldom flashed across the television news back in England. July, in Northern Ireland, was the traditional time for these marches, celebrating the victory of the Orangemen, the Protestant Scottish over the indigenous masses of a Catholic Ireland. We would visit the Bridge of Boyne later in the tour. For many years since, the Catholics in the north were discriminated against in every form of social standard. In healthcare, education, housing and employment, the followers of the Pope came off second best. Areas in Belfast became delineated on strictly sectarian lines,. with whole streets flying either the Union Flag or the Irish Tricolour; even kerbstones painted in the appropriate colour combinations. The formation of the Irish Republican army on one side, and Ulster Voluteers on the other; paramilitary groups from both sides committing atrocities on a tit-for-tat basis, forced the British Government to establish the B-Specials police force, and eventually, the British Army to restore some form of order.the serious situation was exacerbated by the rantings of the ultra-Protestant politician, the Reverand Ian Paisley, as his booming voice of hate harangued around the streets of Belfast, his whole demeanor at odds with his wearing of dog collar and cloth. How, in later years, his hypocrtical, cavern-mouthed jocularity would lighten

289

the halls of Stormont? How, in false friendliness, he rubbed shoulders with that other posturing, self-serving buffoon, that grinning and lying Tony Blair? The parade of fat, suit-clad businessmen marching down from Drumcree Church, with bowler hats and orange sashes, marching to the beat of a drum, had always seemed a little portentous and rather silly to me.

We were ushered to the pavement, crushed at the back of a burly, surly crowd, as the marching band passed by. We caught the fervent seriousness of the event. There was no jolly carnival atmosphere where participants and onlookers threw flowers or flour. No pretty American drum majorettes with their short dresses, long legs, and baton-throwing, coquettish pomposity. This was a threatening display of warlike intentions; where only gruff shouts of encouragement could be heard above the skirl of the pipe, and beat of the drum. As the band faded down the street, and into the distance, we were left with just the sound of rhythmic stamping footfalls; a metronomic beat of booted feet on granite cobbles. And, we didn't even know which side they were rooting for.

Ralph and I cycled through County Down, taking in several historic sites, and staying at youth hostels in Minerstown, Slievenaman, Omeath and Bridge of Boyne, on the border with the Irish Free State. From Minerstown, on the shores of Dundrum Bay, the view of the Mourne Mountains over a sandy shore at sunset had me reaching for the camera. The Mournes and Slieve Donard, at 2,796 feet (852m) in particular, certainly did 'sweep down to the sea'. Ralph, switching from touring mountainous places, began a tour of history as we visited Monasterboice, Melifont Abbey and the long barrow at Newgrange. Celtic stone crosses, elaborately carved with swirling coils, cloaking groups of ancient, armour-clad warriors, thrust out of the tangle of choking ground ivy. Graves surrounded by rusting spiked railings provided the resting place for crumbling partisan bones. The crawl into the tunnel entrance at Newgrange long barrow revealed runic messages scrawled by Neolithic graffiti artists. Chambers off the main passage held an air of gloomy finality. Ralph's pursuit of history was inexhaustible; his desire to absorb the past was as strong as his desire to reach a summit first. I was impressed, becoming limp with culture overload. But it was all so interesting to follow the paths of saints, despite lack of guides or printed literature.

We cycled south, to the coast of Kilkeel, overlooking Dundalk Bay, and the shore of Carlingford Lough at Portaferry. The view over Carlingford Lough to the Mournes was of singular beauty. From Bridge of Boyne, site of William of Orange's famous battle with King James, in 1690, we pedalled towards Dublin, and a softer brogue. We were now in the Wicklows; familiar country for me since my tour in 1962 with Geoff Cartlidge, and passing the Powerscourt Demesne near Enniskerry, we were soon climbing to General Wade's Military Road. From Sally Gap, the unfenced road; undulating and invigorating, bowls along whilst maintaining a lofty elevation, passing the head of Glenmacnaas, and finally dropping to Glendalough. Here, Ralph topped-up his search for Celtic history; exploring the ancient site of Saint Kevin's Bed, the whole area littered with crosses, and the curious, pencil-thin Rattoo tower. His appetite for geography was satisfied on reaching the Upper Lough; a burst of evening sunlight rays animating the classic scene. We had walked through a copse of waterside willow trees, striding over a network of streams, to the very edge of the Lough. Ralph and I stood on the pebble beach alone, and drank in the solitary scene. The evening sun was lowering in the west causing sunbeams to shaft at an angle down to the water, barely clipping the surrounding hill slopes. The sun lit up the rocky heights opposite, and placed a wash of russet over the hilltop bracken above, and all beneath a clear blue sky. The water was still and dark-green in this evening light, and we could discern pock marks on the surface where insects deigned to briefly touch the glassy surface. We heard a few plops as the hungry, rising fish left mouthed 'Os' to swirl and disappear in the ever-changing mirror of water. I decided there and then that this was one of my favourite places ever, and had to be faithfully recorded on still camera.

Our last night in Ireland was spent at Glencree YH, after a day of pottering through the hills, stopping to admire the views, smoking an occasional Sweet Afton cigarette, and finally absorbing the atmosphere of the region. With the fresh, late September air tasting like wine, we freewheeled down into the Glencree Valley, the Sugar Loaf Mountain, distinctively pointed, rising in the distance, near Enniskerry. We caught the evening ferry, the *Caledonian Princess,* from Dun Laoghaire, crossing to Holyhead and making a last overnight stop off the A5 road, at Cynwyd youth hostel.

Having toured through parts of Northern Ireland and witnessed the barely disguised animosity across the sectarian divide in Belfast, I could now understand the fervent singing of those Irish rebel songs. Lively patriotic songs of nationalism that celebrated the exploits of Fergal O'Hanlon, Sean South and Michael (Captain) Farrel, roared out over a pint in the pub, suddenly made sense. The IRA songs, *Patriot Game, Sean South from Garryowen* and *Whisky in the Jar* would remain some of our sing-song favourites.

The only instance of antagonism on this holidayoccurred in Ulster – and by the children too. Ralph and I were sitting on a promenade bench, me cutting bread slices with my carving knife, and Ralph opening a tin of luncheon meat, when a gang of rag-arsed boys approached, and started hurling curses through rotting teeth. They were gradually becoming a nuisance, becoming tiresome in the way some unruly, cheeky kids do. When they started throwing gravel, in exasperation, I grasped the carving knife, and with a manic expression, chased them away at the point of a blade. Fortuneately, they fled with a rasp of boot hobnails on the paving and a final curse thrown over the scruffy jerkin shoulder. These street urchins had probably had a tough upbringing. I glanced around for some bystander, some parent but none existed, and all was peaceful.

The by-passing of Shrewsbury, as already described, prompted us to find other favourite alternative routes. The main road from Welshpool to Shrewsbury was often crowed with traffic returning from the seaside resorts of Borth, Aberdovey, Towyn, and particularly, Barmouth. A crowded road full of tired and frustrated motorists could be an accident waiting to happen for riders cycling two abreast. Although we would get into single file quickly, and immediately when traffic approached from the rear, a motorist trying to keep the kids from fighting wasn't the best scenario. Most drivers would blast the horn, but lacking the skill and acceleration to pass efficiently, could be held up for a few seconds. The mystifying reticence of most drivers to cross that double-yellow line, despite a danger of running a cyclist over, will never case to perplex any sensible person. They would rather kill or maim someone than break the laws of Big Brother by crossing the lines, even for a teeny-weeny distance, and in the blink of an eye. The section of the road that climbed along the side of the Breidden Hills was a particular hazard. It rolled in carpet folds of blind crests, and deep, hidden hollows, tempting the head-on crash or wiping-up of a group of orderly cyclists.

We devised an alternative route to Shrewsbury, starting between Newtown and Welshpool, at Abermule. A right turn off the main A458 road took us under the single line railway near Abermule, close to that site of the railway disaster in January,1921, when two trains met head-on, both on the same section of tablet-controlled line. Early photographs show a scene of utter carnage. Locomotives went at a hell of a speed, even in those days. Confusion arose when a station porter assumed someone had performed a safety procedure involving the signalling block system, and released the trains on a collision course, and passengers to certain death.

We steered through an undulating route of twisting, narrow lanes, passing an isolated mental institute, before reaching Montgomery. This lonely backwater; this cluster of cottages and a shop did, however, boast an ancient castle as a backdrop, with ruins sprouting from the overgrown bluff. Basically, we were skirting the side of Long Mountain, following one of those southwest to northeast valleys encroaching over Shropshire's borders, through Chirbury and Marton. A large, isolated pool, Marton Pool, could be glimpsed through the hedge; pleasantly undiscovered by the wind surfers and water skiers, close by a fork in the lane, and a very detached country pub, a convenient watering hole, and a definite place for a wayside opening of the packed=lunch sandwiches on the outward journey.

Following the B4386, we passed Brockton and Worthen; quiet farming communities with the ancient roadside barn or useful Post Office, and with always a supplementary road surfacing of crusty cow dung. Narrow-necked lanes diverged off the main route, signposted

Binweston, Rowley and Aston Rogers to the north, while to the south, somewhere beyond the unkempt hedgerows, the wilder country rising to Corndon Hill, Black Rhadley Hill, and the crest of the Stiperstones ridge. Soon we joined a wider road at Westbury, headed due east through Stoney Stretton and Yockleton; the latter's school and adjoining church spire, yet another milestone in our journey to Shrewsbury, and teatime at that small café in Frankwell's back streets. When the place closed, we have to continue another seven miles (12k) on the A53 to Edgebolten, and Mrs Haines' welcoming CTC meals.

*

Many public houses in the 1960s, particularly in Shropshire, were basic in the extreme. Shropshire is a county on the edge of England – a veritable wilderness in comparison to the Home Counties – with many of its western villages having the obscure Welsh spelling. Shropshire was where, as portrayed in period films, the rich, landed gentry took their holidays, away from the riff-raff of the working class. In *Howard's End,* everyone took their vacation in distant Shropshire. In the film, *Remains of the Day,* a member of Lord Darligton's family refers to the village of Stanton Lacy, in South Shropshire. Television comedy writers exported John Challis, Boysie of the series, *Only Fools and Horses* from Peckham, London in a remote spot in south Shropshire to be a gentleman farmer in *Green, Green Grass of Home.* Shropshire is vitually still unknown to many, and being so, retains its air of mystery, not to be overrun by mass tourism. Although we are back of beyond, we don't, as Boysie declared, 'eat mice and sleep in ditches'! The county was, and is, easy to reach from Stoke-on-Trent.

A few years later, when new members joined the crowd, Phil Norcopp used to cycle all the way to Bridgnorth on every cycling weekend before even looking at his map and no matter his final destination. Beyond here to the west lay the unknown. Beyond here there be dragons.

We cycled to Bridges youth hostel, set deep in the Onny valley, between the Long Mynd and the Stiperstones. The Hugh Gibbons

Memorial Hostel was yet another disused schoolhouse, its middle-aged, wizened, somewhat fussy warden with his shock of white hair maintaining a friendly, efficient place to stay. We always paid a visit to the small inn, the Horseshoes, it being a matter of yards down the leafy lane. Very popular in summer when folks sit outside, where the only sound is the chatter of the nearby Onny stream, and the occasional lowing of a lonely cow. Rustic enough for Boysie anyway. Next day we sat out on a memorable rough-stuff route that started on the Stiperstones, crossed the Long Mynd, and finished on the back slopes of Caer Caradoc, near Church Stretton.

The Stiperstones ridge is a line of quartzite outcrops linked by a boulder-strewn footpath. The highest cluster is known as the Devil's Chair, and affords a beautiful distant view of those blue remembered hills. Corndon Hill in the west straddles the English/Welsh border. The intervening landscape is one that has been pock-marked with Roman lead mines. The Long Mynd scarp and dip slopes; stretching to the south-east, is circled by insect-like gliders, just one of the many serried ranks of long hill edges that fade into a mysterious, hazy horizon. Jennifer Jones playing Hazel Woodus in the film of Mary Web's story, *Gone To Earth*, is seen grieving on the Stiperstones rocky heights, under a dark, and disturbed thunderous sky.

From here, we plummeted back into the valley, and climbed through Ratlinghope, to the broad top of the Long Mynd. Ratlinghope is a quiet, lonely backwater of a village with an appearance of a medieval settlement, locked into a time warp of servile serfdom. The high point of the Mynd's broad, windswept expanse of moorland is over 1,690 feet (516m) The highest point in the country is to the south-east, on Brown Clee Hill at 1,770 feet (540m). Instead of taken the easy way down from the Mynd, the long, steep and exposed Burway, we found the boggy stream at the head of Ashes Hollow. This narrow valley, constricted by rocky buttresses and tangled shrub, cuts steeplydown to Little Sretton, and offers a visitor-free, secluded route, in contrast to the popular Cardingmill Valley. The interlocking valley sides squeeze the view east to just the wooded slopes of Ragleth Hill, and, if one was fortunate, the sight of the long wingspan of an over-flying buzzard. Our day of rough-stuff ended with a climb to the back of Caer Caradoc. Leaving the cycles on the track, we scrambled up the summit, and paused, resting within the grassy embankment rings of the ancient, Stone Age fort. This summit at over 1,500 feet (459m) provides a view of the conical Lawey, seeming to be too immediate, but pointing further to the north-east, and the lone cone of Shropshire's sentinel – the Wrekin.

This epic day of sharp rocks, rough tracks, and steep slopes was interrupted when we called at Picklescott for a well-deserved lunch. The Bottle and Glass Inn, majestically isolated in these days before going out for a pub meal became popular, was approached by squeezing past an enormous mound of manure. The towering mixture of cow shit and straw wept an oily liquid over the midden cobblestones; an effluvium of indescribable nastiness; a mixture so volatile, it virtually pulsed with heat, while clouds of steam rose from its heaped crest. We negotiated a way past this concentration of agricultural fallout, and, mounting the entrance steps, lifted open the latch of the planked front door, and with a dragging squeak, swept it aside to stumbled inside.

The small room was deserted but for a giant of a landlord, old Mr Chidley, propped up behind his bar. Rough Windsor chairs were scattered across the quarry-tiled floor. A slow fire glimmered in the deep inglenook, and a few horse brasses hung from rusty nails hammered into the stout ceiling beams. The landlord had a crutch jammed under the armpit, and hobbled over to the beer engines in order to pull pints. A sheep huddled at the opposite end of the bar, blinking with doleful eyes; a mournful stare, following his keeper, maybe wondering where *his* drink was. The back wall seemed to be piled high with past copies of *Farmer's Weekly*, yellowing and moth-eaten, together with the sheep, leaving little room for manoeuvre. The landlord, we soon learnt, had only one leg and spent most of the time perched on a high stool, uttering sentences in an uncomprehending Shropshire burr. One of our younger members ordered a plate of cheese and onion sandwiches.

Before long, a rotund lady swept into the bar and presented him with a veritable tower of sandwiches. He had expected thin sliced bread, and having worked up an appetite, had ordered four rounds or two doubled slices. Each slice of bread was as thick as a doorstep – eight slices of one inch thick bread plus massively thick layers of cheese with onion rings created this swaying heap of eats. I remember that we all fell to helping him consume this mammoth lunchtime snack. The bar filled with local farmers, discussing, we could just about gather, the latest market prices for sheep. Dress was of the working farm labourer: flat cap and overalls, although I fully expected someone to come in wearing a Victorian smock. The atmosphere was friendly enough with old codgers smoking their pipes, and downing pints of Wem Bitter. Aromatic smoke curled up to the low ceiling. The scrubbed pine tables were cluttered with the paraphernalia of a drinker's lunchtime. The cheese and pickle of a ploughman's lunch was as exotic as any meal went. The gents' toilet was out the back, under a corrugated shelter, wedged between the pub's rear wall and a high stone boundary.

We left this peaceful inn; this fine example of a long, low, country cottage alehouse, fully replete, thirsts quenched, and ready to tackle the roughstuff routes of the Long Mynd and Caer Caradoc. I have visited the Bottle and Glass on many occasions in the intervening years. In a group, the Wayfarers have been in the pub long past closing-time, sharing drinks with two members of the local constabulary; two patrol policemen, in their blue and white mini, covering hundreds of square miles of this far-flung landscape. They sat on tall stools downing free shots of spirit while the clock by the optics rack showed 12:30am. On another occasion, again after legal closing-time, the local travelling gypsies burst through the door and stayed many a hour. They dressed in holed, scruffy denim, wore Casey Jones pillbox hats; hair escaping down their necks like distressed scarecrows, and communicated with a series of grunts. We thought that we'd been instantly transported into a scene from the outback film, *Deliverance*. Only the banjo was missing. In later years, we arranged camping in a fallow paddock yards down the road from our favourite alehouse. We would hold slide shows, taking over and filling the back room. Pints were quaffed while the projector beamed wonderful scenes of our extended tours. The Stoke cyclists' dry humour became louder as the drink disappeared, resulting in stomach-aching hilarity. On one time when the local vicar was conducting his harvest festival in the bar, we were asked to keep the noise down as he couldn't make himself heard. Landlord Mr Maurice Chidley Junior ran the Bottle and Glass at the time. His wife kept the place when he was out and about, operating his mobile discotheque, most Saturday nights in some far-flung Shropshire village. Now, the manure has gone, the midden tarmac-surfaced, and made into a car park, the pub serves meals, tables can be reserved, and everybody is happy. Or are they? I last heard that the pub had since ceased trading.

I describe this rural retreat so as to compare it with the same place today in our brave new millennium. It wasn't the fact that the Bottle and Glass was run-down and dirty. It was a friendly meeting place; clean but basic, and we liked those sort of places. Back in history, the wayside inn was to provide a simple meal, and change the traveller's carriage horses. Other services could be provided according to Henry Fielding's *Tom Jones* but that's another matter. In the 1960s, the local was for locals; a meeting place to exchange news, have a drink and a peaceful smoke – a coming-together of the age-gap. I believe that we just caught the tail-end of that character, that atmosphere on our tours into the countryside. Subsequent, successive Governments; the latest in particular, Liberally Labour, have fully put paid to all that. We have descended into a nannyish, paranoid, blame society, a controlled-by-the-State people, totally observed, who took to rules and regulations, conditions of contracts, and lead by the sweaty palm to the complete abandonment of common sense. Countless public houses have been turned into pretend exclusive restaurants, serving ghastly set meals – high in quantity and low in quality. Drink-drive laws, although in some cases sensible, have been applied with Spanish Inquisition enthusiasm, and maniacal severity. Motorists now go out for a drink, knowing that they're forced to consume heaps of stodgy gunge before daring to sup the mere half pint of tasteless lager. The pub and the people suffer accordingly. A latterday visit to the Bottle and Glass were 'Reserved' cards displayed on every tabletop. It looked at first glance like the dining car on the Orient Express. The inglenook fireplace was cold with just a weak red light glimmering from a cheap, brassy, pretend lantern.

And definitely no ashtrays! My goodness, No Smoking signs litter bar, wall and table – by law, Smokers who for years swelled the

Chancellor's coffers through high tax are herded out the back door and treated like cattle, aliens, the unclean and considered 'despicable pariahs'. Our ruling masters at Westminster wanted to have their cake and eat it. Surely some ventilated back room could be set aside for smokers? Away from food, away from folk of a delicate nature, with a spittoon for the old soaks. Old men, locals who had enjoyed a pint, and a pipe over the ages, were considered as if they were diseased, having leprosy. Companionship for them was over. They couldn't stand the ignominy of huddling under a cheap awning, open to winter's temperatures, in order to enjoy their pipe, cigar or cigarette – a snatched, subversive inhaling of that terrible, terrible weed. They would just have to go home and die in silent loneliness. Play the violins for goodness' sake!

Consequently, with these sanctimonious restrictions in place, the country inn has lost its character. Become sanitised in our nanny-interfering, over-caring times of control. Most have been spoiled – gone forever and I'm glad that I've had the opportunity to experience, and enjoy them in their original state. This was the time when the Campaign for Real Ale was becoming established. CAMRA ensured a decent, chemical-free product would be available, although some of the skull-splitting strengths were, perhaps, too much of a good thing, too strong, where one pint would derail the body's gyroscope. Generally they did a great thing and dispelled the Watney's Red Barrel image to the sunny Coasta's. they didn't, however, make comments about the character of the pubs, apart from stating if a real fire was in the grate. At work in the latter 1960s, I met colleague Ken Gaul. When asked what car he drove, he replied, "A red one!" I admired his Potteries-style, dry humour. He was of bald head and free spirit and persuaded me to join CAMRA. I joined the local Western Subsection, the county west of the A49 main trunk road, and designed their glass transfers and real ale festival programme covers.

Other drinking hostelries of substance saw us prop the bicycles against their rustic walls. I have mentioned places like the Unicorn, Hanley, the Nag's Head, Edale, the Cobweb, Boscastle, darts at the Horse and Jockey, Stottesden, the Lord Nelson, Oakamoor, our Annual

Dinner in the Black Lion, Consall, high in the Yorkshire Dales at Tan Hill, the Blue Lion, Cynwyd, sitting on the wall at the Mainwaring Arms, Whitmore, the Blacksmith's Arms, Loppington, that cider-serving inn near Gidleigh, Darrtmoor, all drinking houses of character. Some of these places still exist – but only just. Massive companies like Wetherspoons, Punch Bowl and Magners, having acquired strings of, formerly, free houses across the country, will finally destroy the character and diversity of the typical English village pub.

*

I bought a car shortly after touring Ireland but never got to drive until early the next year. It was a black Triumph Mayflower, and Sheila and Fred used it to drive down to Plymouth. There was a hole in the floor of the boot, and their luggage got soaked on a particularly rainy journey. I would later buy a Morris Traveller, dark-red, with a registration number, 1261VP. Later, I part-exchanged it for another Traveller, mid-green, in better condition, with a plate showing CDA406H. Now I could motor to Stoke-on-Trent on a Wednesday evening, and join the group for drinks at the Roebuck Hotel in Leek New Road, near Glebe Street railway bridge. My friends called the car a shooting brake, giving it the quaint flavour of the American Mid West. However, instead of shotguns, fishing rods and picnic hampers, I would load my chariot with the Harry Quinn bicycle.

The Morris Minor saloon; the stereotypical midwives car was introduced in 1948. Designed by Sir Alec Issigonis, it became very popular and the estate, timber-framed Traveller version, even today, still retains its sleek lines. The smell of the old leather seats, the ticking of the petrol pump when the ignition was switched on, the cranking of the starting handle on freezing mornings, all these things bring fond memories. I had to be careful not to catch my thumb when a compression kickback occurred. The handle was useful to free the pistons when the oil was thick due to overnight freezing conditions. A tap with the hammer on the starter motor casing solved a jamming problem. A healthy trumping of the exhaust always used to sound when moving through third gear. In fact, I didn't use the clutch when changing into top. With road speed and engine speed in synch, the merest nudge of the gear lever saw a smooth change. The double opening rear doors facilitated the easy loading of the bicycle, I added a cycle roof rack later but never felt entirely confident that it would stay on when buzzing along the motorway at a sedate 60mph (100kph). The bolted gutter clamps never seemed solid enough to provide a guaranteed secure fit when loaded.

Mushrooms of an unknown species grew in the grooves between sliding window glass and woodwork. Pale grey mounds of fungi that thrived on a reaction between the damp conditions and the ash framing. I passed my driving test first time, without a hitch and in subsequent years, taught others to drive. But in the late 1960s, there were far fewer cars on the road; traffic was lighter generally and went at lower speed. However, motoring still managed to retain a slight friendliness, a sense of camaraderie between users. Things really did change on entering the new decade, be they drinking houses or travelling our roads – on or off the bikes.

*

Although the Wayfarers became motorised, the interest in cycling lasted for a few years to come. The change was gradual. From using youth hostels to camping, from cycling all the way there and back to using the car, and finding fresh fields, this was our transformation. Cycling and motoring became combined. The use of cars and bikes has, today, turned full circle. Many cars speed along motorways with a collection of bikes strapped to the rear boot. With the tightening of drink-driving laws, maybe this mixture is the solution. Get there quickly and in comfort before offloading the bikes and daring to visit the pub for that well-deserved drink.

We spent yet another Christmas at Cynwyd with more names adding to the jollity of the occasion. More names, more characters and more voices to sing our songs in the back lounge of the Blue Lion. Irish rebel, *Young Roddy McCorley* was belted out with even more intent, feeling and meaning. The *Wild Colonial Boy* left his native Ireland for the sunny shores of Australia. We continued to use the bikes and our horizons were expanding with the pressing of the foot on the accelerator pedal.

Chapter Ten
1969

Tour of the Pyrenees – Man On The Moon – An Argument At Clun – Poem:
The Stoke YHA Cyclists – Verse Explanations – Cycle Camping at Gradbach –
A Journey's Ending

Age: 28.
Home: Shrewsbury Road, Bomere Heath, Shrewsbury.
Work: Shropshire County Council, Abbey Foregate, Shrewsbury.
Government: Labour.
Prime Minister: Harold Wilson.
Jan: Students from the London School of Economics demonstrate.
Feb: Yasser Arafat becomes leader of the PLO. Boeing's jumbo jet takes to the skies.
Mar: Anglo/French Concorde's test flight.BOAC pilots' strike.
Apr: QE2 embarks on maiden voyage. President Charles de Gaulle resigns.
Jul: Neil Armstrong first man on the moon. Sectarian rioting in Londonderry.
Aug: British troops deployed in Northern Ireland. Gadaffi seizes power in Libya.
Sept: N.Vietnam's Hoe Chi Minh dies.ITV transmit in colour.
Nov: Huge anti-Vietnam war demonstration.
Film: *Midnight Cowboy.*
Television: *Monty Python's Flying Circus.*
Music: Woodstock hippies pop festival in New York State, America.

Harold Wilson's times of the white heat of technology were, in this last year of the decade, certainly being realised. The American 747 jumbo jet, lifting its enormous bulk into the skies, contrasted with the sleek, supersonic Anglo/French Concorde. The elephantine jumbo added to global pollution while the heron-like Concorde proved, finally, to be the white elephant. Obstinate Charles de Gaulle, wartime leader of the former Free French, resigns, much to the relief of British government leaders. The July marching season erupts into violence as the Derry Apprentice Boys insist on sectarian provocation. The increasing trouble in Ireland sees the deployment of British troops, initially to keep Protestant and Catholic paramilitary factions apart, who are met with friendliness by all the people. This would not last. The 1970s would become the decade of the bullet and the bomb, both in Ireland and England. Ralph's and my tour of Ulster in the previous September would be our last in that country.

The year, in fact the decade and millennium, would be dominated by the Apollo moon programme. Folk from every walk of life, be they dunce, dustman or doctor, were captivated by the fascination of man setting foot on another world, albeit a dry, dead one with no breathable atmosphere. With such blanket exposure on television, everybody in home, office and street became a virtual expert in astrophysics. The space programme culminated with the moon landing itself and from that instance in time, further exploration would become common-place, even boring. Contrasting with all this science and technology was the pinnacle of the laid-back, hippy culture. The growing mass concert scenario saw a milestone at the Woodstock Festival, where music and protest indicated a general rejection of present policies and past conventional values.

*

After the usual winter and springtime cycling weekends, John Bradbury and I decided that it was about time for another adventure into the Pyrenees. He had probably overheard us exchanging anecdotes of our 1965 tour. His friends in the Lyme Racing Club showed sufficient enthusiasm to warrant arranging a fairly testing route from the Basque Country, crossing into the wilder foothills region inside Spain and a spectacular flourish along the Route de Haute-Pyrenees, ending again in the Basque Country, at Bayonne. At one point there were a dozen members from the Lyme who showed an interest of ear-pricking intensity, but the initial enthusiasm soon waned. As March led into April, the racing clubmen dropped out one by one, until only John and I remained. I duly booked through the Cyclists' Touring Club our travel tickets and nominal holiday insurance, and with the usual CTC efficiency, received all in time for our departure in late May. Passport, tickets and foreign currency in order, I was looking forward to revisiting the High Pyrenees by way of an unknown Basque Country and a sortie into the mesa or tableland country to the south of the great range. I'm sure John would be suitably impressed. I cycled to Stoke, starting at 7:30pm on the Friday evening and after meeting John at his Trent Vale home, we caught the early Saturday morning train from Stoke Station, bound for Stafford and a direct link to London. After the usual cross-city jaunt through streets deserted but for a few late party-goers, we ambled from Euston to Victoria to catch the 9:50am train to Newhaven and the early afternoon Channel crossing to Dieppe. By the time we had docked and found our SNCF express, it was teatime and after checking the *Wagon-Lits* destination board marked Paris, clambered aboard and settled into an otherwise empty compartment.

As in 1965, we crossed the Paris streets and River Seine from Gare Saint Lazare to Gare d'Austerlitz. This Saturday, being *Le Weekend* in France, the late afternoon's hectic traffic had subsided, but we still found the journey difficult. At a junction on the riverside freeway, we took to the pavements rather than chance the underpass tunnel. Traffic speeding at well over 60mph (100kph).would have had scant regard for two wobbling, laden cycle tourists, however keen the nation was on all things cycling. We arrived at Austerlitz and had no problem with the bikes; merely handing over a ticket and attaching a destination label. At 10:45pm precisely, our express glided away through the Paris suburbs bound for Bayonne. We crawled into our bunks and left the night journey to rushing, unknown, dimly-lit stations; flashing lights squeezing around the window blinds, the sudden slam of a corridor door and the rocking and rolling dull roar of our mobile sleeping pit.

By next morning, Sunday 25th May at 6:30am, we were rolling into wet and misty Bayonne. Rainwater glistened off the streets' granite cobbles and setts; city surfaces distinctively arranged in typically French fan patterns, making bike control tricky. The mist hardly lifted and torrential rain bounced off the dodgy surfaces, making us struggle under our plastic capes, careful not to slip and concentrating on keeping to the right-hand side of the road. The occasional pap-papping of passing traffic was lost under the swishing of car tyres on wet road surfaces. We took a minor road towards the Spanish border control. On approaching opposing roadside booths, raised barriers, French tricolour flags and statuesque gendarmes seeking what little shelter they could find, we concluded that we were nearing the customs post – miles from the actual border on the summit of the Puerto Otsondo. A gendarme shuffled across, a Gauloise, brown and soggy, dangling from the corner of the mouth. Heavy rain pattered off his pillbox hat and streamed off his black cape, bouncing off gabardine to join the rushing runnels of storm water in the roadside gutter. After a cursory glance at the bikes, he gestured with a yank of the head, indicating that we were free to proceed and let him regain the damp, smoky fug of his border shelter. Apart from the heavy rain, it was damn cold. After hundreds of miles travelling south, one was looking forward to being bathed in sweltering sun. Cold rain dripping off the chin is not what one expected; disappointing, making any cool weather feel more intense. The rain eased for two hours around lunchtime. After the Puerto Otsondo, we climbed the Puerto Velate, two passes of modest altitude on a wet day through scrubby, undulating countryside. Descending into Spain and Pamplona, the weather improved; the temperature climbing and cloud cover rolling back to reveal a town of narrow alleyways lined with tight, jumbled, flat-roofed buildings. The famous (or infamous) bull running was for fiesta days later in the year.

We had covered seventy miles (112k).yesterday and today had to cover a similar distance, pedalling due east, running parallel with the Pyrenean foothills to reach Jaca. The immediate countryside was open, arid, sparsely-covered with low scrub and dotted with isolated, conical hills topped with huddled villages. A curious mesa or tabletop type of landscape littered with several of these hilltop settlements, gathered houses sitting high and aloof from the surrounding flatlands, as if under threat of siege. The road wound between knolls and outcrops where at one point I caught the interest and attention of a snarling dog. The frantic scrabble of paws on tarmac and the sight of slavering jaws and vicious teeth persuaded me to sprint away from this canine adversary. One word only, RABIES flashed through the mind, persuading me to pedal frantically, not bothering to see that I'd drifted over to the wrong side of the road. The booming air horns of an approaching quarry truck made me swerve back in haste to my own side. My pooch friend gave up the chase and slunk back to whence it had sprang from. Halfway along our day's travel, we arrived at Tiermas, yet another hilltop community overlooking the fifteen mile (24k).long Embalse de Yesa. The Rio Aragon flows from this elongated reservoir south through the plains of Navarre, to join the mighty Rio Ebro. It is not a particularly attractive part of the region. A distinctive cone of a mountain in the far distance, the Peña de Oroel, marked the location of Jaca. Glimpses of this peak came and went until we arrived at its stony foot, the 5,800 feet (1,768m).peak overlooking Jaca's ancient town. A historic site, this settlement, when viewed from a distance and with a backdrop of the Pyrenees, resembled a garrison town on the edge of the Sahara desert. As Marrakech in Morocco would look against a background of the high Atlas Mountains. A key location in the Spanish Civil War, Jaca's cluster of flat-roofed buildings, warm, brown stone reflecting an afternoon sun, appeared as an oasis in this otherwise bleak, dry and exposed landscape.

From Jaca, a main road leads directly north over the Col de Somport and into France, passing the mysteriously abandoned railway station of Canfranc-Estacion, high on the border. We stayed in the comparative wilderness of Spain by taking the minor roads east, crossing the lower foothills and through lonely settlements along the way. At Biescas, a remote road climbed to Panticosa along the Valle de Tena, rising towards the central Pyrenees and the small hamlet of Baños de Panticosa. This elevated spot was, presumably, a health spa set high in the mountains, nestling in the hanging valley to the side of the main pass. Today, Tuesday, it had been raining heavily for most of the morning and afternoon, restricting our view to close quarters and hiding any sight of the secret hidden valley of health-giving springs. We booked into a hotel at Panticosa and had to be satisfied on peering from the room window into the mysterious gorge full of boiling, clinging mists. Our hotel was cold and cheerless; having just opened for the season and probably not expecting any guests so early in the season. We even had to use our own soap and towels. The cost for room and meals here for one night was 272 pesetas (£1-16s-0d-£1.65np at the then rate of exchange)., by far the most expensive of all our stays in Spain on this tour. This would appear ironic, as our adventures next day would prove.

Panticosa was at an elevation of 3,885 feet (1,184m). and on this Wednesday morning, the road up the valley was being resurfaced. Heavy plant bordered the road, garish yellow bulldozers and earth scrapers stretched down the valley with working gangs tearing up the existing road surface. Yesterday's rain, instead of abating, had developed into a full-blooded thunderstorm. The Pyrenees are subject to violent thunderstorms; hot air from the central Spanish plateau colliding with cool, wet Atlantic air over France and forming into thunderheads, bringing rain and ice storms. Lightning flashes and thunderclaps rolled around the mountains. This morning, curtains of torrential rain quickly turned the dirt road surface into liquid mud. This was rain of monsoon intensity. We needed to get down to Biescas as soon as possible, so, we struggled past the road repairs with utmost care, astride the bikes but with one foot planted into the gooey slough to remain upright and balanced. Workmen crouched under heavy tarpaulins, chatting in shouts to be heard against the drumming of the rain and growling thunder. We cleared the road works and regained the metalled surface once more, but conditions worsened. Freewheeling down the pass, we were half-blinded by the still torrential rain and noticed flood water rushing off the hill slopes to our right, across the road, to gush into the valley bottom on our left, hundreds of feet below. Lines of powerful rushing water gouging out the potholes made cycling extremely dangerous. The flows were so strong that small rocks were being carried along; our road seemed to be disappearing before our eyes.The chaotic roar of rain and flood, together with the littering of soil mounds and rock, brought us virtually to a weaving standstill. At several points where the road cut through excavated cliff walls, heavy rocks were being washed away, falling from above before bouncing across our path and freefalling over vertical drops. We imagined the whole side of the mountain sliding away, such was the concentrated downpour. One image and one word flashed through my mind: slipping spoil and Abervan. We could manage an occasional summer storm but didn't expect a tempest of Biblical proportions.

Hair soaked and flattened to the forehead, squinting as water stung our eyes, trying to avoid the larger rocks and heaped soil banks, fearful of stones hitting the head and struggling to slow with wet wheel rims made cycling, at that point, extremely uncomfortable. As we finally approached Biescas, I noticed a figure, caped in black against the rain, sauntering into the middle of the highway and looking towards us with inscrutable intent. It was only then that I realised he was a policeman. He gestured with a sweep of the hand, ordering us to the side and towards an arched entrance of what turned out to be the local police station. The solid stone building, an impregnable edifice of village control, displayed a fascia sign – *TODO PARA LA PATRIA* – emblazoned across a background of patriotic colours in red and yellow. This wasn't the local bobby but a member of the dreaded Guardia Civil. The olive-green uniform, leather hip holster and particularly the black, shiny headgear with the distinctive flattened back; the teeming rain made his hat look even shinier. At first, we thought it was something to do with customs but when our saddlebags and panniers were searched, it was evidently something more serious. It seemed that the hotel at Panticosa had reported a theft of their bathroom towels, phoning ahead to the local cop shop. We had visions of rotting in a Spanish dungeon for countless years – an impression of Spain's unforgiving penal system, still widespread as late as the 1960s. Summoning up my best Castilian Spanish and delivered with an almost schoolroom correctness, I managed to tell the police that last night's hotel hadn't even provided us with bath towels. Not sure of the past tense 'weren't', I just spread my arms and protested that there were no towels provided. *"Pero, no hay toallas en sus cuartos!"*Besides, we carried our own and wouldn't be interested in carrying extra heavy and bulky bath towels. Far too luxurious. Surrounded by police, dripping wet and wearing shorts showing exposed knees blue with cold gave us a decidedly naughty boy appearance – not a position of strength when faced with Spanish authority.

Obviously, nothing stolen was found, despite extensive searching. The police made another call to the hotel before a senior officer, leaning across his desk and out of his kiosk hatchway, indicated that we were free to leave. His glowering expression, narrowed eyes flashing in a shadowed, olive-complexioned face, showed his displeasure at his officers' time being wasted, not by us but by the hotel's inefficiency and false accusations. We lingered under the station's entrance arch, waiting for the rain to ease while a junior officer admired the bikes. He was friendly enough and I detected a faint smile at the corner of his mouth. Evidently, the station chief wasn't amused; our stay wasn't warmly welcomed, so, we had to carry on cycling under heavy rainfall. Thankfully, the storm eased to a drizzle and we proceeded on our route, climbing the Puerto de Cotefablo under clearing skies. The summit of the pass at 4,667 feet (1,422m).afforded expansive views of the higher peaks, still covered with substantial amounts of snow. We entered the Ordesa National Park and moved a few miles north on a minor road leading to the lonely hamlet of Torla. We found accommodation in the village; its simple houses clustered upon a rocky bluff gathered around a central, square churchtower, as if for divine protection, with a spectacular backdrop of vertiginous, terraced peaks. The narrow, cobbled alleyways in this outpost; bordered by walls splattered with cow shit, gave it an almost medieval atmosphere. Even the least imaginative would have no problem in conjuring up a vision of clog-wearing serfs driving oxen up these steep passageways towards their winter sheltering.

A spacious Parador, owned by the Spanish Tourism Office, stood at the opening of the deep gorge but it was closed – empty, locked and barred, waiting for the start of the tourist season. Our day was spent in the gorge of the Ordesa National Park admiring the towering peaks, taking photographs, but mainly drying out the socks. Opposite Gavarnie on the

French side of the range, this hidden area resembles, geologically, a mini Grand Canyon. Monte Perdido at over 10,000 feet (3348m). resembling the sheer rock faces of the Sella Group in the Italian Dolomites, forms a full-stop to the view. The name Monte Perdido means Lost Mountain in Spanish, an apt title for this lonely, gigantic buttress of a land mass. Being the only visitors to this wonderful area on the day, gave us a sense of being truly privileged.

We progressed east, at all times within view of the high central range, pedalling along lonely roads and through several deserted settlements. The general landscape was one of low hills, shallow gorges and numerous empty hamlets; rude, stone cottages, barns covered with orange pantiles and ruined church bell towers, all served by dusty, narrow tracks. A Wild West film could have easily been staged within these forsaken outposts – just add horses, hitching rails and a sad, tolling bell! Oh and some tuneless whistling!

Boltana, Fuendecampo, over the Collando de Fordada at 3,345 feet (1,019m)., Campo and to Castejon de Sos, following the Rio Ara and through the Gorge de Ventamillo. We found bed and breakfast in Castejon and stayed two nights, giving us a day to explore the Esera valley leading north to Benasque. At Baños de Benasque, a spa for health-giving waters and a former hospice for the weary foot traveller, we had penetrated to the base of the highest Pyrenean peaks. The Montes Malditos (Mountains of the Damned).contain the Pico de Posets at 11,060 feet (3,371m).and the highest of all, the Pic d'Aneto at 11,168 feet (3,404m). Eventually, the Port de Venasque at 8,032 feet (2,448m).would be constructed to take the traveller across the range and directly to Bagneses de Luchon, on French soil. We had only moved some fifteen miles (24k).into the range at Benasque but from hereon, in the late '60s, we would have needed boots, crampons, ice-axe, rope and an expert local guide to push on further.

East of Castejon, crossing the Coll de Fadas (4,822 feet,1,470m).a view opened out of the curiously detached outlier, El Turbón. Several miles due south of our road, this attractive mountain cluster, rising above successive pine-covered hillocks and interlocking, scrub-covered scarps, topped 8,176 feet (2,492m). Turning north at Pont de Suert, we finally crossed back into France through the Vielha Tunnel. A noticeboard at the entrance gave all the dreaded details; Opened to traffic in 1948. Length: nearly 3.25 miles (5,133m). Width: 20 feet (6m). Height: 19 feet 6 inches (5.5m). Altitude at south end: 5,333 feet (1,626m). Altitude at north end: 4,560 feet (1,390m). According to these figures, we had a downhill journey in front of us – falling 773 feet (236m). The clouds were down to near road level; spitting with rain, it was beginning to get cold; I pulled on my anorak. No, I didn't, but I did close the zipper to the neck on the cycling jacket. I'm neither an anorak, a geek nor a trainspotter.

The tunnel entrance was not a grand arch, but a portal carved into the sheer rock face. Not Brunel's attractive Box Tunnel abutments near Bath, but an elongated worm of an avalanche shelter that protruded a hundred yards or so outwards in front of the rise of the mountain slopes. We ran inside where the curve of roof lights arced into the unknown. An occasional heavy truck roared past, climbing from the opposite direction, our ears deafened by the echoing howl and clamour of its belching exhaust. Naturally, it had to show us the penetrating volume of its echoing, tripletone air horns and the ear-shattering clash of released air brakes;air brakes that are designed to scare fragile young ladies as they cross the road. The road surface, protected from winter's snow and ice, was silky smooth. The sullen orange lighting above flashed past with a staccato frequency as we gathered speed on the falling gradient.

Bursting out of the north entrance, like peas from a pea-shooter, we free-wheeled into Viella and booked two nights bed and breakfast accommodation within the town. This gave us a full day to climb the fifteen miles (24km).of the Puerto de La Bonaigua; still unsurfaced and as stony as it had been in 1965. We took a leisurely lunch whilst admiring the Valle deArán and the jagged Monte Saburedo peaks; alpine grass deep in the valley bottom, turning to forestry pines, to screes and finally rising over snow banks to harsh, triangular mountains. The quintessential Big Country landscape, as seen in many a living room wall print, and an advertisement for a cowboy smoking a Marlboro, from the many hairpin bends of this wild, lonely pass. Dropping down from the Bonaigua summit, 6,796 feet (2,071m).on the return run and slowed by the need for caution on the numerous gravely bends, I had to rub and blow on my cold hands to restore circulation. I could understand why racing cyclists would shove a newspaper under their jerseys when racing down from these alpine heights.

Next day, in contrast, was steamingly hot. From Viella, we cycled through Bosost and climbed the steep, but short, tree-lined Col de Portillon. The frontier post was empty; free of officialdom, be it Spanish or French, the barrier pointed skywards.We descended to Luchon. Tomorrow, we would be joining the usual route of the Tour de France, climbing the Col de Peyresourde at 5,126 feet (1,562m)., and the Col d'Aspin at 4,884 feet (1,489m). These two passes, although high and affording dramatic distant views, lacked the immediate harshness of those imagined in early accounts of Le Tour. Scraggy, sunburned, ill-looking men wearing a spare tyre round the armpits and back of neck, climbing ever upwards on stony, unsurfaced roads evoked circumstances of utter punishment. Wearing goggles and cloth hat, twisted, dusty faces streaming with sweat and surrounded by buzzing flies, open wounds oozing blood from thigh and knee, indicated a *REAL* sport! A sport for *REAL* men. Everyone should consider this when watching millionaire footballers writhe in agony, supine on the turf after the slightest of taps, or if an opponent happens to blow on them. Overpaid prima donnas, labelled Kleenex (soft and expensive).by the rugby union-playing fraternity.

In 1916, Eugene Christophe broke his bike on the Col du Tourmalet, so, shouldering his machine, he ran down the pass to a blacksmith's shop in Sainte-Marie-de-Campan and using the basic tools available, managed to mend it. He was given a massive time penalty by the race officials for receiving outside assistance. A boy had helped him by operating the forge bellows! We glided down the Col d'Aspin; tyres thrumming on the immaculate, metalled surface and stopped in the wet, cold streets of an out-of-season Sainte Marie. It was closed. We looked everywhere for a night's accommodation. Most guesthouses where closed – some even bolted and barred, with shutters firmly closed. With a light drizzle making the streets shiny, we finally, and in desperation, knocked at the solid doors of the local convent. A nun, wimple of starched linen and rosary with crucifix swinging at the waist, ushered us into the cold, echoing great hall. We learnt, using very basic French, that we could stay the night but they couldn't provide an evening meal. After a quick wash and brush-up, we walked the streets in this attractive town looking for suitable sustenance. A back street premises, dimly-lit behind the plate glass window, we thought, would reflect my, and particularly John's, limited spending money.

He and I were ushered into a back room and treated to a slap-up meal; the starter, a giant tureen of pea and ham soup, mopped up with chunks of fresh, crispy baguette, ensued a stomach-cramping fullness. The smiling French maid, coquettishly bouncing up to the table and serving with cheerful efficiency, made this feast an evening to remember. Her mother, peering at intervals from behind a room curtain, checked that her daughter was serving us well. We felt it a great pity to have so little a grasp of the language. Two dashing blades touring so early in the season would have been a delight for any French *mademoiselle* serving wench – especially in the closed season. Two hours later, we had forced down the other courses and crawled back to sleep it off in replete satisfaction.

We had returned to the nunnery and after the heavy doors had been dragged open, crept into the cold and echoing, religiously reverent, grand hall. Our room (cell).was chilled and bare. Raising myself off the low palliasse, I joked with John, asking him if he had prepared himself for punishment from the novice nun. A fervently administered whipping for raising the household at such a late, ungodly hour. It's quite amazing what one thinks about when pedalling for hours along an empty road. John gave his usual deep, lecherous chuckle.

We sat at the long refectory table for breakfast. Weak light filtered down from the high windows as we played with the slivers of bacon on our plates – thin, cold and raw. A watery, half-fried egg stared up like a sad, rheumy eye from the plain, cracked plate. We collected the raw bacon rashers and wrapped them in brown paper for cooking later.

Thursday 5th June and we were well over the halfway point in our tour. We unwrapped the raw bacon and threw it into the dixie pan for frying; sizzling in butter and eaten with a hunk of stale baguette. After

314

this paltry breakfast and a mug of tea, we were ready for the long climb through La Mongie, to the summit of the Col du Tourmalet, 6,936 feet (2,114m).high in the middle of the Haute Pyrenees. As we climbed, leaving the tree line and emerging onto open alp grasslands, light snowflakes floated down from a sullen grey nimbus cloud base. Thankfully, a heavy snowfall didn't happen but, high on the contorted hairpins, recent snow banks crept across the road. We pushed for a short section, wheeling the bikes over compacted snow and crossed the pass; devoid of visitors, serene, silent and surrounded by cruel, jagged peaks. Tourmalet translates as 'bad detour' and the twisting approach to the pass by the rough, potholed road, particularly from the Valle de Bastan direction, together with the overpowering, severe mountains, makes this an apt description. The dirt road from the summit towards the Pic du Midi de Bigorre Observatory was closed, impossibly blocked by deep and dirty snowdrifts. The Col du Tourmalet has always been a high spot of Le Tour despite, in recent years, extra 'add-on' climbs to high level stage finishes having been added. A welcoming sun accompanied our long, fast descent to Luz-St-Sauveur and winding through the forested gorge country here at low level, we turned south again for a stay in Gedre, on the road to Gavarnie.

The Cirque de Gavarnie had been a high spot on our 1965 tour. Today, in early June, it did not disappoint. The approach alongside the chattering Gave de Pau stream was most spectacular; magnificently draped in winter white, snow slopes on the upper ramps shining against massive grey and cream cliffs, the Cirque displayed a scene of epic grandeur. The whole arc of mountains, gracefully curving and resembling a Malham Cove times a hundred, was of a truly breathtaking scale. We wheeled the bikes to a lunchtime picnic spot by the river and continued on foot to the very base of the abyss. Apart from the last section of drop, the Grande Cascade had frozen into organ pipes of blue ice, the 1,000 feet (305m).of waterfall stuck in a time-stopping cluster of solidified tubes. Lesser waterfalls around the rim had frozen too; spears of ice forming tracery patterns against the limestone walls. The snow banks below the cliffs revealed dark, threatening crevasses where dark water trickled into a subterranean world. We gave this area a wide berth. We returned to the cycles and pumped the Primus into life for a brew of tea. I even risked plunging my bare feet into the stream, thinking the cool water would ease the aches and pains of our days of cycling in tight shoes. The coldness of this meltwater instantly anaesthetised not only my feet, but my legs up to knee level. The sharp pebbles in the stream bed went unnoticed – all feeling was nullified. Another brew of tea and a cigarette, thoughtfully inhaled, gave us time to savour the grandeur of this place and before returning to Gedre, I had the scene captured on emulsion for the sake of posterity. The Cirque de Gavarnie, high on the border with Spain at 4,450 feet (1,356m).at its base, is certainly included in my Boys' Book of Natural Wonders.

Our next day, Saturday, was to be almost as spectacular. Warm, sunny weather greeted us on the road from Gedre to Pierrfitte, Cauterets and along the ascending road to Pont d'Espagne. We twiddled up a narrowing, steep route, following a tributary of the Gave de Pau. White waterfalls and cataracts leapt down the river course, wild water draining the Lac de Gaube high above. Our road ended at the lakeside with only faint, rock-strewn tracks leading up the valley and towards the border; smugglers' routes perhaps, secret ways fit only for pack mules, their minders and their illicit merchandise. Our view towards the Spanish border was of a lofty Pic de Vignemale, 10,820 feet (3,298m)., distantly shimmering in the midday haze and framed perfectly between incredibly steep valley slopes. Bulky, long-horned cattle, tails swishing away the eternal flies, complemented the alpine picture. More Himalayan than alpine, however, as the distant lofty peaks, completely covered with deep snow, provided a scene suggesting staggering altitudes of dazzling intensity. We picnic-lunched at the Lac de Gaube, enjoying the scale of this perfect hanging valley, perched on rocky slabs and chattering about this and that. A distant, muted rumble filtering down the long valley interrupted our conversation; an indication of distant avalanches. A chief factor adding to the magnificence of these high places was the sheer silence of the surroundings. An almost tangible lack of sound, save that of natural sources; wind, water and bird-cry complemented the whole experience. With no other visitors, we were fortunate, indeed, to be in the middle of such a sound of silence. One could only stand and stare. We finally tore ourselves away from this idyllic location, passing through Cauterets and Argeles-Gazost, to find accommodation in Arrens. On a much later reading of Agatha Christie's autobiography, I learned that the Pont d'Espagne was one of her most favourite locations.

The Pyrenees west of Arrens showed a cleaner geology. Gone were the shattered and jagged black peaks of the central range, to be replaced by the more rounded, buttressed faces of grey and cream limestone. We left Arrens with a warm sun softening the tarmac, rising during the day to a hot 80 degrees Fahrenheit (27 degrees Centigrade). We climbed steadily to the Col de Soulor, passed along the La Corniche section of road as it clung to the mountain walls, negotiated the several tunnels and continued to the summit of the Col d'Aubisque. I had cycled this road in the reverse direction on our first tour of the Pyrenees but, so as John could enjoy the high altitude views, I considered it essential to make a return visit. On attaining the summit, we absorbed the expansive panorama before making an about-turn in the road and plunging back down to the Col de Soulor. Taking a different road north through Asson, we reached Louvie-Juzon, eventually arriving in Laruns after a day of superb weather and equally superb scenery.

On this tour neither of us wore a wristwatch. This wasn't a disadvantage, although we occasionally had to peer through my binoculars at distant village church towers in search of a clock face to find out whether it was too early or late to book into guesthouses or take meals, etc. The fact of not having the exact time about us when catching trains or ferries never seemed to matter. Staying two nights in Laruns gave us a day to climb the main road south to the Col de Portalet. The day was overcast, ruling out any views and the climb to 5,873 feet (1,790m).was purely an exercise of pass-grabbing.

From Laruns, our route wound in a westerly direction,undulating through and over hills of lesser height and greener hue. This region of the Basque Country was scattered with quaint villages, each one containing its own distinctive church with broached spire and square, enclosed hard court for the curious local game of pelota and the more well-known, petanque (boules.). We cycled in cool, changeable weather through the lower Val d'Ossau to Oloron-St-Marie, Sainte Engrace, Mauleon, St-Jean-Pied-de-Port and to the coast at Saint-Jean-de-Luz. Further bed and breakfast overnights after Laruns were at Mauleon and Cambo. We diverted to a strange area named the Kakouetta Gorges; a system of limestone, maze-like passageways, flooded and accessible by boat only, with columns of rock rising out of the still, grey-green waters. The geology appeared strange – mysterious, almost dreamlike, if not of a nightmarish quality, particularly in this afternoon's dull, overcast conditions. There were no other tourists around and the stacked piers, topped with straggled vegetation, could have figured, for example, in a Salvador Dali, surrealist painting.

We finally reached the coast at St-Jean-de-Luz, below Biarritz-Plage and Bayonne. Staring out to sea, enjoying the sunshine and breathing wafts of ozone between drags on a cigarette, two *mademoiselles* sitting on the seawall hailed us with the laughing cries, *"Tres, tres sportive, n'est-ce que pas!"*John, with an even more lecherous chuckle, commented that it was *they* who were the sporty ones. The final miles up the coast to Bayonne were soon covered, closing the circle of our Pyrenean tour. We caught the 11:30pm Thursday express to Paris, crossed the city and arrived in Dieppe thirteen hours later. The ferry, SS *Falaise,*docked in Newhaven at 5:00pm and we arrived in London Victoria, two hours later, on Friday evening. I cycled from Stafford to Bomere Heath, arriving home in darkness at 1:00am, very early on Saturday morning. Total outward travel time was thirty-five hours, and twenty-five hours on the return. All things considered, the holiday had been a complete success; even our choice of dates, touring in early June with the threat of some of the higher passes being blocked with deep snow, proved advantageous with fewer, if any, other tourists present. Unmelted snow and ice, particularly in the Haute Pyrenees, had provided scenery of a most spectacular nature. Some accommodation was hard to find due to it being so early in the season. Maybe the fact of so many dropping out from this tour at the outset was fortuitous. Accommodation prices were certainly low. Total cycling distance covered in France and Spain was approximately seven hundred and eighty-two miles (1,250 kilometres). All-inclusive holiday cost was approximately £80.00. A full breakdown of itinerary, mileage, passes, costs, etc. can be found in the Appendix.

Soon after returning from the Pyrenees, my and everyone else's attention was turning to the television with its increasing interest in science. The world, particularly in the West, looked forward to America's attempt to make a manned moon landing. At least their intentions were swinging away from invasion and an intense paranoia of spreading Communism, to a journey of real adventure, perhaps into unknown worlds. Although, considering the amount of junk being blown into orbit, this also could be considered an invasion – a littering of space. Overnight, viewers started using such technical terms as escape velocity, orbital apogee, translunar insertion, extra-vehicular activity and re-entry radio blackout. Television presenters, like Cliff Michelmore and James Burke, became nightly celebrities; Burke, with his thick glasses and unruly hair, being the science expert and Michelmore providing a critical, acerbic tone to the proceedings, questioning the morality of it all. Patrick Moore, the fast-talking expert on interplanetary movements, told it how it really was,placing our small satellite moon in its correct order of things. Suddenly, everyone had become a rocket scientist!

The actual landing occurred in late evening on the 20th July and the actual walk on the moon's surface was in the small hours of July 21st GMT. The spacecraft didn't sink into a quicksand of dust, there were no monsters swooping over the lunar horizon, but we were treated to a feast of patriotic, flag-waving and unmitigated posturing. Norman Mailer wrote in his book, *Fire on the Moon,* that while the astronauts were saluting the stiff, planted flag and receiving a message from President Nixon, the scientists back at base were muttering, "For f**k's sake, just get the rocks!" The image on our television sets was of blurred astronauts, zig-zagging across the screen in a glaringly severe contrast of deepest black to dazzling white. All intermediary tones were burnt-out by the savage glare of the sun. All vocal transmissions were accompanied by a regulation telemetry bleep. As if a bleep was needed before every vocal point of detail – however insignificant. James Burke was in throes of excitement and Cliff Michelmore brought everyone back to earth with his typical wet blanket, BBC-British approach to the whole thing. Nevertheless, these were brave times of exploration; a noble quest, providing there be no drawbacks or colateral damage. Another question flits across the enquiring, sceptical mind. Did it really happen? Having always been a keen model maker, my later efforts included space exploration.

I asked myself this when applying the finishing touches to an Airfix model of the Apollo 11 lunar module. I had set it on a silver-grey painted plaster base and enclosed the diorama within a small Perspex cabinet. The surface was suitably pitted with small craters formed by the rounded end of a screwdriver handle. With a close-up converter lens on the camera and low-level lighting from an anglepoise lamp, I photographed the montage and printed the negative to a high contrast. The resulting picture could have been so easily mistaken for the real thing. This achieved by a plastic model and just simple equipment. Would it not be an impossibility to fake the whole thing in some multi-million pound filming laboratory?! The difficult task of maintaining secrecy throughout the thousands of support personnel seems to prove the point of it all really happening.

We cycled to several youth hostels in the following autumn. Corris in mid-Wales, followed by runs to Bridges, in Shropshire. As the year drew to a close, I was making more use of the Traveller. I drove to Stoke and gave Tony Ross and his girlfriend a lift to Cynwyd. Yet another year ended with Christmas celebrations for four nights at our favourite hostel. However, we were entering a new decade; a different period of changing styles, club touring and overall circumstances. Most of the group owned their own transport by now and before long, started to acquire camping equipment and use tents instead of youth hostels. In 1970, the very first tour made without cycles was overland, through France and Spain, to Morocco, hiring a minibus and using shared tents. The singing went from strength to strength; ever popular within the group and for fellow travellers alike, the active and social scene just widened its boundaries. Compared with the decade before, the 1970s were different again, established, no doubt, by the adventures and camaraderie of the past.

Our definitive break with youth hostelling came, I suspect, when we were technically banned from the YHA for that usual felony of returning late from a night's carousing. Not directly from a public house, but from a village discotheque at the community hall in Clun. The young lady warden had gone away for an evening at her canoe club dinner. She told us that she would be late returning and it wouldn't matter if we were late back at the hostel. I remember a swinging night at the village hall following a good evening in the Sun Inn. Dougie Alcock gave a brilliant impersonation of Mick Jagger of the Rolling Stones – I think it was the track, *(I Can't Get No). Satisfaction* – prancing on the stage, swinging his t-shirt and waving to the village girls. He was remarkably good. When we finally arrived back at the hostel, a group of walkers, arriving after we'd gone out for the evening, objected at being awakened. The warden had to agree with them, if only just for keeping to the rules. A bitter argument ensued; they considering us as dirty stop-outs, wild yobbos, with no interest in the spirit of hostelling and we thinking them as whining, toady, old farts. It's surprising just how quickly usually adventurous, peaceful country lovers can become carping critics spouting conforming rules in mouthed, vitriolic tones. We knew our record of hostelling weekends and we doubted if anyone else could be as enthusiastic. Maybe both parties held extreme opinions that were wildly exaggerated in the heat of the moment. Apart from the occasional hostel visit, members became motorised; it wasn't long before we changed to camping weekends.

As regards our future yearly Christmas breaks, youth hostelling became unavailable. Cynwyd and the memories of the Blue Lion would fade into history. From hereon, our festivities would be continued through the 1970s in rented country cottages and, in one case, a mansion. Cottages as diverse as youth hostels having no juvenile rules to cramp the style.

The ending of the decade was an opportune moment to recall some of the many anecdotes surrounding the Stoke-on-Trent youth hostelling cyclists. Verse in the most basic of forms, fell quickly and easily under the pen, using the most basic style of rhyming doggerel.

THE STOKE-ON-TRENT YHA CYCLISTS

1: *Ten years have passed and its time to record,I hope that this story will not leave you bored.It's time to record some places we've been.To tell of the antics and sights we have seen.*

2: *My tale begins in the earliest days;around nineteen-sixty – the start of the craze.*
Roy set it rolling, supported by Eric.
With Joannie and William, Ken, Geoff and Derek.

3: *Yes, Latham, Barnish, Walshaw and Hall were some of the guys who started it all.Soon they were joined by the short and the tall.Biking in the wake of intrepid Joe Ball.*

4: *Geoff on tour near the mountains of Snowdon,Couldn't go fast for he had a fair load on.Wasn't quite sure how much money to take.So, into each pannier, ten cans of stewed steak.*

5: *A tramps' run to Rudyard, via Leek with no care.Straight into Woolworth's, see the crowd stare.The poor, pink-faced lassie, she hardly could cope,With Phil Hughes as he purchased a bar of best soap.*

6: *Marian Vyse had a mighty-fine swerve.To ride close behind needed plenty of nerve.On ev'ry steep rise she would crash through the gears,Scaring the life out of peaceful old dears.*

7: *From High Cup Nick to the Wayfarer's Track,Upon the high crossings with no turning back.From the loch in Glen Affric to the Kintail side,To follow these lads – take a fell walker's guide.*

8: *In Cartwright House, Hanley, we were toast of the day.For with slides and with tape, it was quite a display.They clapped and they cheered even more so,At the colour and texture of John's legs and torso.*

9: *Wiry Paul Leese was a climber at heart.On ev'ry steep hill he would soon play his part."Come down, come down you fool," we'd beg,as he climbed on the road up the devil's trouser leg.*

10: *"Are you in the big party?" asks the warden at Glascwm."Wait on a second, luv, I'll just go and ask 'em."When you hear the distant roar, there's no need to fluster,for she's tearing up the valley on her MV Augusta.*

11: *Through Paris streets with the hooting and jangles,Cars approached from impossible angles.We dived and we swerved and we ran through the red,While many unsavoury French curses were said.*

12: *Roy in the Pyrenees, with their snowy-white caps.A bunch of crunchy celery fixed in his cape straps.Ralph sees the food – across the road he shoots,To take a big mouthful of asparagus roots.*

13: *The stars were bright, the moon beamed out.This was the All Night Ride, no doubt.Over the Wayfarer's and far away,To meet the red dawn of a brand-new day.*

14: *The motorists came from miles around.They thought it was a free playground."Roll up, roll up, see the riders in shorts,""As they go through their paces at the Pickmere Sports."*

15: *Some talk of Ben Nevis, Cairngorm or Stac Polly,Others of Liathach and Ben Macdui.I'd like to conquer a MOUNTAIN for a change.So, I'm cycling down south to the Poldens Range.*

16: *A few years ago, a badge hit the scene,With a wheel and a beer mug where 'YHA' had once been."Quite the wrong image," cried the court of head-shrinkers. "Rubbish," replied the Committee of Drinkers.*

17. *Dave Hope's quite quick with a joke and a grin, When he talks of this comical world we live in. On the road with the bike, you'd have to be a stayer, To keep in touch with Dave, the company's brick layer.*

18. *On all of my travels, I've seen many fine meals. Name them, I've had them, except jellied eels. But one meal for sure had me scratching my head.'Twas Ralph with his beans and his jam on fried bread.*

19: *For some in the group who happened on leading, Must be versed in the art of careful map reading. For Sunday in Wales makes you grumble and sigh, When a line on the map means the pubs are all dry.*

20: *Clive is a brave and most breathtaking rider,Especially when tanked-up with Guinness and cider.I hope and I pray that his cones do not seize,At the foot of the Burway whilst pulling 6 'G's.*

21: *Up and up and up we climb, just like an alpine pass.Until we reach small Picklescott and the rustic Bottle 'n Glass.The landlord squats behind the bar,* *selling ales so cheap and looks out of his window to the steaming cow dung heap.*

22: *One Sunday in April, above Callow Hollow.The track, it was narrow and tricky to follow.Chris lost his saddlebag, it rolled like a dream,Three hundred feet down and stopped by a stream.*

23: *Riding along in the bunch, after tea.A sound issues forth, quite a dubious key.John Hall's larynx is beginning to rattle,Shocking the crows and stampeding the cattle.*

24: *One foggy night, a few miles from Whitchurch.The road disappeared and Dave gave a quick lurch.A pile-up ensued, the dread of the Club,But the worst thing of all, we were late at the pub.*

25: *At Dimmingsdale hostel, one fine Sunday morn,All manner of work clothes, they had to be worn.We dug a deep hole 'til the blisters gave pain and the very next day it was filled-in again.*

26: *Off the shores of south west Spain, Lord Nelson spanked his foe.Down in sleepy Oakamoor, to his pub', we always go.For with all the locals in the bar, we sing and laugh and swear and there's always a friendly welcome from the landlord over there.*

27: *Would-be Hitlers of the YHA,Shake in their shoes when Ralph has his say.Oh, how they rant and oh, how they bicker,For Ralph has a brother named old Harry Hicker.*

28: *To the south of the Wye, just close upon Hay.The noble Black Mountains, in sunshine they lay.To climb to the summit, we found quite a job,But ahead of us now – Lord Hereford's HEAD.*

29. *Somewhere down south lies a village called Broom. To be there and be thirsty can spell out your doom. For cider, like acid, will poison your brain. Makes you stagger and roll and water the lane.*

30. *At darts, Ralph and Roy can be kings of the board. Hark, the glad cheering – one-eighty is scored. But scorer watch out, for when Chris takes his go, He's apt to throw wide and he always aims low.*

31. *Llangollen's the place, Birks jams the door, While Roy in the window gives drinks to the poor. Phil Hughes, a strong lad, all string vest and muscle. Well, a door plus Ms Johnson, boy what a tussle.*

32. Way down the road like a twisting thin snake, With never a thought for the use of the brake. Cars, carts and motorbikes, all left behind. It's been seven long hours since the last time we dined.

33. *Poor Kenny Birks had cycled for miles. To Harlech he'd come, just to sleep on the tiles. By evening, our Kenneth, he'd found a cheap pitch, While the warden, the poor fool, hadn't noticed the switch.*

34. *Boating at Ludlow, on the Teme, smooth and wide. Two naked bathers slipped over the side. Whalley and Hall, I'll bet a pound, spoiled the fishing for miles around.*

35. *On to the Glyders, up a steep snow gully. With a drop like that, we should've used a pulley. Geoff bridged the gap with a movement astute, while I clung for dear life to a welcome left boot.*

36. *One dark, windy night in the quaint streets of Clun, We'd been drinking a little, just to keep up the fun. The warden on his rusty bike was put to quite a stress, for approaching, shouting, singing, rushed the whisky-fired express.*

37. *A crowded summer's boating, upon the River Avon, If you give the oars to Christopher, you're certainly a brave 'un. But it's not the bobbing ducks and the swans that he's after, you can tell by his high-pitched and lecherous-sounding laughter.*

38. *Chris has always been a well-dressed rover and he ordered some smart plusses from his tailor, Ossie Dover. Back came the garment, made to Chris's own size, But Ossie had wrong-cut the body length rise.*

39: *Tony, the tar, is surely no sailor. With the rolling boat, he turns a shade paler. The cruel, wind-blown sea whips over the side, While the toilet on 'C' Deck remains occupied.*

40: *Norway's food is on a groaning table. Help yourself to everything, so runs the fable, Dig in my hearties, don't give a damn, For there's platefuls and platefuls of more eggs and jam.*

41: *Tesco and Finefare don't stand a chance, When you walk the glass floors of the Big S ranch. Food for the taking, but what a price tag. Thank heavens for John and his red duffel bag.*

42: *Good old Sprint Henry rode a puzzling style, A lateral shift, twenty times to each mile. Off the bike, too, he could do many tricks, Like standing inverted and driving artics'.*

43: *Foulkstrath Castle, a bastion tall,Sees Fred looking down from the battlement wall."Come down," cries the warden, "Come down 'fore you fall."Fred's always been the worst of us all.*

44: *In Buttermere, drinking, we lost track of time,So, back to the hostel to face a stiff fine.After cursing and paying, through the door we all went.Next time in this region we'll bring our own tent.*

45: *We sometimes lose Dave Joynson, his mind upon a tune, So it was at Ellesmere, one summer day in June."Hey, Dave," I shout, "Get quickly out, you may well cause a stew.""You'd better get a grip of yourself; you're in the ladies loo!"*

46: *The cold, yellow moon shines on Ystumtuen School.The sleeping Welsh lady rocks back on her stool."Some more late arrivals, they best sign-in tomorrow,"But it's only the boozers back from the George Borrow.*

47: *Way down in Shropshire's rural charms,A Christmas drink at the Bridgewater Arms.They cock up their ears, the yokel and the squire,Just to listen to the singing of the first Urinal Choir.*

48: *Dave, on guitar, has many fine licks.Roy, on mandolin, plucks harmonious tricks.Clive runs a merry dance, along the keyboard,*
And Ralph in the choir, sounds the starting key chord.

49: *Every year on the side of the Berwyn,The good folk of Cynwyd are starting their stirring.For Christmas is nigh, get out while still sane,For the Bats out of Hell are roosting again.*

50: *Down south as a loner, I met big-headed folk.With their handbooks and cocoa and cans of flat Coke.But out from the Potteries, the Stoke Group they came and I doubt if yoy'll see such a fine troupe again.*

Not John Betjeman by any stretch of the imagination, but a collection of verses that attempts to describe some of the incidents in our misspent youth. A cursory reading might indicate a time when we disliked the YHA's rules, pursued Bacchanalian orgies and behaved like a load of uncouth yobs. Acting, in fact, like those early Edwardian cyclists who toured the country lanes, terrorising the peaceful local men and women; modern chaps pursuing their new-fangled pastime, revelling in their new-found freedom and mobility. We were never that bad. We enjoyed a drink, yes, but never taken to Hogarthian depths of depravity. Some of us partook of the dreadful tobacco, but never chain-smoked ourselves into bouts of emphysema. The whole cycling scene was one of shared conviviality – a social thing and not a sanctimonious demonstration of keeping the planet green or keeping ourselves fit at all costs.

Although reasonably descriptive and factually correct, some of the verses need further explanation and description

V4 Geoff Cartlidge, present on our Christmas in 1966, Boots 'n Saddles tour in Snowdonia, carried numerous tins of stewing steak in his panniers. As self-cooking facilities were, at best, basic, these meals were probably the best he or anyone else could muster. Care had to be taken as the saucepan bases would be dented and rounded, proving to be unstable as they teetered on the grease-encrusted gas burners. Yes, Geoff did remember to pack a tin opener.

V5:On our Tramps' Weekend in 1965 (part of the New Year's Party with the Walking Section at Rudyard Lake hostel)., we were photographed at Limekiln Bank Filling Station in Leek New Road, Bucknall and provided a good photograph for the *Evening Sentinel,* our local newspaper. Cycling Section Secretary, Roy Hazeldine, must have tipped them off. We cycled over snow-covered roads to Leek where Phil Hughes made his sensible purchase in the local Woolworths – much to the amusement of staff and other customers.

V6:Marian Vyse, stocky, of ruddy complexion and sporting tight denim shorts stretched over lusty, pink thighs, was a keen cyclist of Boudiccaian resolve. She wore large, horn-rimmed glasses, looked like a melding of both Dame Edna Everage and Mary Whitehouse, and handled her bike with consummate alarm. She would swerve violently at the last possible moment, literally at the drop of a hat, leaving everyone following to find the offending pothole or pile of horse shit. However, Marian was a keen cyclist who allowed a brave Bill Barnish to court her.

V8: The Cycling Section gave several slide presentations to the local YHA at Cartwright House, using a synchronised tape commentary. We showed *A Cyclists' Year* in December, 1964 where a slide of John Hall revealed him skinny dipping at a remote Berwyn location – Swch Cae Rhiw pools. The commentary asked Dorothy, Laurie Landon's wife, if she wanted to sit closer to the screen. Because none of us were bold enough to stand at the front and make a speech, we recorded the commentary and played the Grundig TK20 alongside the slide projector. Despite the innovative presentation, there were mistakes to be made. Ralph, in mentioning the height of a mountain as being _approximately_ three thousand two hundred and forty-nine feet above sea level was, therefore, stating a contradiction in terms. Geoff and I presented a slide/taped show on cycling in Ireland and had a far too long a gap between slide changes. Time to take in a scene is about three seconds, and definitely not thirty seconds. BBC imaging has cut down the time of exposure to a mere blink of the eye. The blanket background music of Beatles hits didn't help the matter either. But both Geoff and I were immersed in Beatlemania in the mid-sixties and couldn't resist the temptation to use the music for every slide, whatever the mood. Overall, our shows were a success and we even gave a showing of _A Cyclists'Year_ to Stone Wheelers Racing Club in January, 1965. Their Secretary sent a letter of thanks, enclosing a Postal Order to the value of £1, a donation for expenses.

V9:Paul Leese, aquiline, powerful, swarthy and compact, was built for hill-climbing. He would be at the top of a hill first on all occasions. A joker at heart, Paul could not resist half-wheeling when at the front – just making sure that his front wheel was a few inches in front of the companion alongside. Obviously, if that other person had a racing streak in his mindset, the overall speed of the group would continue to accelerate until one (not Paul).would be forced to cry, "Slow down, enough is enough!"

V10:The lady warden of Glascwm youth hostel was old, wizened and very proud of her motorcycle. She would travel up the mountain road from Hundred House each afternoon to sign-in any passing hosteller. She probably owned a big, black bicycle with a Cyclomaster miniature engine set within the rear wheel. Nevertheless, Dave Hope, who was keen on racing motorbikes – he had owned a Manx Norton – painted a picture in mind of the dear old lady; clad in tight leathers and fully-enclosed crash helmet, roaring up the pass in a cloud of Castrol R, burning rubber as she brought her Italian MV Augusta to a shuddering halt. Mick Bennett, with his laid-back attitude, non-existent respect and cheeky chuckle, using his own words, described the warden as a toothless hag, a crinkly, old crone, imagining her to be roaring past the hostel's chequered flag with a flapping black cloak and lank hair streaming out from under a conical witch's hat. Panting, her black cat would catch up much later.

V11:Crossing the multi-junction of the Place de La Concorde in Paris, transferring from the Gare St.Lazare to the Gare d'Austerlitz – everybody for themselves and all on the right-hand side of the road for the first time.

V14: Wasting time on the beach at Pickmere Lake, near Delamere Forest. Games of throwing and catching plastic feeding bottles. A similar game was played on a grassy patch by the roadside in the valley of the River Onny, between Bridges and Wentnor, Shropshire. However, it hasn't yet been declared an Olympic sport.

V15: Geoff made fun of the severity of the climb of the Polden Hills in Somerset. I had warned him, in sarcastic tones, of the incredible height of these hills; rising to 250 feet (76m).above mean sea level after noticing them marked on a map – rising out of the ultra-flat plains of Sedgemoor. Of course, cycling over them, any uphill was hardly noticeable; we crested the summit as if on a flat road.

V20: The road dropping from the top of the Long Mynd to Church Stretton in Shropshire, known as the Burway, is long, narrow, steep and with no guard rails. Many a car has run off and bounced down the severe slope into Cardingmill Valley. The gradient steepens near the bottom and cyclists,by now travelling at virtually supersonic speed, have to cross a cattle grid. One feels weak at the thought of a crashing rider's injuries if his wheel should jam in this agricultural barrier. Another fast descent was of Cat Tor Hill, passing the Ramshaw Rocks and towards Leek. I remember Ralph performing a swirling swerve in order to overtake slower, descending cars. An arcing manoeuvre, taking him into the opposite carriageway in front of approaching traffic, before swinging back to narrowly avoid cars and kerbstones.

V21: The Bottle and Glass, high in a fold of the Long Mynd, was, in this decade, a very, very basic country public house. The giant pile of farm manure in the midden alongside extruded its bovine juices in pools of brown effluvia; almost seeping up to the entrance steps. The landlord had only one leg; he kept a sheep behind the bar and the police patrol would make it one of their stop-off spots hours after closing time. The place and our visits deserve a chapter all to themselves. How times have changed.

V28: The high point of the Black Mountains used to be named on the Ordnance Survey maps as Lord Hereford's Knob – causing instant amusement to Joan Hall and Ann Hassall. Later map editions showed it un-named or labelled The Twmpa.

V32: The road dropping from the Milltir Cerrig Pass on the Berwyns, to Llangynog is long and fast. We would be the quickest form of transport on this descent, passing cars, coaches and even motorbikes. The severe right-hand bend when entering Llangynog's main street required an accurate foreknowledge and rider positioning. It has since been widened and straightened. There are many examples of roads being widened and straightened. Transport planners seemed to believe that to do so increased road safety. Not so for the cyclists, however, where they are further exposed to even faster traffic. The design of cycle paths and where they join with these faster roads makes one ask if any of the planners have ever ridden a bike in town. To place a cycle route alongside an existing road as standard practice without visualising problems at junctions and roundabouts is totally irresponsible.

V38:Chris Warren, short and tubby; the all-round cyclist, made sure that he had all the correct cycling equipment. Part of the dress was plus-twos and long socks. Cycling tailor, Ossie Dover, made a pair to Chris's submitted measurements but they proved to have a waist rising as high as his nose. Chris certainly did have a unique body shape.

V39:Tony Ross was an awful sailor; most sea crossings saw him entombed in the toilets suffering from extreme *mal de mer*. A lad who joined us much later, Geoff Pepper, was an even worse sailor; he'd get seasick whilst still on the harbour jetty.

V43: Fred Maitland was a quiet, introspective character who would never dream of getting into trouble. He was a true pioneer of cycling in Stoke-on-Trent. Geoff and I met him while at Foulkstrath Castle, near

Kilkenny, Ireland when Fred had wandered high onto the castle's battlements – apparently out of bounds.

V44: The Lake District hostels seemed to have more rules than any in other parts of the country. A high number of visitors, many from foreign lands, probably was the reason for so many regulations. Us cyclists considered most of them to be petty and demanding the bleeding obvious. The golden rule, however, that one about travelling under one's own steam was the one so often broken.

V46: The George Borrow Inn is on the main road to Aberystwyth, near Pont Erwyd. Named after the famous 19thcentury traveller who risked meeting the indigenous locals and their dogs in his book,*Wild Wales,* this hostelry is an oasis in an area short of watering holes – or anything else, for that matter.

V48: When folk singing became popular within the group, we had several musicians; Dave Joynson, Bob Walker, Trevor Sowerbutts and myself on guitar (not all at the same time!). Bob also played the 5-string banjo and the penny whistle. Dave Joynson also played the harmonica, Bob Dylan style, on a neck halter. Clive Salt, apart from playing the piano by ear, was very good on tambourine. Roy Deakin played mandolin and much later, the bass guitar. Clive Cooper played the guitar (D tuning).and with his friend, Ian Brereton, both sang in the Dalian Singers – a competition choir from Stoke-on-Trent. Ralph was our singer par excellence! In short, we comprised a formidable music group, playing in long, evening sessions and, we believed, pleasing landlords and customers alike.

*

Sometime at the end of the ten years of hostelling, we tried a weekend camping expedition. Despite having a reputation for miserable conditions, cooking accidents, making do and looking ridiculous, we knew there existed a definite spirit of freedom. The chosen destination was Gradbach in the Peak District, in a farmer's field close the River Dane. The run in autumn was kept short to see how we would manage the camping equipment on the bicycles. Geoff Cartlidge used his recently acquired motor scooter and helped out with the extra tackle. I had recently bought a Blacks of Greenock Good Companion bell tent. It was of orange canvas, included a flysheeet and was supported by a single centre pole.

We pedalled north to Leek and continued on the A53, passing the Ramshaw Rocks, up Cat Tor Hill to Upper Hulme and the windy, exposed settlement of Flash. The village, famous for being a leading candidate for the highest habitation in England and also for coining its own currency called, surprisingly, 'flash', was just one of the bleak moorland places where shelter was sought behind strong stone walls, shielded from the cold winds in any season. We arrived at the camping field beyond Gradbach, a flat area of waterside meadow by the River Dane, still not much more than a stream and with enthusiasm, erected the simple tents in a somewhat casual order. I remember Clive Salt throwing up his basic bivouac tent, not much more than a greasy canvas sheet, as we laughed, joked and assembled the small Primus stoves. All this was a liberating adventure where no overbearing rules and regulations existed.

The tang of fried bacon on fried bread, tinged with the faint smells of meths and paraffin, was an unforgettable memory. The baked beans bubbling in their thick tomato sauce, lovingly wiped from the aluminium dixies with a slice of white bread, were, for us, the pinnacle of *haute cuisine.* We smoked cigarettes within the confining curved walls of Ralph's tent. Exhaled smoke collected, danced and drifted, blown this way and that in ghostly, ethereal wisps. A shower of rain pattering on the thin canvas over our heads, with the sense of being protected, made our fragile shelter an even more pleasant experience.

Before returning to the Potteries, we explored the rocky depth of Lud's Church, supposedly a meeting point of unbelieving stick-in-the-muds of long ago. The Luddites who opposed the introduction of machinery into their cotton mills. Thick moss covered the vertical walls of this split in the bracken-covered hillside; a secretive hiding place where, no doubt, anarchic, evil, ungodly sermons reverberated off the hard, unforgiving walls. Or was it old mill workers, complaining about their new machinery, eventually leading to mass redundancy? We broke camp, carefully packed the gear and retraced our route to the Potteries, and a solid roof over the head.

Whereas before, the thought of loading our lightweight cycles with camping equipment was anathema to easy touring, now the practice was possible. The cycle-camping weekend had been a great success, providing the extra equipment was shared. Tent, flysheet, poles, basic cooking stoves and utensils could be shared between two riders. It offered an alternative method of touring and could be used when we had outgrown the YHA. Steadily, we would change from purely cycling to using motor transport and tents. Gradbach had whetted our appetites for the relative freedom of camping; be it the smell of the seasons or the novelty of eating *al fresco,* we were at the place we wanted to be and closer still to the great outdoors.

The End of a Journey

In those ten years, years of revolutionary design, when the fashion changed from 1950s primness to letting it all hang out, when exposure was de rigueur, to impropriety in high places and days of revolt, our band of friends threw a leg over the crossbar and pedalled down the winding highways to discover new experiences. When cars moved from ponderous, boxy conveyances owned only by the well-off, to zippy mini cars and sleek E-type Jaguars that sped along straight, uniform motorways, our group of characters chose the bicycle, spinning down narrow lanes and teetering across indistinct tracks. In the times when hippies preached peace; blokes regressed into psychedelic dreams and girls in gossamer-thin dresses, threaded flowers down gun barrels, we knew only of a long, drawn-out war, a war of attrition, far away in the Far East. Vietnam was thousands of miles away but organised marches protested against nuclear proliferation at home. We shared their philosophy. When some folk, male, moustachioed and kaftan-wearing, adopted the fashions of Carnaby Street and insisted on travelling to India to read the Karma Sutra or learn the whining sitar in transcendental ecstasy, we pedalled through all weathers, dressed in the khaki shorts akin to those worn by Lord Baden-Powell. I remember wearing a woollen cardigan/smoking jacket and ordinary street shoes while on an early tour in Devon, although black shorts, black cotton cycling jackets and red, tartan flat caps became the normal wear. We had moved on from the 1950s, marked by severe short-back-and-sides haircuts, flapping flannel trousers and severe, uptight moral standards. Thank goodness for that! We had moved into a decade of looser morals – some may think too loose. While many people were preoccupied with fashion, music and being noticed, we plotted weekends on the bikes, following lonely routes between youth hostels and having a good time in our own way; well away from work and the smoky, industrial environment of the Potteries conurbation. Family and neighbourly friendships apart, the City's grim environs did nothing to encourage homesickness.

Now, in the new millennium, cycling has gained a massive respectability, becoming the thing to do. Even the image of naturism has changed from elderly folk playing tennis, frying sausages or operating a circular saw, to groups of young people cycling naked through London. The target charity would surely benefit handsomely. I must admit, the latter image of nudists is far more satisfying than the former. There can be no more direct or simpler method of excited atoms transferring from bike saddle to human being, or vice versa, than that.

Throughout those ten years of momentous events dominated by America: the first man in space, the Cuban missile crisis, the assassination of Kennedy, England winning football's World Cup (yes, for England, that was momentous)., and the first landing on the moon, we bunch of cyclists, in a strange, anachronistic style, chose to discover the tracts of countryside not normally found by the tourist. A photograph of the Grand Canal in Venice, taken from the vantage point of the Ponte Rialto in 1967, shows a scene that could have been taken a hundred years before. The busy waterway was full of life with boats of every description, but there were no signs of corporate advertising or obtrusive, public signage that often spoils our modern tourist locations. How often have we, after arriving at a scenic spot, been disappointed by a discarded Coca-Cola can or the scattering of a half-full carton of McDonald' s fries? We knew so well that if it took some effort to reach a certain location, it would be free of the litter of human traffic and disgusting human detritus.

In choosing the bicycle, we were lucky. We were fortunate to find places that had, as yet, escaped the trappings of mass tourism. We had been just visitors, gliding along the lanes; quiet, pollution-free, unassuming, easily pleased and, above all, unobtrusive. This was the beauty of it all. In times still a little free of today's suffocating rules and regulations, we could enjoy a late drink, experience quaint local traditions, find spots that hadn't yet succumbed to the commercialism of the tourist trap and live in the last vestiges of a quaint, slightly quirky society. Therein lay the source of anecdotes. We took from the countryside only experiences and photographs.

In that time, our horizons expanded and we made several excursions on the continent and to Ireland. Following the Emerald Isles, we ventured into the Pyrenees of France and Spain, into the Dolomites and down to Venice, and into the Norwegian fjord country. In choosing such a basic form of transport and seeking unknown, unfamiliar places, we possibly relived the earlier times and experiences of the original Thomas Cook traveller. Peering at detailed maps like consulting a Baedeker Guide, going to locations not advocated by the glossy travel brochure, but by a chance conversation between drinking companions or fellow cyclists met along the road.

As the decade drew to a close and we moved into the 1970s, we hired minibuses and toured Morocco, Pyrenees, Dolomites and the South of France, all, Morocco apart, we had covered on previous cycling tours. We made several epic cycling tours thereafter; the French Alps, Provence, Tarn Gorge, Loire Valley, Picos de Europa and Portugal, cycle-camping with and without motorised assistance, but all stemming from those initial ten years in the 1960s. Nothing would better those carefree days of understated camaraderie. The spirit of adventure had been created in those bicycles-only tours and youth hostelling weekends of that unforgettable decade.

Discovering a still unspoilt Peak District, Shropshire and Mid-Wales, we rode into areas that had not been beautified. We found forgotten places where local customs and even more local 'locals' provided victuals for the hungry traveller, offered experiences of a unique, different way of life. Being a keen photographer, I had many opportunities to record landscapes in glorious black and white; catching the subtle lighting of the changing seasons and get close up to show compositions and textures of those unaltered, diverse, non-clinical lands. The pace of the bicycle allowed me to see the photograph and capture it. Having the means to take and process photographs led me to getting such interesting work. Map-making and illustration work were a natural progression, resulting in a virtually ideal occupation in architecture, town planning and cartography – a very rewarding and, yes, cushy job.

At the close of the decade, my pastime of cycle touring, hobby of photography and work at the drawing board had inevitably and happily combined – bringing together the three strands of interest. The glimpse and oily smell of that efficient Viking Mileater bicycle in a cool architect's basement gave me enthusiasm to start cycle touring in a big way. That sleek, stripped-down machine, standing quietly in cool, crepuscular light, seemed to me to be trembling with potential speed, itching to burst into full daylight, hit the road and bear its rider into a far away world of magic.

From struggling with heavy, sit-up-and-beg borrowed bicycles to eventually affording and buying a high specification, lightweight touring machine, showed me the pleasures of the pastime. From visiting local places of interest to making cycle tours over continental cols in spectacular landscapes fired my imagination. Recounting memories, swapping jokes and retelling experiences. We clearly remembered the 1960s, including the Summer of Love, 1967 and, contrary to the popular saying, we definitely *Were There!!*

Meeting friends and sharing adventures had seen me pass through many a junction and pass by many a signpost – taking decisions, turnings and directions over the many miles of the rapidly changing times – all in a momentous decade.

I was at the ending of a journey – or was it just a pause at the roadside?

Glossary

Some cycling terms explained, either in this book and/or heard in the local bike shop, plus some maintenance tips. Some terms apply to cycle racing but still can be used by the plodding cycle tourist. Based on the 1960s touring bicycle,modern bikes may have more sophisticated equipment and attachments.

ANKLING – a fluid pedalling style where the foot slopes slightly back on the downward stroke and slightly forward on the (idling).upward stroke. An adopted clawing action, supposedly to make long-distance cycling easier. Difficult to sustain, so, needs practise.

BAR PLUGS – plastic or rubber plugs fitted inside the handlebar ends. Helps to prevent serious injuries from bare, protruding metal. A £5 note (dependant on inflation).is sometimes slipped into the handlebar tubing in cases of emergency, although usually forgotten about in the daily joys of cycle touring!

BLOCK – the centre core of the freewheel assembly on which various toothed sprockets are screwed. An occasional light oiling is only necessary. Disassembly is only needed when the pawl springs have broken. A chain jammed between block and wheel spokes can sometimes be freed by loosening the circular centre cover plate. However, extreme care is needed so as not to lift the sprockets and lose the ball bearings.

BIDON – a bottle for carrying liquids.Fitted into a down tube cage or from a cage hanging from the handlebars.

BIT AND BIT – Cycling at the front of a group for short periods, taking turns to break a strong headwind. Used more in club cycling and road racing.Riders usually fall to the back of the group for a rest after doing their turn on the front.

BONK – hypoglycaemia. A sudden drastic drop in bloodsugar levels causing instant exhaustion. Also referred to as 'The Knock' or 'Snakebite'. A rapid intake of sugar helps.

BOTTOM BRACKET – the threaded shell assembly at the meeting of down tube, seat tube and chain stays. Takes the bottom bracket cups and pedals spindle. Can include gear cable guides.

BRAKE HOODS – fixed to the handlebars. The pivot points for the brake levers. Soft, rubber sheaths covering them prevent blisters to the rider's hands when adopting this popular, on the tops, riding position. Also prevents black alloy staining.

BRAKE SHOES – metal holders for the brake blocks. Attached to the brake stirrups.A closed end, facing forward, prevent blocks from shooting out when braking hard. Whole assembly should be positioned in line with wheel rims when brake levers are pulled.

CABLE COVERS – drip light oil down into cable covers to keep cables operating freely. Trim excessive cable cleanly to prevent fraying, or wind into a tight circle.

CADENCE – the speed of pedalling. Too low a gear produces a wild, spin-dry rate of pedalling. Too high a gear produces a slow, laboured action. Both are incorrect, inefficient and energy-wasting.

CALLIPER – a mechanical lever device applied to brakes.

CAMPAG ENDS – fork ends manufactured by Campagnolo from Italy, well-tooled and with wheel-centring adjustment screws, and attached rear gear arm hanger.

CENTRE-PULL BRAKES – brakes operating from a centre pivot and applying equal pressure to both sides of the rim. A basic squeezing action, like the motorcar and motorcycle disc brakes.

CENTERING – a tendency for the steering to find and adopt a central position. Caused by the seating of ball bearings within the worn cups, probably due to incorrect headset adjustment and a rocking motion when braking. Makes balancing difficult.

CHAIN PUNCH – a specific tool to facilitate the removal and insertion of link rivets when splitting the chain in order to adjust its length. Dirty chains need cleaning in paraffin before dipping into a light oil bath. Over-lubricating is counter-productive – the chain liable to pick up extra dirt.

CHAIN RING – attached to the pedal cranks, these are available in various sizes. Smaller for a low gear, large for a high gear.

CHAINSET – the combined unit of cranks and chain rings.

CHAIN STAYS – the tapered rear forks. Hetchins Cycles produced a frame with curly rear chain and seat stays to give a very distinct appearance.

CLEARANCE – the gap between rear wheel and back of seat tube. Also between wheels and fork blades, and mudguard and tyre.

CHROME ENDS – the last 9 inches of front and rear forks can be chromed for decoration, and/or to prevent wear and tear to paintwork when removing and fitting wheels.

CLEATS (PEDAL). – devices on pedals to fix feet accurately into position.

CONES – convex, adjustable wheel bearings that thread on to spindles. Have flats incorporated to take thin cone spanners.

COTTERLESS (as in chain set). – pedal cranks and chain ring formed in one unit. More bulky than steel chain rings and cranks, therefore made from light alloy to save weight.

COTTER PIN – a threaded, tapered bolt with nut and washer to fix cranks to bottom bracket spindle. Usually used on older cycles, these steel pins needed hammering into position. A block of wood wedged underneath the spindle could be used for support to prevent undue shock and strain on the bottom bracket cups. Sometimes flats needed filing down to facilitate fitting.

CRANKS – the levers between chain wheel and pedals.

CUPS – used at headset, in wheel centres and at bottom bracket, dished to take the ball bearings races.

DERAILLEUR – the gear arm to transfer the chain sideways from one rear sprocket to the next. Clearly looked upon by the mechanical purist as an abomination! Nevertheless, it works!

DERNEY – light motorcycle used in paced track racing (see Keirin)., and long distance one day road events.

DEVIL-TAKE-THE-HINDMOST (DEVIL) – a race where the last rider on each lap is ruled as eliminated and has to drop out.

DISHING – in order to accommodate the gear block, the wheel builder will flatten, or dish the spokes on the gear side to gain that extra clearance.

DOUBLE BUTTED – a thickening of the frame tubes in section for extra strength where its needed, where they join at the lugs.

DOWN TUBE – the tube between headset and bottom bracket.

DURALINIUM – a lightweight tubing used in aircraft construction. Developed in WWII for maximum lightness and strength.

ECHELON – a stagger along the line of racing cyclists to cut down wind resistance.

ENDRICK (RIMS). – a wheel rim section found on earlier bicycles.

ENDURANCE EVENTS – long distance trials where maximum distances are attempted over set times, such as 10, 12 and 24 (hours).

EVENS – travelling at an average speed of 20mph (32kph). .

FIXED WHEEL – fixed single sprocket threaded on to rear block. Enables rider to brake by bearing back on the pedals. Used by purists for time trials and mandatory for all track racing. It encourages rhythmic pedalling but needs experience. Don't forget to keep pedalling!

FREEWHEEL – the device for a sprocket or cluster of sprockets to be fixed in one direction of rotation (clockwise)., and free in the other (anti-clockwise).Causes the familiar ticking sound.

FRONT CHANGER – the curved, gated device at the bottom bracket to transfer the chain between different chain wheels.

GEAR RATIOS – stated in inches. Over 100 inches would be considered a high gear. Under 40 inches, considered low. The equation: number of chain ring teeth divided by number of sprocket teeth, times the wheel diameter (27 inches). [685mm]. Therefore, a 16 teeth rear sprocket and a 46 teeth chain ring, using 27 inch wheels, would be a gear of 77.625 inches. 77 inches travelled along the road for one full rotation of the pedals. Geoff Cartlidge, however, swore by the use of a 66 inch gear ratio (46T front chain ring x 19T rear sprocket).

HALF-WHEELING – the habit of insisting that your front wheel is just ahead of your companion's alongside. If neither wants to give way, the speed gradually but inevitably increases.

HANDLEBAR STEM – angled bracket to connect handlebars to front forks. When adjusting handlebar height and alignment, unscrew centre bolt a <u>few turns only.</u> Tap down bolt using a piece of wood for protection, thereby freeing the bottom, tapered expanding nut.

HEADSET – the front steering assembly, frame and cups, holding the ball-bearing races at top and bottom. A too loose an adjustment can lead to juddering when braking, pitting to the cups and the steering to eventually find centre. This makes bike handling and the rider's balance difficult.

HONKING – standing upright on the pedals to exert extra downward pressure. Usually used for brief periods to, maybe, top a rise in the road. Toe clips should be fitted to prevent feet slipping off pedals. When riding in a group, an extra gap should be allowed for this by the following rider.

HOOKED (TEETH) – when old and worn, the chain ring's individual teeth become curved (hooked).causing the chain to unship or to jump and slip.

INFLATOR – or bicycle pump. Clipped to frame or fixed between frame pegs. Remember, bicycle pump shops are few and far between! Posh alternatives (compressed air or foot pumps).can be used but I consider them unnecessary.

JOCKEY WHEELS – the two, small guiding wheels in the rear gear cage arranged through springing to take up excessive chain slack.

KEIRIN RACING – light motorcycle (Derney).paced track races. Bike also used in some classic, long distance road races, e.g.: Bordeaux to Paris.

KNOCK – as the 'Bonk' or 'Snakebite'.

LOCK NUT – an extra nut threaded up tight against an existing one to prevent the former loosening.

LUGS – the plain or fancy-cut metal shells forming the joints between different tubing. An all-welded frame doesn't use lugs, the tube ends being shaped, pinned and brazed-up with bronze welding before final filing.

MADISON – a multi-lapped track race where pairs team up, turn and turn about – one to race and the other to sling his partner into the fray before resting on alternate laps. Points gained on various primes (nominated finish lines throughout race).

MAES BENDS – handlebar shape named after famous Belgian Tour de France rider. Cycling equipment takes the names of famous racers or trade products,e.g.: Christophe for toe clips, Binda for toe straps, Campagnolo for musettes and just about everything else. Eddie Merckx, The Cannibal, rider and winner in the early 1970s had his name on a complete cycle frame. I proudly carried an Evian (spa water).feeding bottle to maintain the pretence of being a famous racer!

MONOCOQUE – futuristic, single moulded frame design used in track events. Tubing and equipment formed into aerodynamic sections where strength isn't compromised.

MUSETTE – light cotton bag worn around the neck to hold emergency food when riding.

PANNIERS – large bags attached to each side of front or rear carrier.

PAWL SPRINGS – two fine hair springs to keep ratchet dogs open in a freewheel assembly.

PELOTON – a racing term. A large group of racing cyclists behind any breakaway leaders.

PITTING – dips and scars worn into the surface of ball-bearing cups caused by bad adjustment and/or lack of oil or grease.

POSITION – the ideal riding position, adjusted by the saddle height, is when sitting on the saddle and the ball of the foot is resting on the lowest pedal in the bottom position, that knee should be slightly flexed. Alternatively, both feet should be flat on the ground when standing astride the top tube. Distance between saddle tip and handlebars should be gauged by placing elbow on saddle tip and outstretched fingers reaching centre of handlebars.

PRESSURES – high pressure touring tyres with a shallow tread and wire inserts in walls to seat within the wheel rim.

PRIME – an intermediate mountain top finish line or sprint point along the route where bonus time points can be won. Any village sign can be treated as a prime when club riding!

QUICK RELEASE – hubs fitted with adjustable levers instead of nuts for fast wheel removal and fitting.

RAKE – the offset angle between a line drawn down the side of the front forks and the centre of the wheel nut. Used to provide some suspension cushioning. Bates frames, to be different, had forward-stepped front forks called (something like).duo-dihedral blades.

RANDONNEUR – a type of handlebar shaped for efficiency and named after well-known cycle tourist.

RAT TRAP (PEDALS) metal pedals with non-slip, serrated plate top edges.

REAR CHANGER – rear gear arm mechanism to transfer chain up and down sprockets.

RESPONSIVENESS – cycle frames differ. Some are as dead as a donkey and others are as lively as a straining stallion. The skill in producing a lively product lies with the frame builder. Generally, a short wheelbase machine used for racing is more responsive, but more uncomfortable than a tourer, with a longer wheelbase giving a gentler ride.

REYNOLD'S 531 – well-known strong, light cycle frame tubing. Main triangle and front forks. Developed from tubing used in earlier aircraft construction.

RIM TAPE – woven cotton or rubber tape set around wheel rim to protect inner tube from rough, protruding spoke nipples. File spoke-ends and nipples (those in the wheel rim).down if and when wheel building.

ROD BRAKES – brakes operated by a system of jointed rods before control cables became popular.

ROUGH-STUFF – cycling off-road along tracks. Now known as the popular sport of mountain biking.

SEAT PILLAR – an alloy or steel tube connecting saddle with frame. Do not extend too far out. Safety line usually marked.

SEAT STAYS – thinner tubing between seat tube and rear fork ends. Sometimes an arched bridge is included for the fitting of a centre-pull cable stop.

SEAT TUBE – the tube between bottom bracket and seat cluster.

SIDE PULL BRAKES – brakes operating from a side position.Preferred by racers.

SNAKEBITE – see the 'Bonk' and the 'Knock' as above.

SPINDLES – the threaded rods to take the adjustable cones for front and rear wheels. The bottom bracket spindle is forged with flats to accept the cranks/cotter pins or splined and internally threaded to accept the alloy chain set.

SPOKING – types of wheel spoking, usually tangentially arranged to give a small amount of suspension. Number of spokes vary, with less used for racing.

SPOKE KEY – a winged and slotted tool to engage the spoke nipples when wheel building.

SPOKE NIPPLES – threaded caps fixing spokes to wheel rims.

SPRINT ENDS – special fork-ends with horizontal slits to prevent wheel pulling over to rub against forks when exerting extreme force, particularly in sprinting.

SPROCKET – a single gear ring of teeth, normally ranging from 12T (high gear).to 28T (low gear).

TIME TRIAL – race against the clock. Riders start at time intervals and ride over a 10, 25, 50 or 100 mile course. Usually held on an early Sunday morning to avoid traffic congestion, on an out and return basis.

TOE CLIPS – springy steel guards to keep the foot in the correct position on the pedals. Used with leather straps so that pedals can be lifted as well as pressed down.

TOPS (ON THE). – a favourite position for the hands. Holding the brake hoods whether racing or touring as against holding down on the drops in a low, racing position.Improves breathing.

TOP TUBE – the tube between head tube and seat cluster. Originally referred to as the crossbar. Burly policemen even rode bikes with a double crossbar!

TRACK (OUT OF). – sometimes a cycle frame will be pulled out of alignment by sustained, powerful riding over a long period. Sight frame from the rear and between forks.

TRACK MITTS – soft, fingerless gloves with chamois palms and stringed backs. Cuts down staining from alloy, increases grip and looks racy – the real deal!

TRACK NUTS – large nuts threaded onto spindle to fix wheels into fork ends.

TUBS – ultra-high pressure tubular tyres with virtually no tread, usually cemented to wheel rim. Used in racing where road resistance is reduced to a minimum.

TWIDDLING – pedalling in a low gear. Can be sustained for long periods when climbing a high pass or when a rider is fatigued.

TYRE LEVERS – angled rods to ease tyre off wheel rim. If unavailable, spoons will do! Avoid trapping inner tube when using. When putting tyre back on, position it into the well of the rim around its circumference, partly inflate inner tube and lever tyre into position in short sections, using thumbs only. Always carry a spare inner tube and mend puncture at leisure. Puncture mending has risen from stuffing the outer cover with grass, to become a tongue-poking-out-the-corner-of-mouth fine art!!

TYRE SAVER – a sprung wire device fitted to the seat stays or front forks to drag lightly on the tyre tread and flip any persistent gravel or glass splinters away. However, I find most punctures arise from thorns, particularly after hedgerow flailing.

WHEEL BUILDING – a highly skilled art – fascinating, satisfying but time-consuming. Old front forks fixed in a vice can be used as a building jig. Drill holes in forks at rim position to insert adjustment guides.

WING NUT – an old-fashioned nut designed to be loosened and tightened with hand pressure only. Seen in sepia prints of Tour de France racing cyclists' bikes, on dirt roads and on mountain passes! Wearing goggles, a spare tyre round the shoulders and looking close to death!!

Appendix i

STOKE-ON-TRENT YHA CYCLING SECTION JAN. 1960 to DEC. 1969.

(Hostels attended by CG, including some walking weekends/holidays).

Chronology of weekends, bank holiday weekends & tours.

Other members' names abbreviated to initials:

DL: Derek Latham. DH: Dave Hope. KH: Ken Hall. KHo: Ken Hodgkinson. GC: Geoff Cartlidge. RS: Ralph Salt. CS: Clive Salt. PL: Paul Leese. DB: Dave Booth. BW: Brian Whalley. PB: Pete Boardman. BB: Bill Barnish. CW: Chris Warren. CL: Clive Lewis. TR: Tony Ross. DJ: Dave Joynson. JB: John Bradbury. (CG: Colin Green).

1960

Living at Bank House, Hanley Road, Sneyd Green, Stoke-on-Trent.
Cycle: Halfords Sports.
Cycled solo to Plymouth and return.
Cleeve Hill YH (Cotswolds).
Street YH (Somerset).
Bampton YH (mid-Devon).
Bridport YH (Dorset coast).
Croscombe YH (Mendip Hills).
Duntisbourne Abbots YH (Cotswolds).
Home (Malvern Wells hostel full).
Autumn: Moved to Cherry Tree Close, Trentham, Stoke-on-Trent.

1961

Cycle: Sun Cycles Tourer, nicknamed Maud.
Cycled solo around Mid-Wales.
Shrewsbury YH.
Clun YH (South Shropshire).
Glascwm YH (Herefordshire/Radnorshire).

Pentre Cwrt YH (Towy Valley).

Poppit Sands YH (Cardigan).

Borth YH (Mid-Wales coast).

Corris YH (South Snowdonia NP).

Bala YH (Mid-Wales).

Late Summer.Joined local YHA group meetings at Cartwright House, Hanley.

Christmas in the Peak.

Edale YH (Peak District).[& in Nag's Head PH in village] with DL, DH, KH.

1962

Jan: Rudyard Lake YH (Leek).New Year's Party with Walking Section.

Jan: Edale YH (Peak District).

Jan: Wandon YH (Cannock Chase).

Feb: Hartington Hall YH (Peak District).*to survey building for Drawing Course.*

Feb: Shrewsbury YH (Shropshire).

Cynwyd YH (Corwen).

Feb: Oakenclough YH (Peak District).

Feb: Dimmingsdale YH (North Staffs).*Adopted Hostel Working Party.*

Mar: Maeshafn YH (North Wales).

Cynwyd YH (Corwen).

Mar: Chaddesley Corbett YH (Bromsgrove).

Mar: Cynwyd YH (Corwen).

Mar: Shining Cliff YH (Peak District).

Apr: Lichfield YH (Mid-Staffs).

Cleeve Hill YH (Cotswolds).

Windgather YH (Peak District).

Easter Weekend in Mid-Wales.

Apr: Shrewsbury YH.

Ystumtuen YH (Mid-Wales).

Llandeusant YH (South Wales).

Clun YH (South Shropshire).

Apr: Shrewsbury YH.

Wheathill YH (South Shropshire).

May: Shrewsbury YH.

Bala YH (Mid-Wales).

Cycle tour to West Country, with DL & DH.

Ashton Keynes YH (Cotswolds).

Bampton YH (Edge of Exmoor).

Gidleigh YH (Dartmoor).

Instow YH (North Devon).

Holford (North Devon).

Cheddar YH (Mendip Hills).

Cleeve Hill YH (Cotswolds).

Ludlow YH (South Shropshire).

May: Bretton YH (Peak District).

Jun: Llangollen YH (North Wales).

Whitsun Bank Holiday in North Wales.

Jun: Shrewsbury YH.

Harlech YH (Snowdonia NP).

Bala YH (Mid-Wales).

Jun: Shrewsbury YH.

Ystumtuen YH (Mid-Wales).

Jun: Shrewsbury YH

Dinas Mawddwy YH (Mid-Wales). Jul: Edale YH (Peak District). Jul: Shrewsbury YH

Maeshafn YH (North Wales). Jul: Chester YH (Cheshire).

Oaklands YH (Llanwrst).

Jul: Glascwm YH (Herefordshire/Radnorshire border).

August Bank Holiday in Mid-Wales.

Aug: Shrewsbury YH.

Glascwm YH.

Ystumtuen.

Aug: Edale YH.

Annual holiday in Ireland (Wicklow, Cork & Kerry).with GC.
Train to Holyhead &ferry to Dun Laoghaire.

Aug: Knockree YH (North Wicklow Mtns).

Baltiboys YH (Blessington Lakes).

Glendalough YH (Mid-Wicklows).

Aughavannagh YH (South Wicklows).

Foulkstrath Castle YH (Kilkenny).

Ballydavid Wood YH (Galtee Mtns).

Cork YH (County Cork).

Glengarrif B&B (Bantry Bay).

Killarney YH (Kerry).

Black Valley YH (Kerry).

Glencar YH (Waterville).

Glencar YH.

Glin YH (Knockmealdown Mtns).

Foulkstrath Castle YH (Kilkenny).

Ferry – Dun Laoghaire to Holyhead &train to Stoke.

Sep: Shrewsbury YH.

Nant y Dernol YH (Mid-Wales).

Sep: Shrewsbury YH.

Sep: Windgather YH (Peak District).

Sep: Leam Hall YH (Peak District).

Oct: Dimmingsdale YH (Working Party – North Staffs).

Oct: Bridges YH (Mid-Shropshire).

Oct: Hartington YH (Peak District).

Nov: Delamere Forest YH (Cheshire).

Nov: Snowdon Ranger YH (Auto-Ramble).

Nov: Buxton YH (Peak District).

Dec: Bridges YH Mid-Shropshire).

Dec: Rudyard Lake YH (North Staffs).

1963

Jan: Rudyard Lake YH (New Year Party).

Jan: Dimmingsdale YH (Working Party). Feb: Shrewsbury YH

Feb: Wandon YH (Cannock Chase).

Feb: Ilam Hall YH (Peak District).

Feb: Shrewsbury YH.

Clun YH (South Shropshire).

Mar: Maeshafn YH (North Wales).

Mar: Cynwyd YH.

Mar: Matlock Bath YH (East Peak District).

Mar: Shrewsbury YH.

Ystumtuen YH (Mid-Wales).

Mar: Cynwyd YH.

Apr: Dimmingsdale YH (Working Party).

Dimmingsdale YH.

Easter weekend around Cader Idris.

Apr: Shrewsbury YH.

Apr: Corris YH (Mid-Wales).

Apr: Dolgellau (Mid-Wales).

Apr: Bala YH.

Apr: Buxton YH (Peak District).

Apr: Bridges YH.

Bought Harry Quinn Cycle (Harry).

May: Shrewsbury YH.

Bala YH.

May: Shrewsbury YH.

Ystumtuen YH.

(Crashed new bike on this weekend).

Whitsun Bank Holiday in Wye Valley, with GC, RS, CS, PL, DH, DB.

May: Shrewsbury YH.

Jun: St Briavels Castle YH (Wye Valley).

Staunton-on-Wye YH (Wye Valley).

Jun: Shrewsbury YH.

Llangollen YH.

Jun: Shrewsbury YH.

Dolgellau YH.

Jun: Shrewsbury YH.

Newtown YH (Mid-Wales).

Jul: Shrewsbury YH.

Cynwyd YH.

Jul: Shrewsbury YH.

Wheathill YH (Mid-Shropshire).

Jul: Shrewsbury YH.

Glascwm YH.

August Bank Holiday in Black Mountains & tour to Pembroke coast, with group & BW.

Aug: Shrewsbury YH.

Capel y Ffin YH (Black Mtns).

Glascwm YH.

Storey Arms YH (Brecon Beacons).

Pentre Cwrt YH (Carmarthen).

Pwll Deri YH (Pembroke Coast).

Pwll Deri YH.

Ystumtuen YH.

Dinas Mawddwy YH.

Holiday in western Ireland (Connemara) Achill & Donegal).with GC, BW, PB.

Train to Holyhead, ferry to Dun Laoghaire, cycle to Dublin, train-Dublin to Galway. Aug: Lettermullen YH (Galway).

Lettermullen YH.

Killary Harbour YH (Connemara).

Killary Harbour YH.

Killary Harbour YH.

Currane YH (Achill Island).

Currane YH.

Currane YH.

Sligo B&B.

Carrick YH (Donegal).

Carrick YH.

Carrick YH.

Poisoned Glen YH (Donegal).

Poisoned Glen YH.

Train-Strabane to Dublin, cycle to Dun Laoghaire, ferry to Holyhead, train to Stoke.

Sep: Bridges YH.

Sep: Clun YH.

Oct: Hartington YH.

Oct: Lledr Valley YH.

(Autoramble on Moel Siabod).

Oct: Ewden YH (Ladybower).

Nov: Ilam YH.

Nov: Bridges YH.

Nov: Wandon YH.

Nov: Delamere Forest YH.

Nov: Ilam Hall YH.

Dec: Hartington YH.

Dec: Wilderhope YH (Wenlock Edge).

Christmas Tour of Snowdonia, with RS, CS, GC.(Boots 'n Saddles long weekend).

Dec: Chester YH.

Idwal Cottage YH (Nannt Ffrancon).

Llanberis YH (Nant Peris).

Bryn Gwynant YH (Nant Gwynant).

Cynwyd YH .

1964

Jan: Buxton YH.

Oakenclough YH.

Jan: Rudyard Lake YH.

Jan: Dimmingsdale YH (Cyclists' Dinner).

Jan: Earl's Court YH (London) for Auto-Ramble on Chiltern Hills.

Feb: Elton YH (Eastern Peak).

Feb: Oakenclough YH.

Feb: Wandon YH.

Feb: Chester YH.

Feb: Cynwyd YH.

Feb: Shrewsbury YH.

Llangollen YH Mar: Dimmingsdale YH.

Mar: Ravenstor YH (Peak District).

Mar: Ilam Hall YH.

Easter long weekend down Towy Valley.

Mar: Shrewsbury YH.

Ystumtuen YH.

Llandeusant YH (Lower Towy).

Ludlow YH.

Apr: Buxton YH.

Apr: Shrewsbury YH.

Dinas Mawddwy YH (Mid-Wales), *(with Palm Beach girl on very windy weekend)*.

Apr: Shrewsbury YH.

Nant y Dernol YH (Mid-Wales).

Apr: Shrewsbury YH.

Bala YH.

May: Wheathill YH.

May: Shrewsbury YH.

Clun YH.

Whitsun weekend in Cotswolds.

May: Lichfield YH.

Broom Hall YH (Ledbury).

Rushall YH (Herefordshire).

May: Shrewsbury YH.

Newtown YH (Mid-Wales).

May: Snowdon Ranger YH (Snowdonia NP).

Snowdon Ranger YH (Auto-Ramble).

Holiday in Devon & Cornwall, with GC, BW, BB, CW, CL.

Jun: Shrewsbury YH *Train to Plymouth.*

Plymouth YH (South Devon).

Lostwithiel YH (Bodmin).

Boswinger YH (South Cornwall).

Falmouth YH (South Cornwall).

Mullion Cove B&B (Lizard). + Land's End YH.

Phillack YH (NorthCornwall).

Truro YH.

Treyarnon YH (North Cornwall).

Tintagel YH (North Cornwall).

Boscastle Harbour YH (North Cornwall).

Gidleigh YH, (edge of Dartmoor).

Bellever YH (Dartmoor).

Dunsford YH (Dartmoor).*Train-Exeter to Shrewsbury.*

Shrewsbury YH.

Jul: Dinas Mawddwy YH.

Jul: Chester YH.

Jul: Shrewsbury YH.

Corris YH Jul: Hartington YH.

Jul: Lichfield YH.

Stratford-Upon-Avon YH (Arden, Warwickshire).

August Bank Holiday weekend & holiday in Mid-Wales, with group & BW.

Jul: Chester YH.

Aug: Lledr Valley YH (Snowdonia NP).

Capel Curig YH (Snowdonia NP).

Corris YH.

Ystumtuen YH.

Ystumtuen YH.

Blaencaron YH (Mid/South Wales).

Nant y Dernol YH.

Newtown YH.

Aug: Leam Hall YH.

Aug: Wilderhope YH.

Aug: Wilderhope YH.

Sep: Cynwyd YH.

Sep: Cynwyd YH.

Sep: Copt Oak YH (Charnwood Forest).

Oct: Clun YH.

Oct: Elterwater YH (Lake District Auto-Ramble).

AGM & Cyclists' Bednights Award.

Oct: Slide Show (Devon & Cornwall).

Oct Delamere Forest YH (joint weekend with Walking Section).

Oct: Bridges YH.

Oct: Cynwyd YH.

Nov: Wheathill YH.

Nov: Wandon YH.

Dec: Ravenstor YH (joint weekend with Walking Section).

Dec: Slide Show (A Cyclist's Year).

Dec: Cynwyd YH.

Christmas holiday in Berwyns.*Travel in Bedford Van.*

Dec: Cynwyd YH.

Cynwyd YH.

Cynwyd YH.

Cynwyd YH.

1965

Jan: Rudyard Lake YH (Tramps' Weekend and New Year's Party).

Jan: Dimmingsdale YH (Cyclists' Annual Dinner).

Jan: Wilderhope YH.

Feb: Bretton YH.

Feb: Bridges YH.

Feb: Cynwyd YH.

Feb: Shrewsbury YH.

Mar: Clun YH.

Mar: Shrewsbury YH.

Ystumtuen YH.

Mar: Ludlow YH.

Mar: Eric Hazeldine's Puzzle Pictures.

Mar: Chaddesley Corbett YH (Bromsgrove).

Apr: Colwyn Bay YH (Auto-Ramble on Carnedds).

Apr: Llangollen YH.

Easter holiday in Isle of Man.

Apr: Chester YH.

Ferry – Liverpool to Douglas.

Ramsey YH.

Port Erin YH.

Laxey YH.

Ferry – Douglas to Liverpool.

Apr: Cynwyd YH.

May: Dimmingsdale YH.

May: Shrewsbury YH.

Broom Hall YH (Ledbury).

May: Shrewsbury YH.

May: Newtown YH.

Whitsun tour of Roman Steps from Harlech, with RS, GC, TR, PB, DH.

Jun: Shrewsbury YH.

Harlech YH (Snowdonia NP).

Bala YH.

Jun: Lichfield YH.

Houghton Mill YH (Cambridgeshire).*Weekend race with Honda 50.*

Jun: Cynwyd YH.

Jun: Shrewsbury YH.

Dinas Mawddwy YH.

Jun: Dimmingsdale YH.

Jul: Shrewsbury YH.

Ystumtuen YH.

Holiday in Pyrenees, France & Spain. Jul. 9th-25th

RS, RD, CW, GC, TR, DH, PB.

Bed & Breakfast.

Train to London & Newhaven, ferry to Dieppe, train to Paris & Pau.

Arrens (via Col d'Aubisque, Soulor).

Gedre (via St Sauveur Gorge).

Bareges (via Cirque de Gavarnie).

Ste Marie de Campan (via Col du Tourmalet).

Bagneres de Luchon (via Col d'Aspin, Peyresourde).

Viella (via Col de Portillon).

Esterri d'Aneau (via.Puerto de Bonaigua).

Seo de Urgel (via Col del Canto).

Andorra-La-Vielle.

Andorra-La-Vielle.

Ax-Les-Thermes (via Port d'Envalira).

Alet-Les-Bains (via Col de Chioula).

Carcassonne.

Train to Paris & Dieppe, ferry to Newhaven, train to London, Stafford & Stoke.

Aug: Bretton YH.

Aug: Bridges YH.

August Bank Holiday weekend in Wales.

Aug: Shrewsbury YH.

Bala YH.

Corris YH.

Holiday in Devon & Cornwall, with DH.

Sep: Shrewsbury YH.

Train- Shrewsbury to Plymouth.

Plymouth YH.

Boswinger YH.

Tintagel YH.

Tavistock YH.

Plymouth YH.

Train – Plymouth to Stafford.

Moved to Bomere Heath, Shropshire.

Undated.

Wheathill YH.

Dimmingsdale YH.

Hartington YH.

Ludlow YH.

Cynwyd YH.

Maeshafn YH.

Llangollen YH.

Christmas at Dimmingsdale YH (Churnet Valley).

Dimmingsdale YH.

1966

Rudyard Lake YH (New Year's Party).

Dimmingsdale YH (Annual Cyclists' Dinner).

Bridges YH.

Cynwyd YH.

Dimmingsdale YH.

Bangor YH (Auto-Ramble to Carnedds).

Clun YH.

Easter weekend on Lleyn Peninsular.

Llangollen YH+ Llithfaen B&B (Lleyn Peninsula).+ Lledr Valley YH (Bettws-y-Coed).

Copt Oak YH (Charnwood Forest).

Bala YH.

Shrewsbury YH + Ystumtuen YH.

Whitsun weekend in Yorkshire Dales (High Cup Nick).& Lake District.

Train – Crewe to Lancaster.

Ingleton YH (Lune Valley).

Middleton-in-Teesdale B&B.

Patterdale YH (Ullswater).

Train – Lancaster to Crewe.

Holiday in Scotland,with GC, CW, BW. (RS, CS, TR, PB, RD; went to Cape Wrath).

June.

Train – Crewe to Inverness.

Cannich YH (Loch Ness).

Glen Affric YH.

Ratagan YH (Glenshiel).

Broadford YH (Isle of Skye).

Glen Brittle YH (Isle of Skye).

Kyle of Lochalsh YH.

Kishorn YH.

Lonbain YH (Applecross).

Inverness B&B.

Train – Inverness to Crewe & Shrewsbury.

Colwyn Bay YH (North Wales coast).

Shrewsbury YH + Broom Hall YH.

Llangollen YH.

August Bank Holiday weekend in Wye Valley.

Staunton-on-Wye YH.

Crickhowell YH (Brecon Beacons).

Glascwm YH.

Penmaenmawr YH (North Walescoast).

Walking holiday in Lake District, with GC & Steve?

Motor to Windermere.
Sep: Windermere YH.
Elterwater YH.
Elterwater YH.
Buttermere YH.
Longthwaite YH.
Longthwaite YH.
Patterdale YH.
Patterdale YH.
Motor to Stoke.
Cynwyd YH.
Christmas at Cynwyd.
Cynwyd YH.

1967

Dimmingsdale YH.
Shrewsbury YH.
Easter weekend in Isle of Man.
Chester YH.
Ferry – Liverpool to Douglas.
Ramsey YH.
Port Erin YH.
Laxey YH.
Ferry – Douglas to Liverpool.
Cynwyd YH.
Bala YH.
Dinas Mawddwy YH.
Llangollen YH, Shrewsbury YH + Ystumtuen YH, Shrewsbury YH + Broom Hall YH, Roewen YH (Llanwrst).
Walking holiday in Lake District, with RS, TR, DJ.
Train – Crewe to Oxenholme.
Kendal YH.
Patterdale YH.
Wastwater YH.
High Close YH.

Keswick YH.

Buttermere YH.

Black Sail YH.

Grasmere YH.

Train – Oxenholme to Crewe.

Dimmingsdale YH.

Chester YH.

Nant y Dernol YH.

Holiday to Dolomites & Venice, with RS, RD, TR, DJ, GC, CW.

Holland Park YH (London).

Train, ferry, train to Bolzano, Italy.

Bed & Breakfast accommodation.

Bolzano.

Passo di Tonale.

Bormio.

Prato alto Stelvio.

Nova Levante.

Canazei.

Canazei.

Cortina d'Ampezzo.

Cortina d'Ampezzo.

Cencenighe.

Venice.

Venice.

Train from Venice to Paris & Dieppe. Ferry to Newhaven. Train to London & Stafford.

Dinas Mawddwy YH.

Bridges YH.

Wilderhope YH.

Outbreak of Foot & Mouth disease.

Christmas at Bomere Heath (Shrewsbury & Shropshire).

1968

Feb: Shrewsbury YH.

Mar: Shrewsbury YH.

Mar: Cynwyd YH.

Mar: Maeshafn YH.

Easter weekend in Isle of Man.

Chester YH.

Ramsey YH.

Port Erin YH.

Laxey YH.

Apr: Cynwyd YH.

Apr: Llangollen YH.

May: Wheathill YH.

May: Llangollen YH.

Undated

Newtown YH.

Bala YH.

Bala YH.

Holiday in Fjords of Norway from Bergen, July 12th- 22nd, with RS, GC, PB, JB, KHo.

Train to Carlisle. Ferry – Newcastle to Bergen.

Carlisle YH.

Floyen YH (Bergen).

Gudvangen B&B.

Skjolden YH.

Lom YH.

Olden YH.

Hellesylt YH.

Geiranger (Christian Centre).

Montana YH (Bergen).

Ferry – Bergen to Newcastle. Train to Stoke.

Newtown YH.

Malvern Wells YH (Worcestershire).

Chester YH.

Penmaenmawr YH.

Holiday in Northern Ireland with RS.

Train to Lancaster.

Ferry – Heysham to Belfast.

Minerstown YH.

Slievenaman YH.

Omeath YH.

Bridge of Boyne YH.

Dundalk YH.

Glendalough YH.

Glencree YH.

Ferry – Dun Laoghaire to Holyhead.

Cynwyd YH.

Christmas at Cynwyd.

Cynwyd YH.

1969

Dimmingsdale YH.

Bridges YH.

Holiday in Pyrenees,May 23rd- June 15th, with JB.

May/June.

Train to London via Stafford, ferry from Newhaven to Dieppe, train to Paris & Bayonne.

All Bed & Breakfast.

Pamplona (via Puerto Otsondo, Velate).

Jaca.

Panticosa.

Torla (via Puerto Cotefolbo).

Torla (via Ordessa NP).

Castejon (via Collando de Fordada).

Castejon (via Benasque).

Viella (via Viella Tunnel).

Viella (via Puerto Bonaigua).

Luchon (via Col de Portillon).

Ste Marie de Campan (via Peyresourde & Aspin).

Gedre (via Col du Tourmalet).

Gedre (via Cirque de Gavarnie).

Arrens (via Pont d'Espange).

Laruns (via Col de Soulor & Aubisque).

Laruns (via Col de Portalet).

Mauleon.

Cambo (via Col d'Osquich).

Bayonne.

Train to Paris & Dieppe, ferry to Newhaven. Train from Euston to Stafford.

Corris YH.

Bridges YH.

Christmas at Cynwyd.

Cynwyd YH.

Appendix ii

YHA CYCLISTS' PROGRAMME

OCTOBER 1963 – SEPTEMBER 1964

HOSTEL BEDNIGHTS COMPETITION

Key to Names

AH: Ann Hassall. BB: Bill Barnish. BP: Bob Proctor. BW: Brian Whalley. CW: Chris Warren. CY: Cliff Yates. CL: Clive Lewis. CS: Clive Salt. CG: Colin Green. DB: Dave Booth. DH: Dave Hope. DJ: Dave Joynson. DL: Derek Latham. EH: Eric Hazeldine. GC: Geoff Cartlidge. JH: Joan Hall. KB: Kenny Birks. MS: Maurice Such. PL: Paul Leese. PB: Pete Boardman. PBr: Peter Brocklehurst. PH: Phil Hughes. RS: Ralph Salt. RP: Rod Peterson. RD: Roy Deakin. RH: Roy Hazeldine. TO: Terry Oakden. TR: Tony Ross.

1963

October

Buxton YH (3).

BW, JH, MS (clashed with Auto-Ramble to Moel Siabod, Snowdonia).

Hartington YH (6).

EH, DJ, PH, RD, GC, CG.

Ewden YH (5).

EH, DJ, RD, CG, RS.

November

Bridges YH (6).

DJ, RD, GC, CG, KB, CY.

Delamere Forest YH (11).

BW, EH, DJ, RD, GC, CG, RS, CS, KB, TR, CL.

December

Ilam YH (Hartington). (8).

RD, GC, CG, RS, CS, KB,CL, PBr.

(Dave Goodhall should have led).

Wilderhope Manor YH (8).

BW, RD, GC,CG, RS, DH, DB, PB.

(John Hall should have led).

1964

January

Rudyard Lake YH (16).(New Year Party).

BW, EH,DJ, PH, RD, GC, CG, RS, CS,KB, TR,CL, DH, RH, TO, BP.

Dimmingsdale YH (16).(Cyclists' Dinner at Consall).

BW, JH, MS, EH, DJ, PH, RD, GC, CG, RS, CS, KB, TR, DH, PB, DL.

February

Elton YH (11).

BW, EH, DJ, PH, RD, GC, CG, RS, KB, DH, PL.

Wandon YH (11).

BW, EH, DJ, PH, RD, GC, CG, RS, KB, CY, PB.

(Paul Leese should have led).

Chester (Llangollen). (9).

BW, PH, RD, GC, CG, RS, KB, CL, BB.

(Eric Hazeldine should have led).

March

Ravenstor YH (7).

BW, PH, RD, GC, CG,RS, CS.

Easter Weekend

Shrewsbury YH (10).

BW, EH, PH, GC, CG, KB, CL, DH, DL, BB.

Ystumtuen YH (12). (+PL, DJ).

Llandeusant YH 13).(+RD).

Ludlow YH (13).(For Clun YH & Glascwm YH).

Total bednights = 48.

(Dave Booth should have led).

April

Shrewsbury YH (6).

DJ, PH, GC, CG, RS, KB Dinas Mawddwy YH (9). + BW, RD, DH.

Shrewsbury YH (5). DJ, PH, GC, CG, RS.

Bala YH (Plas Rhiwaedog). (9), + BW, RD, KB, DH.

May

Wheathill YH (9).

BW, DJ, RD, GC, CG, RS, KB, DH, CW.

Whitsun Weekend Lichfield YH (6).

GC, CG, RS, CS, KB, CW.

Broom YE (8). (+BW, RD).

Rushall YH (8).

Total bednights = 22.

Newtown YH (8).

BW, RD, GC, CG, RS, KB, DH, BB.

June

Chester YH

Hostel booking cancelled.

Shrewsbury YH (8).

BW, DJ, GC, CG, KB, DH, BB, CW, CL.(BW, GC, BB, CW, CL, CG to Devon & Cornwall).

July

All Night Ride (7).

BW, DJ, RD, GC, CG, BB, CW; Eric Hazeldine should have led).

Shrewsbury YH (5).

GC, CG, RS, DL, CW.

Corris YH (5).

Hartington YH (4).

BW, GC, CG, BB.

(Others taking holidays).

August Bank Holiday

Chester YH (7).

GC, CG, KB, DH, BB, CW, AH

Lledr Valley YH (9). (+BW, RD).

Capel Curig YH (9).

(BW + CG continue on holiday).

Mystery ride (Leam Hall YH). (8).

DJ, RD, GC, CG, RS, KB, DH, BB.

Wilderhope Manor YH (4).

BW, CG, KB, DH.

(Clashed with CTC York Rally).

September

Cynwyd YH (7).

BW, PH, RD, GC, CG, KB, CW.

Copt Oak YH (10).

BW, DJ, PH, RD, GC, CG, RS, KB, TR, CW.

(Clive Salt should have led).

Stratford-upon-Avon YH (12).

BW, DJ, RD, GC, CG, RS, KB, TR, DL, CW, AH, RP.

TOTAL NUMBER OF WEEKENDS = 31.

TOTAL NUMBER OF HOSTELS = 39.

TOTAL NUMBER OF BEDNIGHTS = 321.

Names/Bednights

CG: Colin Green (38). 1st.

GC: Geoff Cartlidge (36). 2nd.

KB: Kenny Birks ((29). 3rd.

BW: Brian Whalley (28). 4th.

RS: Ralph Salt (27).= 5th.

RD: Roy Deakin (27).= 5th.

DJ: Dave Joynson (21). 7th.

DH: Dave Hope (18). 8th.

PH: Phil Hughes (17). 9th.

CW: Chris Warren (15). 10th.

EH: Eric Hazeldine (11). 11th.

BB: Bill Barnish (9). 12th.

CL: Clive Lewis (8). = 13th.

CS: Clive Salt (8).= 13th.

DL: Derek Latham (8).= 13th.

TR: Tony Ross (5). 16th.

PL: Paul Leese (4).= 17th.

AH: Ann Hassall (4).= 17th.

PB: Pete Boardman (3). 19th.

JH: Joan Hall (2).= 20th.

MS: Maurice Such (2).= 20th.

CY: Cliff Yates (2).= 20th.

PBr: Peter Brocklehurst (1).= 21st.

DB: Dave Booth (1). = 21st.

RH: Roy Hazeldine (1).= 21st.
TO: Terry Oakden (1).= 21st.
BP: Bob Proctor (1).= 21st.
RP: Rod Peterson (1).= 21st.

Appendix iii

CYCLING HOLIDAY IN PYRENEES

July 9th – July 25th 1965.

Present (8).

Geoff Cartlidge, Ralph Salt, Roy Deakin, Chris Warren, Pete Boardman, Tony Ross, Dave Hope, Colin Green.

Friday

2.10pm: Meet at Roebuck Hotel, Stoke.

3.10pm: Train depart Stoke.

3.35pm: Arrive Stafford.

3.42pm: Depart Stafford.

6.10pm: Arrive London Euston.

Cycled across London to Victoria.

Met with Roy Deakin.

10.20pm: Depart Victoria.

11.30pm: Arrive Newhaven.

Saturday

12.00midnight: CF *Villandray* sailed from Newhaven.

3.15am: Arrive Dieppe Maritime.

3.30am: Depart Dieppe.

6.30am: Arrive Paris St Lazare.

Cycled across Paris to Gare d'Austerlitz.

8.05am: Depart Paris.

4.25pm: Arrive Pau.

Itinerary

Sun: Pau – Arrens, via Col d'Aubisque.

Mon: Arrens – Gedre.

Tue: Gedre – Bareges, via Cirque de Gavarnie.

Wed: Bareges – Ste Marie de Campan, via Col du Tourmalet.

Thur: Ste Marie – Bagneres de Luchon, via Col d'Aspin & Col de Peyresourde.

Fri: Bagneres de Luchon – Viella, via Col de Portillion.

Sat: Viella – Esterri D'Aneau, via Puerto de La Bonaigua.

Sun: Esterri D'Aneau – Seo d'Urgell, via Col del Canto.

Mon: Seo d' Urgell – Andorra-La-Vielle (Las Escaldes).

Tue: Rest day in Andorra-La-Vielle.

Wed: Andorra-La-Vielle – Ax-Les-Thermes, via Port d'Envalira.

Thur: Ax-Les-Thermes – Alet-Les-Bains, via Col de Chioula.

Fri: Alet-Les-Bains – Carcassonne.

I0.55pm: Train depart Carcassonne.

Saturday

8.20am: Arrive Paris Austerlitz.

Cycled across Paris to Gare St Lazare.

10.15am: Depart Paris.

1.15pm: Arrive Dieppe Maritime.

2.00pm: CF *Villancay* sailed from Dieppe.

6.00pm: Arrive Newhaven.

6.30pm: Depart Newhaven.

8.00pm Arrive London Victoria.

Cycled across London to Euston.

10.10pm: Depart London Euston.

Train broke down at Rugby.

Sunday

12.50am: Arrive Stafford.

1.00am: Depart Stafford.

1.30am: Arrive Stoke.

2.15am: Arrive Trentham.

Cycling.

Number of Days Cycling: 12 +1 Rest Day. Total Miles Cycled: 365 (585km).

Average Mileage/Day: 30.5.

Topography

Total Feet Climbed: 27,553 feet (8,398m).

Total Feet Fallen: 26,992 feet (8,227m).

(For heights of passes, see 1969 Pyrenees Tour).

Photography

Camera: Yashica 35mm.

Kodachrome 64ASA colour slide Ffilm. Photographs for Dave Hope: 98.

Personal Photographs: 185.

Total: 283.

Rates of Exchange

France: Francs – FF13.30 to £1. Spain/Andorra: Pesetas – Pts160 to £1.

Cost of Accommodation.

France: 8 nights/£9-4s-0d (£9.20np).

Spain & Andorra: 5 nights/ £2-19s-0d (£2.95np).Total Accommodation Cost: £12-3s-0d (£12.15np).

Weather

Dry Days: 12.

Wet Days: 3.

Sunshine on 11 days. Overcast on 4 days.

Highlights   * *

Col d'Aubisque *****

Cirque de Gavarnie *****

Col du Tourmalet ****

Col d'Aspin ***

Col de Peyresourde ***

Las Bordas (Spanish Village).

Puerto de La Bonaigua ****

Col del Canto *****

Port d'Envalira ***

Col de Chioula ****

Carcassonne Old Cité **

Travel Time

Time of Outward Journey: 25h.15m. Time of Return Journey: 27h.20m.

Appendix iv

HOLIDAY IN PYRENEES
May 23rd – June 15th 1969.
<u>Present (2).</u>
John Bradbury, Colin Green.
<u>Friday</u>
7.30pm: Depart Bomere Heath.
Cycled to Stoke-on-Trent.
10.40pm: Arrive Stoke-on-Trent.
<u>Saturday.</u>
1.23am: Train depart Stoke.
4.15am: Arrive London Euston.
Cycle across London.
9.50am: Depart Victoria.
11.05am: Arrive Newhaven.
11.35am: Ferry depart.
3.40pm: Arrive Dieppe.
3.50pm: Depart Dieppe Maritime.
6.20pm: Arrive Paris St Lazare.
Cycled across Paris to Gare d'Austerlitz.
10.45pm: Depart Paris.
<u>Sunday.</u>
6.35am: Arrive Bayonne. Total: 35 hours.
<u>Itinerary</u>
Sun: Bayonne – Pamplona (70m), via Puerto Otsondo & Puerto Velate.
Mon: Pamplona – Jaca (68m).
Tue: Jaca–Panticosa (30m).
Wed: Panticosa – Torla (28m), via Puerto de Cotefablo.
Thur: Rest day in Ordesa National Park.
Fri: Torla – Castejon (70m).

Sat: Castejon – Castejon (30m), via Benasque.

Sun: Castejon – Viella (43m), via Viella Tunnel.

Mon: Viella – Viella (30m), via Puerto de La Bonaigua.

Tues: Viella – Luchon (28m), via Col de Portillon.

Wed: Luchon – Ste Marie de Campan (36m), via Col de Peyresourde & Col d'Aspin.

Thur: Ste Marie de Campan – Gedre (30m), via Col du Tourmalet.

Fri: Gedre – Gedre (18m), via Cirque de Gavarnie.

Sat: Gedre – Arrens (48m), via Pont d' Espagne.

Sun: Arrans – Laruns (55m), via Col d'Aubisque & Col de Soulor.

Mon: Laruns – Laruns (53m), via Col de Portalet.

Tues: Laruns – Mauleon (69m).

Wed: Mauleon – Cambo (46m), via Col d'Osquich.

Thur: Cambo – Bayonne (30m), via St Jean de Luz.

11.29pm: Train depart Bayonne

Friday

8.00am: Arrive Paris.

Cycle across Paris to St Lazare.

10.00am: Depart Paris.

12.30pm: Arrive Dieppe Maritime.

1.00pm: SS *Falaise* depart Dieppe.

5.00pm: Arrive Newhaven.

5.35pm: Depart Newhaven.

7.00pm: Arrive London Victoria.

Cross London to Euston.

8.00pm: Depart Euston.

9.58pm: Arrive Stafford.

10.15pm: Depart Stafford.

Cycled to Bomere Heath.

Saturday

00.55am: Arrived Bomere Heath.

Total: 25.5 hours.

Cycling.

Number of Days Cycling: 19.

Miles in France & Spain: 782miles (1,250km).

Average/Day: 41 (65km).

Topography

Puerto Otsondo: 1,974 feet (602m).

Puerto Velate: 2,777 feet (846m).

Puerto Cotefablo: 4,667 feet (1,422m).

Collando de Fordada: 3,345 feet (1,020m).

Benasque 3,733: feet (1,138m).

Collando de Fadas: 4,822 feet (1,470m).

Collando de Espina: 4,614 feet (1,406m).

Viella Tunnel: 5,333 feet (1625m).

Puerto de La Bonaigua: 6,796 feet (2,071m).

Col de Portillon: 4,290 feet (1,308m).

Col de Peyresourde: 5,125 feet (1,562m).

Col d'Aspin: 4,884 feet (1,488m).

Col du Tourmalet: 6,936 feet (2,114m).

Col de Soulor: 4,740 feet (1,445m).

Col d'Aubisque: 5,608 feet (1,709m).

Col de Portalet: 5,877 feet (1,791m).

Col d'Osquich: 1,062 feet (324m).

Panticosa: 3,883 feet (1,183m).

Cirque de Gavarnie: 4,450 feet (1,356m).

Pont d'Espagne: 4,910 feet (1,496m).

St Engrace: 2,066 feet (630m).

Cost of Accommodation

9 Nights in Spain

Rooms: Pts 684 (£4-3s-Od-£4.15np). Dinner: Pts 800 (£4-17s-Od-£4.85np). B'fast: Pts 105(13s-Od-65np).Total: Pts 1,589 (£9-13s-Od – £9.65np).Average/Night: £1-Is-6d (£1.07np). Rate of Exchange: Pts 165 to £1.

9 Nights in France

Rooms: Ff 76 (£6-1s-8d – £6.06np). Dinner: Ff 132 (£10-14s-2d – £10.70np).Total: Ff 208 (£17-5s-10d – £17.30np).Average/Night: £1-18s-6d (£1.93np). Rate of Exchange: Ff 12.5 to £1.

Overall Cost of Tour

CTC Rail Fare: £31-0s-Od.

Fare London to Stafford: £2-17s-6d (£2.88).
Foreign Currency: £38-0s-0d.
Travel Expenses: £9-0s-0d.
<u>Total: £80-17s-6d (£80.88np).</u>